SECURITY
AND
DETENTE

SECURITY
AND
DETENTE

Conflicting Priorities
in
German Foreign Policy

Helga Haftendorn

Library of Congress Cataloging in Publication Data

Haftendorn, Helga.
  Security and detente.

  Bibliography: p.
  Includes index.
  1. Germany (West)—Foreign relations.
2. Detente. 3. Germany (West)—National
security. I. Title.
DD258.8.H34 1985   327.43   84-18341
ISBN 0-03-069886-3 (alk. paper)

Published in 1985 by Praeger Publishers
CBS Educational and Professional Publishing, a Division of CBS Inc.
521 Fifth Avenue, New York, NY 10175 USA

© 1985 by Helga Haftendorn

56789 052 987654321

Printed in the United States of America on acid-free paper

INTERNATIONAL OFFICES

Orders from outside the United States should be sent to the appropriate address listed below. Orders from areas not listed below should be placed through CBS International Publishing, 383 Madison Ave., New York, NY 10175 USA

Australia, New Zealand
Holt Saunders, Pty. Ltd., 9 Waltham St., Artarmon, N.S.W. 2064, Sydney, Australia

Canada
Holt, Rinehart & Winston of Canada, 55 Horner Ave., Toronto, Ontario, Canada M8Z 4X6

Europe, the Middle East, & Africa
Holt Saunders, Ltd., 1 St. Anne's Road, Eastbourne, East Sussex, England BN21 3UN

Japan
Holt Saunders, Ltd., Ichibancho Central Building, 22-1 Ichibancho, 3rd Floor, Chiyodaku, Tokyo, Japan

Hong Kong, Southeast Asia
Holt Saunders Asia, Ltd., 10 Fl, Intercontinental Plaza, 94 Granville Road, Tsim Sha Tsui East, Kowloon, Hong Kong

Manuscript submissions should be sent to the Editorial Director, Praeger Publishers, 521 Fifth Avenue, New York, NY 10175 USA

Preface

Throughout the years following World War II commentators have wondered about the stability and reliability of the Federal Republic of Germany as a member of the Atlantic alliance. Might it not be tempted to strike a deal with the Soviet Union if this would help bring about reunification? All West German administrations have emphasized close ties with the West, but they also had to have some form of Ostpolitik. Security through close association with the West and some sort of limited cooperation with the East have been the recurrent themes of German foreign policy; the implicit conflict of priorities has weighted the outcome.

This book is written for the student of modern Germany and for the expert who wishes to relate Bonn's foreign policy to its broader national experience and international approach. It deals with West German foreign policy since 1955, the year in which the occupation ended and Bonn emerged on the international stage. It analyzes the latent conflict of priorities between Western orientation and policies directed to the East.

Changes from the 1983 German edition include dropping of the case studies on the CSCE, MBFR, and non-proliferation; placing references to multilateral arms control in the analytical chapters, and adding references to recent developments.

Whenever possible, English-language documents and publications have been given as sources; but in a number of cases references to German publications had to be made.

In writing this book I have very much benefited from my experience as a visiting professor at various American universities, most recently, during the academic year 1982–83, at Stanford University, teaching American students about German foreign policy. In addition, I am indebted more than I can tell to numerous colleagues and institutions for support, advice, and stimulation, both in Germany and in the United States. I would particularly like to thank Gordon Craig and Alexander George for their encouragement to plan this English edition. A very special debt of gratitude I owe to Catherine Kelleher and Stephen Szabo, long-time German hands, and to "The Harts" for providing a base in Washington, D.C.

Many thanks go to Dennis Mercer, who did a superb job as translator, to Lynne Jordal, who toiled at the footnotes, and to Karin Eifert, who prepared the index and bibliography. I also want to express my appreciation for financial support to the Deutsche Forschungsgemeinschaft, the Freie Universität Berlin, and INTERNATIONES.

Helga Haftendorn
Berlin, June 1984

Contents

SECURITY
AND
DETENTE

1

The Foreign Policy of the
Federal Republic of Germany:
A Framework for Analysis

Nowhere is the past a more telling prologue than in the Federal Republic of Germany. Three strains of its European history have made their indelible imprint on the Federal Republic's political system: the uncertain democratic tradition, the unsolved national question, and the emergence of the two German states under the impress of the cold war. These are central to an understanding of the self-image and the guiding principles informing West German policy. Germany's geographic situation at the heart of Europe also accounts for specific political realities. European history has always been in part a battle for control of the center, and Germany has been either too weak or too strong to be a stabilizing factor in the European concert of powers. Today, Germany is split by a border that divides Europe into two opposing social, political, and military systems.

Less a formative element than a consequence of historical development, geographic situation, and economic orientation are the close integration of the Federal Republic into the security and economic systems of the West and the resulting interdependencies bearing on its foreign policy.

An enumeration of the determinants of the Federal Republic's foreign policy would not be complete, however, without mention of the helmsmen who have firmly and farsightedly guided the ship of state through the shoals of the postwar era. Deserving of special note are Konrad Adenauer, the first chancellor of the Federal Republic and architect of its policy of integration into the West; Willy Brandt, the first Social Democrat to occupy the Schaumburg Palace and the author of Bonn's Ostpolitik, and finally, Helmut Schmidt, who faced both the world economic crisis and the crisis in detente and who foundered when domestic policy began to call for a change of direction.

HISTORY'S PROLOGUE: UNCERTAIN DEMOCRATIC TRADITION, UNSOLVED NATIONAL QUESTION, AND THE PARTITION OF EUROPE

Germany is one of the few Western industrial nations without its own democratic revolution. Neither a "Glorious Revolution" nor a "Storming of the Bastille" are part of its democratic tradition. The failure of the Paul's Church Assembly in Frankfurt demonstrated the political incompetence of the educated German middle classes; the half-hearted revolution of 1918–19 and the Weimar constitution were discredited by the "stab in the back" legend from within and the "dictates of Versailles" from without. The democratic republic, tainted with the national humiliation and founded on only very tenuous popular acceptance, was worn down by fascism from the right and communism from the left. For most Germans Hitler initially was not a criminal dictator, but a leader toward national renewal who slew the Hydra of the multiparty state and upon its ruins raised the vision of a thousand-year Reich, beyond the wrangling of parties and the politics of special interest.[1]

After the defeat at Stalingrad, the bombing of Cologne, Berlin, and Dresden, and the stream of refugees from the eastern territories, the Germans gradually began to discern their fate. Consumed with the needs of physical survival, yet summoning moral courage to develop new political models, they attended the reemergence of German state structures in the years 1945–49. The founding of the Federal Republic, however, was not an act of free will on the part of the Germans, but was a decision of the Western allies and a consequence of the cold war. This defined the parameters in which democratic institutions could be built in government, society, and economy—partly restorative, partly innovative, carefully welding old and new. The democratic structures thus formed enabled the West German state to effect political consolidation at home and to gain international recognition abroad.[2]

The reemergence of German state structures had its origins, then, in the cold war and the partition of Europe. The founding of two German states preserved the Germans' national problem and transported it to the international level as a new "German question." However, the causes of the national problem lie deeper in German history. The decision of the Paul's Church Assembly in favor of a smaller-German solution and Bismarck's founding of the Reich at the point of bayonets are as much part of its scar tissue as the cession of German territories under the terms of the Treaty of Versailles or Hitler's fatal drive for lebensraum.

The dismemberment of Germany after the Second World War is primarily a product of the war of aggression unleashed by Hitler and of the consequent need for security and self-assertion on the part of his wartime adversaries, amplified by the developing power-political, economic, and ideological struggle between East and West. Their national identity profoundly shaken, the Germans west of the Elbe and Werra reduced their concept of nation to a moral postulate and to a legal claim, while those Germans east of the demarcation line were henceforth giving "nation" an ideological foundation as the first Workers' and Peasants' State on German soil—both, however, commemorating the unity of the nation primarily in rhetoric for popular consumption. Those other roots of national identity, the history endured—or forfeited—in common, the traditions in moral and cultural values, the needs and hopes of people, were blocked up.

Germany's economic development into the strongest industrial power on the continent came about largely independently of the national development. The formation of the German Customs Union in 1833 and the building of the railroads produced a more lasting impact than the founding of the Reich in 1871. The German economic system bore the features of state capitalism before there existed a full German state. Direct involvement of government authorities in key sectors of the economy as well as virtually complete government supervision gave rise to a mixed economic system strongly influenced by the public sector. With the introduction of worker protection and social security laws the German Reich presented to the rest of the world a model road to reform. These social reforms were designed to safeguard society against revolutionary tendencies; the laws against the Socialists, on the other hand, embodied the other, repressive strand of Bismarck's strategy for stabilizing the system.

Recalling the two great economic crises of the Weimar Republic, the catastrophic inflation that culminated in 1923 as well as the world economic crisis that struck Germany severely at the beginning of the 1930s, and under the still vivid impact of hunger and misery in the immediate postwar period, the West German state considered itself bound to uphold economic stability as foundation and prerequisite for a durable democratic order.

Aided by credits from U.S. GARIOA aid and the Marshall Plan, the nation inaugurated a policy of stability through economic growth (a policy initiated by the Frankfurt Economic Council and supported by the bulk of the population) and it proved to be a powerful motor for postwar reconstruction. Released prisoners of war and refugees from the east provided a strong force of skilled workers. With social peace arrived at domestically, they provided the basis for the "economic miracle" and its internalization as a distinctive mentality geared to material prosperity.

But the founding of the Federal Republic of Germany was attended by a number of uncertainties. The tenuous democratic tradition, the outstanding national question, and the fear of a military conflict between East and West engendered doubts as to whether the "Second Republic" would have sufficient staying power and protection against the dangers threatening its existence.[3] Most imperative was giving the new West German democracy a stable political and economic foundation, first by means of a constitution that avoided the mistakes of Weimar, and secondly through the economic instrument of the "social market economy," with which market forces were controlled and social tensions mitigated. The Federal Republic's close link—political as well as economic—with the Western democracies provided a further support.

For the restoration of German unity there was no solution in sight that would not have meant giving up or at least endangering the course of political and social development launched with the founding of the Federal Republic. The only conceivable possibility seemed to be an agreement among the Four Powers by which the Soviet Union would allow the German Democratic Republic to leave the Soviet sphere of influence and proceed to reunification through *anschluss* with the Federal Republic. A politically solid and economically flourishing West German state would exercise a "magnetic effect" on the people of Eastern Germany, accelerating this process, but above all making it increasingly costly for Moscow to maintain the communist regime against the will of the people. The "economic miracle" was thus part of the West German version of the "policy of strength" originally formulated by U.S. Secretary of State John Foster Dulles. In the Treaties of Paris and Bonn this policy was complemented by the Federal Republic's claim to sole representation and the three Western allies' commitment to the goal of German reunification.

How, then, could the security of the Federal Republic, situated at the fault line between East and West, be ensured? How could the Federal Republic avoid being drawn into a military conflict where it would become the battlefield? In view of its internal and external weaknesses the Federal Republic could escape such a fate only through close political ties with the West, above all with the United States, and by rejecting the risks of neutrality—even at the expense of reunification. The Federal Republic's entry into NATO and the establishment of the Bundeswehr were as much a political as a military answer to the perceived security dilemma. No other way would enable the Federal Republic to protect itself against an attack from the east (which seemed a very real possibility in the wake of the Korean War) and to develop and maintain a stable democracy. Finally, voluntary integration into the West was also a means toward terminating the occupation regime and gaining a greater measure of international equality.

In line with the basic values of unity, peace, and freedom proclaimed in the preamble to the Basic Law, the first West German governments pursued a policy aimed primarily at internal stabilization and external security. These aims complemented each other in that political and economic stability was a prerequisite for international recognition just as it promised to facilitate reunification, while security policy would not only afford protection agaist military aggression but also ensure an autonomous political and social development within the contours of Western integration. In political practice, however, a security policy understood primarily in terms of Western integration and a national policy aimed at reunification proved to be mutually incompatible. From a correct appraisal of the new structures of international affairs, priority was given to securing freedom and preserving peace, and thus harmony was maintained between West German and allied interests. The goal of national unity had to take a back seat. Yet the triad of "peace-freedom-unity" was maintained in the political rhetoric, as reunification was declared to be the end result of a consistent security policy.[4]

Amidst the cold war, the Federal Republic had no alternative to security through Western integration; at the same time, maintaining the status quo—including the division of Germany—became a prerequisite for the Western powers' protective guarantee. When in the mid-1950s the first thaw in East-West relations set in, the German question seemed to become negotiable again, though only at the expense of Western integration. Yet this was not acceptable to the Federal Republic, for its democratic system as well as its economic prosperity rested upon its strong ties with the Western democracies. True detente seemed possible only through reunification, namely through the GDR's union with a Federal Republic rooted in the West. Hence, Bonn blocked any reconciliation of the world powers possible only at its expense.

When a nuclear stalemate and the new global dimensions of conflict prompted the United States and the Soviet Union to intensify their efforts toward a modus vivendi based on the status quo in Europe, just as the Federal Republic was seeking to keep this status quo open to change, Bonn was confronted with the danger of becoming isolated internationally. It also faced the threat of falling behind economically as its West European partners began to strengthen their trade relations with the East European nations. The Federal Republic had to make significant adjustments in policy if it were not to risk seriously straining its relations with its Western allies. This meant giving up the goal of reunification in favor of a modus vivendi based on the status quo; in security policy, the concept was broadened to encompass, besides deterrence and defense, elements of negotiation and cooperation with the other side.[5] However, this change of position in the foreign policy of the Federal Republic was conditional and consequent upon a lasting detente in East-West relations that could not be limited to Central Europe but had to include the United States and the Soviet Union.

Security and detente thus became the dominant concepts of West German foreign policy, expressive of autonomous and/or adapted aims and objectives. The question then was how to manage the inherent conflict of priorities between alliance and security policy on the one hand and Ostpolitik and detente on the other, how to take into account the domestic political equation and the international constellation of power, and how to gauge the Federal Republic's room for maneuver in foreign affairs.

1955 AS A WATERSHED IN THE POST WAR PERIOD

The year 1955 marks a watershed in European postwar history and as such offers a clear point of departure for an analysis of West German foreign policy. First, the Paris Treaties and Bonn's integration into the Western alliance gave the Federal Republic of Germany its sovereignty and a say in world affairs. Secondly, the incorporation of the two German states into their respective alliance systems essentially completed the formative process establishing postwar European structures. As of 1955 the Federal Republic's future role in the international system had been delineated. One of the main results of the Second World War was the destruction of the European center as an independent political force and the emergence of the United States and the Soviet Union as the new world—and thus European—powers of the first order. The political and military presence of these two powers in Europe as well as the partition of the continent and inclusion of the two parts of Germany into the two opposing spheres of hegemony became the decisive structural features of postwar Europe.

At the heart of this development was Germany. On the surface the conflict between the two world powers was over the future of Germany and Central Europe; yet at a deeper level there was the question of the global order, of the two competitors' freedom of political action worldwide, and moreover, the United States' desire for advantageous foreign economic relations in the face of the Soviet Union's efforts to construct socialism in its own domain.

At the end of the war neither of the two powers had a clear conception of Germany's future. However, roughly in the years 1946–47— key moments here are Secretary of State James Byrnes's speech in Stuttgart on September 6, 1946, the formation of the Bizone on January 1, 1947, the proclamation of the Truman Doctrine on March 12, 1947, and finally the announcement of the Marshall Plan on June 7, 1947— the United States, for reasons of domestic as well as foreign policy, decided to pursue the consolidation and incorporation of the Western zones into its own sphere of influence. In contrast, the Soviet Union at first pursued a dual strategy of demarcation and confrontation (Stalin's speech of February 9, 1946, Zhdanov's theses on the founding of the Cominform in September 1947, and the decision on the Berlin blockade of June 1947) *and* of offering reunification of Germany at the price of its neutralization (Molotov's press statement of July 10, 1946, Vyshinsky's proposals of May 23, 1949, and the Soviet notes on Germany of March and April 1952). Thus, the Soviets wanted both to nail down their own sphere of influence and to prevent the formation of a West European bloc closely allied with the United States and inclusive of West Germany.[6]

Under the initial protectorate of the victorious powers the Germans in the four occupation zones had very little potential for shaping political matters. Even after German state structures had been reestablished, first at the *länder* and zone levels, then in the Economic Council for the United Economic Region, and finally in the Federal Republic of Germany in the West and as the German Democratic Republic in the East, the German governments were bound by the directives and provisos of their occupying powers. The Basic Law worked out by the Parliamentary Council in Bonn and approved by the allies, as well as the Occupation Statute issued by the latter, were carefully balanced so as not to permit independent development to exceed allied potential for intervention. On the domestic level, a parallelogram of political forces evolved in which, within the scope of action tolerated by the allies, the Conservative-Liberal coalition government led by Konrad Adenauer including the CDU/CSU, FDP and German Party sought to establish a market economy and fostered the political concept of integration into the West. Once Washington had made its fundamental decision for a European presence and the incorporation of the Federal Republic into the Western system, Bonn no longer had a choice between Western integration and reunification. Hence neither the negative response to the

Soviet notes of 1952 nor the Adenauer government's proclaimed "fateful decision" for Western integration and against an uncertain neutrality was a "missed opportunity." Adenauer's greatness lay rather in his insight into the historical necessity of such a decision that avoided a conflict with the allies and moved the Federal Republic onto the road to sovereignty; his failure, however, came from cloaking it in strong words that contributed to making legends and for a long time prevented the Germans from accepting the division as political reality.

By the mid-1950's the institutional organization of the blocs had been completed on both sides, with the two German states included in them. In the West the Federal Republic was accepted into the North Atlantic Pact. NATO membership not only meant a termination of the occupation regime but also gained Bonn a say in the Western system. The price for this was the establishment of German armed forces fully integrated in NATO and a web of arms limitations and controls as part of the Western European Union, as well as an explicit renunciation of force vis-á-vis the Western powers. The West German government believed it could keep the German question open once the United States, Great Britain, and France had reaffirmed their responsibility for restoring the unity of Germany and the Federal Republic had committed itself to pursuing this goal solely by peaceful means.[7]

A more tangible goal than reunification, now distant politically, was that of a political union in Western Europe. Despite the breakdown of the European Defense Community, this project was to be the result of the policy of integration. Steps in this direction included the founding of the European Coal and Steel Community (ECSC) in 1952, the decisions of the foreign ministers of the Six at the Messina Conference in the summer of 1955 on creating a Common Market, and the March 1957 signing of the Treaties of Rome establishing the European Economic Community (EEC) and the European Atomic Community (EURATOM). This was paralleled by the Federal Republic's integration into the international economic system with its accession to the General Agreement on Tariffs and Trade (1951), to the International Monetary Fund and the World Bank (1952), as well as to the European Payments Union and the European Monetary Agreement (1955 and 1958).

At the same time there had developed in the East a political, military, and ideological bloc oriented to Moscow. In 1949, the Council for Mutual Economic Assistance (COMECON) was founded, and in 1955 the Warsaw Pact, with the GDR being progressively integrated into both of these. By the mid-1950s the copestones had thus been added to the bipolar power structure. Its stability was not seriously shaken either by Stalin's death (1953), and the change in U.S. administrations from Truman to Eisenhower, or by the crises within the blocs—the June 17, 1953 uprising in the GDR, the Suez crisis in the fall of 1956, or the Soviet intervention in Hungary in October 1956. Both world powers had established themselves for the time being as European powers of the first order.[8]

However, both sides also recognized that the actual conflict—the domination of Central Europe—could not be won. While the ideological competition persisted and the arms race intensified, the two world powers began to strive for a modus vivendi on the outstanding controversies in Europe. A first result of these endeavors was the Austrian State Treaty, which gave Austria a neutral status and enabled it to pursue its own political development while imposing upon it an explicit ban on union with Germany. A settlement of the German question was postponed; an "Austrian solution" would have implied for Moscow the danger of an unraveling of its sphere of domination especially with memories still fresh of the June 17 uprising in the GDR, while Washington would have lost substantial reserves of men, material, resources, and territory for its security policy, and, by dismantling its military presence in Europe, would have forfeited significant potential for exercising influence on the continent.[9]

In the face of mutually antagonistic interests, the negotiations undertaken by the four powers for establishing a European security system yielded no substantial results. Yet the spectacular summit conference of the four heads of state and government and the much-acclaimed "spirit of Geneva" demonstrated that despite the persistence of the fundamental conflict between East and West there did exist a partial identity of interests between the great powers as well as a desire on both sides for detente in international relations.[10]

In the eyes of Bonn, however, the relaxation of tensions emanating from the Geneva Summit Conference entailed enormous dangers for the Federal Republic, threatening to jeopardize what had already been achieved. A subsiding of the cold war tended to diminish the political importance of Bonn's defense contribution; a waning fear of Soviet aggression would reactivate misgivings among Bonn's neighbors about a rearmament of the Federal Republic. Above all, Adenauer feared an accord among the victorious powers of the Second World War at the expense of the Federal Republic.[11] From this standpoint his trip to Moscow and the establishment of diplomatic relations with the Soviet Union in September 1955 were certainly designed, in part, to give the West German government direct contact with the Soviet leadership, even if this act of emancipation signified another step toward acceptance of the European status quo.

Two other events in 1955 underscored this movement toward acceptance of the status quo: the third Eden Plan of July 21, 1955, in which proposals for an inspection zone in Central Europe were not coupled with steps toward reunification of Germany, and thus the military dimension of European security was given priority over the political (i.e., the division of Germany was no longer judged to be the main danger), and Khrushchev's statement on July 26, 1955 in Berlin on the existence of two sovereign German states.[12] After that all attempts to keep the German question open—the formulation of a policy of nonrecognition of the GDR, in the form of the Hallstein Doctrine; declaratory acts such as the Berlin Declaration of July 1957, and the devising of various plans for Germany—were essentially "damage prevention measures" or were designed to shield politically (especially in the domestic arena) against de facto acceptance of the status quo. The year 1955 thus marked an incisive turning point: it was stamped by the recognition that the German question would no longer head the agenda of international politics and that there were no concrete prospects for its solution in the face of the divergent interests in East and West. Alliance and security policy—alongside European integration—moved to the forefront of active concern. For the Federal Republic this became the most important instrument for articulating its own interests and gaining international recognition.

INTERDEPENDENCE AS THE NEW INTERNATIONAL CONTEXT OF GERMAN FOREIGN POLICY

Since its founding the Federal Republic of Germany has been bound into a tightly woven texture of international relations. While the Occupation Statute was in effect, the German government possessed only very limited room for maneuver in foreign or domestic affairs. The Allied High Commissioners had the authority to intervene in the decisions of the West German state directly, by their own directives, or indirectly, via the Federal government.[13] Moreover, the Federal Republic was integrated into the Western security and economic system created by the United States, a system offering military protection and economic property but also the obligation to a policy of Western orientation.

The Atlantic Alliance as "Security Network"

Developing out of the special historical situation at the end of the Second World War, the Atlantic alliance and West European integration became the mainstays of the Federal Republic's international interdependence. First, they tied the Federal Republic closely to the Western democracies and thus constituted a kind of safeguard for its political and social system; secondly, the close interdependence with the military and political potential of the United States offered protection against external threat; and thirdly, West European integration opened up to the Federal Republic a broad economic field, subject to ample infusions of American capital and closely interwoven with the international economic system. This, then, established some of the basic preconditions for a reconstruction of the West German economy and the rising prosperity of its society.

NATO, as one of the institutional supports in this network of interdependence, is first of all an alliance of sovereign states that includes a partly integrated civilian and military substructure, the North Atlantic Treaty *Organization* in the stricter sense. This rests upon the understanding that in the event of conflict the member states will place their assigned or otherwise predesignated armed forces under an integrated command. Other important components include the binding of North America to Western Europe through the U.S. and Canadian military presence on the continent as well as the linkage in strategy and military policy of the conventional potential in Central Europe with the tactical and strategic nuclear forces of the United States via the triad. At the same time the U.S. presence has for the Federal Republic a tripwire function by means of which the United States is directly and at an early juncture drawn into a conflict.

In addition, NATO is an instrument for crisis management and political coordination among the 15 (16 since May 1982) or, as it were, 14 states taking part in the integrated defense program of NATO. Since the end of the 1960s this political function of the alliance, which is accentuated in the Harmel Report on ''The Future Tasks of the Alliance,'' has become more important for East-West relations and particularly for the conduct of a multilateral detente policy.[14] Thus, the two parts of the NATO modernization decision of December 1979 were prepared in two ad hoc bodies of the alliance, the High Level Group and the Special Group. The latter also served to coordinate the negotiating position of the alliance on the limitation of long-range theater nuclear forces (LRTNF), although the negotiations proper have been conducted by the United States and the Soviet Union.

The Atlantic alliance restricts its members' room for maneuver in various ways. For the Federal Republic it is significant that it has fully integrated its armed forces and the planning for their use into the alliance; pulling out of the NATO organization as France did or going it alone militarily á la Suez in 1956 is not possible for Bonn. The realm of military strategy presents a similar picture. The development of the strategic discussion since the mid-1950s shows to what a great extent the Federal Republic is affected by changes in U.S. strategic thinking. Thus, Bonn endeavored very early on to participate in the operational planning of the alliance's nuclear potential, as was shown by its tenacious adherence to the Multilateral Force (MLF) as a possibility for nuclear codetermination. However, there is no alternative to adaptation to the U.S. military strategy, for on its own the Bundeswehr could not fulfill its mission: deterrence and defense. The current debate on the role of Eurostrategic nuclear weapons in Western Europe illustrates the security policy dilemma of the Federal Republic, which for the sake of the credibility of deterrence and defense is faced with the risk of its own nuclear destruction in the event of conflict.

Also, it should not be overlooked that the extensive integration of the Federal Republic into the Atlantic alliance and the strong U.S. connection not only have a protective function for the Federal Republic, but are also designed to guarantee its European neighbors protection *from* the Federal Republic. France consented to the arming of the Federal Republic and its entry into NATO only after the United States and Great Britain had declared their readiness for a long-term stationing of troops on the continent. The anxieties feeding upon historical experience may have a diminished importance today, but it should not be overlooked that of the ground forces on West German territory at present, the 335,200-man Bundeswehr (excluding territorial army) is flanked by U.S., Belgian, British, Canadian, French, and Dutch forces numbering 336,200 men (excluding Berlin contingents).

For the Federal Republic of Germany the Atlantic alliance is primarily a security network that safeguards its foreign policy. The alliance has exercised this function most notably in the area of policy on Germany. It derives from the responsibility for Germany as a whole and Berlin assumed by the three Western powers in the context of the Paris Treaties and complemented by a renunciation of force on the part of the Federal Republic in accordance with Article 2 of the UN Charter. While the Federal Republic has been dependent upon the consent of its partners in matters of policy on Germany and Berlin, it has also been able to draw from this obligation the demand for support from them. The security network of the Western alliance thus represents more than a mere fall-back position; it binds as much as it protects.

The European Community as Prerequisite for a Say in International Politics

From the standpoint of the Federal Republic, the European Community has always been three things: Common market and Economic community, multilateral framework for eliminating the Franco-German security conflict, and pioneer for a political union of Western Europe. Whereas the EC, ECSC, and EURATOM were designed to foster economic growth and closer relations among the member states—initially the Six, then the Nine, and since 1981 the Ten—and thus political stability, the goals of the political union were more broadly defined. In this union the "unfinished nation" hoped to find a new political identity that made a radical break with the past and removed the historical antagonism with France. Moreover, the Federal Republic expected that an economically powerful, unified Western Europe could make its voice heard on international issues and form a counterweight to the two superpowers.

After 30 years of European integration policy the West Europeans have achieved neither the goal of harmonization of their economic policies nor the degree of political coordination that would allow them to speak with one voice on the international stage. On the positive side of the European Community's political balance there is the development of a common foreign trade policy, the establishment of a European Monetary System, as well as the association with the French- and English-speaking nations of Africa, the Caribbean, and the Pacific in the Lomé Convention; in all three areas the ten EC countries have given up a number of internal control possibilities.

By entering into commitments exceeding the limitations of sovereignty set forth in the Treaty of Rome, the Community nations have limited the scope for national foreign policy. For the Federal Republic this has meant that it could make few trade concessions as part of its Ostpolitik and could not, e.g., meet the demands of the East European states for most-favored-nation status. Similarly, the joint representation of the EC in GATT or in the UN Conference on Trade and Development (UNCTAD) means that there first have to be developed Community positions, which are achievable only by means of a far-reaching harmonization of interests in economic and foreign policy, with a capability for reaching pragmatic compromises.

Still the European Community is far from its goal of a political union. On the contrary, the institutional road to European integration and its attendant formal renunciation of sovereignty have not proved to be durable enough, and so the establishment of the European Council and the European Political Cooperation (EPC) in the 1970s marked a new functional course that did not formally encroach upon the sovereignty of the member states but allowed them considerable scope for harmonizing their policies in various areas. This new mechanism has proved itself particularly with coordination of policy on the Middle East and multilateral detente.[15]

Another challenge to the Community was the initiative of U.S. Secretary of State Kissinger for a "Year of Europe." The response was the December 1973 Declaration of Copenhagen on European Identity, a June 1974 statement of the NATO Council on Atlantic Relations, linked also to the "Gymnich Agreement," in which the EC nations agreed to consult with the U.S. and other friendly nations in working out common positions.[16] Consequently, the EC nations have generally drawn up common positions on international questions, e.g., on the situation in South Africa or in the Middle East. To date, questions of military security and arms control have been excluded because of French objections. It remains to be seen whether the German-Italian initiative of the fall of 1981 for a "European Charter"[17] will lead to greater political coordination encompassing security issues.

Although the process of political integration cannot be regarded as anywhere near completed, there have been consummated within the national systems far-reaching changes in the existing political means, in the technical competencies and their distribution, and in the organizational structures. Today, in a number of highly integrated fields, purely national decision-making processes have already ceased to exist. At the same time the European Community has developed the means for making decisions, differing with respect to form, intensity, and importance of the institutions participating in them, yet producing an extensive multi- and transnational interweaving of decision-making processes.

Economic Integration and Political Interdependence

In part indirectly via the European Community, in part directly, the economy of the Federal Republic has been institutionally meshed with the international system. Bonn is a member of the International Monetary Fund (IMF). Although two key elements of the Bretton Woods Agreement, fixed exchange rates vis-á-vis the dollar as leading currency and partial coverage by gold, were broken by the monetary crisis of 1971, the rules of the IMF have essentially been preserved. U.S. dollars have been replaced by Special Drawing Rights (SDR) as means of payment and reserves. In addition, the mark, franc, pound, and yen have become unofficial reserve currencies. On the IMF Board of Governors, where they have a mean voting percentage of 27.03, corresponding to their quotas for SDRs, the EC states assume a key position. However, in recent years monetary policy has been set less by the Board of Governors or the Permanent Council of Ministers, than by the Group of Ten, or at multilateral conferences such as the various "economic summits."

In the realm of trade policy, the Federal Republic has been working actively within the framework of the General Agreement on Tariffs and Trade (GATT), whose aim is a harmonization of international trade through gradual elimination of tariffs and other trade barriers. In the GATT negotiations, which since 1973 have been led by the EC Commission, Bonn has, because of its high dependency on foreign trade, a particular interest in unhindered access to world markets along with stabilization of the international monetary system. Another important forum is UNCTAD, which furthers the dialogue between industrialized and developing nations and deals with issues of stabilizing prices and profits of raw materials as well as developing a new international economic order.

Beyond these institutional connections, the West German economy is also highly integrated into the world economy by virtue of the large volume of its foreign trade, its international services, and its capital transfer. The share of foreign trade in the gross national product is more than 40 percent, whereas the corresponding figure for the United States, for example, is about 15 percent. The share of exports is similarly high, amounting to 30 percent in 1980. More than half (55 percent) of business abroad is in capital goods; primary and manufacturing goods total about 25 percent. Export dependency increased substantially during the 1970s. The Federal Republic has grown strong competitively in the world market and has been able to raise both value and volume of its exports. The high level of exports has had an impact on business profits as well as the structure of the job market and the rate of employment. In 1980, the export dependency of those employed in the Federal Republic amounted to more than 25 percent, that is, every fourth job was directly or indirectly tied to exports. Domestically this has led to a solid community of interest between business and unions. An ''export pact'' among the most important social groups supports the world orientation of the German economy.

At the same time, the West German economy is greatly dependent on imports of industrial raw materials. Ninety-five percent of gas and petroleum, 95 percent of iron ores, and 94 percent of all other nonferrous metals have to be imported. The enormous price increases for raw materials on the world market—crude oil by nearly 1,000 percent in ten years, nonferrous metals by about 75 percent—have resulted in a sharp decline in economic growth and high rates of unemployment in the Federal Republic.

The integration of the Federal Republic into the international economy has not developed evenly but has been concentrated on a number of countries and groups of countries. Roughly 50 percent of its foreign trade is transacted with other EC countries; the Community thus provides the most important model for the Federal Republic's foreign economic integration. The United States and the other OECD countries are also main trading partners. While the volume of trade with the state trading nations has remained relatively constant in recent years, fluctuating around 5 percent, the flow of commodities with the developing countries has become increasingly important. These latter are not only the most important suppliers of raw materials, but also are active buyers of West German capital goods.

Another dimension of the Federal Republic's economic interdependence is in the international flow of capital. The nation had claims and liabilities amounting to 65 billion marks and net currency reserves of 63 billion marks at the end of 1980. Though the actual sums of maneuverable capital are smaller, the influence on the world economy of transactions emanating from the Federal Republic appears obvious.[18]

The position of the Federal Republic on the international capital markets was especially strong when it enjoyed a steady surplus in its balance of payments as well as large foreign exchange reserves. As a creditor nation it not only had a say in international monetary questions, but also exerted an influence on the economic policy of other countries. By purchasing U.S. dollars in the 1960s the Federal Republic financed the deficit in the United States balance of payments, which originated largely in the Vietnam War; it gave detente-motivated credits to Yugoslavia and Poland, and it supported politically shaky countries such as Turkey, Italy, and Portugal with foreign currency loans.

But the Federal Republic has also been greatly dependent on developments in the international commodity and capital markets. As a result of the worldwide recession and the enormously increased oil prices, its balance of foreign exchange payments went into the red at the end of the 1970s. Similarly, the U.S. policy of high interest rates had a direct influence on interest levels and investment climate in the Federal Republic.

The fact that the Federal Republic conducts roughly 50% of its foreign trade within the Common Market gives the European Community, in addition to its political significance, an economic importance that forces the German government to make various sorts of political concessions. The value of trade with the East, on the other hand, is frequently overestimated. Its importance is chiefly that deliveries from the Soviet Union and other East European countries allow for a diversification of raw materials and energy imports and, at the same time, help form a market for high-cost industrial goods. The increased importance of raw materials suppliers of the third world, especially after the oil crisis of 1973, gives added impetus to the Federal Republic to adopt a positive attitude toward them. This is evidenced in the reorientation of its traditional policy of friendship to Israel, toward a more pro-Arab stance. Above all, however, the Federal Republic feels bound to make a greater contribution to overcoming or at least mitigating the North-South conflict.

Because of its economic strength, Bonn finds itself regularly confronted with demands from its allies in the realm of security policy. It is expected either to raise its own defense spending or else give support to other, more needy allies. Faced with U.S. pressure for increased "burden-sharing," the Federal Republic declared its willingness to provide military equipment and training assistance for countries outside Europe; at about the same time it committed itself to help reduce U.S. balance of payments deficits by means of various offset payments agreements. In the European Defense Improvement Program (EDIP) established in the 1970s and the Long-Term Defense Program (LTDP) the Federal Republic bears the lion's share of the costs. In 1980 Bonn stepped forward as head of the consortium providing aid to Turkey. These forms of aid-giving reflect alliance obligations founded on German economic strength. However, the economic power of the Federal Republic does face limits, and ebbing of this strength implies limitations in foreign policy.

The connection between economic policy and security policy is susceptible to crises for other reasons as well. First of all, the Federal Republic continues to be largely dependent upon the United States in matters of security, and secondly, it is closely integrated politically and economically with its West European partners. Finally, for political and economic reasons it has a strong interest in cooperation with the Soviet Union and the East European states. This wide range of interests entails a latent danger of priority conflicts, which in the past have flared up particularly over trade with the East. In 1962 the German government bowed to a resolution of the alliance and agreed not to supply large-diameter pipes to the Soviet Union; 20 years later, despite vehement criticism from Washington, it stood by the West European gas-pipeline deal concluded with the Soviet Union. This time it was able to come through the conflict, since it found itself in accord with its West European partners and could bring its increased political weight to bear. However, this did not remove the basic conflict, which had its origins in differing appraisals of East-West relations and the political uses of economic instruments.[19] The conflict over the gas-pipeline deal also showed that the Western industrial nations lacked suitable means not only for recognizing in timely fashion the mutual interactions between issues of economic and monetary policy on the one hand and problems of foreign policy and security on the other, but also for developing appropriate compromise solutions.

International Organizations and Conferences as Contexts for Foreign Policy

The Federal Republic's membership in a number of international organizations and its participation in international conferences produce ties and commitments but also additional political possibilities. Alongside the European Community and the Atlantic alliance, the United Nations with its specialized agencies and conferences is currently one of the most important contexts for West German foreign policy. The Federal Republic has been a full member since 1973, once the Basic Treaty with the GDR had established the basis for joint membership of the two German states in the world organization. However, the Federal Republic had already been active in the UN system since the 1950s. It was a member of several subcommittees as well as all UN specialized agencies and took an active part in numerous international conferences of the United Nations. As one of the leading industrial nations it made high-level financial and material contributions to the organization. Since 1973 it has participated as a member of equal standing in the sessions of the General Assembly; in 1974 it was selected as a representative of the West European group of states to the Economic and Social Council; in 1977-78 it belonged to the Security Council of the United Nations; in the 35th General Assembly of 1980-81, Bonn's ambassador to the UN, Rüdiger Freiherr von Wechmar, held the presidency. Today there are no UN specialized agencies or conferences of importance in which the Federal Republic is not represented.[20]

In line with the goals of the United Nations, German UN policy concentrates on peace-keeping and disarmament as well as global development. Bonn makes an important financial, material, and political contribution to international crisis management through its support for UN peacekeeping missions and forces. Since 1973 the Federal Republic has also been a part of the Committee on Disarmament (CD) in Geneva; but it had already, before this time, been following the work of this committee and its predecessors, in part through its own expert observer in Geneva. Whereas in the 1960s it found itself more the object of international disarmament efforts and strove to avoid negative consequences for the German question, in the 1970s it directed itself to the goal of achieving peace worldwide and came forward many times with studies and proposals of its own.

There have been discernible shifts in emphasis in the area of de-

velopment aid also. In the 1950s and 1960s, bilateral technical assistance and private economic aid were predominant, and support for
Bonn's position on the German question was expected in return. The
Social-Liberal coalition then largely abandoned the political conditions
of cooperation with countries of the third world. At the same time the
multilateral elements of this policy assumed greater importance: the
European-Arab dialogue, cooperation with the "Group of 77," efforts
to achieve a New International Economic Order at UNCTAD. However, under the pressure of the recession, the long-term goal of narrowing the gap between rich and poor nations again receded in favor
of promoting jobs at home and of assuring imports or raw materials
and exports of industrial goods.

The high degree of interconnectedness among states and the close
interdependence of decision-making processes have given the Federal
Republic a range of possibilities for exerting its influence. Geographical
situation, population, and military potential, but above all its prominent economic power—which prompts many observers of the Federal
Republic to speak of an *économie dominante*[21]—contribute to a situation
where international decisions as a rule are possible only with, not
against Bonn. In many instances the initiative comes from the Federal
Republic, or Bonn supports certain political strategies through its close
rapport with one of its partners—usually the U.S. or France—or else it
makes solutions possible because of its financial and economic
strength. It does this in no way disinterestedly, but rather in pursuit of
its own interests and objectives, as well as in recognition that historical
continuity, central geographic position, and worldwide economic interdependence do not allow for an autonomous policy, but permit only a
flexible adaptation to international structures and skillful influencing of
them.

THREE PERIODS OF POSTWAR GERMAN POLICY
AND THEIR ARCHITECTS

A description of the foundations of German foreign policy would
be incomplete without reference to the contributions made by individual political figures. The potential for playing a formative role was
especially great in the early years of the republic, as the constitutional
framework preserved room for maneuver, the foreign policy
bureaucracy had attained little weight of its own, and the constraints of
traditions and established ways of doing things had yet to take hold. In
subsequent periods the latitude for individual action always opened up
when new fields of foreign policy were pioneered, as with the Brandt-

Scheel government in Ostpolitik and the Schmidt-Genscher government in foreign economic policy.

The "Adenauer Era": The Constitutive Phase of Postwar Policy

The first phase of German postwar policy was shaped primarily by the basic structures of the international order and by the paramount influence of the Federal Republic's first chancellor, Konrad Adenauer. Such was his influence that one can justifiably speak of an "Adenauer Era" (Schwarz). At that time a number of directions in foreign policy were set that were of enormous importance for the further development of the Federal Republic. The central element of this policy was that of Western integration, a policy pursued by Adenauer out of inner conviction and external necessity and consisting essentially of four aims:

1. To support and strengthen the as yet unsolidified democracy at home through close ties with the Western democracies;
2. To supersede the occupation regime and the restrictions of allied control with obligations voluntarily assumed;
3. To overcome the historical strains between Germany and its western neighbors by means of a close economic and political integration of Western Europe;
4. To ensure the protection of the Federal Republic against military aggression or political subversion by means of a durable alliance with the United States.

Toward the East, Adenauer's policy was confined to establishing diplomatic relations with Moscow and then using these lines of communication for sounding out under what conditions the Soviet Union might be prepared to entertain a relaxation of European tensions— whether allowing reunification, by a truce of limited duration, or by an "Austrian solution" for the GDR.[22]

The Adenauer Era was also shaped by the economic concepts of Ludwig Erhard. Domestically, this meant the establishment of a "social market economy"—a combination of market economy and social policy that characterizes the West German system to the present day; externally, its far-reaching integration into the world economy. Finally, the new regime would not have been so effective without the knowledgeable and committed support of politicians and civil servants devoted to Adenauer, figures such as Heinrich von Brentano, Walter Hallstein, and Wilhelm Grewe.[23]

In the founding phase of the Second Republic, there were also created and developed political structures and institutional tools that would shape Bonn's foreign policy in future. The paramount importance of the chancellor in the political system of the Federal Republic was derived more from the personal force and effectiveness of its first incumbent than from the powers set forth in the Basic Law. In Adenauer's day the Foreign Office was an instrument to be used by the chancellor, if need be, over the head of Foreign Minister von Brentano. Von Brentano's successor, Gerhard Schröder, was the first to establish for the ministry the principle of departmental competence founded in the Basic Law and to provide the Foreign Office a greater measure of influence. However, his time in office coincided with a weakening of the role of the chancellor—after 1961 Adenauer's days in office were numbered as a result of the Berlin crisis and the Spiegel affair, and he was followed as head of government by the luckless Erhard. The position of foreign minister did not attain a weight of its own until this office was conferred on the basis of coalition agreements to the smaller coalition partner—in 1966 to the SPD, since 1969 the FDP.

As long as security policy was primarily a function of foreign policy, Adenauer reserved its conduct to himself; Theodor Blank, his first minister of defense, was essentially his agent. However, Blank's successor, Franz Josef Strauss, soon gained a political weight of his own, in part as a result of his quickly acquired military expertise, in part because of his independent and dynamic personality, which then tripped him up in 1962 in the Spiegel affair. Adenauer did not hesitate to acknowledge the superior expertise of a cabinet colleague, so long as the latter operated within the framework laid down by "the old man." This also marked his relationship with his economics minister, Ludwig Erhard, whom he gave largely a free hand in foreign economic policy. Conflict between the two did not emerge until Erhard set about to succeed Adenauer.

At the peak of his power—essentially from 1953 to 1961—Adenauer proved a master at harmonizing the three constitutionally defined and inherently divergent principles: responsibility for general policy guidance, principle of departmental competence, and cabinet policy-making—not only reducing them to a common denominator, but directing them toward his person. Moreover, he was able to impart government responsibility upon potential competitors or critics—e.g., representatives of the trade unions, industry, or the churches. It also did help that the dominant position of the Christian Democratic Union (CDU), and its Bavarian sister party, the Christian Social Union (CSU), was never seriously challenged. The result was a political field of forces in large measure oriented toward Adenauer, yet substantially less effective after the chancellor's capacity to act had been diminished in the wake of the domestic and foreign policy crises of 1961–62.

Analogous to this sort of centralized system of government orientation to the dominant personality of the head of government, the party system was also highly personalized during this initial phase of the Federal Republic. In Kurt Schumacher the Social Democratic Party (SPD) had a politically effective opposition leader, whose illness and untimely death in 1952 was a major setback for party leadership and direction. Under his successor, Erich Ollenhauer, the Schumacher course of a principled anti-communist and Western orientation that would give priority to restoring Germany's unity over its integration into the Western bloc was not put forward convincingly enough, especially not for gaining a parliamentary majority. Not until the end of the Adenauer Era did the SPD regenerate its top leadership and adapt the party's course to changed international parameters. It was essentially the work of Fritz Erler that laid the conceptional basis for the change of course, which Herbert Wehner publicly consummated with his sensational Bundestag speech of June 30, 1960.[24] Willy Brandt, who had gained in political stature as governing mayor of Berlin during the crisis of 1958–61, could then as SPD candidate for chancellor offer an alternative to Adenauer. But it was the Grand Coalition of CDU/CSU and SPD, replacing the Erhard government at the end of 1966, that first gave the SPD the opportunity to demonstrate its ability to govern.

Adenauer's success, at least up to the height of the Berlin crisis in 1961, rested on the fact that he and the policy he pursued in large measure accorded with the interests of the Western allies, especially the United States. His policy of Western integration coupled with greater international status for the Federal Republic suited the U.S. containment policy toward the Soviet Union; in this context the Federal Republic became an important ally. The "thaw" in East-West relations in 1955 and the attempts that same year to resume the four-power dialogue on European security and the future of Germany put this rapport to the test. But it did not break until, at the height of the Berlin crisis in 1961, Washington began to seek a modus vivendi with Moscow.

With East-West detente, the Adenauer government became a prisoner of its own "policy of strength," which was set upon solving the national question through unconditional integration into the West and nonrecognition of the political changes in Europe as a result of the Second World War. The Hallstein Doctrine, in which Bonn sought to deny the GDR international recognition, ultimately became the rope with which Bonn tied its own hands. This policy became completely untenable when the other Western nations began endeavoring to normalize and devolop their political and economic relations with the East European states and the Soviet Union.

The "policy of small steps" pursued by Foreign Minister Gerhard Schröder as of 1962 attempted to adapt to the new international tendencies without, however, giving up Bonn's basic positions on the German question and without realizing that the allies had already irreversibly distanced themselves from these. Thus, more and more the Federal Republic was running the risk of isolation—the very danger that Adenauer had sought to prevent with his policy of Western integration. Adenauer's resignation in the fall of 1963—for reasons of age and domestic politics—thus coincided with the end of an epoch in German foreign policy of which the distinguishing feature was the way the political objectives of the German government paralleled those of its most important ally, the United States.

The 1960s were a period of transition. One phase of German foreign policy was coming to an end and a new one was heralding its arrival. Key episodes were the discussions on breaking the deadlock in relations with the GDR; Gerhard Schröder's efforts toward a "new Ostpolitik," which were reflected in the "peace note" of 1966; and the Grand Coalition's dialogue with the Soviet Union on a renunciation of force. The tactical character of the alliance between CDU/CSU and SPD—allowing the former to remain in office while opening it up to the latter—was reflected in the contradictions in the policy pursued by the Grand Coalition. Whereas the CDU/CSU held that nonrecognition of the GDR and of the border changes in Central and Eastern Europe had to be maintained, the SPD was prepared to accept the status quo if that were to make possible reconciliation with the East.

Willy Brandt and the Social-Liberal Coalition: Rising to New Frontiers

The formation of the Social-Liberal coalition between the SPD and Free Democratic Party (FDP) in the fall of 1969 opened up the possibility of a new direction in foreign and domestic policy.[25] The election of Gustav Heinemann as West German president in March of that year had augured not only the change in coalition but the emergence of a widespread desire for reform. The election of Willy Brandt as chancellor, a representative of the "other Germany" that had not compromised with Hitler in any way, and his act of homage at the memorial in the former Warsaw ghetto signaled that from that point forward the Germans were facing up to their past and were prepared to accept its consequences.

Willy Brandt's Ostpolitik started from the "situation as it really exists" in Europe and acknowledged it without giving away anything that had not been forfeited long before by Hitler. The decisive new element of this policy was the endeavor to reach a modus vivendi with the Soviet Union and the East European states on the basis of postwar realities. Both sides adhered to their different legal standpoints but precluded any change of the territorial status quo through the use or threat of force. The renunciation of force pertained chiefly to the European postwar borders, e.g., the Polish western frontier on the Oder and Neisse and the intra-German border on the Elbe and Werra.

The West, however, expected that the Soviet Union would in return respect the status quo on Berlin and agree to a settlement through which the situation in and around Berlin could be defused. With the Quadripartite Agreement on Berlin, the viability of West Berlin and its ties with the Federal Republic were placed on a treaty basis. Thus, too, the four victorious postwar powers created a framework that could be used by the two German states for normalizing their relations.

The core of the modus vivendi, however, was the de facto recognition of the GDR, enabling a closer cooperation toward solving the problems resulting from the partition, or, if and as long as this was not possible, at least a regulated coexistence. The goal of national unity was subsumed in the vision of a European order of peace, with which the partition of Europe and thus the division of Germany would be overcome.[26]

Brandt's historical achievement consisted in having recognized the necessity of giving up what had become a hollow policy of reunification and seizing the opportunity to effect a reconciliation with the East. His success rested on the fact that he—like Adenauer before him—could operate in harmony with the interest of the Western allies. Thus, his policy did not jeopardize the fundamental Western orientation of the Federal Republic but rather strengthened it by bringing Bonn into line with the West's detente policy and by freeing the allies of what had become an onerous duty of paying lip service to German unity, which in reality was no longer in their interest. The problematic side of this policy was that it aroused hopes that detente would lead to a significant and permanent reduction of political tensions and open up the possibility of reducing military potentials in Europe. This expectation, however, remained unfulfilled.

Toward the West the Social-Liberal coalition reinvigorated the efforts to develop the EEC into an economic and monetary union encompassing Great Britain and other nations willing to join. The founding of the European Political Cooperation (EPC) was a new impulse designed to put the European states in a position to speak with one voice on political matters. In the realm of military security, greater efforts were made within NATO and at the national level. One result was the European Defense Improvement Program (EDIP), another the strengthening and modernization of the Bundeswehr, which reached a peacetime strength of 495,000 troops and obtained a modern armament.

On the surface, Willy Brandt's resignation following the uncovering of the Guillaume espionage was a very personal step. However, in historical perspective it appears to be also an acknowledgment that the long-range goals of the Brandtian peace policy were not redeemable. This was the case for detente policy, whose dynamic was being retarded by political opposition within the Federal Republic, but also in the United States and presumably in the Soviet Union as well. Reform policy, affecting the basic principles of the meritocracy upon which the economic prosperity of the Federal Republic was based, was stagnating, just as financing it was becoming increasingly difficult in the face of worldwide recession.

The Schmidt-Genscher Government: Continuity and Reliability

Willy Brandt's successor as chancellor, Helmut Schmidt, found himself confronted with a twofold task: ensuring both the continuity of alliance and security policy anchored in the West and that of detente policy toward the Soviet Union and Eastern Europe. To that end the results of Ostpolitik had to be consolidated and safeguarded in the West. At the same time it was imperative to bring about, in close collaboration with the other Western industrial nations, a reordering of the world economy, which had been shaken to its foundations by the oil price dictates of the OPEC states. And finally, these diverse strains of policy had to be kept mutually compatible.

Whereas for Brandt detente had been the leitmotiv of peace policy, with Schmidt security policy in the broadest sense came to the fore. Its aims were stability and equilibrium in the East-West relationship. Its most important elements were the political dialogue, which must never be broken off even in times of crisis; negotiations on a balanced reduction of troops and armaments, which did not, however, preclude one's own "counterarmament," or modernization, if such was necessary to restore the balance of power; and finally economic cooperation, if and as far as this was in the interest of both sides and did not create any unilateral dependencies for the Federal Republic.

For a security policy understood in these terms Schmidt had already created the concept of a "strategy of equilibrium."[27] This could be carried out only on a multilateral basis; its vehicle was necessarily the Atlantic alliance. Hence, for Schmidt close coordination with the United States and amicable cooperation with France had priority. The multilateral context of the Federal Republic's security and detente policies ruled out any independent national course but did not prevent the Federal Republic from reaching bilateral accords, e.g., with the GDR, if these operated within the framework of jointly agreed policy. A further prerequisite for the success of such a policy was the internal stability and economic strength of the Western industrial nations. Helmut Schmidt therefore saw his particular responsibility in devising common action with the other Western powers to get the battered international economy going again.

Under Schmidt the Federal Republic carried out the self-conscious policy of a second-tier power. This policy was grounded in economic strength, geopolitical situation, and proven reliability as an ally, but was also shaped by an awareness of the Federal Republic's ties with its partners and its dependence on global developments. This perception of the limits of German policy led to moderation in pursuing national interests and rejection of a predominant international role. The result was, nevertheless, an enormous increase in the Federal Republic's political potential and importance in international affairs. Yet at the same time the bounds of its freedom of movement became clear as the East-West antagonism distinctly sharpened at the beginning of 1980 after the Soviet intervention in Afghanistan. It turned out that the German chancellor simply could not act as "interpreter" between the two contending parties when these in fact were the two global powers. Thus, it became evident that the political effectiveness of the Federal Republic was greatest within the alliance and with the United States, not against them. This did not rule out limited conflicts with the leading Western power, e.g., on the question of the natural gas-pipeline deal with the Soviet Union, when Bonn found itself in agreement with its European allies.

The institutional framework of foreign policy had changed in a number of ways since the Adenauer Era. Since 1961 no party has enjoyed a majority in the Bundestag, so governments have always been coalition governments. As a rule the agreed political strategies as well as the distribution of offices have been the product of tough bargaining and compromise. Since 1966 the junior partner has always been allowed the posts of foreign minister and economics minister, besides that of vice-chancellor, and has thus attained a central role in foreign policy. In place of the chancellor, who lays down the course of foreign policy on his own, on the strength of his personality and office, there has developed a four-tiered policy structure, in which the head of government, of course, continues to assume paramount importance. The other essential elements are the foreign minister and the economics minister (who both belong to the coalition party), and the defense minister (who in turn comes from the ranks of the larger governing party). Further, because of the importance of foreign economic and monetary policy, the finance minister and the president of the German Federal Bank also play an important role. Owing to the structure of the government as well as the nature of the problems to be surmounted, the decision-making process within the federal government has been built much more around teamwork than was the case in the 1950s.

At the same time, there has developed a functioning ministerial bureaucracy that outlasts changes in government and attempts to master the growing technical problems through organizational routine. The hierarchical structure within the individual "houses" combines with a strict adherence to the principle of departmental authority, which frequently has degenerated into egoistic departmentalism. This has tended to produce relatively deeply entrenched channels of decision-making processes. Yet because the policy domains are in large measure interdependent, there have developed at the lower working levels unorthodox interministerial processes of coordination, or else it happens that the problems first emerge in cabinet consultations and are then often worked out in personalized ways.

The possibilities for parliamentary control in the area of foreign policy have dwindled down to a supervision of general direction.[28] Parliamentary parties and representatives simply lack the staff expertise that heads of government and ministers have at their command. Moreover, a great many decisions have shifted to supranational bodies. On the other hand, the transnational contacts have developed to such an extent that individual representatives have been able effectively to put forward foreign policy positions in Washington or Moscow without these being conveyed by the government or the parties. (In this way, e.g., the CDU, then in opposition, with the aid of the Konrad Adenauer Foundation, was able to establish close contacts with important political figures in the United States so that at the right time the CDU leaders could present themselves to the Reagan administration as a political alternative in the Federal Republic.) In a number of ways industry, banks, associations, and trade unions have been involved in this process of arriving at foreign policy decisions. All in all, the Federal Republic's system of foreign policy has become a great deal more sophisticated.[29]

However, the increased complexity of both substance and process in foreign policy has had the effect that questions have become clouded and more difficult to follow. Thus, when the experts themselves are unable to reach a consensus on the East-West military balance, the public suffers from the dearth of standards for assessment and it becomes an object of manipulation. People can no longer follow the difficult logic of deterrence, e.g., that their own destruction is to be prevented by its being taken into account. One consequence of this "impenetrability" of central political axioms has been a feeling of powerlessness and frustration which has led to political alienation, especially of the young and committed, and has fostered the emergence of a "green" movement that sees itself as an alternative to established politics. Inadequate legitimation of security policy thus is seen to lead to the development of a political "counter-culture," calling into question the political and social consensus of the postwar period.

The formation of an active protest potential, which has taken place partly within the SPD, partly to the left of it, has had direct consequences for the party system at the federal and state levels. The development of a political force outside the established political system has jeopardized the existence of the FDP and complicated the majority-building process. The FDP's switch in coalition, which brought about the downfall of Helmut Schmidt, was primarily a tactical move to ensure survival. It was also an indication that the impetus of the new departure of 1969 and the coalition's raison d'etre had been exhausted.

Thus, the year 1982 also marks a watershed and a turning point. It was more than simply a change from a Social-Liberal coalition to a Conservative-Liberal coalition. Following the phase of integration in the West in the 1950s and the opening to the East in the first half of the 1970s, Helmut Schmidt helped the Federal Republic, not least by his great personal effort, to attain an unprecedented influence in international affairs. This leadership was grounded in economic strength and the reliability of Bonn's political course. Unlike Adenauer or Brandt, Schmidt viewed his primary mission not in overcoming historical burdens but in mastering the challenges of the present. The Federal Republic had become a normal state.

Epilogue

The Federal Republic entered a new political stage when Helmut Kohl and his coalition of CDU/CSU and FDP came to power on Oct. 1, 1982, and general elections in March 1983 confirmed the new government for another four years in office. The Kohl government's proclaimed "change of direction" was to consist in the priority of security policy over detente and of performance over provision in social policy. In this way the Federal Republic was again to become a politically reliable and economically strong partner in the Western alliance.

In soon appeared, however, that a new government team does not alter the international framework within which the Federal Republic must operate. In security policy the government carried through with the deployment of the Pershing II on German soil in accordance with the NATO dual-track decision of December 1979—while the SPD opposition could afford the luxury of rejection. At the same time, Bonn called upon Washington to make new efforts with the arms control negotiations. Relations with the GDR were not frozen but rather experienced a new blossoming, to which a private bank loan of billions to the GDR no doubt contributed. Despite differing party colors, European relations were distinguished by a new Franco-German rapprochement. The declared priority of security policy was crumbling away under the exigencies of German politics and the constraints of quotidian affairs. Under the surface of close ties with Washington, muddling through and avoiding any clear-cut choices became the order of the day.

2

Western Integration, European Security, and the German Question

As the Federal Republic had come into being as a result of Europe's division into spheres of interest conditioned by cold-war power politics and ideology, it necessarily followed that Bonn would be closely tied to the Western democracies. And the Western powers would have an interest in renewed German sovereignty only when assured that German political, economic, and military potential would benefit and strengthen the West in its conflict with the Eastern bloc. Western integration and anticommunism thus became the Federal Republic of Germany's *raison d'état*.[1]

At the same time the division of Europe into two hostile camps was a source of tension that brought with it the danger of a military conflict along the fault line of Europe. In the mid-1950s it became clear that the struggle between East and West, a struggle for control of Europe's center, could not be won by either side. The danger was perceived that both sides could become embroiled involuntarily in a war that, in view of the long-range weapons systems, would not remain localized. Hence, greater efforts were made to find ways of stabilizing the military situation in Europe. The result was a number of proposals for a European security system, zones of limited armament, military disengagement, or regional disarmament measures. But as the fault line in Europe ran straight through the middle of Germany, all these plans—whether coupled with steps toward reunification or based on the status quo—affected the future of the two German states, their status, and the political contexts in which they operated.

The conception of the Federal Republic as a provisional state and the concern about the destabilizing effects of the division prompted the West to seek solutions combining a reunification of Germany with arms limitation in Central Europe. These endeavors produced the first Eden Plan, the Herter Plan of 1959, and various other plans for Germany. While the Bonn government gave integration in the West and reunification priority over arms limitation and hence created a linkage between the two, the opposition SPD tried to bring into play, as leverage and context for a reunified Germany, proposals for a collective security system in Europe designed to ensure both "security for Germany and security from Germany" (Fritz Erler). The other Western states were striving primarily for military stabilization; under the umbrella of global deterrence, military confrontation in Europe would be defused by steps toward arms limitation. The different priorities between Bonn and its Western allies made any substantial progress in the area of European security impossible.

THE CONSOLIDATION OF THE EUROPEAN SYSTEM

The End of the Occupation Regime and the Federal Republic's Admission to NATO

In 1955 the Paris Treaties both terminated the occupation regime in the Federal Republic and ensured Bonn a voice in the Western system. The price was the deployment of German armed forces integrated in NATO, the acceptance of arms limitations and controls in the framework of the Western European Union (WEU), and an explicit renunciation of force toward the Western powers. The German question was left open in a way that saw the United States, Great Britain, and France expressly affirming their responsibility for restoring the unity of Germany while the Federal Republic committed itself to pursuing this goal exclusively by peaceful means.[2] Despite the collapse of the European Defense Community (EDC), the possibility of a close political and economic association with the states of Western Europe seemed more tangible than the now politically remote prospect of reunification. However, rearmament, arms control, and renunciation of force were more than simply the Federal Republic's quid pro quo for sovereignty, security guarantee, and the prospect of a European option: they constituted an enormous augmentation of political power and political options for the West German state.

The Soviet Union had been able to delay the development of the Western alliance system by diplomatic initiatives, which contributed to the rejection of the EDC treaty by the French National Assembly. However, it could not prevent German rearmament. Most importantly, it was unable, with the offer of reunification in exchange for German neutrality, to divert the Federal Republic from its Western course and thus remove the cornerstone from the Western alliance system. The West German government, which under Konrad Adenauer's leadership pursued a resolute policy of Western integration, was aided by the fact that after the traumatic experiences of the war and postwar years the German people were more intent on security and prosperity than on national unity, and by the fact that its room for maneuver toward the East was narrowly limited by the alliance policy of the U.S. and the latent mistrust of Germany's western neighbors. The Soviet Union, in turn, used this political defeat to implant its own system of European hegemony by establishing the Warsaw Pact and politically upgrading East Germany—which was now declared "sovereign" and admitted into the Warsaw Pact "counteralliance."

The Establishment of Diplomatic Relations with the Soviet Union

The consolidation of the European system did, however, open up new possibilities for movement. At the global level, the Geneva conference diplomacy of 1955 heralded the beginning of a thaw in East-West relations; at the European level, the Austrian State Treaty and the establishment of diplomatic relations between Bonn and Moscow signaled an end to the forced rigidity in the bloc structures of the cold war.

From the Federal Republic's standpoint the establishment of direct relations with the Soviet Union had become possible once Bonn had joined NATO and thus raised itself above the lurking suspicion that it could conduct a *schaukelpolitik* playing off East and West "à la Rapallo." Also, it appeared advantageous to establish relations once the four powers set about reviving the old wartime alliance and negotiating on European security and the German question. However, care had to be taken that paving the way for diplomatic contact could not be interpreted as recognition of the status quo—and thus of the existence of the GDR. To this end the "Hallstein Doctrine," named after Walter Hallstein, state secretary in the Foreign Office, was designed to accentuate the exceptional nature of twofold German relations with Moscow and to prevent international recognition of the GDR.

Bonn did not overestimate its possibilities, however; Adenauer knew that reunification would come about only with the consent of the four powers. His trip to Moscow would simply enable him to probe firsthand to see whether the Kremlin was prepared to make concessions—which meant giving up the GDR—and to demonstrate at home his willingness to negotiate and so counter the opposition's insistence on an active reunification policy. The enduring outcome of this trip—besides the release of the prisoners of war detained in the Soviet Union—was the insight that with the new political and military structures in Europe a reunification on Western terms was not achievable in the foreseeable future, but that, regardless of political antagonisms, the Soviet leadership was interested in reducing tensions and diminishing the danger of war.[3]

The Geneva Four-Power Conferences

The Geneva Conferences of 1955—the Summit Conference in July and the Foreign Ministers Conference in October and November—likewise demonstrated the stability of the political structures developed in Europe after the Second World War. East and West alike were interested primarily in consolidating, not altering the status quo, yet they endeavored to achieve a political detente and to diminish the dangers of conflict emanating from the military confrontation. In the eyes of the West the Geneva summit was a complex mixture of foreign and domestic exoneration and hope, alloyed with skepticism, that once the status quo in Europe had been assured, a political modus vivendi could be reached with the Soviet Union. It was thus a response both to the repeated calls from Moscow to settle the outstanding problems at a conference of the highest level and to the expectations forcefully articulated in West European domestic politics that stronger political initiatives ought to bring a reduction of tensions and of armaments. For the leaders in the Kremlin the decisive consideration may have been more that of regaining lost ground by means of diplomatic activity designed to point out the narrow room for maneuver of the West—should the latter want to maintain what had been achieved with the Paris Treaties—and to exploit the differences in interests in the West.

The four points on the Geneva agenda—reunification of Germany, European security, disarmament, and development of contacts between East and West—were a product of the way the conference came about and of the mixture of Eastern and Western interests and constraints. All four powers could refer to proposals that had already been tabled: the West to the Eden Plan for a reunification of Germany in conjunction with a pact with guarantees to be concluded simultaneously; the Soviet Union to its draft for an "All-European Treaty on Collective Security," and both sides to the various phased plans for a general, controlled disarmament. But in Geneva the Western powers laid the main emphasis on quick disarmament steps. The U.S. believed it had the greatest room for maneuver here, that it could make a lasting public impact and be able to fall back on a secure reserve position in the UN Disarmament Commission. Great Britain and France, on the other hand, were more inclined to regard the realm of European security as negotiable and forwarded their own initiatives, such as the "second Eden Plan" of inspection zones on both sides of the iron curtain. With its proposals for a nonaggression pact between NATO and the Warsaw Pact and for a European security treaty, the Soviet Union wanted to gain a formal confirmation of the status quo and at the same time to lay the foundation for subsequently altering it in a European collective security system.[4]

The directive to the foreign ministers for continuing the negotiations inextricably linked the German question with the complex of European security and the disarmament problem and thus covered over the different priorities in East and West. The priority that the Federal Republic's allies had previously accorded a solution to the German question was given up in favor of a balance of reunification and European security. Yet any agreement would come to nought, ostensibly because of the Western demand for free and secret elections in all of Germany and the Eastern insistence on withdrawal of all foreign troops from German territory as well as the dissolution of the military alliances. Essentially, neither side was prepared to accept the shifts in power connected with a reunification of Germany and redefinition of its alliance status, with their repercussions for the two systems of hegemony. The disarmament question was referred back to the Five-Power Commission of the United Nations. Thus, as a matter of negotiating tactics, a distinction was made between the global problem of disarmament and the European issues; but the close political connection between arms control measures and steps toward a European security system again obscured the dividing line. This heralded a certain regionalization in disarmament politics, which reached a peak in 1957-58 in the debate on nuclear-weapons-free zones in Europe.[5]

In the "international modus vivendi" after Geneva, both sides accepted the status quo in Europe for the time being. The Western powers maintained an emphatic protest and the Soviet Union kept to its longer-range goals, but both sides made it clear that they did not contemplate violent intervention in internal affairs beyond the line demarcating the spheres of interest. With the "thaw" in East-West relations, however, the different constellations of interest among the various Western states began to emerge. For the British—and at times for the French government, too—there was a strong temptation to sever the political from the military problems and seek first a solution to the European security question by means of arms limitation measures. Washington adhered the longest to the priority of resolving the German question. At the same time it was trying to differentiate between the political problems of Europe and the global disarmament questions.

This was done not just out of consideration for the West German ally—rather, the United States assumed that the U.S. lead in weapons technology and its strategic nuclear superiority would eventually force the Soviet Union to make concessions, and secondly, Washington intended to isolate the "disarmament connection" from the European problems and utilize it if need be for contacts and agreements with Moscow.

For the Federal Republic the Geneva road was paved with a number of land mines. The Soviet proposals for an all-European security treaty jeopardized the policy of Western integration begun in 1949 and brought to an initial stage of completion with the Paris Treaties. The Soviet proposals would replace NATO with an uncertain collective guarantee system based on division and neutralization. But from Bonn's standpoint even the Western proposals implied the latent danger of an agreement at the expense of the Federal Republic. The linkage it postulated with the German question thus became an instrument with which Bonn sought to gain a voice in the negotiations on European security and disarmament.

SECURITY AND DETENTE IN ADENAUER'S CONCEPTION OF FOREIGN POLICY

The first phase of German postwar politics was stamped on the one hand by the specific international structures, on the other by the prominent influence of the Federal Republic's first chancellor, Konrad Adenauer. This influence was in part the result of the extensive harmony of Adenauer's political ideas with those of the three states that, first as occupying powers, then as protective powers and allies of the Federal Republic, accompanied it on its way into international politics; it was also the product of the virtuoso handling of a foreign policy decision-making system tailored to the head of government.[6] Moreover, the Federal Republic in 1955 stood, so to speak, at the beginning of its foreign policy career.

Western Integration as Dominant Element of Security Policy

Adenauer's thinking on foreign policy[7] was conditioned by concern over the Soviet Union's expansionist drive, which was grounded in power politics and ideology. Here Adenauer saw the cause of the tensions in world politics and the main threat to the Western states. The military confrontation of the two alliance systems as well as the division of Germany were symptoms, not causes of the East-West conflict. To this he brought skepticism, motivated by history, as to whether the German people, indeed whether the Western democracies as a whole, would possess the moral substance and inner strength to be immune to totalitarian and nationalistic temptations. Only the close ties of the Federal Republic of Germany to the Western community of nations would give permanence to its free democratic social order and put the West German state in a position to withstand the dangers emanating from Soviet Russia. In Adenauer's view "unity and consistency of the world's free peoples" were "the most effective guarantee for maintaining the security and freedom of the Western nations."[8]

This line of thinking had three basic elements. First, the security of the Federal Republic could not be guaranteed exclusively or primarily by military means, for the threat consisted just as much in internal instability and mutual distrust as in external aggression. The close connection of the Federal Republic with the Western democracies was to be instrumental in creating the foundation for a political community of West Europeans. Adenauer wrote in his memoirs:

> We could again realize the good things that we Europeans had inherited from our forefathers over the centuries: European thinking, Western thinking, Christian thinking, and again secure the European countries a role in the world economy and in international politics only if Europe were bound together in unity. Standing up for the cause of a strong, united Europe was the urgent task of contemporary Europeans.[9]

One important prerequisite for this was overcoming the old antagonism between Germany and France, even if this were to demand painstaking effort and sacrifice, e.g., on the Saar question. At the same time, the Europeanization of the various spheres of political action offered a way of accelerating the economic reconstruction, taking into account the security requirements of West European neighbors, and leading the Federal Republic back into the community of nations as an equal member.

Secondly, concerted political action in Western Europe called for the creation of certain institutional foundations, with which national responsibilities would be transferred to community organs and through which the union would be given a greater degree of permanence. Tasks and structure of a European Community could, indeed should, be flexible so as to be adaptable to prevailing political conditions. This approach was reflected in the European Coal and Steel Community (ECSC), instituted in 1950-51 with the aim of replacing the

Ruhr Statute and jointly regulating the production of coal, iron, and steel; the European Defense Community (EDC), which, however, broke down in 1954 over continued French mistrust toward Germany; the Western European Union (WEU), conceived as an alternative to the EDC and reorganized into a West European "security network" for Bonn's defense contribution, and finally, the European Economic Community (EEC) and the European Atomic Community (EURATOM). What had been accomplished in the formation of a European community must not, however, obscure the fact that Adenauer's goal remained political union. "I was well aware that the development needed time. The goal, however, had...to be kept steadily in mind: the political unity of Europe."[10]

The Federal Republic's entry into the community of nations as an equal partner and the building of a West European community were prerequisites for the third pillar of Adenauer's security policy, that of the Atlantic alliance. However, the link with America was qualitatively different from that with the West European neighbors. Adenauer saw "that in fact the basic interests of America and Europe are the same, but that not all vital interests of the European states need be vital interests of the United States as well, and conversely, that this inevitably results in differences in political views, which in certain situations necessarily lead to independent courses of action." Western Europe was no longer a great power, only the United States was in a position to establish a powerful political counterweight to a Soviet Union perceived as predominant. On the other hand, "in the long run the countries of Europe could...not fully develop their strengths if they continued to find their well-being and security solely through the patronage of the United States."[11] This required: first, a certain political distance from America; second, the necessity for Europe's own political and military efforts; third and finally, the endeavor to establish a security link between the United States and Western Europe.

NATO fulfilled these purposes in a particular way. The North Atlantic Pact was not an integrated defense community like the unsuccessful EDC; rather, it was an alliance of sovereign states, which nevertheless, in contrast to classical alliances, disposed of its own military apparatus. Thus it offered an organizational framework into which the Bundeswehr could be integrated. The special security measures, without which a rearmament was unacceptable to Germany's neighbors, could be arranged without inordinate discriminations in the context of the WEU, which was limited to the West European states. Even the failed EDC would have been geared with the core of NATO, through guarantees pronounced by the United States and the three allies responsible for Germany, and also through consultation agreements between the two organizations. In this way it would have been clear that a reliable protection for Western Europe was impossible without U.S. engagement.

The promises of mutual assistance according to Article 4 of the NATO Treaty were strengthened by declarations from the U.S. and Great Britain that they would leave in place their armed forces stationed on the continent and would employ them for the defense of alliance territory in accord with their partners. This presence of allied troops in the Federal Republic had a "trip-wire" function; it was a guarantee that in the event of conflict the nuclear potential of the U.S. would extend its deterrent effect or in the case of aggression would come into use. With much anxiety Adenauer followed the various changes in U.S. strategy as they came forth with the Radford Plan and the criticism of the strategy of massive retaliation. The chancellor was always concerned that the link between the conventional forces in Europe and the strategic nuclear forces in the United States could be weakened.

Not only was the West German defense contribution inseparably linked with the termination of the occupation regime and the attainment of sovereignty; in it Adenauer saw the essential prerequisite for the Federal Republic's participation in the strategic deliberations of the West. His policy was aimed at preventing war by demonstrating the unity and strength of the West. In this sense he conceived of the Bundeswehr and NATO primarily as political and not as military instruments.

For Adenauer, proposals for arms reduction or disarmament that would have called into question the Bundeswehr as a factor of political influence, the Federal Republic's integration in the West as "security network," or the U.S. presence as counterweight to the Soviet Union were no alternatives to the emerging system of European security. Moreover, since about 1952-53 he had assessed the risk of a military conflict with the Soviet Union as relatively slight. Hence, he viewed these sorts of proposals as a danger to his policy of Western integration and to the Federal Republic's social and political order secured by its ties with the West, but not as a possibility to create alternative security structures.

Conflict of Priorities between Integration and Reunification

Yet the central problem of European security was the German question. It was the key point of all proposals from the Stalin note of 1952 to the Herter Plan of 1959; it was also a lever used mainly by the Soviet Union to generate movement in the increasingly stable system of European security and to change this system as it would have it. Soviet policy on Germany combined in various versions the offer of a reunification with the condition of a neutralization of Germany; its goal was to weaken the Federal Republic's ties with the West and consolidate, potentially also to expand, the Soviet realm of domination. The various Western proposals for a disengagement or a neutralized zone in Central Europe, on the other hand, were designed to reduce the danger of conflict at the iron curtain and stabilize the situation in Europe.[12] Moreover, they were an attempt to underscore the consequences of the Second World War in the ledger of history.

For the Adenauer foreign policy, such proposals implied dangers of a special kind. They confronted it with the domestically controversial question of whether priority should be given to integration into the West or to reunification. For all the verbal declarations professing the goal of reunification, Adenauer had already, with the decision for rearmament (actually even earlier, with the decision to create a separate West German state, contrary to Jakob Kaiser's bridge idea),[13] decided in favor of Western integration. "Adenauer...was not interested in a reunification that would have detached Germany from close association with the West."[14]

Adenauer regarded the Soviet thrusts—whether they were designated proposals for German reunification as in 1952 or plans for a European security system as in 1954 and 1955—as maneuvers to disrupt the process of West European unification. Their timing, coinciding with the EDC ratification debates and Bonn's entry into NATO, supported such a suspicion. In Adenauer's view a breakdown in the work of West European unification would have not only raised the danger of reviving centuries-old rivalries, but also signified Western Europe's ultimate renunciation of having a say in global politics. If European integration did not become a reality, then there was the risk of U.S. disengagement from the European continent.[15] "Russia" would then "intensify its influence on the Federal Republic of Germany and ultimately harness the Federal Republic of Germany permanently for its own ends."[16] Hence, there was just one possibility: "The German road had to lead to Europe and not into a national solitude that would also be isolation in world politics."[17]

Had Adenauer thus abandoned reunification? By 1955, after his visit to Moscow, he was aware that a reunification without weakening ties with the West was not to be realized in a short- or medium-term perspective.[18] For him there remained only the hope that the Soviet Union, for political and economic reasons—in view of its limited economic resources and greater domestic pressure for raising living standards—would one day release the GDR, or at least grant the people a greater measure of freedom in order to gain a breathing space in the competition with the West over arms technologies and power politics. This was the purpose behind the proposal in the spring of 1958 of an "Austrian solution" for the GDR and the offer aired in 1963 of a ten-year "truce" on the German question linked with the condition of greater human rights in the GDR.[19] Such proposals were based on a twofold calculation. First, there was a recognition of the priority of—to use a slogan of that time—"Freedom over unity" (Jaspers),[20] i.e., national unity was assigned a back seat to more freedom for the GDR. Secondly, in these sorts of proposals there was always some expectation that the communist regime in the GDR would not be able to hold on if political conditions were relaxed, and that the people—as in the Saarland—would in free elections opt for a union with the Federal Republic. Only in the so-called "Globke Plan"—an internal working paper developed in 1959-60 amidst Western preparations for the Paris Summit Conference—were a (temporary) recognition of the GDR, measures of humanitarian relief, and a plebiscite on reunification in both German states bound up in one package.[21]

Adenauer's proposals were distinguished from the Foreign Office's position on the German question by a high degree of flexibility; yet the question remains, under what conditions would the Soviet Union at that time have been prepared to give up the GDR or the party leadership it supported? Perhaps offering not to equip the Bundeswehr with nuclear weapons would have been a way of testing the Soviets' willingness to negotiate; but alliance and domestic considerations prevented Adenauer from thinking out loud about that. Moreover, what advantage would the Soviet Union have had from a standstill agreement on the German question? What could have moved Moscow to agree to a temporary arrangement with which it would—at least explicitly—recognize the subsequent need to settle a question that it claimed had long been settled, or else was a matter for the Germans themselves to work out. Adenauer also knew that Germany's neighbors saw a lesser danger for European security in a continuation of the division than in an economically potent and politically self-confident reunified Germany.[22]

If, in Adenauer's view, the one danger was a political vacuum in Central Europe that would make Germany an easy prey for the Soviet Union, then the other consisted in a reconciliation of the victorious powers of World War II at Germany's expense. "Germany must never again fall between two stools, for then it would be lost."[23] This anxiety about a renewed isolation similar to what had happened before the First World War or after the debacle of 1945 has been termed by Hans-Peter Schwarz as Adenauer's "Potsdam complex."[24] The chancellor eyed proposals for summit conferences of the four powers with suspicion, particularly when he was not certain that the West had a harmonized position for these. Adenauer himself proposed four-power conferences only when the West could negotiate from a position of political strength: in 1953, after the signing of the EDC, when it was necessary to parry Soviet reunification initiatives, and in 1957, when integration in the West had been formally assured with the Treaties of Paris and Rome, Bonn's coordination with the Western powers seemed guaranteed, and Adenauer perceived a relaxing of the Soviet attitude following his correspondence with Bulganin.[25]

In order to prevent a reconciliation at the expense of the Federal Republic, Bonn had to conduct an alliance-oriented foreign policy and persuade its partners to "stick to its guns."[26] Adenauer was aware what sort of a role "the specter of a German seesaw policy, a Rapallo policy," continued to play among its allies. Germany "had to remain true to itself, and it must not entertain the almost criminal idea of fashioning some sort of political line now with the East, now with the West, of conducting a *schaukelpolitik.*"[27] Policy toward the East, he believed, could be carried out only on the basis of close ties with the West. In view of the mistrust toward any kind of German dynamic, Adenauer confined himself to a defensive strategy that was often artful yet not very constructive. If the allies should threaten to deviate from the common political line, then Adenauer would admonishingly remind them of the obligations entered into, in particular with respect to Germany as a whole, or lure them back to the path of virtue through intimations of disturbing domestic developments in the Federal Republic or in some other Western country. Nor was he averse to playing off one against the other and seeking support with Dulles vis-à-vis Macmillan or with de Gaulle against Kennedy. When he himself took the initiative, e.g., in establishing diplomatic relations with Moscow or the contacts with Smirnov and Mikoyan, he carefully covered these moves with a series of consultations with the Western partners. For him there was no question that the ties with the West must not be jeopardized by an active Ostpolitik, that a—hypothetical—reunification was acceptable only if Western Germany were not in the process wrenched out of the West European-Atlantic alliance system.

Security and Peace in Europe

In the contemporary assessment of the Soviet threat, Adenauer's "policy of strength"—willingness to negotiate on the basis of political unity and sufficient military capability of the West—was not an offensive but a defensive policy. This is evidenced by his position maintained during the Polish October and the popular revolt in Hungary and finally with the construction of the Berlin Wall. Particularly in talks with Soviet political figures, the chancellor never tired of pointing out the German people's desire for peace. Thus he told Mikoyan that he regarded it as his lifework "to secure the peace in Europe and to unite Europe."[28] In connection with the Geneva Summit Conference he expressed his conviction that "the issue of controlled disarmament is the decisive element for whether or not we will achieve peace in the world at all." In the same paragraph, however, Adenauer was quick to point out that as long as the division of Germany persisted, "tranquility, order, and peace could not be established in Europe, because this division violated the balance of power."[29] If these statements are placed in the overall context of Adenauer's Eurocentric and anticommunist world view, then peace was ensured only if Soviet expansion could be stopped. Peace was possible solely on the basis of freedom; as a political maxim, therefore, the maintenance of peace was subordinated to the guarantee of freedom.[30]

From a conviction that the tensions in Europe were first and foremost caused by the division of Europe and of Germany, and less by the military confrontation along the line of demarcation, Adenauer attached no particular importance to measures for arms control and disarmament. For him these were solely instruments of his security policy and policy on Germany. This of course did not prevent him from coming out on various occasions for a general and controlled disarmament; even Adenauer did not find it opportune always to array himself in the garb of a "cold warrior." On the other hand, he was careful not to play the problems of disarmament too much into the limelight and so unintentionally give support to the domestic opposition in its fight against rearmament. For him it was important that the disarmament negotiations set in motion in 1956 did not interfere with the development of the Bundeswehr, upon which the Federal Republic's alliance value depended. However, since time-consuming negotiations were to be expected, statements of principle on the will to achieve disarmament could not hurt if at the same time Bonn took care to obviate any contemplation of isolated solutions for Central Europe that would limit the political or military status of the Federal Republic.

Adenauer took a particularly skeptical view of proposals for European zones of inspection or limited armament; to him these were acceptable only on condition that they

- did not hinder the development of the Federal Republic's ties with the West or its integration into Western Europe;
- did not imply any political discrimination against the Federal Republic;

- did not make the stationing of U.S. troops in Western Europe militarily worthless;
- did avoid the danger of recognizing the status quo, i.e., were not based on the demarcation line as a midline.[31]

Since neither the various disengagement proposals nor the diverse Rapacki Plans met these demands, Adenauer regarded them as "dangerous ideas"[32] that consequently had to be blocked by attaching conditions, such as simultaneous steps toward reunification, or by referring to more urgent problems, such as general disarmament and detente.

Although Adenauer tended to view the various proposals on European security and arms limitation as a danger rather than as an asset for his policy, he did not ignore the justifiable security needs of Germany's neighbors. In the event of reunification he was prepared to give them—especially the Soviet Union—assurances that Germany would not call into question the political terms of the Paris Treaties and would accept limitations on its armed forces.[33] Moreover, there were thoughts in the Chancellor's Office about proposals designed to guarantee that the military potential of a reunified Germany would not accrue one-sidedly to the Western bloc. But such deliberations were also a reaction to the plans, sprouting like mushrooms in the wake of the Austrian State Treaty, for an all-European security system encompassing a neutralized Germany or a belt of neutral states in Central Europe.[34] "For us this was a dangerous subject," wrote Adenauer in his memoirs. "In my opinion such a belt would mean the end of Germany and of Europe."[35] The United States would pull back over the Atlantic and the ensuing vacuum at the center of Europe would entice Soviet intervention. With a combination of public statements and diplomatic démarches, Adenauer reacted sharply to these sorts of proposals. "The most effective way I saw of counteracting the Western ideas of neutralization was in having my own plan worked out, one that accommodated the often cited Soviet 'security need' but also made it possible to continue the deployment of American and Western troops on the territory of the Federal Republic. At my instigation concrete plans were developed on the German side for an arms limitation in Central and Eastern Europe that would create the preconditions for a detente."[36]

These plans reflected a continuation of ideas that had been developed by Adenauer's aides Adolf Heusinger and Herbert Blankenhorn in August 1953 prior to the Berlin Conference and entailed a demilitarized zone in the eastern part of Central Europe. In a study which Heusinger submitted in early June 1955 to Blankenhorn (in the Foreign Office) and Ulrich de Maizière (in the newly established Defense

Ministry) the creation of a troop-free area in Central Europe on both sides of the Stettin-Prague-Vienna-Trieste line was suggested. In this zone neither national nor stationed troops or military facilities would be maintained. East and west of it there would be two additional arms limitation zones. In Zone II, delimited in the west roughly by the Rhine and in the east by the Riga-Brest line, both sides could maintain balanced ground forces (40 divisions for NATO and 50— numerically weaker—for the Warsaw Pact) including the necessary air support, but could not station any long-range weapons systems. In Zone III, ranging to the Atlantic in the west and to the Dnieper in the east, armed forces equivalent in number and kind could be maintained.[37]

The premises of the Heusinger Plan were the reunification of Germany and the continued existence of the Atlantic alliance. However, the design contained neither a timetable nor concrete measures for reestablishing the unity of Germany. In effect, Heusinger's proposals would have essentially demilitarized the territory of the GDR and eliminated the conventional preponderance of the Eastern forces in Europe, while the defense planning of NATO would not have been impaired. Great Britain and Spain were excluded, since U.S. and British strategic air bases were located there. The lines of demarcation of the individual zones were laid down according to military criteria; but at the same time they were not to coincide with political borders and not to prejudice a border settlement in a peace treaty with Germany.

Upon closer examination and comparison with similar proposals from this period, Heusinger's ideas reveal a distinctly defensive character. There is a direct relation between the Heusinger Plan and the Eden Plan, also with the ideas of Belgian Foreign Minister Paul van Zeeland. In 1953, and again in 1955, van Zeeland made various proposals for settling the East-West conflict. These provided for the creation of a demilitarized zone on the territory of the GDR along with a limitation of troop strengths in the areas east and west of it.[38] At the Geneva Summit Conference in July 1955, British Prime Minister Anthony Eden proposed a mutual security pact between the four victorious powers and a reunified Germany together with an agreement on a limitation of forces and armaments on both sides in Germany and in the neighboring countries. Then the concept of a demilitarized zone between East and West was put forward. Though this second Eden Plan still started from the reunification of Germany and was thus more or less acceptable to the Federal Republic, this was no longer the case with Eden's third proposal for a joint inspection system of the forces confronting each other in Europe.[39] And from America there came word that plans were being drafted in Washington for a neutralized area in Central Europe.[40]

Adenauer was extremely alarmed. Realization of these sorts of plans would mean giving up the linkage between security and reunification as well as one-sidedly discriminating against the Federal Republic and weakening the military defense of the West. At first the German government was not successful in registering its grave concerns in the Western working group preparing for the Geneva Conference of Foreign Ministers. Only when Adenauer intervened in person with Eden and Dulles was the plan from the Berlin Conference for step-by-step reunification of Germany, i.e., the first Eden Plan, combined with the security pact of the second plan, which itself was concretized by some of the central elements of the Heusinger Plan. Thus, Paragraph 3 of the Treaty of Assurance provided for the establishment of a zone of arms limitation:

> In a zone comprising areas of comparable size and depth and importance on both sides of the line of demarcation between a reunited Germany and the Eastern European countries, levels for armed forces would be specified so as to establish a military balance which would contribute to European security...There would be appropriate provisions for the maintenance of this balance. In parts of the zone which lie closest to the line of demarcation, there might be special measures relating to the disposition of military forces and installations.[41]

With a combination of military and political arguments Adenauer was able to remove from the discussion concepts that were based on West or all-German neutrality and that threatened to weaken the Federal Republic's ties with the West. Several times the chancellor had his staff prepare discussion papers with the express proviso that they give him "good statements" for his negative position. Adenauer got these from Hans Globke, Wilhelm Grewe, Adolf Heusinger, and Franz Josef Strauss. And in subsequent years he sustained a tactic forged at the Geneva Conference of Foreign Ministers in 1955, that of a flexible linkage between reunification of Germany and measures of regional arms limitation.

However, since the mid-1950s Adenauer had come around to the view that the Soviet Union would not agree to a reunification of Germany at the price of neutrality for either the GDR or all of Germany. Henceforth his strategy was directed at inducing Moscow to accept a liberalization in the GDR or to agree to a truce on the German question for a limited period of time. At the same time, with the introduction of long-range nuclear weapons by NATO and the Warsaw Pact, zones of limited armament in Europe lost their military value. Thus, Bonn's proposals and counterproposals on the German question increasingly acquired a dilatory character, and its pressing for a general disarmament had in this context the function to prevent the West from making isolated concessions in European security under the pressure of the Berlin crisis. This emerges quite clearly from the Western preparations for the Geneva Foreign Ministers Conference in 1959, as the Western powers argued on the basis of a phased plan for reunification and arms limitation in Europe, but Adenauer wanted to offer the Soviet Union an agreement on general and controlled disarmament as quid pro quo for a truce in Germany.[42] Similarly, the so-called Globke Plan was less a plan for restoring the unity of Germany than it was a tactical device to wrest from Moscow the ''Berlin lever'' with which Moscow could again and again call into question the Federal Republic's ties with the West. In addition, it was an attempt to achieve a truce, perhaps even a modus vivendi, with the Soviet Union on the German question without giving up legal positions and to make this acceptable to international and domestic opinion by declaring it an ''intermediate station'' on the way to reunification.[43]

For Adenauer ''European security'' was primarily a political entity, not a product of defense programs or disarmament plans. (Western) Europe was ''secure'' when the West had political unity and sufficient strength to prevent Soviet aggression—or when Soviet Russia renounced its expansive foreign policy and permitted the East European states and the GDR a greater degree of political liberty and self-determination. Then an East-West detente could come into being, not at the expense but with the inclusion of the Federal Republic.

THE POLITICAL CONCEPTIONS OF THE SPD ON SECURITY AND THE GERMAN QUESTION

For the SPD the year 1955 was much less a watershed than it was for the CDU/CSU and Chancellor Adenauer. It could not claim the ending of the occupation and the Federal Republic's entry into NATO as outcomes of its policy; nor did it appear that the Federal Republic's integration in the West gave it new options for realizing both security and reunification of Germany. The period from 1952 to 1959-60, from Kurt Schumacher's death to the adoption of the Godesberg party program, was clearly a transitional phase for the SPD in terms of personalities as well as concepts. While in Adenauer's foreign policy all goals were subordinated to that of gaining freedom through integration into the West, the Social Democrats were striving, with equal emphasis, for the restoration of Germany's unity, the preservation and expansion of basic democratic rights, and the guarantee of the Federal Republic's security—in fact, in an international situation in which these three axioms could no longer be reduced to a common denominator.

Schumacher's Legacy

The heart of the foreign policy concept of Kurt Schumacher, chairman of the SPD and great political opponent of Adenauer in the formative years of the Federal Republic, was the development of a democratic and socialist Europe to which a free and united Germany would belong as an equal partner.[44] However, his ideas on the way to this goal underwent major changes subject to international developments.

In the initial postwar period Schumacher championed a pan-European confederation that would include a democratic and socialist Germany participating on an equal basis and that, as a "third force" in international politics, would constitute a counterweight to the (Stalinist) Soviet Union as well as to the (capitalist) United States. However, when it appeared that the unity of Germany could not be attained by negotiation and accommodation as he had advocated—at least not in the short term—Schumacher supported the moves toward West European integration (chiefly the Marshall Plan and the formation of NATO), at least as long as the SPD, in association with the other socialist parties of Western Europe, could play a substantial role in determining the political, economic, and social structure of the integration. A united and economically strong Western Europe would exert a pull on the people of Central and Eastern Europe; by the "force of circumstances"[45] the Soviet Union could then be induced to release its zone in Germany, possibly the other East European states also, from its sphere of influence. The restoration of Germany's unity was, however, primarily the task and responsibility of the victors of the Second World War. For their part, the Germans were not to do anything that could contribute to a worsening of the situation. This was then the basis for the SPD's negative position on German rearmament.[46]

Under the influence of the Korean War and hence the need for security in Europe, the SPD began to revise its positions on the security question. But Schumacher dropped his categorical no to German armed forces less from concern about an imminent military conflict than from the recognition that a German defense contribution could be used to commit the Western powers to an active reunification policy. However, he attached to rearmament the precondition that "the Americans and the other Western powers forcefully demonstrated their full power, [that] they be ready not to regard the Rhine as the line of defense, but to protect the entire German territory from possible aggression."[47] A military contribution by the Federal Republic made sense, in his view, only if the West defended Germany offensively to the east to save it from the heaviest destruction.[48]

A second condition was an equal political and military role for the Federal Republic, reduced to a simple motto: "equal risk, equal sacrifice, and equal chances."[49] Yet the Pleven Plan did not meet these conditions: in Schumacher's view, the planned army of Europe was too weak to prevent Germany from becoming the theater of war; the Germans were denied political equality of status, they were allowed only the "chance to shed their blood." But above all, the way the German government was falling into line with the Western rearmament plans jeopardized Schumacher's most important goal: forcing the Soviet Union to accept reunification politically on the basis of military strength.[50]

By the end of 1951 it had become clear that the West's plans amounted to essentially a defensive preservation of its own sphere of influence and were not accompanied by an active and concrete policy of reunification as Schumacher understood it. With that the antinomy between defense contribution and German question again came to the fore. When at the same time the East—first the GDR with its slogan "Germans to one table," then the Soviet Union—initiated a large-scale diplomatic offensive with concrete proposals for the reunification and neutralization of Germany,[51] Schumacher, too, came out once again for quadripartite negotiations, particularly for a serious testing of the Soviet note of March 1952.[52] However, the SPD made it clear that a neutralization of Germany was not a reasonable alternative. A reunified Germany had to have the right to determine its place in Europe. In this regard Schumacher and other leading figures of the SPD left no room for doubt that this Germany would stand politically with the West. In place of hostile military alliances, peace in Europe would be guaranteed by a collective security system. This idea of a European security system was an essential correlate to the Social Democratic policy on reunification.[53]

For Schumacher security policy was a function of his policy on Germany, a policy geared toward restoration of Germany's unity (*nota bene*: in its borders of 1937). The political opposition to the EDC and the Bonn Agreements of 1952—which also had domestic motivations—signified neither a rejection on principle of a defense contribution nor an option for a politically neutral Germany between East and West; this position was far removed from the widespread *ohne mich* (count me out) postwar attitude. Schumacher's rejection of the Western Treaties, primarily because of the inequality of status accorded the Germans and their disregard for a perspective on reunification, had elements of principle and of tactics, with the latter calling for constant adjustment to the changing international and domestic situations. However, after the death of Schumacher in 1952, the demand for reunification through free elections guaranteed by the four powers and the rejection of the Western Treaties turned into a dogma that circumscribed the SPD's room for maneuver.

The Proposal of a Collective European Security System

In its efforts to find a solution for both the security problem and the unresolved German question, the SPD returned to ideas discussed back in the 1920s and 1940s about a European security system.[54]

Its proposals were first of all designed to develop a political alternative to the Federal Republic's entry into the European Defense Community; after that they were an invitation to Moscow to demonstrate its readiness to accept the reunification of Germany and provide guarantees for its freedom and security; finally, they were to serve as the political framework for a reunified Germany, ensuring both "security for Germany and security from Germany."[55]

As long as the proposal was no more than a tactical device in the fight against the EDC, it remained vague and open to interpretation. In the course of the discussion, Carlo Schmid and Fritz Erler—in December 1952 the latter was named chairman of a commission on security instituted by the SPD's executive committee—made the concept of a European security system more precise, namely that it would be a system of collective guarantees according to Articles 52, 42, and 43 of the UN Charter and would necessarily include the political aggressor—i.e., in the European context, the Soviet Union. U.S. membership would likewise be indispensable. Schmid and Erler spelled out in detail what would have to be demanded of such a system:

- it could not offer less security than the EDC;
- it would have to make possible German reunification in peace and freedom;
- it would have to assure the Soviet Union that German divisions would not be incorporated into a hostile alliance system and at the same time to safeguard the Western powers and Germany against domination by the Soviet Union;
- it would have to give a united Germany the possibility of self-defense in the event of aggression and to ensure that an attack on Germany would trigger the third world war;
- except for the ban on military alliances, it must not hinder Germany from forming close ties with all free peoples.[56]

The principal element of this sort of collective security system was the assurance to the Soviet Union that a reunified Germany would not belong to any military alliance. But to lend weight to this offer and thus give it a chance of realization—the necessary correlate, in Erler's view, was a willingness otherwise to consider the Federal Republic's membership in NATO (after the EDC's collapse). Erler did not want to grant Moscow a veto position on the question of rearmament, but rather to use the latter to compel the Soviet Union to negotiate in earnest on reunification. Hence, he also demanded a revision clause in the Western Treaties so that in the event of a restoration of German unity the then necessary alternative security concepts could be realized. For Erler the "gain in sovereignty through the elimination of occupation status, connected with preparations for entry into NATO, and a *simultaneous* new negotiating offer to the Soviet Union [were] two sides of the same coin."[57]

In line with the dual strategy sketched by Erler for defense contribution and negotiating offer, the SPD's Berlin party congress in 1954 adopted an action program in which it intimated that in the absence of an East-West agreement on reunification of Germany it would under certain circumstances approve a West German defense contribution.[58] However, it did not concretize this any further, just as it did not take up the Soviet reunification offers—in January 1955 the Soviet Union had reiterated its proposals of 1952 and had offered "free elections" as well. The SPD position became completely incredible when the party resolved to make common cause with the Paul's Church Movement. Supported mainly by trade unionists, church representatives, and intellectuals, the Paul's Church Assembly adopted in January 1955 a "German Manifesto" that warned against ratification of the Western Treaties and declared that the deployment of German armed forces would destroy the chances for reunification for a long time to come.[59] This ingratiation with the *ohne mich* movement, which Schumacher had always opposed, brought upon the SPD the carefully cultivated charge of its opponents that it was pandering to pacifist tendencies.

Prior to the Geneva Summit Conference in 1955, the SPD presented a reassessment of its ideas on the complex of questions pertaining to European security and German unity. In view of the impending four-power negotiations it demanded that "consolidating and guaranteeing European security and restoring the national unity of Germany are to be regarded, treated, and realized as an intrinsic whole."[60] Therefore, the international status of a reunified Germany would have to be determined simultaneously with an agreement on reunification, which could be effected only on the basis of free, universal, secret, and internationally controlled elections. Germany should not belong to either military bloc but should be a partner with full rights and responsibilities in a European collective security system. This was based on the recognition that Moscow would agree to reunification only if Germany rejected military ties with the Atlantic pact. Therefore, the German government ought to declare immediately that a reunified Germany would permit no military bases on its territory except for those that derived from the responsibilities of the regional security system. Until the latter were established the four powers should conclude an agreement with the all-German government that would guarantee territorial inviolability and peaceful resolution of conflict.

Unlike in the discussion of a military disengagement, in which the case was made for a belt of neutral states between the two blocs, the proposals of the SPD envisioned a transformation of the evolving alliance systems and the institution of a collective security system guaranteed by the four powers present in Germany, though if possible by the United Nations. This would ensure that a reunified Germany could determine its own political and social development in freedom.

After the failure of the Geneva conferences of 1955, the SPD was faced with the question of whether and in what way it ought to adapt itself to the new situation. It testified neither to a sober assessment of the political realities nor to great political imagination that the opposition essentially clung to its old demand that the four powers should come to terms on the reunification of Germany and its incorporation into a European security pact in which it would participate with equal rights and obligations. The "Ollenhauer Plan for Security and Reunification" of May 1957 also contained, in essence, the familiar elements of a European security system:

- participation of reunified Germany and its neighbors in the East and West;
- multilateral commitment to nonaggression;
- peaceful settlement of disputes by arbitration;
- system of arms limitation and arms control;
- regional system in the framework of the UN Charter;
- automatic obligation of mutual assistance;
- guarantees from the United States and the Soviet Union.[61]

As to the desired change of European structures, a new element was introduced into the discussion by the SPD's security expert, Fritz Erler: the idea that appropriate measures for disarmament and detente could not only reduce the acute threat to security in Europe but also qualitatively alter the relationship of the two superpowers. With that Erler was responding to trends in the international discussion. It had not escaped his notice that the allies were beginning—even under the impact of the Soviet intervention in Hungary—to give disarmament measures priority over steps toward reunification. In his view, however, disarmament and reunification were two sides of one problem; the one marked the way, the other the goal.[62]

The SPD's "German Plan" of March 1959 was a—last—attempt to bring about a restoration of Germany's national and economic unity by means of closely coordinated steps toward military detente and arms limitation. Security for all-Germany was to be provided by embedding it in a collective security system. The "German Plan" thus took up the SPD's familiar ideas on the connection between European security and reunification, linking them, however, with the proposal of the Rapacki Plan for creating a zone of detente and arms control in Central Europe, and spelled out the individual steps for its realization.[63]

With the worsening of the East-West situation by the Khrushchev ultimatum and the Berlin crisis,[64] European detente was viewed as a prerequisite for resolving the political and military issues. Such thinking clearly showed the hand of Erler. However, the phased plan for reunification reflected mainly the ideas of Herbert Wehner.[65] In a break with the SPD's previous notions that the reunification process must begin with free elections, in the first phase an all-German conference would be convened, composed of equal numbers of representatives from the two German governments, which would discuss how the two parts of Germany could be joined together again politically and economically. Then in a second phase an all-German parliamentary council would be instituted, the memebers of which were to be popularly elected half by the Federal Republic, half by the GDR, and entrusted with full legislative powers, primarily in the areas of economy, currency, transportation, telecommunications, and postal system. At a third stage of the reunion this all-German council would prepare legislation for adjusting the economic, financial, and social policies of the two parts of Germany and order elections for a national constitutional assembly. Once an all-German constitution had gone into effect, then universal, free, and secret elections would be held to elect an all-German parliament, from which an all-German government would emerge. As the European security system became effective, the two German states would withdraw from NATO and the Warsaw Pact; the security of all of Germany would then be ensured by a collective agreement and by guarantees from the United States and the Soviet Union.

But how did the SPD expect to have the plan accepted as a basis for negotiation by West and East and how could it ensure that the end result would be a united Germany closely allied with the West politically, nonaligned militarily, but protected by a collective security system? The West would be attracted by the prospect of eliminating a permanent source of crisis in Central Europe, and the East would look forward to West Germany's withdrawal from NATO, in fact without Moscow's having first to give up the communist regime in the GDR. Leading SPD politicans were convinced that the problem of the GDR would take care of itself in the course of the reunification process. While Wehner was counting on the "German patriots" in the party apparatus, Erler assumed that after the withdrawal of all foreign troops from both German states the GDR would be open to political solutions along the lines of SPD conceptions, once it could no longer rely on the presence of Soviet occupation troops. The transformation of the existing alliance systems in conjunction with the withdrawal of foreign armed forces was thought not only to make reunification acceptable to the Soviet Union; it was also seen as real leverage for effecting the transformation in Germany itself.

However, in its programmatic orientation to the goal of reunifying Germany, the SPD lost sight of the fact that the European as well as the international situation had fundamentally changed since the first half of the 1950s. In the first place, the status quo had come to be a powerful force. In both parts of Europe political, economic, and military systems had been developed on the basis of close cooperation with the respective hegemonic power, and thus the European situation had been stabilized. For security reasons the United States did not want to give up its European glacis, nor could the Soviet Union afford to sacrifice the GDR without serious repercussions in its own alliance. Secondly, Moscow had achieved strategic parity with the United States and could now counter a West European threat with a strategic counterstrike against U.S. territory. With that, concepts of European neutralization had lost much of their military significance for the Soviets. On a trip to Moscow a few days after the "German Plan" had been made public, Erler and Schmid discovered that the chances of setting the reunification process in motion by solving the security problems in Central Europe were very slim. They therefore decided not to bring up the "German Plan" for discussion in the Bundestag. The negative outcome of the Geneva Foreign Ministers Conference in 1959 confirmed this skepticism. The following year, in the course of its foreign policy reorientation, the SPD officially shelved the "German Plan."[66]

Peace Policy, Disarmament, and the German Question

The failure of the Geneva talks of 1955, the convulsions in Eastern Europe in the fall of 1956, and the determination evidenced by Moscow to assert its claim over its sphere of influence, as well as the flagging of the Western powers' interest in combined security and reunification initiatives, diminished the prospects for a comprehensive European security system and left the SPD to seek other possibilities for resolving the German question and securing peace in Europe. Most promising seemed to be various proposals for arms limitation zones, which the debate on European security in the 1950s had brought forward in ample diversity. Although most of the proposals did not meet the criteria that the SPD had set in connection with its own proposals for a European security system, it did emphatically support such concepts. For one thing, it held the view that the process of reunification could be facilitated by a reduction of the military confrontation at the center of Europe; also, it regarded the proposals developed by British Labor Party leaders Hugh Gaitskell and Dennis Healey for a zone of reduced armament in Europe[67] as a confirmation of its own thinking. But most importantly, the SPD gradually came around—initially with Fritz Erler and Helmut Schmidt—to the view that the Germans would not be able to block disarmament measures until the German question had been solved.

The proposals for arms limitation zones acquired an especial urgency when it became known that NATO was planning to introduce tactical nuclear weapons in Western Europe and when word got out that the West German government wanted to equip the Bundeswehr with these very systems. In a vigorous debate in the German Bundestag in May 1957, the opposition appealed to the government to help stop the nuclear arms race by means of a universal agreement on the limitation of forces and armaments. It feared both the catastrophic effects of a conflict with tactical nuclear weapons in Europe—where there would be, in Erler's words, "nothing left of the German people"—and the negative consequences for the German question—"The time bomb of the German division is dangerous enough for everyone, not just for us. This bomb will become even more dangerous if it is filled with atomic explosives."[68]

The issues of an arms limitation zone in Central Europe became even more prominent with the proposals of Polish Foreign Minister Adam Rapacki, who first proposed in October 1957 the creation of a nuclear-weapons-free zone encompassing the Federal Republic, the GDR, Poland, and Czechoslovakia. The following year this plan was detailed and supplemented first by the inclusion of a ground and air control system, then by the proposal of a reduction in conventional forces in a second phase.[69]

The SPD welcomed the Rapacki proposals, as the creation of a nuclear-free zone in the heart of Europe "could contribute to reducing tensions, increasing our security, and in this way clearing the way for the solution of our political problems."[70] At first this support was a tactical instrument for preventing the Bundeswehr from being equipped with nuclear weapons. Yet when it came to discussing the substance of the Rapacki Plan it became clear that for the SPD, security and unity were still two sides of the same coin. Although the Eastern proposals were not coupled with steps toward reunification, they represented, in the SPD's view, a first step on the road to detente, a course that would facilitate talks on the German question. At the same time the SPD hoped that the realization of a nuclear-free zone would have a beneficial impact on the other disarmament negotiations and would lead to a reduction of the stationed forces.[71] The bayonets behind Chairman Walter Ulbricht, prodding him and underpinning his power, had to be removed; if not, it would be impossible to overcome the regime in the GDR.[72]

But could the SPD expect that the Bonn government and the West would take up the Polish proposals and come to terms with the East on an arms limitation zone in Central Europe? For many on the party board who thought in Schumacher's categories, e.g., for Ollenhauer, it was enough to be convinced of the correctness of their adhering to the primacy of reunification. In so doing they overlooked the fact that the basic structures of international affairs had changed considerably since the time of Schumacher. However, for the "reformers" (Ashkenasi) in the party—Erler, Carlo Schmid, Wehner—it was not just a matter of *being right*, they also wanted *to get their right* (Erler). They realized that "once the Soviet Union had caught up with the United States in the military field, perhaps even overtaking them in some areas...there was no longer a short road to reunificaiton."[73] From this two conclusions could be drawn. First, German defense policy had to be directed toward maintaining and stabilizing the existing international balance. To that end, NATO had to have a credible deterrence strategy and the means for an effective defense should deterrence fail. However, this did not include the Federal Republic's having control over nuclear weapons. Secondly, there followed an obligation to wage a tough and persistent struggle for disarmament. Supposedly the German question could be better approached "if in the course of controlled arms limitation Central Europe ceases to assume the same importance for the two systems."[74]

This new conception of security policy was first presented in a speech by Helmut Schmidt in the Bundestag in November 1959.[75] Schmidt proposed a Central European arms control zone that would comprise the Federal Republic of Germany, the GDR, Poland, Czechoslovakia, and Hungary; in this zone an approximate balance of national military potentials (armed forces/territory/population/economic strength) would be established and the foreign troops withdrawn except for symbolic units. This would also mean a withdrawal of tactical nuclear weapons. Observance of the stipulated limitations would be safeguarded by a monitoring and control system supplemented by an early warning system. In contrast to previous Social Democratic plans—in particular the "German Plan" made public eight months before—this proposal was not coupled with steps toward reunification, nor did it presuppose the withdrawal of the Federal Republic from NATO and that of the East European states from the Warsaw Pact. While the political structures in Europe were to remain essentially intact, the security of the Federal Republic was to be enhanced by reducing the danger of a surprise attack or of an accidental war. The SPD was thus taking up proposals that had previously been brought forward by East and West in the discussion on preventing surprise attacks. Only in a long-term perspective did it seem conceivable that a Central European zone of detente could be a preliminary stage for a collective European security system.

Helmut Schmidt's speech of November 1959—supplemented by a number of similar statements by Fritz Erler—indicated a fundamental change in the order of priorities among the SPD's security policy objectives. With Schumacher and his successors, security policy had been oriented primarily to the goal of restoring the unity of Germany. Proposals for a European security system or nuclear-free zones were assessed according to their consequences for the German question. In the 1960s this approach was supplanted by a perspective oriented to the security requirements of the Federal Republic and the goal of securing peace. In this conception arms control measures assumed an important place. Thus, the SPD supported proposals for a nuclear test ban and for non-proliferation (it had done so since 1958, though at the time primarily as a tactic in opposing atomic weaponry for the Bundeswehr) as well as for regional arms reduction in Europe.

This gave rise to a general political conception again in the mid-1960s. The Eight-Point Program, which had been formulated by the SPD parliamentary group in November 1966 as a basis for coalition talks with the CDU/CSU, stated that "promoting international detente is in the interest of Germany. The federal government has to take appropriate initiatives in its foreign, defense, and Germany policies. This is the way to uphold our security, which at present only is safeguarded in the framework of the Western alliance."[76] Along with steps toward stabilizing the alliance and normalizing relations with the East European states, specific measures for detente were to include negotiations on a reduction of forces and armaments in East and West, support for a non-proliferation treaty, and the exchange of legally binding renun-

ciation-of-force statements. Of interest here also is the linkage—or ambivalence?—of objectives in security policy and those of policy on Germany. One of the purposes of arms reduction was to afford points of
departure for progress on the German question, just as it did not appear possible to gain a lasting world peace without eliminating the political sources of tension in Europe.

THE POLICY OF LINKAGE BETWEEN EUROPEAN SECURITY AND THE GERMAN QUESTION

The web of the Paris Treaties was finely spun. As quid pro quo for
Western integration and rearmament the Federal Republic had been accorded national sovereignty and international recognition, while the
three Western powers had explicitly recognized the West German
government's claim "to speak for Germany as the representative of the
German people in international affairs" and declared that "the
achievement through peaceful means of a fully free and unified Germany remains a fundamental goal of their policy."[77] With that Bonn felt
that it had gained for itself a say in European matters and at the time
kept the German question on the international agenda. After the disappointment of the Geneva Foreign Ministers Conference there was no
expectation of a rapid East-West accord; rather, official Bonn was bet-
ting that in view of the strength and solidity of the Atlantic alliance the
Soviet Union would one day find the costs of maintaining the communist regime in the GDR too great and would seek some arrangement with the West.

The Western attempts to reach an agreement with the Soviet Union
on measures of disarmament and arms control—since an accord on the
German question was not possible—jeopardized Bonn's policy in two
ways. First, the German government feared that if the German question were put on the back burner there would be tendencies toward
recognizing the status quo, and secondly, that West German rearmament would be questioned and impediments placed in the way of raising the Bundeswehr. Moreover, proposals for regional arms limitation
implied the danger of a diminished status for the Federal Republic—a
situation the Federal Republic thought it had just overcome.

To counter these dangers the Bonn government in 1955 and 1956
formulated a flexible linkage between disarmament, European security,
and the German question, whereby agreements in one area would be
linked with progress in the others.[78] At the same time, this linkage
could be used to meet the demands of the domestic opposition for a
more active policy on Germany. It was subsequently the most impor-

tant instrument of West German foreign policy for defending the policy of Western integration and keeping the German question open. Still, the Federal Republic could not expect the other allies' unconditional support for this policy of linkage; it therefore had to be ready to bear the costs of adhering to it and accept limitations of its political maneuverability in other areas.

Western Proposals for Disarmament and Disengagement in Europe

Following the interlude of summit diplomacy in 1955, East-West activity shifted to disarmament negotiations in the framework of the United Nations. The London Five-Power Committee had before it a Franco-British plan for general disarmament and the so-called "Gromyko Plan," in which the accent was on a freeze of conventional forces and armaments within a proposed zone of limited armament. In early 1957 the United States put forward a package of partial measures. It was not until August of that year that the Western negotiating partners were able to find a common denominator for their divergent interests and submit a common program for disarmament—shortly before the negotiations broke down.[79] The submission of the Western proposals had been preceded by difficult consultations in the NATO Council, where the German government wanted to see a linkage established with progress on the German question. Bonn's desires were taken into account in that initial disarmament steps were to serve as a test of Soviet willingness to reduce tensions and the transition to more extensive measures was made dependent on progress in resolving political questions. It was only with reservations that Chancellor Adenauer, on a visit to Washington in late 1957, consented to this formula that did not fully take German considerations into account.

While disarmament negotiations held priority at the operative level, at the declaratory level the German government gained assent to a joint declaration by the three Western powers and the Federal Republic on reunification, in which the linkage between disarmament, European security, and the German question was once again affirmed. Thus the "Berlin Declaration" reads:

> The reunification of Germany accompanied by the conclusion of European security arrangements would facilitate the achievement of a comprehensive disarmament agreement. Conversely, if a beginning could be made toward effective measures of partial disarmament, this would contribute to settlement of outstanding major political problems such as the reunification of Germany. Initial steps in the field of disarmament should lead to a comprehensive disarmament

agreement which presupposes a prior solution of the problem of German reunification. The Western Powers do not intend to enter into any agreement on disarmament which would prejudice reunification of Germany. Any measures of disarmament applicable to Europe must have the consent of the European nations concerned and take into account the link between European security and German reunification.[80]

With the assertion of linkage the German government wanted, first of all, to block distinct tendencies in the disarmament talks to discuss regional measures for Europe besides steps toward general disarmament. The Soviet proposals for an arms limitation zone in Europe had found a receptive hearing, particularly in Great Britain and France. For economic and domestic political reasons both governments were interested in agreements with the Soviet Union on arms limitation. So it seemed natural to set aside the difficult German question or at least to put it at the bottom of the foreign policy agenda. Also, in the United States the Sputnik shock and the budget pressures from new military programs and expenditures had prompted greater consideration of how the arms race could be brought under control. However, U.S. foreign policy under John Foster Dulles did not go so far as to assign priority to an agreement with the Soviet Union over the alliance interests of the United States. Its disarmament proposals consisted of carefully coordinated measures into which sufficient safeguards were built so as to ensure a political control of the whole process. Yet any, even the most timid, consideration of regional measures by Washington regularly generated a crisis of confidence in Bonn, which only repeated declarations of alliance solidarity could resolve.

Secondly, in 1957 and 1958 Bonn regarded the international profusion of proposals for a military or political disengagement in Central Europe as a special kind of danger. These plans for a military moving apart of the blocs or a politically neutral belt of states in Europe were aimed at defusing the situation in Central Europe militarily, enabling the peoples living in this area to attain an independent national existence, and at the same time incorporating Germany into an East-West accord.[81]

Particular notice was taken when George Kennan, considered an experienced authority on the Soviet Union, put forward in the BBC's "Reith Lectures" in November 1956 the idea of a withdrawal of Soviet and U.S. forces from Europe in conjunction with the reunification of Germany.[82] From the standpoint of the Bonn government, these sorts of proposals threatened the past policy of Western integration, discriminated against the Federal Republic vis-à-vis its allies, and appeared to be a risk to its security. To this was added a domestic political perspective. The affinity of many of these plans with the SPD's ideas for a European security system could not be overlooked. The CDU/CSU-led government was not willing to abet an implicit international recognition of the opposition's concepts, especially as 1957 was an election year.

Eastern Proposals for a Nuclear-Weapons-Free Zone (Rapacki Plan)

In October 1957 the Polish Foreign Minister Rapacki proposed to the United Nations the creation of a nuclear-weapons-free zone in Central Europe comprising the two German states, Poland, and Czechoslovakia. The plan was outlined in a speech before the Sejm in mid-December and in a memorandum presented to the states affected on February 14, 1958. Thus, the states in the zone were to commit themselves "not to manufacture, maintain, or import for their own use and not to permit the location on their territories of nuclear weapons of any type as well as not to install or to admit to their territories of installations and equipment designed for servicing nuclear weapons, including missile launching equipment."[83] For their part the stationing powers should agree not to maintain warheads and nuclear delivery vehicles in this zone or pass them on to these states. Also, the nuclear powers should commit themselves not to use any nuclear weapons against targets within this zone in the event of conflict. These obligations could be entered into either through unilateral declarations or through an international treaty and were to be accompanied by an effective ground and air control system.

The Rapacki Plan was subsequently altered so as to take into account various objections raised by the West. Thus, in November 1958 provision was made for a reduction in conventional forces. The plan also was divided into two stages: in the first stage a freeze on nuclear weapons was envisaged, and only in the second was there to be a denuclearization and thinning of troop levels in Europe.[84]

The German government was doing the Gomulka regime an injustice when it viewed the latter essentially as "Moscow's messenger," particularly in this phase of Polish striving for independence. The Polish plan has to be regarded as an independent initiative, even though it fits in logically with the Soviet disarmament proposals of the preceding years, proposals directed toward preventing any further integration of the Federal Republic into the security system of the West. In particular, it took up ideas from the "Gromyko Plan" of March 1956, in which the Soviet government had proposed an arms limitation and nuclear-free zone in the territory of the two parts of Germany and neighboring states. Also, in two communications from Premier Bulganin to Chancellor Adenauer in December 1957 and January 1958 and in various notes from the Soviet government to other Western states during the same period, the question of a nuclear-free zone in Central Europe was addressed.[85] The timing of Rapacki's speech was well chosen. A few weeks later the NATO Council was to decide on the deployment of U.S. medium-range missiles in Europe and on the arming of the Bundeswehr with nuclear launchers.[86]

The German government therefore regarded the Rapacki Plan primarily as an instrument of the Soviet policy of preventing the Bundeswehr's equipment with nuclear weapons. It suspected that Moscow wanted to achieve structural changes in Western Europe via arms control measures, especially as the proposals were put forward at a juncture when the West was setting about to offset its existing conventional inferiority in Europe through a conversion to nuclear arms. Because Warsaw's action ran parallel with the Soviet regime's initiatives for a limitation of conventional and nuclear armaments in Europe, Bonn saw no reason to keep the Polish ball rolling.

Above all, the German government feared that a nuclear-free zone in Central Europe could weaken the political cohesion of the West, first through differential treatment of the allies, particularly discrimination against the Federal Republic, and second through reinforcement of the U.S. inclination, already manifested in connection with the Radford Plan, to reduce its conventional troops in Europe. With the founding of the European Community, which had come into being with the active participation of the Federal Republic, the German government and the Western powers had stitched a second seam—after the Paris Treaties—into the Federal Republic's Western integration. In the short term, at least in talks between Bonn and Paris on nuclear collaboration, the project of a European Defense Community had again moved into focus.[87] Thus, the German government feared that with the Rapacki Plan the Federal Republic was to be severed from the West. Added to this was the concern that these or similar proposals could serve to solidify or even validate the division of Europe. The proposals put forward more or less simultaneously by the Soviet Union and the GDR for a confederation of the two German states[88] strengthened Bonn's view that Moscow was first and foremost concerned with a recognition of the changes on the political map of Europe resulting from the Second World War.

Moreover, the German government held the view that any political compromise between East and West would have to start from Moscow. However, since it doubted whether the time had come for that, Bonn was more inclined to let things take their course than to influence developments through initiatives of its own. Replying January 21, 1958 to the letters from Premier Bulganin, Chancellor Adenauer confined himself to stressing the readiness of the German government to conduct serious discussions with the Soviet government on questions of disarmament and security, but otherwise supported the U.S. proposals on this complex of issues. With reference to a comment by Bulganin that the use of nuclear weapons knew no geographic bounds, he suggested that instead of dealing with the divisive issue of atomic weapons deployment, the nuclear powers should concentrate on an agreement to ban their production.[89]

Moscow's diplomatic actions documented the largely instrumental character of Soviet security policy. Within a few weeks and months in 1958 Soviet support for regional arms limitation in Europe was replaced by proposals for halting nuclear weapons tests and by the call for a summit conference. The rapid sequence of changing plans reflected the methods of a foreign policy aimed at exploiting the great many awkward Western reactions and the differences of interest among the allies, and so to consolidate its own system and strengthen the international influence of the Soviet Union.

In Bonn's military assessment of the Rapacki Plan, essentially two questions came to the fore. How could the creation of a nuclear-weapons-free zone in Central Europe be prevented from increasing the conventional superiority of the Warsaw Pact? The Western conversion to tactical nuclear weapons was aimed precisely at offsetting this disequilibrium. A denuclearization was acceptable, then, only if the geographic area of an arms limitation zone were substantially enlarged and the conventional potentials of East and West also reduced. Secondly, the German government was concerned with the question of how the territory and population of the Federal Republic could be protected from a nuclear conflict. The assurance contained in the Polish proposals—especially in the March 1958 explanations by the Polish foreign minister—that the nuclear powers were to commit themselves not to use nuclear weapons against a country in the nuclear-free zone, was considered insufficient. The German government noted the absence of a concrete guarantee; also it appeared dubious to Bonn whether, in view of the ranges of nuclear weapons and strategies, a territorial exclusion would be possible militarily. On the other hand, because of the Federal Republic's participation in nuclear defense with NATO, Bonn expected a potential say in the targeting that it viewed as essential for the defense of its population.[90]

The decision to arm the Bundeswehr with nuclear weapons thus ruled out acceptance of the Rapacki Plan. However, to counter Eastern criticism, the German government made efforts to produce a common

Western response to the Eastern proposals. It had followed with alarm how the various plans for inspection zones and a military disengagement had found ready acceptance with some of its allies. The German government therefore developed an alert and timely diplomatic activity aimed at blocking all such efforts. Thus, reference was made to the four-power responsibility for the reunification of Germany, as set forth in the Paris Treaties and reaffirmed at the Geneva Summit Conference, or to the overriding importance of a general disarmament as opposed to regional security arrangements.[91] For carrying out Bonn's course of action, the close contact between Chancellor Adenauer and Secretary of State Dulles proved to be very helpful, just as the German government could also count on close collaboration with France in parrying the Rapacki Plan. Differences of opinion with the United States over colonial policy as well as doubts about the credibility of U.S. deterrence had moved Paris to develop its own nuclear force. This decision had resulted in a reorientation of French arms control policy and in rejection of all efforts that could lead to weakening the conventional "shield forces" in Europe or jeopardizing French nuclear policy.

In the Permanent NATO Council the three Western powers and the Federal Republic did not agree on a joint response to Bulganin's letters, but they concurred on a rejection of regional measures and advocated efforts toward resolving the German question as well as various disarmament steps. In the French note an acceptance of the Rapacki Plan was expressly tied to the reunification of Germany.[92]

An "Austrian Solution" for the GDR?

Once the German government had secured its position with its allies, it intensified its bilateral contacts with the Soviet Union. These contacts included Adenauer's talks with the Soviet ambassador in Bonn, Andrej Smirnov, the visit to the Federal Republic of Deputy Foreign Minister Anastas Mikoyan, and the appointment of Hans Kroll, an advocate of an active Ostpolitik, as ambassador to Moscow. Via Smirnov, Adenauer aired the proposal of an Austrian solution for the GDR[93] and thus raised ideas that had already been suggested in the Heusinger Plan of 1955. However, the Soviet government did not take up the offer; Moscow was interested primarily in an international confirmation of the status quo in Europe.

Subsequently the diplomatic activity of the West shifted to preparations for a summit conference, which the Soviet Union was actively promoting. In this connection the Eden Plan for reunification of Germany was revived and broadened to include provision for a zone in which both sides were to reduce their conventional forces and forgo deployment of nuclear weapons. The German government chose not to give its own substantiated response to the Polish government and the plans presented by it for nuclear-free zones, aside from the brief statement that Bonn had conveyed to Warsaw 14 days after receipt of the February memorandum and that had promised a careful examination of the Polish proposals.[94]

Without doubt the Rapacki Plan dealt with considerations the SPD had formulated for a European arms limitation. But the opposition supported the Polish proposals—with a number of technical reservations—primarily in the hope that negotiations on arms limitation in Europe would also contribute to progress on the German question. Moreover, it conceived of agreements on prohibiting the deployment of nuclear weapons as an element of reduction of tension and confidence building in East-West relations. Further, it viewed the proposal as a point of departure for establishing diplomatic relations in which Warsaw was interested at the time.[95]

In the domestic political discussion the Rapacki Plan was soon overshadowed by the debate on equipping NATO forces with nuclear weapons. The opposition set things moving in this direction when on the eve of the NATO conference in December 1957 the SPD parliamentary group introduced in the Bundestag the motion that the German government renounce the arming of the Bundeswehr with nuclear weapons. The motion would not allow any stationing of medium-range missiles in West Germany, and declare Bonn's readiness to negotiate on a nuclear-free zone in Europe as well as a balanced withdrawal of troops stationed in this area. At the same time, the FDP introduced a major interpellation in which it sought to clarify the position of the German government on the question of reunification of Germany and detente in Europe.[96]

In two great debates on foreign policy in the Bundestag, in January and March 1958, the government pursued the tactics of dismissing the Soviet notes and the Polish proposals as troublemaking and of justifying the nuclear armament of NATO forces by the increased threat from Soviet nuclear missiles. If there were an agreement on general disarmament, then the Federal Republic would accede to such an accord. Yet a solution to the German question had priority, since the reunification of Germany was an essential prerequisite for any detente in Europe. In this connection it appealed to the obligation of the four powers to restore the national unity of Germany, and in view of the international situation it declared the solidarity of the Federal Republic with its allies. Chancellor Adenauer brought the issue to a head with the alternative, "NATO yes or no", whereby he equated NATO with a deployment of nuclear weapons by the alliance—including the

Bundeswehr—and military non-alignment with isolation and extreme peril for the democratic system. This was no doubt a gross simplification, misleading the public, since the spokesmen of the SPD and FDP had not questioned the Federal Republic's integration into the West but had suggested supplementing the Western Treaties by a security arrangement with the East in order to clear the way for reunification.[97]

In the debate Foreign Minister von Brentano rejected the Rapacki Plan with the argument that it implied recognition of the GDR, would lead to the withdrawal of Western troops from the Federal Republic, and would mean a military weakening of the West. "The whole thing would take place without our having come even one step closer to detente, to controlled disarmament, to the resolution of the German question. Yet the danger of being exposed to the effects of these means of mass destruction would not be diminished either."[98] In contrast, the SPD and FDP stressed that the Rapacki Plan at least offered an opportunity to negotiate on the military status of Germany and thus to create an essential prerequisite for a reunification of Germany. Speakers from both parties criticized the government, saying that it had ruled out the Polish proposals as well as other detente measures from the start and had not attempted to weigh the possibilities therein. Bonn was demanding security and reunification, but, as Erler said, anyone who wanted that "must do his part to see that the atomic armament is ended, and anyone who wants this must first of all do nothing to intensify the arms race through his own policy."[99]

However, German government and coalition parties confined themselves to verbally supporting efforts towards disarmament and detente and flatly rejected negotiations on the basis of the Polish proposals. Defense Minister Strauss was the only one to take up the idea of a zone of limited armament, but he called for a greater geographical scope, particularly in East Europe, and a linkage with reductions in conventional forces. If an agreement on such a zone were to be possible, then it would have to be tied to an effective control and guarantee system and coupled with concrete steps toward the reunification of Germany.[100] Such ideas, however, did not find acceptance in Bonn's official policy; on the contrary, they were quickly blocked by Chancellor Adenauer. The latter was concerned that the West's defensive front against the Polish proposals could be relaxed and the domestic opposition given a chance to make inroads.[101]

For its part the SPD had to recognize that rhetorical eloquence would not offset the CDU/CSU's absolute majority in the Bundestag. Consequently it turned more to extraparliamentary activities such as the campaign "Against Atomic Death".[102] At the heart of the debate on a military disengagement and/or arms limitation zone in Central Europe was the question of alternatives to the existing system of highly armed military pacts in hostile confrontation. Of course, the Federal Republic was not in a position to choose autonomously between alternative security concepts—it was too heavily integrated into the Western alliance system for that—but it definitely would have been able to exert some political influence on its allies in terms of all-German preferences, since there were in various countries strong currents toward reexamining the alliance system created in 1949-1955. However, the German government stuck to the priority of a military integration into the West and did not even attempt to explore its room for maneuver in changing the European security system—apart from the idea of an "Austrian solution" for the GDR.

But would there have been any chance at all of bringing about an alternative security settlement? The strongest opposition was probably to be expected from the United States, though less from President Eisenhower than from Secretary of State Dulles. A military disengagement and a nuclear-free zone in Central Europe would not have substantially interfered with the U.S. strategy of massive nuclear retaliation yet would have impeded the deployment of tactical nuclear weapons on the European continent, which was initiated in the latter half of the 1950s to strengthen that strategy's credibility. Such plans might also have led to a break-up of NATO.

The plans for deploying medium-range nuclear weapons in Western Europe and the Federal Republic's demand that the Bundeswehr be equipped with nuclear launchers elicited criticism not only in the East. Given the historical experiences with German militarism in the past, there were also in Western Europe influential efforts to prevent a development through which a German state would again become the leading military power in Europe. In the United States as well there were growing doubts as to whether a nuclear-armed Federal Republic was desirable and expedient for East-West relations. Once the Soviet Union had attained nuclear parity and U.S. territory had become vulnerable to Soviet intercontinental missiles, political cooperation with Moscow for purposes of managing crises and avoiding conflict assumed increasing importance for Washington.

For the West a military disengagement failed to come about, primarily for political reasons. As much as the Soviet Union, by supporting and promoting such ideas, was attempting to prevent a strengthening of the Western alliance and, if possible, to force the United States out of Western Europe, the United States was not prepared to allow a homeground advantage to a Soviet Union that continued to be viewed as aggressive and expansive. The bloody drama in Hungary, however, had demonstrated that the "rollback" strategy formulated by Dulles was untenable. And at its Twentieth Party Congress the Soviet Union had taken leave of the strategy of world revolution and declared as political principle the doctrine of peaceful coexistence, which in some sense was a strategy of war prevention. Thus, the nuclear stalemate also forced the superpowers to alter their conduct of foreign policy. In the long run this meant respecting each side's spheres of influence and the political status quo in postwar Europe.

With the plans for an arms limitation in Europe, what could have induced the Soviet Union to agree to a reunification of Germany once the military significance of the European continent as deployment zone for the two superpowers' armed forces had been diminished? Until 1955 there might still have been a chance; after that it was too late. For the Soviet Union the GDR had become in political as in military respects a pillar of its alliance; the GDR's breakout would have had an unforeseeable impact on the entire system. The Soviet Union was ready for changes in security policy only on the basis of the political status quo—unless the latter could be altered to Soviet advantage. This is precisely what it tried to do from late 1958 on, with the aid of the Berlin crisis, once the Soviet willingness to negotiate during 1955-1958 had failed to have the desired effect.

BERLIN AS LEVER FOR SOVIET POLICY ON GERMANY

While the disengagement and disarmament discussion implied the danger of a decoupling of European security and the German question, Khrushchev's Berlin ultimatum was aimed at altering the "open status quo," i.e., the conditions for overcoming at some point the German division through "reunification in peace and freedom." The transformation of West Berlin into a "free city" according to Soviet demands would have meant a change of the postwar political situation in Europe; the alternative of a peace treaty with Germany would have entailed international recognition of the second German state and thus confirmation of the status quo. In the view of the German government both measures would have negatively prejudiced the German question. Though successful in 1955, Bonn's linkage between European security and the German question was not very effective in the face of this challenge. Once the Soviet Union had grown stronger economically and had caught up with the West militarily, it was questionable whether any Western offers and quid pro quos could move Moscow to make concessions on Berlin and accept a new political order in Europe corresponding to Western conceptions.

Khrushchev's Ultimatum of November 1958

Moscow demonstrated this newly won strength when Premier Nikita S. Khrushchev, in a speech on November 10, 1958—one year after the launching of Sputnik—called for a peace treaty with Germany and a review of the four-power status of Berlin. In notes to the three Western powers, the Federal Republic, and the GDR on November 27, 1958, Moscow specified that West Berlin should be turned into an independent political unit, into a "free city." If no agreement on a new status for Berlin had been reached within six months, the Soviet Union would transfer its former occupation rights in and in relation to Berlin to the GDR. On January 10, 1959 Moscow put forth a draft peace treaty with the two German states, combined with the proposal to handle this issue at a summit conference of the states involved. On February 17, 1959 Khrushchev finally threatened that the Soviet Union would conclude a separate peace treaty with the GDR and transfer to it all rights and obligations with respect to Berlin.[103]

These Soviet initiatives and the diplomatic activities up to the building of the Wall in 1961 made it clear that Moscow wanted primarily a confirmation of the status quo, including the division of Germany, and was using Berlin, as the weakest point of the Western position, to achieve this goal. Terminating the four-power status of Berlin was a lever as well as a greatly desired side effect, if it were to succeed in removing the "thorn in the side of the GDR"—the status of West Berlin bolstered by the allied presence—its place in the Western social and political system, and the attendant possibilities for the people of the GDR to compare and flee, which hindered a consolidation of the GDR. Finally, the Soviet course of action served domestic political purposes, such as securing the Khrushchevian dictatorship in advance of the Twenty-first Party Congress, scheduled for the spring of 1959.

The Soviet ultimatum on Berlin confronted Bonn with the dilemma "that on the one hand the Western allies were waiting for and desirous of an initiative from Bonn, on the other hand such an initiative on Germany was capable of arousing their mistrust only too quickly as soon as—and this was inevitable—it envisaged changes in the Western security system and affected the Federal Republic's integral position in the Atlantic alliance."[104] The base line of Heinrich von Brentano's Foreign Office was to demonstrate firmness and commit the allies to the defense of their rights in Berlin, in part because it was felt that in this dilemma there were no other political alternatives. Chancellor Adenauer held a more flexible, though also ambiguous position. Throughout, he saw the tactical elements in the Soviet course, just as he was aware of the narrow room for maneuver of the West on the Berlin question. For these reasons he was particularly desirous of avoiding isolated negotiations on Berlin. First of all, he attempted to reestablish a connection between the German question and the problems of disarmament and to induce the West to put forward an initiative in this area. At the same time he had State Secretary Globke work out his own plan for Germany, one which contained quite a number of "unconventional ideas" (H.-P. Schwarz). Thus, Bonn would for a time accept the existence of two German states as well as a free city of Berlin, if immediately or within a year greater freedom were guaranteed in the GDR and in the foreseeable future the German people had the possibility of exercising self-determination with regard to reunification.[105]

However, the ideas in the Globke Plan were not accepted in the official policy of Bonn. Rather, the latter noted with great skepticism statements such as those of Secretary of State Dulles that under certain circumstances the United States might look upon representatives of the GDR as "agents" of the Soviet occupying power, e.g., in the Berlin traffic, and might accept their control function. Responsible persons in Bonn were likewise irritated by ideas such as those of Walter Lippmann that recognition of the GDR might be considered as a quid pro quo for international safeguards for the status of Berlin—e.g., by the United Nations. The British government, which had once again raised the idea of an arms limitation zone in Central Europe, was even accused by the chancellor of making too extensive concessions to Soviet policy on Germany; after their trip to Moscow he charged Prime Minister Macmillan and Foreign Secretary Selwyn Lloyd with having undermined the common position of the West by their "extra tours." Only in the case of President de Gaulle and the French government did Bonn find support for its uncompromising rejection of the Soviet plans, though less for objective reasons, but rather because Paris did not want to give up its rights in Berlin and its potential say on the German question; and also because it had no interest in an East-West rapprochement that could result in the restoration of Germany's national unity. The result was a fairly rigid negotiating position on the part of the Federal Republic, which was bent primarily on safeguarding—and not altering—the "open status quo."[106]

It took considerable effort to develop among the four powers a common Western negotiating position for the foreign ministers conference planned for May 1959 and designed as a step toward a summit meeting. Several times Adenauer had intervened personally in the preparatory talks of the Four-Power Working Group, and he did not shrink from disavowing his foreign minister before the allies. To the end he tried to thwart the two Anglo-Saxon allies' proposed combination of a European control zone and phased plan for the reunification of Germany; the British portion of the overall plan, the idea of a European arms control zone, seemed to him stupid and dangerous, the American portion, that is the attempt to work for reunification via an all-German federation, he considered unrealistic, outmoded, if not antiquated. Rather, he seemed to believe that the Soviet Union was interested in a comprehensive disarmament and might be prepared to conclude a 'standstill agreement' in Germany.[107] Thus, Adenauer was pursuing ideas upon which the Globke Plan was based and which he took up again three years later with his proposal for a "truce" with the Soviet Union on the German question. Other politicians in Bonn were more disturbed by the idea of an all-German confederation—an idea that had also been considered in Bonn—since such a confederation did not appear compatible with its policy of nonrecognition of the GDR. The German government was able to effect substantial changes in the Western proposals—e.g., the idea of a federation between the two German states was given up and a geographical limitation of the proposed arms control measures dropped—not, however, to move the Western powers from their negotiating concept, which, in fact, consisted in the linking of the German question, European security, and general disarmament.

The Geneva Conference of Foreign Ministers, which met from May 11 to August 5, 1959, with two breaks, did not yield any convergence of Eastern and Western points of view. First, the West presented as its negotiating proposal the "Western Peace Plan" (Herter Plan).[108] The Soviet Union repeated its call for concluding a German peace treaty and making West Berlin a free city. The two German "advisory delegations"—participating for the first time in an East-West conference—confined themselves to supporting the proposals of their respective blocs. Although the foreign ministers of the four powers had agreed to give priority to seeking an interim solution for Berlin, the Soviet Union intensified its pressure tactics with respect to the city. It linked a time-limited recognition of residual occupation rights and regulations in Berlin to the formation of an all-German committee, composed of equal numbers of representatives of the GDR and FRG, that would work out the fundamental principles for reunification and the conclusion of a peace treaty. If a German peace treaty were not concluded within one year, the Soviet Union threatened to sign a separate peace treaty with the GDR. The Western powers did not accept the new Soviet ultimatum (which a few days later was extended to 18 months), but submitted their own interim solution on Berlin, in which they declared their willingness to reduce their armed forces in Berlin, provided the Soviet Union would guarantee free and unimpeded access to Berlin and between the two parts of the city. These proposals were later made more specific. After 25 full sessions the conference came to a close without result—with an arid final communiqué and the announcement of a visit by Premier Khrushchev to the United States.[109]

A four-power summit conference planned for May 1960 in Paris foundered even before it got started—ostensibly because of the U-2 reconnaissance flights over the Soviet Union, possibly because the West had been able, despite divergent interests reflected principally in German and French objections, to agree once again on the negotiating position already taken in Geneva in 1959, but probably because Moscow had recognized that progress in negotiations could be expected at the earliest following the U.S. presidential elections in the fall of that year.

Superpower Bilateralism

Fourteen days before the Kennedy administration came into office the Soviet premier again stepped to center stage. In a major speech on international affairs, notably on problems of war and peace, Khrushchev took up the question of Berlin and declared that the position of the three Western powers in West Berlin had proved to be "particularly unstable" and that they would have to be compelled to take account of the real situation. "If they are stubborn," Khrushchev said, "we will adopt decisive measures. We will conclude a peace treaty with the GDR because we are fully determined to ensure the conclusion of a peace treaty with Germany at last, to do away with the occupation regime in West Berlin, and, thus, to eradicate this splinter from the heart of Europe."[110] On February 17, 1961 the Soviet government sent a memorandum to the German government. In tone obliging but in substance uncompromising, the memorandum stressed that it was high time to sign a peace treaty and end the occupation regime in West Berlin by establishing a "free city." With that the West was to be confronted with the alternatives of either resolving the problem of Germany and West Berlin according to Soviet conceptions or else forfeiting its position in the city. At the same time Moscow rejected all attempts to establish a linkage between a peace treaty and disarmament. It maintained that such a connection would only serve to hinder the solution of either problem.[111]

In the subsequent months, while the government in Bonn was mainly seeking to gain time, Washington was still preoccupied with reviewing its foreign and security policy. The new administration found itself confronted with the task of developing workable options for such complex issues as the redefinition of military strategy, negotiations on nuclear arms control, and solutions to the problems of Laos, the Congo, Cuba, and, of course, Berlin.

While Khrushchev, from a position of military strength based on the capability to launch a nuclear counterstrike against U.S. territory, was primarily trying to consolidate his East European sphere of influence, Kennedy was first of all concerned with adapting U.S. strategy to the loss of strategic superiority and regaining the initiative in foreign policy. Secondly, he wanted to mobilize American society for a new awakening, with the "New Frontier" designed to restore the old self-confidence (e.g., through an ambitious space program). At the same time—like the Soviet Union—the U.S. was striving to strengthen its influence in the third world and offer itself to the young nations as partner in the decolonization and development processes. The newly enflamed ideological and political rivalry stamped by the dynamic personalities of Khrushchev and Kennedy precipitated an intense bipolar relationship between the two superpowers.

Shortly after his inauguration Kennedy had proposed to Khrushchev a personal meeting, which ultimately took place in Vienna on June 3 and 4, 1961. If Kennedy had hoped to have first decided the situation in Cuba through U.S. intervention, and then be able to negotiate with Khrushchev on Berlin from a position of strength, the Bay of Pigs fiasco shattered these hopes. And despite the amicable sounding communiqués it could not be ignored that between the United States and its most important allies these existed differences of opinion on how to defend the Western position in Berlin.[112] But Khrushchev was also under pressure. In the previous weeks the Berlin problem had been amplified by a steadily swelling stream of refugees from the GDR, one that the GDR was not able to curb by travel restrictions and increased controls. Party Secretary Ulbricht repeatedly pressed for a joint action by the Warsaw Pact states designed to cut off the stream of refugees and prevent a "bleeding" of the GDR.[113]

The Vienna meeting between the U.S. president and the Soviet leader served primarily to let the two sound out and take measure of each other. While Kennedy had come to Vienna to probe Soviet willingness to negotiate on the various international problems and at the same time to communicate the U.S. determination to defend essential positions, Khrushchev was bent on achieving a settlement of the Berlin question and demonstrating to his negotiating partner that if it were not possible to do this harmoniously, the Soviet Union would then proceed unilaterally. He presented Kennedy a "Memorandum on the German Question" in which the Soviet government called for a peace treaty with Germany—in fact, within six months—as well as a normalization of the situation in West Berlin. It further stated that it is not pursuing the goal of harming the interests of the United States or the other Western Powers in Europe. It does not propose to change anything in Germany or in West Berlin in favor of any one state or group of states. The USSR deems it necessary in the interests of consolidating peace formally to recognize the situation which has developed in Europe after the war, to legalize and consolidate the inviolability of the existing German borders, to normalize the situation in West Berlin on the basis of reasonable consideration for the interests of all the parties concerned.[114]

These obliging formulations could not, however, obscure the fact that the Soviets had again laid their maximum demand on the table and that the United States could not accept this without giving up a number of fundamental positions and risking a deep rift in the alliance. Kennedy's way of trying to maintain the status quo but make it more stable by new modalities was ill-conceived. When Khrushchev threatened that if the West were not prepared to negotiate the Soviet Union would take unilateral steps to solve the Berlin question, Kennedy could only counter that the United States was determined to defend Western rights in and on the access routes to Berlin by all means—if necessary by the use of military force. Threatening war was apparently the only way of preventing war.

Thus, after the initial months of the ultimatum in the winter of 1958-59, the Berlin crisis had reached a new climax. Under U.S. leadership the West utilized the time following the Vienna summit to

- define its basic positions on the Berlin question,
- demonstrate its determination to defend these positions, and
- develop its own negotiating position.

Particular significance was attached to the "essentials" spelled out by President Kennedy in a radio and television address of July 25, 1961 on the Berlin question:

- the presence of the three Western powers in West Berlin,
- the free access of these powers to West Berlin, and
- the guarantee of the security of West Berlin's people and of their right to decide freely upon their own way of life.[115]

Particular attention was paid to the fact that these "essentials" related to West Berlin and not to Berlin as a whole—a point that had always been left open in the West's previous statements.[116] Here the U.S. position differed fundamentally from that of the German government, which always spoke of "Berlin." Moreover, Bonn insisted on: (1) Berlin's belonging to the legal, financial, and economic system of the Federal Republic, as well as (2) the preservation of Berlin's function as a meeting place between East and West.[117]

As it strengthened its conventional armed forces in Europe and improved its emergency planning, the United States demonstrated that it was prepared to defend its rights in the city and to free access, if need be militarily. There were greater problems in developing a common Western negotiating position. American ideas on an international access authority or a corridor solution did not meet with approval among the allies, nor were the latter—particularly the Federal Republic—prepared to recognize the Oder-Neisse border as a quid pro quo for Eastern guarantees of Western rights in Berlin. At a special session of the NATO Council in early August 1961, the foreign ministers of the three Western powers and the Federal Republic could agree only that they would make further efforts to develop a common negotiating position.[118]

The policy of the Federal Republic was primarily set on not accepting any diminution in the present role of Berlin as constituent part of the Federal Republic, though with a special status, or in the long-term possibility of making Berlin the capital of a reunified Germany. In this there were dangers emanating from the East and the West. In Bonn's view, Khrushchev's threat of a separate peace treaty giving the GDR control over the connecting routes to Berlin amounted to a status quo minus no less than the limitation to West Berlin in Kennedy's three "essentials" or the search for a negotiated settlement that implied a limited recognition of the GDR. From its perspective, Berlin was as much the symbol of all Germany as it was the "window on the West" that exerted a force of attraction on the people of the GDR and thus hindered a consolidation of the communist regime. Berlin was an essential element of the "magnet theory" underlying many hopes for reunification. Considerations along the lines of an "Austrian solution" for the GDR or a "truce" necessitating a recognition of a second German state always presupposed internal changes in the GDR.

The West German ideological offensive could not, however, obscure the fact that Bonn did not have at its disposal the political or economic means to impose its will on the other side. The preceding year's suspension of the Interzonal Trade Agreement had turned out to be a weak instrument for preventing the GDR from imposing restrictions and impediments on the access routes to Berlin. Following its termination in September 1960, the agreement was again put in force on January 1, 1961, without any decisive improvements for the status of Berlin. But above all, tough talk could not obscure the fact that the geographic situation put the West on the defensive in Berlin. The West did not dispose of political measures to counter the Eastern "salami tactics" of impediments and restrictions on the access routes; it was left solely with recourse to military force to uphold its position. In this situation Bonn saw little promise in negotiations on the German question, even less so on an isolated Berlin agreement. Faced with the U.S. determination to leave nothing untried to reach a negotiated settlement, and faced with a revived interest in arms control agreements, Bonn found it useful to reverse the order of priorities in the linkage and refer to the positive effects of general and controlled disarmament, which would then "create future preconditions for a permanent and just solution to the German question based on the German people's right to self-determination."[119] With that linkage had become a dilatory formula.

The Building of the Wall on August 13, 1961

The closing of the sector border in Berlin by the GDR authorities in the morning hours of August 13, 1961,[120] followed by the building of the Wall all around West Berlin in the next few days, was perceived as a massive provocation that posed a fundamental threat to the policy of the "open status quo." In the United States, however, it was noted that the GDR, which had proceeded in close coordination with the Soviet Union and the other Warsaw Pact states, had not violated any of the Kennedy "essentials" nor encroached upon the rights of the Western powers in West Berlin. Attempts by the GDR to refuse the Western allies access to East Berlin or to exercise control over the air corridors were frustrated by the stubborn insistence on observance of the occupation agreements. Because Moscow had continued to call for a peace treaty with the GDR yet had named no date for it, there remained the fear in the West that the 13th of August was merely the prelude to a repudiation of Western occupation rights. Hence, from a Western perspective it seemed necessary to defend these rights with firmness, but also to develop a common Western negotiating concept with which the status of West Berlin could be safeguarded in the long run.

However, negotiations on Berlin were burdened with a twofold difficulty. First, it remained to be clarified among the Western allies what the object and purpose of negotiations were to be, and secondly, Moscow had to be sounded out to see whether there was a modus vivendi with which the lever of "Berlin" could be wrested from Khrushchev without impugning the basic Western positions on the Berlin question. The United States especially wanted to cross Berlin off its crisis calendar—in part to be able to turn its attention again to other international problems—and was therefore willing to make concessions in other areas, e.g., on the question of European borders, for the sake of securing West Berlin.

The German government, most recently Chancellor Adenauer on his visit to Washington in November 1961, had to realize that it could not sustain its strategy of dilatory negotiations in the face of U.S. determination to engage in a dialogue with Moscow. The two sides found a compromise to the effect that Bonn gave up the linkage between Berlin settlement, German question, and European security. It not only agreed to isolated negotiations on Berlin but now insisted that the exploratory talks be confined to this question. In the Berlin Contingency Group the German government had with some reservations agreed to the U.S. proposal of an international access authority, yet it made no bones about the fact that it regarded such proposals as a danger to the rights of the four powers and would under no circumstances agree to a de facto recognition of the GDR.[121] At the same time, as a kind of ''reinsurance,'' Bonn attempted to maintain a direct dialogue with the Soviet Union via the German ambassador in Moscow, Hans Kroll.[122] France rejected negotiations entirely, as it feared that these would diminish its potential say in all questions pertaining to Germany.

Various rounds of talks were conducted, in part in Washington between Secretary of State Dean Rusk and Soviet Ambassador Anatoly Dobrynin, in part in Moscow between Foreign Minister Andrej Gromyko and U.S. Ambassador Llewellyn Thompson, and in some instances directly between the two foreign ministers outside the UN General Assembly or the Geneva disarmament conference. Both sides were trying to see whether there was a promising foundation for East-West negotiations. In these exploratory talks, however, it soon became apparent that the Soviet Union was not interested in an international access authority, at least not in the form envisaged, as Moscow also rejected a solution limited to modalities of the Western presence. Therefore, in early April 1962 the U.S. government developed a new proposal that again placed the Berlin problem in the context of the German question and European security. This proposal contained the following elements:

1. Establishment of an international access authority;
2. A treaty between Washington and Moscow on the non-proliferation of nuclear weapons;
3. Exchange of nonaggression declarations between NATO and the Warsaw Pact, guaranteeing the inviolability of existing borders and lines of demarcation;
4. Appointment of joint technical commissions, with three representatives each from the Federal Republic and the GDR, and

5. Establishment of a permanent conference of deputy foreign ministers of the four powers, which was to deal with the German and Berlin questions on an ongoing basis.[123]

These proposals were evidently aimed at offering the Soviets an assurance of the status quo in Europe in exchange for recognition of the Western status quo in Berlin, as far as this was possible without a peace treaty and without formal recognition of the GDR under international law.

These proposals caused a row between Bonn and Washington not only because the United States was about to go beyond the compromise worked out between Adenauer and Kennedy and—from Bonn's standpoint—make far-reaching concessions in the area of European security, but also because of the way the internal Western consultations were handled. The request for approval of this negotiating package within 24 hours was perceived in Bonn as an ultimatum; on the other hand, press disclosures in Bonn about the content of the Western proposals rubbed Washington the wrong way. The leaks were presumed to have been inspired by the chancellor himself, though the German ambassador in Washington, Grewe, was held responsible.

At the NATO conference in Athens, painstaking efforts were made to mend the rifts in the Western alliance. Foreign Minister Schröder expressed the German government's agreement with a continuation of the government-level talks, suggesting, however, that the following principles be adhered to:

- continued presence of the Western powers in Berlin;
- maintenance of Berlin's ties with the Federal Republic;
- guarantee of free access to Berlin;
- no recognition of the GDR as a legitimate German state, no entrusting of control over the access routes to the authorities of the GDR;
- coupling of a final solution of the Berlin question with reunification.

In the meantime a modus vivendi was to be found.[124] Secretary of State Rusk reaffirmed that the United States would submit no proposals that were unacceptable to the Federal Republic. The NATO decision arrived at on this basis was not exactly evidence of a convincing Western negotiating position.

But the main problem of the NATO meeting in Athens consisted in finding a solution amenable to the NATO partners' desire for nuclear sharing compatible militarily with the doctrine of centralized operational control over nuclear weapons and politically with their nonproliferation. Without this having become explicit, surely the connection of this question with policy on Germany and Berlin must have been clear to all those involved: the Federal Republic, which sought to enhance its role in the alliance through nuclear codetermination in the form of a multilateral NATO force; the Soviet Union, which wanted to use pressure on Berlin to bring about a security arrangement in accord with Soviet interests, and especially to prevent the equipment of the Bundeswehr with nuclear weapons, and the United States, which regarded an accord on nuclear non-proliferation, particularly a guarantee that the Germans would not be given control over nuclear weapons, as a prerequisite for a satisfactory solution of the other contentious problems between East and West.

In the subsequent months, however, it became clear that there was no common ground between East and West for an agreement on Berlin, indeed, there was not even clarity as to the respective intentions of the other side. The United States interpreted the Eastern proposals for a free city of West Berlin, the announcement of a transfer of access control to the authorities of the GDR, and the proposal to replace the Western occupation troops with symbolic contingents from other states, primarily as an attempt to drive it out of West Berlin. In perspective it would appear Moscow was using the lever of Berlin mainly to gain a recognition under international law of the changes that had taken place in Europe after the Second World War. To that extent, Moscow was not interested in an isolated Berlin settlement once the borders of the GDR had been sealed off.

At that time, however, the United States was not able to negotiate successfully on broader solutions involving a recognition of the Oder-Neisse line as Poland's western frontier, a respecting of the GDR in international relations, or measures of European security, because—for various reasons—it could not count on either Bonn's support or agreement from Paris. Progress in the disarmament negotiations also turned out to be difficult so long as the military-strategic changes initiated by the Kennedy administration had yet to be completed. Hence, the summer of 1962 did not bring the progress hoped for in the negotiations but rather a renewed sharpening of the Berlin crisis by Soviet disruptive actions on the access routes and in the air corridors to Berlin. These actions as well as shooting at refugees by the GDR's border police and the dissolving of the office of Soviet commandant for East Berlin were intended to demonstrate formally the departure from the four-power status of the city. The United States also strengthened its forces in Germany, and a new conflict appeared imminent.

With developments in Berlin, the confrontation in Cuba presented a double crisis. The installation of Soviet missiles on this Caribbean island was surely designed to bolster the thesis of a global East-West balance of power obviating the use of nuclear weapons in a limited regional conflict. It also gave the Soviet Union added leverage for inducing the United States to compromise on Berlin and Germany. The U.S. government's ability to make credible to the Soviet Union its determination to employ military means of power, while at the same time refraining from a public humiliation of the Soviet Union, forced Moscow not only to give in and withdraw the missiles from Cuba, but to come down a peg in Europe as well. Moscow then intensified its arms programs, particularly in the areas of strategic nuclear weapons and naval forces, so as to be able in the future to back up its global claim to power. But in October 1962 the world had narrowly avoided a nuclear catastrophe.

The Berlin and Cuban crises had been triggered by the Soviet Union's attempt to alter the international balance of power. These crises had dramatically shown to both sides that any forcible change of the status quo entailed the danger of one's own annihilation. But from this insight East and West drew different conclusions. The Soviet Union adhered to its goal of obtaining an international confirmation of the European status quo, though from then on it took to waiting more or less patiently for the West, especially the Federal Republic, to come realize that maintaining the status quo with minimal changes would also be in its own well-understood interests. In the 1960s the campaign for a European security conference was Moscow's most important means to this end. The community of risk with the Soviet Union prompted the United States on its part to pursue a course of mitigating the ongoing political competition through partial security cooperation. The result was a greater effort to achieve agreements on arms control and joint crisis management with the Soviet Union.

For the Federal Republic the building of the Wall meant the breakdown of a long-term reunification concept that had been based on maintaining the "open status quo." In view of the importance its allies attached to defusing the crisis situation in Central Europe and the simultaneous readiness to respect, at least, if not formally recognize, the status quo, the instrument of linkage became useless. Bonn found itself compelled to modify or hold off using this instrument in many instances until it was finally given up altogether in the summer of 1962. What remained was a veto power—the possibility of preventing unacceptable settlements by means of appropriate diplomatic—or journalistic!—countermeasures, which tended, however, to restrict Bonn's room for maneuver in foreign policy.

The difference of interests between the U.S. and the Federal Republic with respect to overcoming or maintaining the status quo led to a serious crisis of confidence in German-American relations, which was reflected in German domestic politics in the conflict between "Gaullists" (such as Adenauer or Strauss, oriented to German and European interests) and "Atlanticists" (such as Foreign Minister Schröder and the SPD leadership, trying to effect a harmonization with the U.S.). If the Federal Republic did not want to lose its accord with the United States, it faced considerable pressures to accommodate in several areas. On security policy it was a matter of accepting in the military realm the new U.S. strategy of flexible response and in the political the doctrine of arms control. With respect to East-West relations, the United States was beginning to press for the Federal Republic's participation in the process of political normalization that was gradually getting under way, demanding of Bonn movement toward a modus vivendi on European problems. Bonn's attempt to merge its interests on the question of Germany with a parallel alliance policy had failed.

3

Security Policy as Alliance Policy

From its inception the Federal Republic conceived of security as a military *and* political category.[1] Security meant preserving an independent course of political development as much as protection against military aggression or coercion. In the 1950s security seemed threatened in three ways:

First, as a consequence of the East-West conflict, there was the Soviet threat. Soviet policy was perceived as offensive and aggressive. The Sovietizing of Eastern Europe, The Berlin blockade, and finally the Korean War gave rise to fears of having to contend with a Soviet military intervention in Central Europe or with an attack carried out by the paramilitary forces of the GDR (the *Kasernierte Volkspolizei* had reached a strength of 50,000 men by mid-1950).

From the point of view of Konrad Adenauer, this military threat could be countered in three ways:

- by an allied security guarantee and stronger allied forces in Western Europe;
- by the development of a federal police;
- by a German defense contribution in the framework of a European or Atlantic army.[2]

The developments of 1950-55 showed that the German government was able to go all three routes. In September 1950 the three powers announced an increase in their armed forces in Western Europe and declared that any attack on the Federal Republic or Berlin would be regarded as an attack on them.[3] The question of a federal police was more complicated, since here Bonn had to overcome not only the hesitations of the Allied High Commissioners but also the reservations of the federal states, which were responsible for police authority. But in February 1951 the Bundestag was able to pass the law creating the Federal Border Police, which was assigned to the Ministry of the Interior, with personnel not to exceed 10,000 (20,000 as of 1953). The negotiations on a German defense contribution turned out to be even more difficult. Parallel discussions in Petersberg near Bonn and in Paris encompassed both a NATO contribution and a European army. Then, because of French concerns, preference was given to deploying German contingents within the European Defense Community. However, once the EDC Treaty, signed on May 27, 1952, was rejected in the French National Assembly, a hastily convened Nine-Power Conference in London in the fall of 1954 resolved to accept the Federal Republic in the North Atlantic alliance. On May 8, 1955, exactly ten years after the unconditional surrender, the West German state became a member of NATO.

Secondly, German politicians were worried that there could be a repeat of Potsdam; i.e., the victorious powers could come to new terms over the heads of the Germans.[4] To prevent this the Federal Republic had to overcome its status as an object of international action and become an actor itself. Thus, for Bonn the military contribution was in part a means for attaining national sovereignty and an equal international status. This instrumentality of rearmament was clearly demonstrated by the linkage between the Bonn and Paris Treaties and the German defense contribution, with the treaties coming into force and terminating the occupation regime in conjunction with rearmament's becoming operative.

Thirdly, the political situation in Europe in the 1950s seemed to be still in flux. The division of Europe had yet to acquire that degree of permanence which today appears constitutive of the postwar period, nor had the role of the Germans in Europe been precisely determined. Not least of all, the Federal Republic saw itself as a provisional entity, as an intermediary on the way to a reunified Germany. Added to this there were questions of German history, questions about the young democracy's stability in the face of crisis, about the reliability of the Federal Republic's Western orientation. In the view of responsible West German politicians this Second Republic had to be safeguarded through strong ties with the Western state system. The notion that Germany had to become a member of equal standing in a democratic Europe united Christian Democrats and Social Democrats, though the two had different ideas as to the structure of the future Europe and the way to get there.[5] Concern about the internal and external stability of the Federal Republic in view of the "catastrophic German historical tradition" led Konrad Adenauer to give integration in the West priority over reunification and to reject categorically any form of neutralization, as put forward in the various disengagement plans. His counterpart, Kurt Schumacher, the leader of the SPD, was moved by the same concern. He claimed that it was paramount to solve the national question, since reunification and equality of status were prerequisites for a secure democratic future. However, what in Schumacher's view was supposed to have a stabilizing effect domestically and prevent a national irredentist movement would have destabilized the postwar structures of Europe. The nightmare of Germany's European neighbors was a nation of 80 million at the center of Europe, a people whose desire for unity would have to be satisfied, but whose incorporation into Europe would be very difficult and whose drive for equality would have to be curbed. Hence, under the given international political configuration, only the road of integration with the West was feasible. The founding of the ECSC, EEC, and EURATOM provided the European, economic, and potentially political counterpart to the Atlantic, military integration.

This development, leading to a German defense contribution within NATO, the political consolidation of the Federal Republic, and the emergence of integrative structures in Western Europe, had essentially three consequences for European security structures. First, the division of Europe and the integration of the two German states into opposing power blocs were firmly set for the foreseeable future. If this resulted in a greater potential for shaping the structure of relations within the Western system, in the East-West context policy was possible only on the basis of the status quo. Secondly, the presence of the United States in Europe was given a lasting foundation in the stationing of its armed forces within NATO as well as in the U.S. rights and duties with regard to Berlin and Germany as a whole. The United States had thus become a "European power." Without its participation, an all-European policy was no longer possible, while this in turn denied it a return to the isolationism of the prewar period. Finally, the disintegration of the anti-Hitler coalition and the subsequent development of the new formations of the East-West conflict led the West Germans out of ostracism and isolation and made them a sought-after security partner, which, because of its geographic position, economic strength, and, not least, military potential (since the 1960s the Federal Republic has been the strongest conventional land power in Western Europe) has come to have a considerable political influence.

The security structures created in Europe in the early 1950s[6] had formed under the impress of the East-West confrontation and were designed to decide the ideological and power-politics conflict in favor of the West. The ways in which this conflict was carried out consisted as much in calculated demonstration of power as in gestures of entente. The 1950s were not a period of uninterrupted East-West confrontation, but in fact included phases of detente: Korean War *and* Geneva Summit Conference, Soviet military intervention in East European states *and* U.S.-Soviet cooperation in the Suez crisis. The dual conflict around Berlin and Cuba was—for the time being—Moscow's last attempt to tip the scales of the global conflict in its favor. As it transpired that in their nuclear stalemate the two great powers could keep each other in check by the threat of nuclear annihilation, East-West relations began to settle into a political modus vivendi with elements of both confrontation and cooperation. Western security doctrine took this change into account, somewhat belatedly, with the "Harmel Report,"[7] in which defense capability and readiness to negotiate were presented as the two goals of security policy. For its part the Soviet Union had replaced its thesis of the inevitability of wars between antagonistic states and social systems by the doctrine of peaceful coexistence.[8]

The change in threat perceptions was also accompanied by a change in the concept of security, which was broadened in that military defense was joined by political detente. Security was to be preserved no longer simply by means of military contributions to the NATO alliance, but also by arms control agreements with the other side. With the Harmel formula the conflicts of priorities in Western policy were subsumed in a new concept of security. At first this proved flexible enough to accentuate now one component, now the other, depending on the general international conditions and the specific configurations of national interests. But by the end of the 1970s the divergence of security priorities on either side of the Atlantic, particularly in the United States and the Federal Republic, had sparked a pseudoconflict of "security or detente." This produced irritations in the Western alliance and in East-West relations, but also tended to obscure the close links between the military and the political elements of security policy.

THE BUNDESWEHR AS WEST GERMAN CONTRIBUTION TO THE WESTERN SECURITY COMMUNITY

The rearmament of the Federal Republic was a complicated business of contribution and quid pro quo. While the Western powers honored Bonn's readiness to deploy a 500,000-man army by terminating the occupation regime and thus their direct influence in the internal affairs of the West German state—at the same time committing themselves to support Bonn's political goal of eventual reunification—Bonn bought itself security and partnership at the price of extensive arms limitations and an institutionalized foreign control over its military forces. These restrictions consisted of a ban on production of ABC weapons, a prohibition of producing heavy weapons—missiles, bombers, larger warships—the observance of which was to be monitored by the WEU, and complete subordination of German units to NATO, so as to render superfluous the institution of a separate general staff.[9] The virtually complete integration of the Bundeswehr into the Atlantic alliance underscored the fact that the former drew its raison d'être from its inception as an alliance army. It is not an independent national army within a classical alliance of states; rather it is the contribution of the Federal Republic to the common defense of an alliance without which neither deterrence nor defense—and thus the essential elements of the Federal Republic's security—can be guaranteed. However, the close integration of the Federal Republic into the alliance also makes the former particularly sensitive to changes in the political objectives, security concepts, and military strategy of its most important allies—primarily, of course, the United States—changes which have compelled Bonn to undergo a number of painful adjustments.

Political and Military Motives for the German Defense Contribution

In the eyes of the German government the development of the Bundeswehr had a political and a military function: the deployment of an armed force of half a million troops—the largest in Western Europe—was to give the Federal Republic a proportionate say within the Western alliance. This strengthening of the conventional forces in Europe was to enable NATO to localize a possible military conflict and to ensure a defense at the intra-German border against a Soviet attack. West Germany was thus to be spared the alternative between capitulation and nuclear destruction. The NATO strategy in force in the early 1950s presented the combination of a direct defense of Western Europe by conventional forces and a threat to use nuclear weapons against the Warsaw Pact states. The main emphasis of deterrence, however, clearly lay in the threat of a nuclear retaliatory strike by the strategic forces of the United States.[10]

In political practice the organization of the Bundeswehr took place in a complex web of social, political, and military interests and considerations. Most evident was the contradiction between the ambitious talk by the federal government, which had committed itself to raising a 500,000-man army within five years, more or less from scratch, and the widespread fear of war among the West German people as well as their *ohne mich* attitude, rooted in the experience of the Hitler Reich. The political gap was further widened when the SPD opposition and large parts of the trade unions and churches accused the government of endangering by its armament the last chance for reunification. They proposed alternative security concepts—ranging from the SPD's plan for German unification to proposals for disengagement and various concepts for a collective European security system.[11] Within the government, too, there existed a strained relationship between those politicians who regarded the Bundeswehr principally as a political instrument designed to assure the Federal Republic an equal say in its security affairs and to establish a close coupling of the United States to the European continent, and those who saw in it primarily a military security factor and wanted to construct the most effective force possible. This debate was sparked above all by the question of force goals, i.e., the size, armament, and deployment tempo of the Bundeswehr. Finally, the conflicts were preconditioned by Bonn's readily accepted role of loyal "vassal of the United States"[12] and the resulting constraint to adapt to changing U.S. conceptions of political and military strategy.

In view of the emerging tendencies toward detente in East-West relations in 1955, Chancellor Adenauer wanted to create faits accomplis with a rapid build-up of the Bundeswehr so as to knock the bottom out of any hypothetical notions of neutralizing Germany. At the same time, the German government was taking pains to demonstrate its alliance loyalty to the United States, in order to induce Washington to take German perspectives into account in international negotiations and to get the United States to commit itself—in the face of countervailing tendencies in the Eisenhower administration—to maintaining a strong conventional presence in Western Europe. Hence, Adenauer was pressing for the raising of at least a symbolic volunteer contingent in 1955, one which would serve as nucleus for the future conscript army.

Before the first West German soldiers could be mobilized in November 1955, the Bonn government had to overcome diverse domestic political opposition and material obstacles. To begin with, there was a dearth of everything: suitable instructors and barracks, weapons and equipment, even uniforms, but mostly, the legal foundation for the armed forces. While Defense Minister Theodor Blank, at Adenauer's insistence, had devoted himself to the task of raising 500,000 troops within three years, many military and political figures— with the Bavarian CSU chairman, Franz Josef Strauss, making himself their spokesman—preferred a smaller but well-trained army equipped with modern technologies, even if it were to take longer to build. Faced with a tight labor market in a boom economy, business leaders also expressed their misgivings about a forced rearmament. The parliamentary opposition likewise rejected a precipitous build-up and wanted assurances that the internal structure of the armed forces conformed to democratic principles. Specifically, it advocated civilian leadership, parliamentary control, and an unimpeachable selection of personnel.[13]

In late May 1955 the government submitted to the Bundestag and Bundesrat a volunteer army bill, hastily thrown together in the chancellor's office, which was to establish a legal basis for the mobilization of armed forces. Opposition was formed in the parliamentary bodies, including a "grand coalition" of CDU/CSU and SPD representatives, who wanted above all to ensure that the new army was subject to political control and that its internal organization conformed to democratic principles. To this end the Bundestag wrote into the volunteer bill a proviso on organization ensuring the lawmakers a prominent part in decisions about the structure and composition of the armed forces. At the same time it decided to appoint an advisory committee on personnel matters, composed of figures from public life who were to assess the personal qualifications of all applicants for leading positions in the armed forces.

The actual military organization was constituted in a series of legal measures. It included an amendment of the Basic Law that provided a foundation for determining a case of military emergency and regulating command authority. A prominent role was given to the defense committee, which obtained the rights of an investigating committee. This legislation was also supported by the SPD, which had demanded that the defense minister be directly responsible to the Bundestag, but settled for the establishment of the office of Defense Commissioner of the German Bundestag, which was to watch over the maintenance of a democratic order in the armed forces. This embodied the concept, developed essentially by Graf Wolf von Baudissin, of *innere führung*, or "moral leadership," which envisaged a model of the responsible "citizen in uniform."[14] At this time the new armed forces were designated the "Bundeswehr."

The parties were not in accord, however, on the size of the Bundeswehr, the length of military service, and whether or not service should be compulsory. Not least at Adenauer's insistence, the CDU/CSU and the military leaders for the time being adhered to their ambitious goal of mobilizing 485,000 troops by the end of 1959, which would necessitate a conscript army with an 18-month service. The SPD advocated a smaller volunteer army. As leading SPD politicians saw it, one argument against conscription was that the planned half-million-man force would deepen the division of Germany and burden the current disarmament negotiations, and a second was that with the greater recourse to nuclear weapons in the event of conflict, a large conventional army was not necessary militarily.[15] The SPD's advocacy of a professional army represented a break with its traditional position on armed forces since the Erfurt Program (1897), in which it had viewed a people's army as a democratic and democratizing element. This break is explicable only in light of the SPD's difficulties in finding the way from "no" to joining NATO to "yes" for national defense.

The debate on the Bundeswehr very clearly brought out the conflict of aims between political and military purposes. The military planning of the Bundeswehr, as conceived by Blank's office and then carried out in the Ministry of Defense under Generals Adolf Heusinger and Hans Speidel, provided for the raising of a conventional army with strong armored forces and armor-piercing weapons, and was largely shaped by experience from the Second World War. Within the dual strategy of nuclear deterrence and conventional defense decided upon by NATO in Lisbon in 1952,[16] the German government assumed that the West German defense contribution in conjunction with the nuclear superiority of the United States would generally make an attack by the Warsaw Pact less likely. But should a military conflict occur, then West German territory had to be defended as far eastward as possible and as long as warranted without recourse to nuclear weapons. The parliamentary opposition, on the other hand, argued that even with a West German defense contribution a military conflict in Europe could not be limited to conventional warfare, especially since the NATO Council in December 1954—in departure from the Lisbon decisions— had resolved "the immediate and direct use of atomic weapons." The fact that Chancellor Adenauer, despite all opposition, stuck with the mobilization of a 500,000-man army underscored the relative importance of political motives for the West German defense contribution.[17]

The Organization of the Bundeswehr Amid Changing NATO Strategies

The "New Look" in defense policy introduced by the Eisenhower administration reflected an altered threat analysis and took into account economic, budgetary, and domestic political aspects. The previous nuclear-conventional dual strategy was to be replaced by a "strategy of massive retaliation," i.e., the threat to use nuclear weapons against targets of one's own choosing. This strategy was to be complemented by a credible regional defense.[18] The U.S. example and the availability of tactical nuclear weapons prompted the NATO Council at its meeting in December 1954 likewise to attach a lesser importance to conventional armed forces and instead reformulate its strategic concept in such a way that even a conventional attack would be repulsed with the use of tactical nuclear weapons. This was the birth of the "sword and shield concept": the conventional forces constituted a "shield" to contain local breaches while the attack itself was to be repelled with the nuclear "sword." This strategy enabled the Western allies to modify the unfulfillable Lisbon force goals and promised them substantial financial savings; in so doing they overlooked the fact that they were bargaining for defense at the price of their own destruction. From the U.S. point of view a European conflict carried out with nuclear weapons might be "tactically limited," but for Europe the damage would be immense in any case.

While this debate was going on in the alliance, the Germans were occupied with their own problems, i.e., with plans for mobilizing the first units of the Bundeswehr. However, the nuclear reality caught up when the "Carte Blanche" maneuver was carried out in July 1955. NATO's first atomic air exercise, Carte Blanche simulated the dropping of 300 atomic bombs on a hundred targets between Hamburg and Munich and assumed losses numbering 1.7 million dead, 3.5 million wounded, and countless other radiation victims.[19] The German public reacted to these reports with shock and outrage; Adenauer's argument that a substantial defense contribution would prevent West Germany's becoming a battlefield in the event of conflict was bared in all its dubiousness. The SPD opposition accused the government of acting irresponsibly, neither educating the public about the risks of a nuclear conflict nor adapting its own military planning to the changes in weapons technology and military strategy. Yet the SPD's own position was also extremely contradictory. While SPD politicians warned of a strategy that would lead to the use of nuclear weapons on European soil and thus entail vast destruction, they also criticized the building of a conventional ground force in a way that could be taken as an argument for an army suited to the conditions of nuclear warfare.[20] However, Carte Blanche had its most lasting impact at the military level, where it revealed the structural defects of a force planning that rested essentially on the experience of the Second World War. Franz Josef Strauss, then minister for atomic affairs, used these weak points in military planning to present himself as a defense expert well versed in modern strategy and to recommend himself as Blank's successor.[21]

With Carte Blanche the nuclear question was now on the agenda for the Federal Republic, too. In December 1955, at the suggestion of Supreme Commander General Alfred M. Gruenther, the NATO Council called upon the United States to place tactical atomic weapons— "the most modern weapons," as the communiqué expressed it—at the disposal of the West European allies.[22] Still, when the Radford Plan became known, it found the German government, which just a week before had carried the military conscription law against strong opposition in the Bundestag, completely unprepared politically. On July 13, 1956 the *New York Times* had reported that the chairman of the Joint Chiefs of Staff, Admiral Arthur W. Radford, was advocating a redirection of defense spending in accordance with the "New Look." In the face of the Soviet Union's advances in weapons technology—the Soviets had detonated a hydrogen bomb in 1954—the main objective from now on had to be attaining a clear superiority of U.S. strategic retaliatory forces; in relation to that, all other programs were to be reduced. In particular, far smaller conventional forces would be sufficient and overseas troops could be cut back.[23] In this form the Radford Plan, which in part reflected U.S. bureaucratic politics and inter-service rivalry, was never realized; it did, however, indicate a reorientation of strategic priorities in the United States, one which called in question the German concept of a strong regional conventional defense and thus led to a serious crisis in German-American relations.

First, the German government sought to clarify U.S. intentions. Although Washington stressed that there was no decision on the part of the U.S. government to alter its force planning, a statement by Secretary of State Dulles at a press conference on July 18, 1956, in which Dulles emphasized nuclear weapons,[24] was not apt to allay German fears. With a series of diplomatic initiatives Bonn attempted to effect a change in the U.S. plans or at least to prevent troop reductions in Western Europe. Adenauer dispatched his military advisers, Generals Speidel and Heusinger, to SHAPE and to Washington; then two other confidants of the chancellor, press secretary Felix von Eckardt and chairman of the CDU/CSU parliamentary group Heinrich Krone, toured the Western capitals. In personal correspondence with Dulles, in which he referred to the U.S. plans' negative consequences for the cohesion of the alliance and to the prospect of a disarmament agreement with the Soviet Union, Adenauer tried to induce the United States to change its course. At a special session of the WEU Council of Ministers, Bonn again expressed its misgivings to the six European allies. Moreover, the chancellor also tried to exert influence on public opinion through a series of newspaper interviews critical of U.S. strategic concepts.[25]

Bonn's reaction to the Radford Plan was so vehement because the plan called into question a number of basic assumptions upon which West German foreign policy was based. The defense contribution was designed not only to enhance the security of the Federal Republic by incorporating it into the defense community of the Atlantic alliance, but also to raise its status internationally. The growing importance of nuclear weapons and the U.S. pronouncement that in future it would place greater reliance on nuclear systems, while the Europeans were to put up the conventional ground forces, amounted to a division of labor within the alliance whereby the two Anglo-Saxon nuclear powers would command the nuclear sword while the West European allies were to employ the conventional shield. The latter would be used to resist smaller local attacks, but primarily would provide targeting for the effective employment of nuclear weapons. From Bonn's viewpoint this division would diminish the influence of and discriminate against the non-nuclear allies, particularly the Federal Republic, which had hoped to avoid precisely this through its military contribution.

The German government had carried rearmament into the domestic political arena with the argument that its defense contribution strengthened the conventional defense of the West and thus largely obviated a recourse to nuclear weapons—and the inevitable destruction this would entail. Moreover, the building of the Bundeswehr was supposed to offer a guarantee that the United States would be permanently tied to Western Europe—not to facilitate a U.S. withdrawal. Reductions in the U.S. military presence would critically weaken both the combat strength of NATO and the hostage role of these troops, their function as "trip wire." The security of the Federal Republic depended on a tight linking of the nuclear and the conventional potentials of the alliance; thus by all means it had to try to prevent a "decoupling" of the U.S. from Europe. Here Adenauer saw a connection with the U.S.-Soviet rapprochement, as evidenced in the cooperation of the two powers in the Suez crisis or with the disengagement proposals circulating in the United States.[26] When Washington recognized the extent of the damage caused by thinking out loud about a reorientation of its security policy in Europe, it schooled itself in gestures of alliance solidarity.[27] For its part the German government began to turn toward the deployment of tactical nuclear weapons.

But the alliance conflict over the role of nuclear weapons had also turned a political flank in the Federal Republic. On September 27, 1956, the cabinet decided to shorten the term of military service to 12 months and justified this with the argument that in view of the U.S. plans for troop reductions an 18-month term could not be carried in the Bundestag. A few days later Defense Minister Blank was replaced by Franz Josef Strauss. This reflected more than simply an adjustment in the German political front, for which the Radford Plan was merely a pretext, but rather indicated a fundamental reorientation in military policy designed, for political reasons, to enable the Federal Republic to catch up with the strategic discussion under way in the alliance. The building of the Bundeswehr was to be slowed down and the new army was to be equipped with the most modern weapons—which meant, under the circumstances, with tactical nuclear weapons. At the same time Bonn assured the allies that it would meet its NATO commitments, without, however, setting any time limits.[28]

Equipping the Bundeswehr with Nuclear Weapons

The plans for equipping the Bundeswehr with nuclear delivery systems—the warheads remained under U.S. control—were based on military and political considerations. One factor was the strategic development within NATO reflected in the "New Look" strategy and in the NATO decision of December 1954 that in future the conventional superiority of the Soviet Union was to be offset by a greater reliance on tactical nuclear weapons. NATO Supreme Commander Lauris Norstad summarized the military rationale more precisely than the spokesmen of the German government:

> So long as the over-all situation does not change, defensive atomic weapons are absolutely indispensable for the strengthening of the defensive power of the Bundeswehr—for the protection of the Federal Republic and all NATO nations; that is the purely military standpoint. Now, however, for the German standpoint: a comprehensive defense contribution by the Federal Republic is coming into being. It is wholly unthinkable that these forces should be condemned to a second-class function, in which they would be practically useless for defense. We cannot give the German forces inadequate arms; the German nation cannot allow its soldiers to be armed with weapons long since obsolete.[29]

Added to this was the fear that units equipped differently would create regional differences in deterrent effect.

The interview with Norstad showed that the German thinking at that time was shared by NATO military. Similar considerations were entertained in other West European countries. At the December 1956 NATO Council meeting an intensive discussion ensued on the role of the new weapons for the defense of the alliance territory. In the course of this discussion several NATO states—particularly France and the Federal Republic—called upon the United States to equip the forces of the West Europeans with short- and medium-range nuclear weapons. Then in April 1957 the United States announced its readiness to place modern U.S. medium-range missiles under the command of the allies—including missiles of the Honest John, Matador and Nike types—and to station such systems in Europe.[30]

Besides this, Bonn was demanding an equal role in the alliance. Uppermost in Adenauer's thinking was the view that the Federal

Republic must neither lose its value as an equal partner in NATO nor weaken the alliance by balking at developments initiated by the other partners. At the same time, it was searching for solutions through which both the importance of the Anglo-American "special relationship" could be made relative and the French hegemonic tendencies, as manifested during the EURATOM negotiations, could be counteracted. And Bonn could never free itself entirely from the fear that the Federal Republic would become isolated internationally and then fall prey to "Soviet expansion."[31]

With Defense Minister Strauss there was a stronger conviction that only military power, nuclear power in particular, would guarantee political influence.[32] While he was fascinated by the military possibilities of the new arms technology, Adenauer took the nuclear road with rather more skepticism. The fear of a destruction of the national substance of the German people in the event of nuclear war in Central Europe led Adenauer, as it did many other political and military figures, to emphasize the deterrent effect of even "small" nuclear weapons.[33]

But was Strauss really striving for national control over nuclear weapons, as his critics charged? Answering this question is complicated first of all by the fact that not all the documents concerning the activity of the defense minister are yet accessible. For another thing, his speeches and interviews yield little information on fundamental views. His pronouncements were to a great extent conditioned by the situation, a mix of allusions to political matters of the day and slogans imaginatively strung together.[34] On many occasions, publically and privately, Strauss has excluded the possibility that the Federal Republic could become an independent nuclear weapons state. Yet just as surely has he thought about other possibilities for a nuclear armament: about obtaining nuclear weapons from the United States under bilateral control,[35] about coproduction with France or other allies,[36] about a common pool of atomic weapons in NATO or a European nuclear force.[37] Independent national control over nuclear weapons may have been a distant goal, but there was never any chance of its realization at that time.[38]

Thus, the German government's position on the nuclear question was marked by three basic patterns: adherence to the nuclear restrictions of 1954; forgoing independent initiatives and operating in the NATO framework, and trying to keep options open as long as possible. Correctly appraising its limited domestic and foreign political room for maneuver, the Federal Republic refused to engage in spectacular actions of its own. In light of strategic developments the U.S. partners would sooner or later be forced to give it nuclear delivery systems.

Within the Federal Republic the issue of nuclear armament led to a political polarization comparable to the debate over the Eastern Treaties in 1971-72. It was triggered by various statements in which the government indicated that the Bundeswehr ought to be equipped with nuclear delivery systems,[39] and was accentuated by a major interpellation of the SPD in the Bundestag in April 1957 as well as by the Göttingen Declaration of 18 well-known physicists warning against a nuclear arming of the Bundeswehr and calling for a voluntary renunciation of nuclear weapons of any kind.[40]

The SPD's opposition to equipping the Bundeswehr with nuclear delivery systems was based on two motives. Like the signers of the Göttingen Declaration, the SPD feared the consequences of a nuclear war on German soil. Moreover, the party felt that reunification of Germany would be possible only in conjunction with arms limitation in Europe. A striving for nuclear weapons on the part of the Federal Republic, however, would block that road. That this line of argument was not entirely consistent with its earlier criticism of mobilizing a mass conventional army did not bother the party in view of the dangers emanating from a nuclear arming of the Bundeswehr. More shortsighted, however, was its demand that U.S. tactical nuclear weapons not be allowed on West German territory. It would surely not be unfair to the SPD to observe that many of its arguments were directed more toward the electorate than toward its political opponent.

In response to SPD's major interpellation, Defense Minister Strauss emphasized that nuclear weapons were an integral part of the alliance's military thinking, but that the Federal Republic was not striving for national control over such weapons. With respect to equipping the Bundeswehr with nuclear delivery systems, the government pulled back into dilatory action in the face of the impending elections to the Bundestag and asserted that the question was not yet ripe for decision.[41] With that it was knowingly telling an untruth, as the decision had been taken as late as April 1956, when the United States promised to make medium- and short-range missiles available to the NATO allies. However, the government's wariness about detrimental domestic political consequences was unnecessary: with its slogan "No Experiments" to cover over all problems, the CDU/CSU won an absolute majority in the Bundestag in the fall elections of 1957.

On March 25, 1958 the Bundestag voted to equip the Bundeswehr with nuclear delivery systems. Against the votes of the SPD (the majority of the FDP abstained), it called upon the government

> to proceed with the building of the German national defense within the framework of the North Atlantic defense community until a general disarmament agreement has come about. In accordance with

the requirements of this defense system and in view of the armament of the potential adversary, the armed forces of the Federal Republic must be equipped with the most modern weapons so that they will be able to meet the obligations undertaken by the Federal Republic within NATO and can effectively make their essential contribution to securing peace.[42]

But the domestic political debate went further: with the protest movement "Against Atomic Death" sustained by the SPD and the trade unions, the opposition was attempting to mobilize public opinion and exert pressure on the government to give up its plans.[43]

Externally, Bonn had to contend first with keen suspicion, even in friendly countries, about German nuclear ambitions and secondly with the plans put forward by Poland and the Soviet Union for a nuclear-free zone in Central Europe, as well as various Western proposals for disengagement. It sought to allay the concerns of its neighbors by pointing out that it planned only to acquire multipurpose weapons, while the warheads would be kept under lock and key by the United States. It rejected all plans for arms limitation in Central Europe or for loosening the ties between the Federal Republic and its Western allies—not the least of whose aims was to contain German nuclear ambitions—arguing that first the causes of the tensions, the division of Germany, had to be removed. It did, however, declare its readiness in principle to join in any international disarmament treaty.[44] This blanket declaration cost little, since the rapid build-up of the Bundeswehr and its modern armament were in fact designed precisely to prevent international agreements on disarmament and detente reached over the head of Bonn. The integration of the Federal Republic into the nuclear defense concept of NATO was thus also a decision against the Rapacki Plan.

Equipping the Bundeswehr with nuclear weapons presented a number of military and political problems for the Federal Republic. In view of the opposition to nuclear armament within the country and the mistrust without, the political costs of such a step were reasonable only if the Federal Republic were able to bring its influence to bear on allied military strategy in such a way that in the event of a military conflict in Central Europe there would be a spectrum of possible responses below the threshold of a strategic counter-strike. From a German perspective the Berlin crisis beginning in 1958 made it abundantly clear that there could be military predicaments in which threatening a nuclear world war was neither sensible nor credible. Hence, greater importance ought to be attached to the function of the shield forces and these put in a position to withstand successfully a local attack. Improving the capability for regional defense became all the more urgent when the Sputnik shock (in October 1957 the Soviet Union had launched its first space satellite) engendered growing doubts about whether the United States would be prepared to launch a nuclear retaliatory strike if it were then to risk the destruction of its own territory. Such fears found confirmation in the theories being increasingly developed by the United States for the waging of a limited war (which for the West Europeans would be an unlimited war!). This strategic debate led to a modification of the U.S. concept of massive retaliation, which was turned into "graduated retaliation," i.e., the threat of a retaliation corresponding to the challenge, yet without the alliance's commanding in practice the requisite spectrum of military responses for it.[45]

In view of these doubts and anxieties it was surely no accident that in 1957, with the Bulganin-Adenauer correspondence, Moscow and Bonn began a dialogue through which both sides worked toward an improvement in German-Soviet relations. In the course of this exchange, which was terminated by the Berlin crisis in the fall of 1958, Adenauer also developed the proposal of an "Austrian solution" for the GDR.[46] Adenauer was able to generate a certain measure of publicity around his talks with the Soviet ambassador in Bonn, Smirnov. In fact, one cannot quite dismiss out of hand the suspicion that the chancellor was seeking to demonstrate publicly—as counterweight to his vigorously pursued defense policy—his willingness to pursue detente and his active efforts toward a solution of the German question. These talks had the added function of developing an independent channel of communication with Moscow parallel to the international disarmament negotiations, in which the Federal Republic was not taking part. In domestic politics, the groundlessness of the thesis that military ties with the West and active Ostpolitik were incompatible had to be demonstrated.

Finally, it was imperative to establish international safeguards concerning the nuclear weapons systems for the Bundeswehr. Who would control, when, and in what way, the release of the atomic warheads whose delivery systems were in the Bundeswehr's possession? How would operational and target planning be governed? Would the Federal Republic have a finger on the trigger or at least on the safety catch? Faced with anxieties about the Federal Republic's possibly going it alone in atomic matters, Bonn supported community regulations over the decision to use nuclear weapons, as these, under the circumstances, would be the optimal way of taking its interests into account. Hence, it responded coolly to U.S. proposals for stationing medium-range missiles under a two-key system in West Germany, but supported all the more emphatically multilateral solutions for the U.S.

medium-range missiles in Europe, namely "because they first of all promised a greater German participation in strategic planning, secondly were well suited to strengthening the U.S. guarantee, and thirdly would have lessened the political role of the *force de frappe*."[47] This applied to the Norstad Plan, the concept of NATO as fourth atomic power, and finally the project for a Multilateral Atomic Force (MLF).

Nuclear Sharing or Joint Control of Nuclear Weapons?

In the early 1960s a number of events made it appear especially urgent to seek a nuclear solution in the Atlantic alliance. In Bonn's view the election of John F. Kennedy as the new U.S. president brought altered priorities in U.S. foreign policy. The Eurocentrism of previous policy was displaced by a global strategy in which Western Europe continued to occupy a place of great importance; yet efforts to reach a limited understanding with the Soviet Union on arms control or to overcome the problems of the developing countries made equal claims on the administration. The fear that the U.S. might no longer perceive the interests of the West European allies in the same way as before was reinforced by the events of the Berlin crisis. The proposals for an international access authority involving the GDR, the limitation of the U.S. "essentials" to the western part of the city, and the hesitant reaction to the building of the Wall on August 13, 1961 were indicators of an acceptance of the status quo by the U.S. ally.[48]

The Federal Republic found itself confronted by special problems as a result of the strategic revolution that was rapidly changing the military-strategic concepts of the Western alliance. After Bonn had, following fierce internal debate and despite the attendant burdens for foreign policy, converted its defense planning to a tactical nuclear defense, the United States began to free itself from its virtually total dependence on nuclear weapons. The strategy of massive retaliation was replaced by one of flexible response. The latter rested on a graduated use, appropriate to the challenge, of a spectrum of military and political means. It necessitated, among other things, strong conventional forces, a mobile or hardened second-strike capability, and the central control of all nuclear weapons. In the political realm this strategy was supplemented by the doctrine of arms control.[49]

The U.S. turn from the automaticity of nuclear escalation led to considerable uneasiness in Bonn, recalling the crisis over the Radford Plan four years before.[50] To prevent any mitigation of the threat of nuclear retaliation, the German government sought to strengthen its influence on NATO's strategic planning. It endeavored above all to gain a stronger say on nuclear questions. In April 1962 Strauss summarized the German demands in three essentials: information on the type and site of U.S. nuclear weapons stationed in Europe; a guarantee that the nuclear weapons stationed in Europe would not be withdrawn against the will of the countries affected, and both a positive and a negative control over the use of nuclear weapons stationed on its territory.[51] Thus the German government persistently supported the plan of "NATO as fourth atomic power," yet it also made procedural proposals for closer political consultation.

During a visit to Washington in the spring of 1961 Chancellor Adenauer submitted to the U.S. government a plan developed by Defense Minister Strauss according to which nuclear weapons would be used in the event of conflict upon the joint recommendation of SACEUR and the country attacked. Another suggestion provided for the creation of a nuclear "steering committee" within NATO, consisting of five members: the United States, Great Britain, France, the Federal Republic, and a "rotating Mediterranean country." Most far-reaching, however, was the idea, developed by Strauss in a speech in Washington, of creating an Atlantic federal state, whereby the problem of nuclear control would have resolved itself. But representatives of the German government, particularly Strauss, were not averse to letting it be known now and then that the Federal Republic could find itself impelled to follow the French and British example if it were not possible to realize joint nuclear solutions[52] (under the circumstances this threat was scarcely more than a bluff).

Intent on both strengthening the cohesion of the alliance and preventing the emergence of nuclear weapons states, the United States gave the allies renewed nuclear guarantees at the NATO meeting in Athens in May 1962 and proposed "guidelines" for the use of nuclear weapons. Accordingly, in periods of crisis the allies were to be informed about planning and in the event of conflict consulted as much as possible; however, Washington was not thinking about sharing with other states the decision on using nuclear weapons. In that same year the United States reactivated a plan developed under Eisenhower for a multilateral nuclear force assigned to SACEUR. This was to consist of 25 surface ships equipped with Polaris missiles, manned and commanded by various nations. The warheads for the missiles were to be under joint custody; however, they would be used only with the consent of all states involved.[53]

There are numerous indications—not least the "essentials" outlined by Strauss on April 6, 1962 and various speeches by opposition politicans such as Erler and Schmidt[54]—that the Federal Republic would have preferred a solution on the basis of joint nuclear consultation and planning. The Athens guidelines did provide a start in this direction, but in view of Washington's restrictive attitude on the question of nuclear control and the faltering realization of the Athens decisions, this road did not appear very promising. Systems involving common possession, common financing, and common planning were regarded as a more promising "second-best" way to joint strategic control.[55] However, the German government was prompted to seize upon the MLF proposals given the political situation at the end of 1962 and beginning of 1963:

> Breakoff of negotiations on Great Britain's entry into the Common Market; Nassau Agreement with all its diplomatic implications, especially its rejection by de Gaulle; conclusion of the Franco-German Treaty, which in this situation inevitably assumed an anti-Anglo-Saxon character, and not least the change in the Defense Ministry in Bonn. Thus, between the United States and the Federal Republic, to a certain degree from mutual misunderstanding and mutual 'appeasement,' the MLF became a symbol of 'reassurance' and only in the course of time did the truer interests of the Americans and the Germans become apparent.[56]

However, the enthusiasm for the alliance project soon gave way in the United States and in the Federal Republic to a more sober assessment, as it became apparent that the other NATO countries had little interest in a collective effort. Great Britain presented its own proposals for a multilateral solution (the so-called "ANF") and France was making no bones about its determination to stick with its *force de frappe* and prevent a Bonn-Washington axis. In Washington, there was growing interest in an agreement with the Soviet Union on the non-proliferation of nuclear weapons which was not to be had simultaneous with the MLF. In the Federal Republic, doubts about the potential for joint planning and increased integration through the MLF were mixed with considerations for the French neighbor. When the MLF was shelved by the U.S. government at the end of 1965, Bonn had in fact come around to fully accept this project. Feeling rebuffed, it accused Washington of giving higher priority to a non-proliferation agreement with the Soviet Union than to a joint nuclear arrangement with its NATO allies.[57]

Instead, the alliance continued on the road of joint nuclear planning. At first, Secretary of Defense Robert McNamara's 1965 proposal of a "special committee" for developing consultation procedures on the use of nuclear weapons was perceived as a kind of consolation prize for the deceased MLF. However, the German government as well as others soon recognized the potential for the non-nuclear allies' participation in nuclear planning, if the existing bodies could be purposefully used and developed. In the fall of that same year NATO's Defense Planning Committee (DPC) instituted three working groups, the most important of which was the Nuclear Planning Working Group (NPWG), whose mission was to initiate the non-nuclear allies into the problems of nuclear policy. One year later the Defense Planning Committee replaced this nonpermanent body with a Nuclear Defense Affairs Committee (NDAC). Twelve NATO countries are represented in this committee; France, Iceland, and Luxembourg do not belong. The DPC commissioned also a Nuclear Planning Group (NPG), with seven states participating. Permanent members are the United States, Great Britain, Italy, and the Federal Republic; the membership of the other three rotates on an 18-month basis. It is the task of the Nuclear Planning Group to work out guidelines and concepts on the use of nuclear weapons. In the past it has dealt primarily with the elaboration of principles for the use of nuclear weapons, the development of consultation procedures, the modernization of existing weapons systems, and contingency studies on the possible employment of nuclear weapons. Further, it has carried out a comprehensive program of study on the use, conditions, and effects of various nuclear weapons systems. The NPG has become one of the most important organs in the alliance. All in all, the German government has assessed its work positively, as it has enabled the Federal Republic to participate sufficiently in nuclear planning, even though transforming this into political decisions has continued to be reserved for the United States.[58]

The debate on nuclear cooperation in the alliance made it clear, first, that the Federal Republic's room for maneuver on nuclear policy was determined by the interests of the nuclear weapons states. In particular, Bonn was not able to make its interests prevail against the United States when the latter wanted to reach a nuclear non-proliferation agreement with the Soviet Union but Moscow made abandonment of the MLF a precondition. Secondly, however, the Federal Republic had become the most important ally of the United States on the continent. It commanded not only an impressive national economy, but now also a modern army, and its desires and expectations had, as far as possible, to be given due regard. These considerations explain the repeated attempts by the United States to find a satisfactory solution to the nuclear question. However, this was made even more difficult by the fact that nuclear sharing was not simply an internal alliance issue, but given the relative importance of nuclear weapons in East-West relations (as instrument of deterrence as well as object of negotiation) the Soviet Union also had at its disposal specific ways for exercising influence. They highlight the countervailing tendencies coming out in the alliance in the mid-1960s: on the one hand, the efforts to preserve the cohesion of the alliance in the face of centrifugal tendencies, underscored by France's withdrawal from NATO integration, and thus to maintain its security function; on the other hand, the strivings of the various allies to ease the East-West confrontation to their own benefit through bilateral agreements with the Soviet Union and the East European states. The result was a series of conflicts of priority that strained alliance relations during the 1960s.

COUNTERVAILING TENDENCIES IN STRATEGY AND ARMS CONTROL

Alliance policy in the 1960s was marked by two countervailing tendencies: while the shift in the global balance of power—the "nuclear stalemate"—had prompted the United States to replace its policy of denial ("containment") with one of limited cooperation with the Soviet Union, though the fundamental political antagonism persisted, the Berlin crisis and the building of the Wall had accentuated the confrontational elements in East-West relations and led to a questioning of Bonn's past policy on Germany. More and more the Anglo-Saxon allies tended to defuse the Berlin problem by trying to find a modus vivendi with the other side on the status of the city; the German government felt that the only way it could resist this was to seek to commit its allies to the legal positions anchored in the Bonn and Paris Treaties of 1954. This in turn restricted Bonn's own options for normalizing relations with the East European states. The consequence was increased conflict between the United States with its policy of bilateral stabilization and the various European interests (France not only was on the point of liquidating its colonial empire, but also had to find a new national identity, which under de Gaulle it perceived in an insistent national sovereignty, based on military means—particularly the *force de frappe*). These different sets of interests came out strongly in the debate on NATO strategy, arms control, and the goals and methods of detente policy.

The Critique of the Strategy of "Flexible Response"

With the development of Soviet intercontinental weapons, the United States at the end of the 1950s had lost its nuclear-strategic dominance. The incipient vulnerability of U.S. strategic nuclear forces, but especially the vulnerability of American cities to a Soviet attack, threw into question the strategy of massive retaliation. The retaliatory strike against the Soviet Union—an assurance to the allies in the event of an attack on Western Europe—ceased to be politically credible. In response to the Soviet challenge, the strategy of flexible response was developed. Its most important elements were a second-strike capability made invulnerable by means of hardening of silos or mobility of delivery systems; strengthened conventional forces to counter and contain aggression below a specific threshold or to force an initial "pause" before nuclear weapons were employed, and finally, a centralization of the command and control authority over the entire military potential of the nation and the alliance so as to be able to direct the deployment, targeting, and operation of this potential with maximum rationality and effectiveness.[59]

The flexible response strategy aimed at stabilizing the strategic balance between the United States and the Soviet Union. It was supplemented by a policy of arms control.[60] This, too, was oriented to the goal of stability. Starting from the assumption that both the United States and the Soviet Union had parallel interests in avoiding a global nuclear conflict, it represented a means toward reducing the risks inherent in military confrontation. This strategy of war prevention—on the U.S. side primarily determined by criteria of rationality and understood in terms of arms technology—was paralleled on the Soviet side by the—there, however, ideologically grounded—thesis of the avoidability of war and the theory of peaceful coexistence.

In the case of the United States, both the strategy of flexible response and the doctrine of arms control tended toward an emphasis on political bilateralism as well as on centralizing military decision-making authority, and ran counter to the emergence of more independent nuclear powers. In contrast, the doubts about the credibility of the nuclear protection generated by the new U.S. strategy and the mistrust toward the superpowers' dialogue strengthened the already existing tendencies in Western Europe for greater independence from the U.S. protective power. The crystallization point of these countervailing interests was the nuclear debate, in which the U.S. side endeavored to neutralize the nuclear ambitions of the West Europeans through the project of a multilateral NATO force, while the European partners pressed for nuclear sharing in order to gain influence over the strategy and diplomacy of the leading power.

These countervailing interests were also expressed in the elaboration of differing concepts of political order. The idea of an "Atlantic partnership" developed by the Kennedy administration was countered by Franz Josef Strauss and his political friends with the plan of a "European Europe," a united Western Europe only loosely tied to the United States, i.e., a third force in international politics. These different concepts led to tensions and irritations in the European-American relationship in the 1960s, without, however, seriously jeopardizing the continued existence of the Atlantic alliance as such. Apart from France, the West European states' military and political dependence on the United States, their limited room for maneuver and dearth of alternatives on the one hand, and the great strategic importance that Washington attached to its engagement in Europe as well as the, in political practice, effective dialectic of confrontation and cooperation on the other, all worked toward preserving the European system.

For the Europeans the reorientation of the U.S. defense and foreign policy entailed a number of military and political problems. The stabilization of the strategic balance between the United States and the Soviet Union did indeed reduce the danger of a "major war," yet below the level of global nuclear war there was still a growing danger of conventional conflicts in the regional theater. The emphasis on conventional options as well as on notions such as "threshold" and "pause," which replaced "active deterrence's" implicit automaticity of a nuclear counterstrike in response to an attack of whatever sort on Western Europe, weakened the credibility of U.S. deterrence. A "limited conflict" from the U.S. standpoint would be a total war for the Federal Republic and would extinguish its national existence. Moreover, it was doubtful whether the Americans and Europeans would be able and willing to mobilize the requisite forces for a conventional defense.

A second problem was the possible political consequences of the U.S. stabilization policy. For the United States the strategy of flexible response and its related arms control doctrine meant transcending the contradiction or the split view of military policy and diplomacy. However, in the eyes of the Federal Republic, the concentration on strategic force relations resulted in a one-sided orientation to security factors, while the political problems, the German question in particular, were bracketed out. The policy of arms control assumed the continued existence of the confrontation and confined itself to reducing the latter's inherent risks. But it avoided coming to grips with the causes of the confrontation. It thus conflicted with the West German view that a prerequisite for reduction of tensions was the elimination of their causes, i.e., the division of Germany.

From Bonn's point of view the stabilization policy pursued by the United States implied a jeopardizing of national interests; it was therefore to be expected that West German criticism of this policy would be especially pronounced. Yet it would probably not have come down to a deep crisis in German-American relations if at the same time there had not been other developments, the concurrence of which gave particular impetus to mutual mistrust. The building of the Wall in August

1961 and the attitude of the United States in the U.S.-Soviet exploratory talks on Berlin, especially Washington's readiness to negotiate on an international access authority and to consider a nonaggression pact between NATO and the Warsaw Pact, fostered doubt within the German government, notably on the part of Chancellor Adenauer and the CDU/CSU parliamentary group chairman, von Brentano, as to whether the United States sufficiently respected Bonn's interests on the German question or whether it gave priority to an arrangement with the Soviet Union that would imply a political stabilization on the basis of the status quo.[61]

The German government responded to the first intimations of a reorientation of U.S. strategy with the same allacrity with which it had in the past reacted to all changes in U.S. policy touching upon either the security of the Federal Republic or its defense contribution. Just a few weeks after the Kennedy administration had presented its first defense program, Defense Minister Strauss, in an interview with the *Frankfurter Allgemeine Zeitung*, criticized the new strategic concept on five main points:

1. Excessively theoretical treatment of strategic problems, wherein the political issues were not sufficiently considered;
2. Lack of consideration for the particular geographical and psychological situation of Central Europe, whereby he warned against a raising of the nuclear threshold and an unrealistic strengthening of conventional forces;
3. The theoretical possibility of a conventional war in Europe, which he regarded as unrealistic;
4. Rejection of changes in the organization of the Bundeswehr, because it was a matter not of more but of better divisions, which would have to have the entire spectrum of modern weapons at their disposal;
5. The absence of a nuclear operational planning that was binding for all NATO units and for which NATO assumed responsibility.[62]

In talks with U.S. politicians, in the NATO Council, and by a number of public statements, Strauss tried to influence the development of U.S. strategy in favor of a nuclear guarantee covering all of Western Europe.

At the NATO conference in Athens in May 1962, the United States informed its allies for the first time in coherent form about the new strategic concept. But it was also made clear that Washington was not prepared to undertake any major changes in it. Rather, the United States called upon the allies to assume a larger share of the defense burden and to strengthen their conventional forces. In a speech in Ann Arbor shortly after the Athens NATO conference, Secretary of Defense

McNamara once again set forth the strategic concept of the United States.[63] However, this speech, the resignation of NATO Supreme Commander General Norstad,[64] and an inflammatory speech by Defense Minister Strauss at the University of Bonn in late June 1962[65] gave rise to renewed speculation about U.S. policy on security and Europe and led to critical commentary in the Federal Republic. After Washington had issued vexed statements intended to dismiss doubts about whether it would stand by its commitments,[66] the German government, too, felt compelled to admonish Defense Minister Strauss to moderate his statements and to bring the public discussion under control again.[67] Continued opposition to the strategic reorientation inaugurated by the United States would have entailed the danger that the Federal Republic would isolate itself internationally and thus also lose its potential for influencing U.S. policy on the German question. The Berlin crisis demonstrated in most dramatic fashion the vulnerability of the Federal Republic to Soviet pressures; for the Federal Republic, there was—in contrast to France—no acceptable alternative to membership in the alliance and to the protective guarantee of the United States. Yet little was altered in the fundamental rejection of the U.S. defense conception by the CDU/CSU. The coalition was undertaking the difficult attempt to emphasize its agreement with NATO policy and at the same time suggest that it was the United States that was not in harmony with the NATO concept.[68] It underscored its confidence in the U.S. protective guarantee, "that alliance territory in its entirety is defended with the same weapons as the U.S.,"[69] but hinted very subtly that there might be other options for the Federal Republic. Here Strauss was thinking more of a "European option," of making common cause with France, than of a national control over atomic weapons.

In practice, however, both sides endeavored to work out a compromise. By extending compulsory military service to 18 months the German government met Washington's demand for strengthening the conventional components,[70] while the United States used the MLF project to appease European desires for strategic collaboration and nuclear partnership. When the U.S. government presented its MLF Plan in January and February 1963, the Federal Republic was one of the states to take up this proposal with a certain enthusiasm, in fact less for military reasons than as political demonstration. It wanted to emphasize the priority of alliance perspectives in its foreign policy and at the same time strengthen U.S. ties with the West European allies through the multilateral project. Also, with its advocacy of the MLF, it wanted to establish a counterweight to the just-concluded Franco-German Treaty. Once Strauss had resigned and Kai-Uwe von Hassel headed the Defense Ministry, Bonn's military orientation to Washington became more precise. Even in basic concepts von Hassel, like Foreign Minister Schröder, proceeded along the course marked out by Washington and thus found himself in close harmony with the SPD opposition.

Uneasiness over the strategy of massive retaliation—founded on domestic and military considerations—had brought the SPD and its security experts Erler and Schmidt very early into the conceptual vicinity of the proponents of the "new strategy" in the United States.[71] Above all they shared the criticism of Western defense policy's one-sided dependence on the big nuclear strike and put forward instead a broad spectrum of deterrence options.[72] With the metaphor that it was scarcely realistic for the European tail to wag the U.S. atomic dog, they rejected the nuclear automaticity that Strauss wanted to institutionalize, but advocated, as did the government, sufficient participation by the Europeans in joint strategic planning. The SPD, however, was reserved and skeptical about the proposals for a NATO nuclear force; in Erler's words, there would not be the means for non-nuclear defense if the Europeans were to stray inopportunely into the nuclear sphere. By strengthening conventional forces the alliance would free itself from the deadly alternative of having only the choice between "capitulation or atomic suicide" in the event of conflict.[73] Consequently, the SPD supported an extension of military service to 18 months. The emphasis on conventional defense capabilities made it easier for the opposition in its discussion within the party to support the U.S. strategy of flexible response as well as the arms control policy developed parallel with it. The latter also suited the continued strong demand in the SPD for arms limitation and disarmament.

The Controversy over Arms Control

The doctrine of arms control was founded on the idea of a security partnership of the nuclear superpowers, according to which the potential for mutual destruction necessitated joint measures for arms control. In practice, arms control policy led to a qualitative change in disarmament negotiations. All too common simplistic assumptions about the arms race as a cause of tension and, since this could not be eliminated with patent remedies, disarmament proposals as propagandistic all-purpose weapons were replaced by a policy that aimed at eliminating the instabilities inherent in a given configuration of armament. However, the Europeans and in particular the Germans argued that the division of Europe was the fundamental cause of East-West tensions; this division would have to be removed if there were to be an international relaxation of tensions. They feared that the stabilization policy being pursued by the United States would solidify the political status quo in Europe. In this they overlooked the dialectic of confrontation and cooperation built into the doctrine of arms control, which in spite of serious crises—Cuba, Vietnam, Czechoslovakia—introduced a new dynamic into East-West relations. Arms control policy gave the United States new political options. With the diversity of interests, however, the pressure for success in the negotiations conducted by Washington restricted the European allies' room for maneuver and demanded of them a conscious disregard for their own concerns, without commensurate compensation, such as a greater measure of security, room for maneuver, or potential for solving their own national problems. The Federal Republic's reticence toward the test ban and non-proliferation treaties is an example of this.[74]

Three premises underlying the concept of cooperative arms control made it difficult for the Federal Republic to accept this intellectually and politically:

- the transcendence of friend-or-foe thinking and the acceptance of a concurrence, however limited, between the superpowers;
- the acceptance of an identity of interests among the United States and its West European allies in the strategic-political realm, empowering Washington to act as spokesman in the bilateral dialogue with Moscow;
- the expectation that through technical manipulations of armament the risks inherent in confrontation could be gradually removed and a relaxation of tensions produced.[75]

The attitude of many West German politicians was conditioned by a great mistrust of Soviet intentions, which did not preclude a truce but did harbor skepticism toward the expectation that if both sides acted rationally it would be possible to achieve a compromise acceptable to East and West. The trauma of Potsdam had a lasting impact on Adenauer and gave rise to the fear that the victors of the Second World War could again come to terms at the expense of Central Europe and institute a nuclear condominium. The U.S. arms control policy confronted the Federal Republic with the dilemma of either risking political isolation—especially since the turn away from the containment strategy toward the Soviet Union and its "satellites" tended to raise the specter of a turnabout to isolation of the Federal Republic—or else entering into such an extensive dependence on the United States that its West European potentialities would have been severely restricted. In this context the Franco-German Treaty was, like various German-

Soviet contacts, an instrument designed to prevent or mitigate this alternative and to avoid a narrowing of the Federal Republic's room for maneuver.

At bottom, however, Bonn's concerns about the consequences of arms control pertained to the German question. Just as in the disarmament negotiations of the 1950s, the predominant fear was that cooperative arms control measures without a simultaneous settlement of political issues would result in a consolidation of the status quo or, if encompassing political elements, assume the character of a peace treaty, but in any case make a solution of the German question more difficult.[76]

In the Federal Republic the discussion of risks and chances with arms control was further burdened by the fact that it was conducted largely with a vocabulary taken from the disarmament discussion of the 1950s. While a slow convergence with U.S. concepts was discernible in the strategic sphere, the Federal Republic's stance on questions of arms control was rather consistently negative, though Bonn was also willing to make tactical concessions, e.g., with the Test Ban Treaty. Another difficulty was that the Federal Republic regarded strategy and arms control as two mutually independent areas. It conceived of the defense contribution as an "immediate task of current policy," while a general, controlled disarmament was more a distant goal. For Bonn, realizing this goal presupposed that the existing balance of forces would not be changed and the potential adversary not provided any advantage. These prerequisites signaled the differences between the German and the U.S. conceptions. This was shown especially clearly by the following statement of the CDU position on disarmament:

> Disarmament must pertain both to traditional and to atomic weapons. The military balance of power must not be shifted in favor of one side;
> disarmament must be universal, i.e., it must not encompass only individual countries or a specific zone. In the age of intercontinental missiles a zone of 'disengagement' is unrealistic. Such zones invite political and military subversion. Besides, military concentration moves to the flanks of such zones;
> disarmament must be controlled. This demand is consistent with a self-evident security need. And yet a control of disarmament is unwelcome to the aggressive character of communism. Thus, up to the present the Soviet Union has put up the stiffest resistance to effective control and so has prevented a controlled disarmament;
> disarmament, however, presents more than strictly a military-

technical problem. It is primarily a political problem. A relaxation of tensions to displace the 'balance of terror' can be achieved only if nations are granted the right to self-determination.[77]

For various reasons the SPD had a very much easier time finding a positive approach to the U.S. arms control policy. First of all, professing disarmament and international detente was traditionally part and parcel of Social Democratic policy. In the Godesberg Program defense policy and disarmament/detente policy were conceived of as a unit, expressed in "security through deterrence, security through understanding."[78] In the first place, openly declaring for disarmament had a political unburdening function within the party. As a correlate of saying "yes" to national defense, it made this yes easier on the consciences of party members. At the same time the continuity of Social Democratic security policy was preserved by confining the need for national defense within NATO to a transitional period, "as long as there are no international treaties in force on arms control and disarmament."[79]

Secondly, a number of objective and tactical considerations induced leading SPD politicians such as Brandt, Erler, and Wehner to seek a close contact with Washington. Especially for the mayor of Berlin during the crisis years 1958-61, it was an incontestable fact that the security of the Federal Republic and West Berlin could be guaranteed only through the United States and the Atlantic alliance, "to whom it makes its contribution in loyal fulfillment of its obligations."[80] However, alliance policy needed to be supplemented by an active disarmament policy that did not exclude Central Europe but, on the contrary, worked toward a mutual and controlled limitation of armaments in this area. And there was another vantage point of a domestic political nature. In adopting arms control thinking the SPD also saw a possibility for replacing the CDU/CSU as Washington's preferred German ally.

In arms control the SPD started from two assumptions. First, it recognized that Germany's neighbors had a legitimate security interest—"security for Germany and security from Germany"—and secondly, it presupposed that the global balance of forces remained intact, the contributions were on a par, and the necessary control measures were functioning.[81]

In this connection the renunciation of national control over atomic weapons had a special importance. Such a stand accorded with the traditional antinuclear attitude of the party's rank-and-file, but it also enabled the SPD to support the Test Ban Treaty and the efforts toward a nonproliferation agreement with less reservation than the government. Finally, it also regarded an unequivocal German renunciation of "the bomb" as a prerequisite for the desired normalization with the East European states. However, this policy did not imply a unilateral ban on nuclear weapons by the West; on the contrary, the SPD supported the efforts within the alliance to develop a joint nuclear solution. It gave preference to a codetermination solution over the MLF, but was prepared to accept the latter as the "second-best" solution. It was primarily concerned with ensuring a say in operational planning for nuclear weapons or a right to veto the use of nuclear weapons in the event of a conflict.[82]

Unlike the proponents of arms control in the United States, the SPD was not oriented first and foremost to the goal of stabilizing the strategic balance of forces. Rather, it shared the German government's fear that such an agreement could reinforce the division of Germany. For the SPD, arms control was a method to be used for defusing the confrontation and initiating detente. This could then create a climate in which a settlement of the German question was conceivable. Hence, it became necessary for German policy to participate actively in the international disarmament discussion so as to influence it in the direction of German interests.[83] As of about 1961 disarmament policy was joined by the demand for a more active Ostpolitik, whereby greater economic, cultural, and political contacts were to lead to a relaxation of tensions in Europe and a mitigation of threat perceptions.[84]

Working from these considerations the SPD pressed for Bonn to come forward with ideas for the international arms control talks and to make a constructive effort toward harmonizing the views on this subject within the West. The reaction to the Test Ban Treaty in the Federal Republic also had shown the inadequacy of the existing institutional means, which in 1963 consisted of a small departmental section in the Foreign Office and one officer in the Defense Ministry. The opposition therefore introduced a motion in the Bundestag to establish a disarmament office, whose task it would be to look into

> the diverse problems resulting from the connections between military security, foreign policy, economic problems and technological development, and the various potentialities for disarmament, arms limitation, and arms control. It should facilitate the German government's assessment of other countries' proposals in the area of disarmament and arms control and develop German proposals in the said area.[85]

To carry out its work it was to make use of other agencies of the German government and of the existing or to be newly created independent research institutions.

The CDU/CSU and the FDP supported the opposition's demand for a strengthening of the government's disarmament apparatus. However, objections were raised to the establishment of an independent office. The Foreign Office proposed strengthening the existing disarmament desk and reorganizing it into a subsection. Eventually all three parliamentary groups settled on a joint draft resolution in which the government was requested (1) to appoint a "Representative of the Federal Government for Questions of Disarmament and Arms Control" within the Foreign Office and to submit in an addendum to the budget law of 1965 proposals for strengthening the existing agencies in the Foreign Office and the Defense Ministry, and (2) to develop proposals for creating an independent research establishment for questions of strategy, disarmament, and arms control as well as related fields.[86] However, because of jurisdictional disputes within the government—most notably with the claims put forward by the chairman of the Federal Defense Council, Minister without Portfolio Krone—it was still several months before the cabinet appointed a first disarmament representative and commissioned the Research Institute for International Policy and Security of the Stiftung Wissenschaft und Politik to attend to the work called for in the Bundestag resolution in the areas of strategy, disarmament, and arms control. It remained to be seen, however, whether institutional innovation could activate what had been mainly a reactive arms control policy on the part of the German government.

Arms Control Policy in the Discord on German and Alliance Policy

By improving its disarmament apparatus the German government had created the institutional means for pursuing a more active detente policy in the mid-1960s. Still, a piano does not yet make a concert; it has to be properly tuned, the pianist must have a command of the instrument and the composition, and finally the orchestra, under the direction of a capable conductor, must work together to produce a harmonic body of sound. There is, then, the question of the quality of the instrument and the pianist as well as of the possibilities for a successful ensemble performance.

The arms control policy of the Federal Republic in the first half of the 1960s was like a concert for two pianos in which the player of the German part and that of the alliance part could not agree on a common key. Hence, a prerequisite for an active and internally consonant detente policy was to remove the blocking of interests between policy on Germany and alliance policy.

The contradiction between these two lines of foreign policy assumed a particular importance as France was now pursuing an active detente policy on the basis of the status quo[87] and thus ceased to provide the Federal Republic's European backing for its criticism of the U.S. policy of stabilization. As long as it was also not prepared to take the step toward acceptance of the postwar realities, it was left with a policy of muddling through and damage limitation. Bonn's ability to act was further constricted by the contradiction between "Atlanticists" and "Gaullists" in the Erhard government, i.e., those politicians around Foreign Minister Gerhard Schröder and Defense Minister Kai-Uwe von Hassel who did not want to risk weakening alliance ties with the United States and were instead willing to make tactical retreats from their position on Germany, and those around former Chancellor Adenauer and CSU Chairman Strauss who called for greater West European influence in world affairs—also vis-à-vis the United States—and opposed any U.S.-Soviet bilateralism.

The self-imposed blockade of the Federal Republic was most evident in Bonn's handling of the U.S. proposal for a system of ground observation posts and in the Federal Republic's accession to the Treaty on Non-proliferation of Nuclear Weapons.

U.S. arms control policy in the 1960s included measures designed to prevent a conflict unleashed by accident or miscalculation. The Cuban missile crisis in the fall of 1962 had revealed to all involved the critical importance of rapid communication in conflict situations. In a document presented at the Geneva Eighteen-Nation Disarmament Conference in December 1962, the United States proposed a series of measures designed to reduce the danger of accidental war, such as advance notification about larger military movements, establishment of a system of ground observation posts, and the exchange of military missions, as well as various plans for improved communication between East and West.[88] With the exception of the establishment of a direct communications link between Washington and Moscow, the so-called "hot line,"[89] which was realized in the spring of 1963, the proposals addressed in the U.S. working paper were motivated by the desire to prevent local military conflicts at points of exceptional military confrontation and remove the attendant danger of escalation to a large-scale nuclear conflict.

These arms control measures were conceived as being applicable to any region of high military confrontation. However, for military as well as political reasons, translating this into political practice was meaningful primarily in Europe. Here the U.S. and Soviet armed forces directly confronted each other, here a system of reassurances could be militarily meaningful. At the same time, only measures related to the European area were negotiable, since here they correlated with a Soviet interest in political stabilization. The Soviet Union's interest in recognition of the status quo also became clear in that all its proposals proceeded from the idea of European arms control zones, either through their geographic delimitation, or in conjunction with demands for a denuclearization of Germany or a reduction of foreign troops in Europe.[90]

The German government reacted to these proposals with undisguised horror, particularly as initial exploratory talks were taking place in connection with U.S. compromise proposals on the Berlin problem, which in Bonn were seen as a Western capitulation to Moscow's demands. In the fall of 1963 and spring of 1964 the proposals for ground observation systems were discredited mainly by the Soviet Union's attempt to link these with a nuclear freeze in Central Europe as was put forward in the Gomulka Plan, formulated by the Polish party and government leader in the tradition of the Rapacki Plan.[91] Essentially, Bonn wanted to avoid the creation of a special arms control zone confined to Central Europe, which would discriminate against the Federal Republic and enhance the status of the GDR. For the rest, it tried to compensate for its reticence toward regional arms control measures by advocating a general controlled disarmament.

Leading elements in the CDU/CSU parliamentary group held the view that the Federal Republic could agree to further arms control measures—especially when Europe in particular was affected by them—only if they were coupled with progress on the German question, for a relaxation of tensions would be inconceivable without eliminating the causes of tension. Foreign Minister Schröder, however, came out emphatically in support of the Western efforts for detente. Besides raising considerations of alliance policy, Schröder maintained that a sheer insistence on the German question would conjure up the danger that the status quo could become a status quo minus. Still, he energetically opposed any measures that would lead to a shift in the balance of forces detrimental to the West. Nor were regional measures—which he supported—to worsen the initial basis for a solution of the German problem.[92]

In view of the divergent priorities in detente policy, the process of establishing harmony in the German government proved to be extraordinarily difficult. It took intensive consultations among the leading CDU politicians before Schröder was able to win acceptance for his view that Western detente policy must not be blocked by insistence on a linkage with progress on the German question. His proposal was along the lines of developing precise German concepts on the specific topics for the specific phases of the East-West negotiations and inserting them into the process.

Upon assuming office, Chancellor Erhard declared that the German government supported a general controlled disarmament but recognized that this could be realized only gradually. The interest of the Federal Republic, therefore, demanded that it "also assist in achieving partial measures, provided they do not affect the balance of forces between East and West to our detriment and do not discriminate against us."[93] Thus, a compromise formula had been found between the conflicting tendencies. Numerous interviews have shown, however, that the differences in appraising detente policy persisted within the CDU/CSU and the German government and gradually grew into differences in priority in policy on Germany, Europe, and the alliance.[94]

For all its outward unanimity, the SPD also had its differing accentuations. For Fritz Erler, the unity of Germany was of the utmost importance—not without good reason did his collected speeches and writings bear the title "Policy for Germany." For him, disarmament and detente were a way, perhaps under the circumstances the only negotiable way, to reach this goal. With Willy Brandt, on the other hand, "the will to peace and conciliation" was foremost. In Brandt's view a solution to the German question—more in the sense of the Germans peaceably living with one another than in the form of reunification under one national roof—could take place only in the framework of an order of peace encompassing all of Europe.[95]

As a result of Erler's untimely death in early 1967 and the political "marginalization" of Strauss,[96] Schröder and Brandt became the exponents of alternative political concepts. Whereas Schröder, from a felt responsibility for all of Germany, wanted to keep open both the German question and the nuclear option, Brandt was prepared in the mid-1960s to accept the status quo and to conduct on its basis a policy of conciliation that encompassed the East European states as well as the GDR. When the Grand Coalition was formed in December 1966, the SPD was to share government responsibility and Brandt was entrusted with the Foreign Ministry in place of Schröder. Under his influence the German government took the road of de facto acceptance of the postwar realities of Europe. The composition of the Grand Coalition did, however, necessitate multifarious compromises. After the Warsaw Pact states' intervention in Czechoslovakia in August 1968, the different assessments of Soviet intentions and of appropriate Western modes of response resulted in a virtually complete foreign policy blockage.

The Grand Coalition's inability to act stood out with particular clarity in the case of the Non-proliferation Treaty. Whereas the CDU/CSU emphasized the treaty's security dimension and wanted to see appropriate measures to strengthen the alliance components in U.S. foreign policy, the SPD regarded the Federal Republic's renunciation of any military nuclear options—thus going beyond the 1954 commitments—as a detente measure prerequisite to the normalization of relations with the East European states. But for the time being the fear of upgrading the GDR even hindered Bonn from becoming a member of the Geneva Disarmament Conference.[97]

The countervailing priorities in policy on Germany and the alliance led to a situation where arms control policy—as well as the detente policy being carried out by Washington—became a burden on security policy, which called for proceeding tactically and defensively. A constructive involvement of the Federal Republic in the detente dialogue was not possible until Bonn had brought itself round to acceptance and de facto recognition of the status quo[98]—once the Social-Liberal coalition had been formed—and, secondly, until the Western alliance had in the Harmel Report eliminated the contradiction between defense capability and readiness for detente in favor of a security concept integrating military and political elements.

THE DUAL STRATEGY OF NATO: DEFENSE CAPABILITY AND WILLINGNESS TO NEGOTIATE

The Harmel Report, a set of guiding principles on the future tasks of the alliance, was adopted by the NATO Council in December 1967. It marked the beginning of a new phase in the alliance policy of the West. Besides ensuring the military defense of the NATO countries against external aggression, henceforth the alliance was also to function as a vehicle for a common detente policy. Specifically, the report stated:

> The Atlantic Alliance has two main functions. Its first function is to maintain adequate military strength and political solidarity to deter aggression and other forms of pressure and to defend the territory of member countries if aggression should occur. Since its inception, the alliance has successfully fulfilled this task. But the possibility of a crisis cannot be excluded as long as the central political issues in Europe, first and foremost the German Question, remain unsolved. Moreover, the situation of instability and uncertainty still precludes a balanced reduction of military forces. Under these conditions, the Allies will maintain as necessary, a suitable military capability to assure the balance of forces, thereby creating a climate of stability, security and confidence. In this climate the Alliance can carry out its second function, to pursue the search for progress towards a more stable relationship in which the underlying political issues can be

solved. Military security and a policy of detente are not contradictory but complementary. Collective defense is a stabilizing factor in world politics. It is the necessary condition for effective policies directed towards a greater relaxation of tensions. The way to peace and stability in Europe rests in particular on the use of the alliance constructively in the interest of detente. The participation of the USSR and the USA will be necessary to achieve a settlement of the political problems of Europe.[99]

Thus, in the future the protective fabric of security policy would be woven with two different yet matching threads: military defense policy and political detente policy. Defense would continue to be the warp thread, through which the alliance now wanted to draw the shuttle of detente policy.

The Consolidation of the Atlantic Alliance

With the Harmel Report, the NATO members wished to reappraise the function of the alliance, which had been clouded by doubts as a result of three developments:

1. The U.S. policy of stabilization had led to a political bilateralism in the relations between the two superpowers and clearly revealed an inclination of the United States under certain circumstances—thus, on the question of non-proliferation of nuclear weapons—to accord an agreement with the Soviet Union priority over the wishes and concerns of the allies.
2. Like the United States, a number of West European countries had been intent upon improving their relations with the Soviet Union and the East European states. De Gaulle's France had gone furthest with its attempt to make itself the preferred partner in the East-West dialogue, at the same time turning against a U.S. leadership role in detente policy.
3. France's withdrawal from NATO integration and the approaching possibility of the NATO treaty's termination in 1969, as well as the preoccupation of the United States with the Vietnam War and the stronger demands being raised in the United States for a reduction of its European commitment, likewise raised the question of the Atlantic alliance's future.

As the East-West antagonism abated, the question was raised as to the future of the organization that had been created at the high point of the antagonism and whose build-up, particularly the inclusion of the Federal Republic, had contributed to deepening it. Should the alliance from then on assume a reduced importance, perhaps in the long run to be made superfluous by the detente process? The thinking of some

Western politicians, including Foreign Minister Willy Brandt, ran in this direction, as did the Eastern argumentation. But could a European security system overarching the alliances guarantee the military defense of the West Europeans and ensure the close connection of the U.S. with the continent? The supposition was not so far-fetched that France could afford to withdraw from NATO integration only because for Paris there was no conceivable military alternative to the NATO alliance inclusive of the European engagement of the United States and a strong conventional contribution of the West Germans. If this alliance, then, had a military task to fulfill that did not become superfluous with a progressive East-West rapprochement, then its role would have to be redefined so that detente policy was not hampered. Moreover, it was essential to use the alliance as a framework into which the national detente policies of the various allies could be integrated and, as far as possible, transformed into a common policy supported by the alliance.

Thus, at the suggestion of Belgian Foreign Minister Pierre Harmel, the NATO Council had, at its session in December 1966, appointed a special working group to draw up a report on the future tasks of the alliance and to examine possibilities for strengthening the alliance's function of preserving peace. Four politicians from member countries—the German Klaus Schütz (replaced after his appointment as governing mayor of Berlin by the Dutchman, Patijn), the Briton Sir Duncan Watson, the Belgian Paul Henri Spaak, and the American Foy Kohler—were instructed to submit reports on the various aspects, which were then combined into the final Harmel Report. This fact, plus the circumstance that the final report was to be acceptable to all states, including France, helps to explain the very summary formulation of alliance goals on the one hand, and the reference to the sovereignty and autonomy of the alliance's members in pursuing the common tasks on the other.[100]

In the report, the alliance's ultimate political purpose was designated as achieving a just and lasting peaceful order in Europe, without any more precise definition or further statement as to how this ought to be realized. As prerequisites for a durable settlement, mention was made of solving the German question in the sense of overcoming the division, maintaining a balance of military forces, as well as taking measures of disarmament and arms limitation, including troop reductions; yet it was left open what steps were to be considered and what remained as long-term goal. These unclarities and contradictions underscore that the Harmel Report was not an alliance program for a common detente policy, but rather an instrument of alliance policy with which the NATO states committed themselves to maintaining the military capability and political cohesion of the alliance, but recognized that both individually and jointly they had a legitimate interest—compatible with the military tasks of the alliance—in better relations with the Soviet Union and the East European states. This then gave rise to the philosophy of the two pillars—deterrence and defense as one, negotiation and detente as the other—upon which the common alliance policy would in future be based.

The Harmel Report assimilated ideas that had previously been developed in the various member states: the notion, first raised by President Johnson, of "building bridges" between East and West,[101] de Gaulle's concept of *"détente—coopération—entente,"*[102] and the scheme developed by Foreign Minister Brandt of a "European order of peace."[103] At the same time the alliance was responding to the detente initiatives of the Warsaw Pact, which in July 1966, in the "Bucharest Appeal," called upon the West to develop neighborly relations based upon the principles of peaceful coexistence, and proposed concrete measures for consideration at a European security conference. This call was repeated in a "Declaration for Peace and Security in Europe," adopted by a conference of Communist Party leaders in April 1967 in Karlovy Vary.[104]

Coming three months after the establishment of diplomatic relations between Bonn and Bucharest, the Karlovy Vary Declaration showed that the East also saw the need for binding the bilateral contacts into a multilateral context. Means to that end were provided by the Ulbricht Doctrine, which was characterized as a "reverse Hallstein Doctrine" because relations with Bonn were made dependent on prior recognition of the GDR, and by the project of a Conference on Security and Cooperation in Europe, which became an important vehicle of the East-West dialogue. All these developments—the desire of the Western states for a normalization of their relations with the Eastern states, the activation by the Soviet Union and the East European states of an all-European dialogue, as well as the constraint present on both sides to channel these efforts in the respective alliances—made the Western alliance an important actor in detente politics. In retrospect, it lent the Harmel Report programmatic relevance.

Harmel Report and "New Ostpolitik"

In the 1960s the Federal Republic also began to improve its relations with the East European states. A first step was the establishment of trade missions in Warsaw, Budapest, and Bucharest; a further step was the offer of renunciation of force statements, which constituted the core of Bonn's "peace note" of March 1966.[105] Such steps were in large measure the German government's reaction to its partners' activities toward the East. For one thing, Bonn did not want to leave the East European market to the French and Italians alone; for another, it feared a "detente downgrade" and an isolation of Bonn on security and German policy if it were not able to introduce its own interests into the detente dialogue. Johnson's speech and the Harmel exercise as well as numerous unofficial contacts were supposed to induce greater German flexibility on questions of arms control and detente. Non-proliferation and European arms control measures were meaningful only if the Federal Republic were involved in them. But since Bonn was not willing to run any risk to its security, the alliance had to be reactivated as backing and reciprocal reassurance.

However, the main problem consisted in moving the Federal Republic to accept the status quo. As the time did not seem ripe for a formal recognition of the postwar realities of Europe, the Western powers wanted to exclude the political issues from the detente dialogue, while at the same time they tried to ensure the cooperation of the Federal Republic by supporting verbally Bonn's position on the German question, which amounted to overcoming the status quo.

The West was spared the oath of disclosure as to whether it gave priority to recognizing or to overcoming the status quo, for in the latter half of the 1960s the Federal Republic itself began moving toward acceptance of the status quo. After the shock of the Wall had abated, there appeared in the domestic political discussion a growing sentiment in favor of normalizing relations with the Central and East European states, including the GDR. The first of the political parties to cross the Rubicon was the SPD at is party congress in Dortmund in June 1966, when it explicitly incuded the GDR in the normalization of relations and distinguished between the immediate goal of humanitarian relief and the distant goal of a reunification.[106] The Grand Coalition continued on this road. Coming out of a political crisis in which the CDU/CSU could remain in power only together with the SPD, the traditional governing party accepted the new coalition partner's demands on detente policy.[107] In his government declaration of December 13, 1966, Chancellor Kurt-Georg Kiesinger placed foreign policy under the heading of peace policy and declared that the Federal Republic would work toward eliminating political tensions and containing the arms race. He stated that Bonn was striving for neither a national control over nuclear weapons nor copossession of them. On detente and Ostpolitik he reiterated the German government's willingness to exchange statements of renunciation of force with the Soviet Union and the other East European states, but now extended them to "the unresolved problem of the German division" and complemented them with the desire for reconciliation and cooperation with Poland

and Czechoslovakia.[108] With that the Federal Republic had joined in the Western detente dialogue and put itself in a position to influence this dialogue in its interests.

In the subsequent years, Bonn worked within the alliance both in drawing up the Harmel Report and in developing position papers on questions of European security. The new Ostpolitik was designed to normalize relations primarily with the Soviet Union but also with the other East European states, so as to create the preconditions for a long-term solution of the German question. This policy consisted of three elements: renunciation of force, force reductions, and non-proliferation. General declarations renouncing the use of force were to facilitate acceptance of the status quo without giving up legal positions on the German question or with respect to the peace treaty proviso on the border question. Negotiations on mutual force reductions were to help guarantee European security at a lower level of forces and at the same time signal a willingness to achieve disarmament. The renunciation of any kind of national nuclear weapons option was to be both an act of accommodation to the U.S.-Soviet arms control dialogue and a confidence-building measure toward the East European states.

However, the complexity of the outstanding problems together with Bonn's hesitation in accepting the status quo prevented rapid progress in negotiations. The intervention of Warsaw Pact troops in Czechoslovakia in August 1968 brought the East-West detente process to a complete standstill—though only for a few months. In the Federal Republic the difficulties in the renunciation-of-force dialogue and a sharper confrontation policy of the Warsaw Pact states led to the disintegration of the foreign policy consensus between the coalition partners; the Grand Coalition degenerated into an alliance for maintaining power. It was the formation of the Social-Liberal coalition that first freed the Federal Republic from this paralysis in foreign policy and opened the way for an active policy of detente with the East.

With the exception of the bilateral renunciation-of-force talks with the Soviet Union and the East European states, which culminated in the Eastern Treaties and the Basic Treaty with the GDR in the early 1970s, the detente policy of the Federal Republic was primarily security and alliance policy. Yet the policy behind the Eastern Treaties also needed the backing and, as the Quadripartite Agreement on Berlin showed, active support of the Western powers. Egon Bahr made particular note of this point:

> Just as our renunciation of force agreement with the Soviet Union needed the alliance, the two superpowers' agreement on the prevention of nuclear war stands in need of the alliance systems, in fact in

a twofold sense. First, the alliance is essential as reinsurance in case the renunciation of force agreement does not function. Secondly, there are greater chances of the renunciation of force functioning because the alliance systems are there. The nuclear pact gives the alliance and its partners additional security, and it gains stability because the alliances on both sides remain credible in their deterrence capacities. They remain reliable because they, like the treaty on the prevention of nuclear war, met the same fundamental interest: the status quo must not be altered by means of force. Transformation demands stability.[109]

Security and detente policy were complemented by an active policy on Europe and the alliance. Following the mid-1960s alliance crisis occasioned by the increased bilateralism of the superpowers, France's withdrawal from NATO integration, and the tendencies toward unilateral troop withdrawal from Western Europe, internal consolidation assumed priority. This was done first by the improvement of the consultation mechanisms in NATO—especially by organizing the Nuclear Planning Group—and secondly through various measures taken by the West European allies—especially the Federal Republic—toward greater burden-sharing. Agreements on the U.S., British, and French troops stationed in West Germany were supplemented by U.S.-German and German-British offset agreements[110] and increased European contributions to the infrastructure program. Also, in 1967 NATO officially accepted the strategy of flexible response and made it the basis for its own force and operational planning. In policy on Europe, the decisions of The Hague summit gave new impetus toward realizing the economic and monetary union and in 1972 the negotiations with Great Britain and the other membership candidates were brought to a successful conclusion. For Bonn, policy on Western Europe was prerequisite and correlate to policy on Eastern Europe; in the Brandtian concept of a European order of peace, the Western steps toward union had an exemplary character just as they were to be elements of an all-European order overlapping bloc and social systems.[111]

The SALT Accords as a Product of U.S.-Soviet Bilateralism

Since the Cuban crisis, the foreign policy of the United States exhibited a two-track structure of U.S.-Soviet bilateralism and multilateral detente policy including the allies. The ideas leading to the Harmel Report marked an attempt to activate the alliance as a common negotiating framework at least for questions of European security. At the global-strategic level, however, a number of developments prompted the two superpowers increasingly to seek bilateral arrangements. For one thing, it appeared that continuation of the current Soviet armaments program would give Moscow an approximate strategic parity by the mid-1970s, thus eliminating the U.S. strategic superiority.[112] At the same time, new developments in arms technology—development and deployment of missile defense systems (ABM) and multiple warheads (MIRV)—were endangering the assured destructive capability of second-strike potentials and thus the stability of deterrence. Finally, both world powers were entangled in conflicts outside the classical fault lines of the East-West antagonism—the United States in the Vietnam War, the Soviet Union in the conflict with the People's Republic of China, dramatized by the shooting on the Ussuri—conflicts in which the good conduct of the other world power was essential to the outcome. Added to this were domestic political constraints. In the United States there were pressures for a reduction of the military commitment, whereas the Soviet Union found itself confronted with problems of resource allocation, which it sought to remedy through increased capital and technology imports.

In this situation the Nixon/Kissinger administration (the latter in the capacity first of national security adviser, then, after September 1973, as secretary of state) attempted to contain the power struggle with the Soviet Union through a broad "strategy for peace" (and, with the Nixon Doctrine, to transfer to U.S. allies greater responsibility for common military security and East-West detente). To this end, the still existing strategic superiority would be utilized and restraint in arms policy—in building and deploying ABM systems and multiple warheads—would serve as quid pro quo for support in ending the Vietnam conflict, but especially for restraint in the crisis areas of the third world.

This strategy of linkage did not work out, however. Moscow did have an interest in formalizing strategic parity (though above all in limiting U.S. ABM programs) and in strengthening economic and technological relations with the West, yet it could not agree to forgo a global foreign policy—which meant precisely intervention in regions outside Europe. This relative incongruence of Soviet and U.S. objectives, however, did not become evident until the middle of the 1970s, mainly as a result of the experience in the Middle East. At first there prevailed a negotiating dynamic between Moscow and Washington basically fed by the arms control dialogue.

The summit meeting between President Nixon and General Secretary Brezhnev in Moscow in May 1972 marked the high point of U.S.-Soviet detente policy. At this meeting agreements were reached in four areas:

1. Both sides agreed upon guiding principles for mutual relations, and they expressed their desire to develop these relations on the basis of equality and in accordance with the principles of peaceful coexistence. At the same time they undertook the obligation to renounce the use or threat of force and to prevent military confrontations, especially nuclear conflicts. This understanding was defined more precisely in June 1973 by the Agreement on the Prevention of Nuclear Wars.

2. The United States and the Soviet Union signed a Treaty on the Limitation of Anti-ballistic Missile Systems and an Interim Agreement on the quantitative limitation of strategic weapons systems—the SALT I treaties, valid for five years. At the same time the talks on limiting strategic weapons systems were to be continued in order to replace the Interim Agreement with a comprehensive SALT treaty.

3. The U.S. and Soviet governments came to procedural agreements on the progress of the European detente dialogue, the most important of which was the decoupling of CSCE and MBFR. In September 1972 this agreement was concretized to the effect that in November of that year multilateral consultations to prepare for a Conference on Security and Cooperation would be held in Helsinki and at the end of January 1973 preliminary talks for negotiations on Mutual Balanced Force Reductions would be initiated in another neutral country.

4. Finally, both sides signed treaties on scientific and technological cooperation and completed work on a trade agreement, which was signed in October 1972. These accords were supplemented by a series of additional agreements on cooperation in a wide range of areas (e.g., outer space, nuclear energy, agriculture, etc.).[113]

The two SALT agreements marked the first time that a quantitative limitation of central strategic systems had been agreed on. In the ABM Treaty the development of anti-ballistic missile systems was limited to two systems on each side—one system for the capital city and one for protection of a missile site. In the Interim Agreement the current level of strategic armament was essentially frozen, though here both sides were allowed to complete systems already under construction and, within certain limits, modernize existing facilities. All in all, the agreement stipulated a ceiling of 1,054 land-based and 710 sea-based (on 44 submarines) launchers for the United States and 1,618 land-based and 714 sea-based launchers (or 950 of these systems, if older facilities were dismantled in exchange) for the Soviet Union.[114] This protocol was to remain in force for five years; by that time both sides hoped to have concluded a comprehensive SALT treaty. Originally they had hoped to have already completed a SALT II treaty by the time of General Secretary Brezhnev's visit to Washington in June 1973. An agreement was made more difficult, however, by the fact that in ratifying the SALT I accords Congress had imposed on the U.S. negotiators the condition that they not accept a comprehensive SALT treaty setting a lower ceiling for U.S. forces than that for the Soviet Union. Further difficulties emerged in determining qualitative restrictions, in particular for the greater MIRV capability of the United States and the greater throw weight of Soviet missiles, as well as in accounting for European systems and those stationed in Europe. This led to both sides' limiting themselves to signing in the summer of 1973 an—empty—declaration on agreed negotiating principles for SALT II.[115]

From a European point of view the existing security structures were not, or not critically, influenced by the SALT accords. Notably there remained an adherence to the existing system of deterrence, resting on the U.S. capability to launch an atomic counterstrike and to ensure nuclear escalation in the event of a conventional attack threatening the existence of Western Europe. In European eyes the components of deterrence were given added emphasis through the limitation of anti-ballistic missile systems, which likewise extended the life-span and viability of the British and French nuclear systems, and through the stipulation of ceilings for offensive weapons, which ensured the continuance of mutual assured destruction despite a certain numerical advantage for the Soviet Union in delivery vehicles, though not in usable warheads.

In the Interim Agreement, the Soviet medium-range missiles (MRBM) and the U.S. forward based systems (FBS) as well as the French and British nuclear forces had been left out of account.[116] The Federal Republic in particular had originally called for inclusion of the Soviet MRBMs. However, it had soon backed off from this when the Soviet Union argued that strategic weapons were all those systems that could reach the territory of the negotiating partner and thus demanded inclusion of the FBS, without, however, wanting to talk about its MRBMs. From a perspective of bilateral stability, the United States could view the forward based systems in Europe as negotiable, but from a European standpoint these systems represented both a counterweight to the superior ground forces of the Warsaw Pact and a connecting link between the conventional potential of Europe and the U.S. strategic systems. U.S. considerations of incorporating parts of the FBS into the MBFR talks or a SALT II agreement gave rise to the fear that the central mechanism of escalation, upon which the security of Europe depended, could be weakened. With reference to the differentiation between global and regional responsibility enunciated in Kissinger's "Year of Europe" speech, concern was expressed that the United States could "decouple" its allies by maintaining its responsibility for deterrence in the strategic sphere but assigning the West European allies the burden of conventional defense.[117]

These anxieties were further strengthened by the accord signed in Washington during the Brezhnev visit in June 1973, the Agreement on the Prevention of Nuclear Wars, in which the two world powers committed themselves to avoid doing anything that could lead to the outbreak of a nuclear conflict, and to consult with each other and take appropriate measures when such a risk could ensue from the actions of another state.[118] The uneasiness generated by the treaty in the Federal Republic had its origin less in the text of the agreement itself, where there was explicit affirmation of the alliance commitments, than in speculation about its intentions. In particular, the agreement was regarded as another step in the direction of a bilateral control of nuclear power, which tended to produce an international condominium of the two superpowers and which Europe would then have to resist by articulating its own interests.

Today, it would appear that the agreement was accorded too much importance not only in these alarmist views, but by those who saw it as a step toward a fundamental reordering of U.S.-Soviet relations or who regarded it as complementary to the Federal Republic's renunciation of force declarations.[119] Its signing was in large measure a substitute action, for the U.S. in place of the desired SALT II treaty, for Moscow in place of a declaration on no first use of nuclear weapons. The agreement was supposed to help keep intact the dynamics of the U.S.-Soviet dialogue, which was increasingly in danger of being grounded by domestic politics, and it was supposed to give a U.S. government weakened by a decline in domestic authority and foreign power a new basis of legitimacy, as the accords with the Soviet Union were made part of the striving for a new international political structure of peace.

The continuation of the SALT dialogue was strained by a series of domestic and foreign developments. There was, for one thing, the decline in power of the U.S. presidency, culminating in the impeachment proceedings against Richard Nixon and his resignation in August 1974. For another, the October War (1973) in the Middle East put a damper on the expectations that the United States could involve the Soviet Union in a network of mutual obligations and restrain it in the third world. The Agreement on the Prevention of Nuclear Wars thus remained without political substance. Finally, the U.S. Congress thwarted Soviet desires for credits by imposing restrictive conditions and tying the granting of most-favored-nation status in the U.S.-Soviet trade agreement of October 1972 to Moscow's facilitating emigration of Soviet Jews to Israel (Jackson-Vanik amendment). The SALT II talks themselves were made more difficult when equal systems ceilings were stipulated as a negotiating goal (Jackson amendment). Within the administration there was disagreement on how to limit the Soviet lead in the throw weight of delivery vehicles and at the same time exploit the U.S. advantage in the number of independently targetable reentry vehicles (MIRV).[120]

Nevertheless, at a hastily convened summit meeting between President Gerald Ford and General Secretary Brezhnev in Vladivostok in November 1974, an agreement was reached on principles for SALT II, documenting the continuity of detente and marking an attempt to reach a new U.S.-Soviet agreement on limiting strategic weapons systems before the expiration of the Interim Agreement in 1977 and the expected immobility in the election year 1976. The agreement stipulated equal ceilings for strategic delivery vehicles (2,200) as well as a sublimit for MIRVable systems (1,320). More extensive qualitative limitations, e.g., with respect to the throw weight of Soviet missiles, were rejected. Long-range bombers were included yet counted as simple systems. The forward-based systems in Europe (FBS) remained excluded.[121] The breakthrough seemed to have been achieved and U.S.-Soviet detente policy seemed to have survived the downfall of Richard Nixon in the Watergate mess. Why then did it take nearly five years before the SALT II accords could be signed in June 1979?

First of all, it should be borne in mind that, since the Moscow summit of 1972, SALT had become a kind of synonym for U.S.-Soviet detente, for which it played a role similar to that of the CSCE for the European detente process. However, by the mid-1970s people in Washington began to realize that bilateral cooperation with the Soviet Union was not producing the degree of Soviet restraint in the third world as had been originally assumed. Likewise, Moscow concluded that it could neither derive the desired economic benefits from detente nor prevent rapprochement between the United States and the People's Republic of China. On the Soviet side this led to a shrinking of the Kremlin's room for maneuver and willingness to compromise, while in the United States there was growing criticism of Moscow's conduct (e.g., on the question of emigration and policies in the third world). And so the SALT negotiations got into the cross fire of domestic politics.

In addition, there were difficulties in the realm of disarmament complexities. In Vladivostok such controversial questions as the verification of ceilings on "MIRVed" delivery vehicles, the definition of "heavy" missiles, and the handling of the Soviet "Backfire" bomber as well as the newly developed cruise missiles of the United States were left open. These issues raised complicated technical problems; yet their solution called for primarily a political decision, from which both sides shied away in view of the uncertain outcome of the 1976 presidential elections.

Upon coming to office in the spring of 1977, the Carter administration undertook a new approach and tried to solve all problems (the strategic and the domestic political) at once with a revised negotiating concept. It failed just as thoroughly and then picked up again where Kissinger had left off in the negotiations in the spring of 1976.[122] Meanwhile the Soviet arms build-up proceeded apace. This was kept within the bounds marked out in Vladivostok, yet it was all the more alarming as President Jimmy Carter was in the process of canceling certain arms programs (B-1 bomber) or slowing down others (MX missile). At the same time, and not unaffected by this development, there was increasingly strong criticism in the United States of the neglect of important U.S. strategic interests. In this regard SALT became the whipping boy for all the negligence that had led to the negative shifts in the strategic balance of power and opened up the "window of vulnerability" predicted by prominent experts for the 1980s.[123]

The SALT II Treaty signed in June 1979 was the product of protracted and laborious, in part highly technical, negotiations. While SALT I had been used by both governments as a means for making a success of the Moscow summit between President Nixon and General Secretary Brezhnev and achieving a breakthrough in U.S.-Soviet detente—as the war in Vietnam had reached a new peak—this summit meeting between Carter and Brezhnev in Vienna in the summer of 1979 was not possible until all the details of the SALT II agreement had been nailed down. It was less an element of the detente hopefully begun in 1972 than an attempt to maintain an alternative to an unchecked arms competition.

The treaty that was to replace the Interim Agreement of SALT I consisted of four parts: the treaty limiting strategic nuclear weapons to ceilings of 2,400 systems (as of January 1, 1981: 2,250), 1,320 of which with MIRV warheads, and including restrictions on modernization, which were defined in greater detail through numerous agreed statements and common understandings; a protocol in which both sides committed themselves until the end of 1981 not to deploy any mobile intercontinental missiles or any sea- or land-based cruise missiles with ranges greater than 600 kilometers; a memorandum of understanding regarding the establishment of a data base for the number of strategic offensive weapons; and finally, a declaration of intent on subsequent negotiations with the aim of achieving a substantial reduction in the number of strategic offensive systems and a qualitative limitation on them. This set of agreements was supplemented by a Soviet statement that the bomber of the TU-22 M type (Backfire) was an intermediate-range aircraft whose radius of action and rate of production were not to be increased and which therefore did not come under the SALT limitations.[124]

But the basic international situation had also changed from what it was in 1972. The SALT II accords could not obscure the fact that U.S.-Soviet relations were in a crisis. In the visit of the Chinese leader, Teng Hsiao-ping, to the United States in January 1979 and in the Camp David accords between Israel and Egypt in April, the anti-Moscow direction was unmistakable. Similarly, Washington interpreted the Soviet activities on Cuba and all the more the intervention in Afghanistan as violations of detente. Under these circumstances the SALT treaty did not generate positive impulses for continuing the detente process; rather the treaty itself would have needed a climate of international relaxation of tensions to ensure its ratification by Congress and create the requisite conditions for more extensive arms control.

Essentially, the SALT treaties failed because of the concern in the United States that the strategic balance of power between East and West could—on account or in spite of the SALT agreements—develop to the disadvantage of the United States. After the Soviet invasion of Afghanistan it seemed impossible to get a majority for the treaties in Congress, so President Carter withdrew them from the ratification process. His successor, Ronald Reagan, had presented himself during the election campaign as a critic of the SALT treaties. His slogan, "America—Second to None," made it difficult to pursue credibly a policy that explicitly acknowledged asymmetrical strategic parity. Like every new administration, the Reagan administration considered it necessary first to develop its own concept for arms control negotiations. It distinguished itself from previous administrations primarily in that understandings with the Soviet Union assumed a substantially lesser importance in its overall political concept. Hence, 18 months passed before it returned to the bargaining table in Geneva. To accentuate the difference in conception from the policies of its predecessors, it gave the negotiations a new name: START, i.e., Strategic Arms Reduction Talks.[125]

SALT and European Security

Ever since the founding of NATO the security of Western Europe has been guaranteed by the close connection between the forces deployed in Europe and the strategic potential of the United States; this alliance unity in security policy was the foundation for a credible deterrence and defense capability. Debates on security policy within the alliance have been sparked primarily by the question of whether changes in the global balance of power had weakened this coupling and thereby made less credible the U.S. guarantee to employ nuclear weapons in defense of Europe. This doubt led to a crisis of confidence in European-American relations at the end of the 1950s and beginning of the 1960s, once neither the automaticity of the old strategy of massive retaliation seemed credible nor the new one of flexible response appeared politically acceptable without suitable ways for the Europeans to have a say.[126] Ten years later, the U.S.-Soviet bilateralism evident in concluding the Non-proliferation Treaty and the SALT I accords once again produced the anxious question of whether the United States would decouple itself from its strategic bond with Western Europe. With the consolidation of parity between the United States and the Soviet Union in the strategic balance of power, which was what the SALT II accords came down to, this question was raised once again and all the more urgently as it was posed rather openly and emphatically in the discussion on the treaty in the United States.

Foremost was the question of whether the United States, in view of the loss of its strategic superiority and the increasing vulnerability of its land-based ICBM potential, could still credibly threaten to use its strategic forces in the defense of Western Europe. In this connection there was talk of a "decoupling paradox" of Europe. If the West Europeans were to forgo stationing additional tactical nuclear systems to cover targets in the Soviet Union, then this would have to be seen as

> decoupling, because it would make them dependent on the not very credible American option of a massive employment of strategic systems; however, if a number of medium-range systems corresponding to the Soviet potential were stationed in Western Europe, then this, too, could lead to decoupling, because the U.S. in this instance could be inclined not to use its central systems any longer for the defense of Western Europe.[127]

(The coupling, then, was effected by the Soviet Union, which repeatedly pointed out that in the event U.S. medium-range weapons were used against targets in the Soviet Union from out of Western Europe the Soviets would strike back against the United States.)

In the Federal Republic's assessment of the SALT treaties, political and strategic aspects became blurred. The German government regarded "the readiness of both parties to the treaty to agree upon strategic parity and thus renounce strategic superiority as an important factor of stability and a significant contribution to detente."[128]

Yet two questions marks had to be added to this assessment. First, the strategic equilibrium was not be be equated with strategic stability; i.e., the crisis stability that resulted from a low first-strike vulnerability and an assured second-strike potential and that had reliably ensured mutual deterrence over the previous years. In view of the increasing vulnerability of the U.S. intercontinental missiles (at least as long as the fixed-site Minuteman missiles had not been supplemented or replaced by better protected MX systems) concern was expressed that the Soviet Union was acquiring a nuclear first-strike capability. Moscow could then be tempted to exploit this politically once the use of the U.S. strategic potential for the defense of Western Europe had lost its credibility.[129] Secondly, it had long been pointed out, particularly by the Federal Republic, that the consolidation of a formal parity between U.S. and Soviet strategic nuclear potentials could in effect politically neutralize these forces and so increase the importance of the Soviet Union's tactical nuclear and conventional superiority in Europe. In his often cited (and seldom read) London speech of October 1977, Chancellor Schmidt had therefore called for eliminating the Eastern superiority in conventional and tactical-nuclear forces in Europe parallel to the SALT talks.[130] Thus, the stipulation of a strategic parity, desirable from the standpoints of detente and arms control, actualized regional military disparities, which, in turn, raised new critical questions.

The concern over the negative political consequences of shifts in the military balance led Bonn to become a most vigorous advocate of NATO force modernization, i.e., the deployment of long-range theatre nuclear weapons systems (LRTNF), if it was not possible to negotiate a dismantling of the Soviet medium-range missiles (SS-20) directed at Western Europe. The purpose was neither to deploy a military potential that could reliably put the Soviet SS-20 out of action nor to establish an equilibrium at the regional level parallel to that at the strategic level of SALT II—neither of which could have been achieved with the number and types of systems provided for—but rather to produce a closer coupling between the alliance's intercontinental and its theater nuclear weapons potentials. This, then, would preserve the credibility of the strategy of flexible response for the defense of Western Europe (including escalation control).[131]

In view of the NATO states' intention of stationing new medium-range weapons in Europe, the SALT accords presented two concrete problems. First, there was the question of whether the treaty's non-circumvention clause (Article 32) would impede U.S. cooperation with the allies in TNF modernization. However, the administration in Washington maintained that this condition applied only to such systems as the United States was in principle barred from possessing, but not to such as were only numerically limited. This question was of particular moment for Great Britain, which hoped to obtain U.S. Trident systems for its Polaris submarines. On the question of transfer of technology and weapons systems that the allies needed for modernizing their armed forces, the United States confirmed, in part at Bonn's insistence, that these would not come under the ban and that decisions on transfer would be made case by case, e.g., on cruise missile technology for the allies.[132] However, this still left some margin for interpretation. Secondly, Washington's acceptance in the SALT II protocol of limitations on cruise missiles gave rise to anxieties and criticism in Western Europe that the United States had consented to a moratorium on ground-launched and sea-launched cruise missiles as well as longer-range air-launched missiles without the Soviet Union's reciprocating in the realm of medium-range systems. But above all it was feared that the protocol could be extended beyond 1981, and thus a deployment of long-range cruise missiles in Europe might be prevented and, in fact, future arms control negotiations negatively prejudiced.

In the Federal Republic, however, these various objections were more often voiced by the opposition than by government spokesmen. They illustrate the skepticism of the CDU/CSU toward any arms control agreement with the Soviet Union as long as such an accord was not accompanied by measures with which the causes of the tensions between East and West could be eliminated.[133] The German government refrained from public criticism of the SALT agreements; rather, it sought to ensure that the allies would be included to a greater degree in the development of negotiating positions for subsequent negotiations. To this end the institutional prerequisites were created by the formation of special consultative groups in NATO (the High Level Group for strategic issues; the Special Group, after 1979 the Special Consultative Group, for arms control questions). Moreover, in its positions and public statements Bonn tried to ease the ratification process by stressing—in the face of criticism of SALT that frequently referred to alleged European hesitations—the importance of the SALT II accords for the East-West relationship and the continuation of the arms control dialogue. In its eyes SALT II was the starting ground from which SALT III could be tackled. These negotiations would also have to encompass the previously excluded European systems—in particular the Soviet missiles of the SS-20 type that covered targets in all of Western Europe. In the view of the German government and leading members of the coalition parties, the continuation of the SALT process was a prerequisite for maintaining the unity of the alliance and ensuring that Europe would not become the theater of a new arms race.[134]

The Federal Republic's reaction to the SALT accords inevitably raises the question of what importance arms control in general assumed in Bonn's overall concept of security policy, that is, what was the relative importance of that bundle of measures that sought to attain security not through more but through less armament? Since the mid-1960s, since Gerhard Schröder's "peace note," arms control agreements, apart from the Non-proliferation Treaty, had ceased to be viewed primarily as burdens; rather, the German government now sought to make them serve its own political purposes. This became particularly clear after the Social-Liberal coalition came to power; as a first step in its detente policy the coalition signed the Nonproliferation Treaty. Along with bilateral renunciation-of-force agreements, negotiations on European security had a high priority in this concept.

Here particular significance was attached to the negotiations on mutual and balanced force reductions (MBFR).[135] For the Federal Republic these talks had a three-fold function: first, to prevent unilateral Western troop withdrawals, which had been repeatedly called for by Senator Mike Mansfield, or to use them as a bargaining chip; secondly, to encompass the military confrontation in Europe by the East-West detente at hand and to stabilize the military balance at a lower level; and finally, to enlarge and support Bonn's bilateral Ostpolitik with a multilateral arms control policy. These different sets of interest, however, complicated both the development of a common alliance negotiating position vis-à-vis the Warsaw Pact states and a steady conduct of negotiations during the talks, beginning in Vienna in 1973.

In March 1971 the German government submitted to the allies a negotiating concept that provided the following elements: (1) statement of principles; (2) advance notification and movement constraints; (3) force limitation agreement; (4) phased reductions; (5) agreement on common ceiling.[136] However, Bonn was not able to win acceptance of these ideas, particularly not with the United States, which unofficially characterized the German paper as "a dignified way of doing nothing" and, for reasons of domestic politics, pressed for rapid reductions.

In April 1973 Washington presented its own position paper on MBFR in which three options were formulated for the Vienna talks:

Option 1: numerical parity of NATO and Warsaw Pact troops in the NATO guideline area through reductions of U.S. and Soviet ground forces by one sixth;
Option 2: phased, equal-percentage reductions of stationed and national armed forces to a common collective ceiling;
Option 3: reduction of various offensive elements of Soviet and U.S. forces (mixed package).

Following a complicated process of reaching agreement within the alliance—and not before the Warsaw Pact states had seized the initiative in Vienna with a draft MBFR treaty—the NATO states in November 1973 presented a negotiating proposal according to which both sides would reduce their ground forces in two phases to a common ceiling of 700,000 men. This proposal represented a combination of the first option, favored by the United States, and the second option, desired by the Federal Republic. In December 1975 the NATO states enlarged their negotiating repertoire with elements of the third option as they offered to disarm 1,000 nuclear warheads if the Soviet Union would counter by withdrawing a complete tank army from the GDR.

These proposals—and supplementary offers—failed to alter the extremely slow progress of the negotiations. Certainly the Soviet Union and its allies were gradually approaching the negotiating concept of the West, yet a number of fundamental problems continued to prevent an agreement. The two negotiating principles of collectivity and parity were especially controversial. Forces were to be reduced to a common collective ceiling for both sides, but following an initial phase of U.S. and Soviet troop withdrawals, the allies would determine internally in the second phase the mix ratio of reductions to be undertaken. Thus, the other side would have no way of interfering in the internal order of battle of the alliance and, specifically, there would be no treaty-based limitation of the Bundeswehr. The reduction to a common collective ceiling and the stipulation of appropriate reduction ratios presupposed that there was agreement between the two sides as to the number of troops present in the reduction area. With substantial differences between the figures given by the Warsaw Pact and the estimates of NATO, there developed fierce discussion of data which turned into the joker on the way to an agreement.[137]

Neither the partial agreement on a first phase of Soviet and U.S. troop withdrawals, proposed by the West in conjunction with the NATO dual-track decision of December 1979, nor the draft treaties presented by each side in 1982 could lead the talks out of the impasse. A new element in these drafts was the Western proposal of associated measures such as advance notification and inspections. A close analysis of the drafts shows, however, that neither side was any longer politically interested in force reductions. The West was striving primarily for a military stabilization agreement—and this without much enthusiasm—while the East was using proposals and negotiating initiatives to demonstrate its peace-loving nature for all the world to see and especially to point out to the West Europeans the problems of NATO force modernization.

THE NATO DUAL-TRACK DECISION OF DECEMBER 1979: ARMAMENT AND ARMS LIMITATION

Two developments activated the problems of European security in the 1970s: first, the Soviet Union's policy of forced arms build-up, in particular the deployment of SS-20 medium-range systems; second, the codification of an approximate nuclear parity of the two super-powers' strategic weapons systems in the SALT treaties, which failed to take the European correlation of forces into account. Hence, especially in the Federal Republic, concern was expressed that there would emerge in Europe a gray zone that was not covered by the current arms control agreements. In turn, the balance of forces could shift to the detriment of the West, with the consequence that Moscow would acquire new options for political pressure.

In his "Alastair Buchan Memorial Lecture" on October 28, 1977 before the International Institute for Strategic Studies in London, Chancellor Helmut Schmidt referred to these imbalances and stated,

> But strategic arms limitations confined to the United States and the Soviet Union will inevitably impair the security of the West European members of the Alliance vis-à-vis Soviet military superiority in Europe if we do not succeed in removing the disparities of military power in Europe parallel to the SALT negotiations. So long as this is not the case we must maintain the balance of the full range of deterrence strategy. The Alliance must, therefore, be ready to make available the means to support its present strategy, which is still the right one, and to prevent any developments that could undermine the basis of this strategy.[138]

Although further on in his address the chancellor advocated restoring the balance in the European area primarily through greater efforts in the realm of arms control, supporting in particular new initiatives in the Vienna MBFR talks, this speech should also be viewed in relation to the discussions within the Western alliance on strengthening medium-range nuclear systems. In historical retrospect Schmidt has interpreted his speech as an attempt to give impetus to an improvement and modernization of NATO's medium-range potential.

At the beginning of the 1970s, however, there had already begun a new debate within the Western alliance on whether, in view of increased Soviet arms efforts, the available military potentials were sufficient and credible for implementing a NATO strategy geared toward war prevention. One result of this debate was the Long Term Defense Program (LTDP), which was adopted by the NATO Council of Ministers in May 1978. With this program the alliance would undertake improvements in the state of military readiness, reinforcement and mobilization capabilities, the rationalization and standardization of armament as well as command control, communications, and logistical systems, plus the modernization of the nuclear forces in and for Europe.

Back in 1974-75 a debate on adapting the strategy of flexible response to the altered global strategic situation had already begun in the United States, with Secretary of Defense James Schlesinger playing a prominent role. Subsequently the concept of a countervailing strategy was developed, designed to expand the West's range of military options in the event of conflict and include to a greater extent the adversary's military forces in its targeting.[139] The NATO partners were only marginally involved in this debate, and public attention beyond the narrow circle of experts was not aroused until 1977. Then, a first phase reached its peak with the debate on introducing neutron warheads as battlefield weapons in Europe. The second phase comprised the discussion that resulted in the NATO dual-track decision in December 1979. The third phase was marked by growing criticism of this decision and by the emergence of a heterogeneous yet publically effective peace movement in Western Europe and the Federal Republic.

The Debate on the Introduction of Neutron Warheads

The decision by President Jimmy Carter to ask Congress to provide funding for the production of new enhanced radiation weapons (ERW) and to call upon the allies to take corresponding decisions concerning the storage and tactical deployment of these weapons systems[140] unleashed a fierce and very emotional debate, particularly in the Federal Republic. It was inaugurated with an article by the SPD's party manager, Egon Bahr, appearing in the July 21, 1977 issue of *Vorwärts*. Bahr characterized the neutron bomb as "a symbol of the perversion of human thinking." This was a weapon that did little or no material damage but "cleanly" killed people. "Is mankind on the verge of madness?"[141] This reaction reflected all those fears and anxieties that had stamped the debate on atomic weapons in the 1950s. In contrast, the Bonn government stressed that ERW did not consitute a qualitatively new system but rather further development of nuclear battlefield weapons, and that their introduction would be decided upon only after thoroughgoing consultation in the alliance. This would necessarily entail an examination of whether the new weapons made deterrence strategy more credible, i.e., whether they were a suitable means of war prevention, and what significance their introduction would have for arms control efforts.

After intensive consultations in the alliance and in light of opposition in public opinion, including parts of the SPD and FDP, the German government developed a discriminating position on the deployment of the new systems, the basic elements of which also entered into the TNF decision of 1979. First of all, the government underscored its commitment to maintaining its renunciation of atomic weapons, as the Federal Republic had reaffirmed in the Non-proliferation Treaty. As a non-nuclear-weapons state it could not take part in decisions on the production of nuclear weapons; such decisions would have to remain a sovereign act of the United States. Secondly, decision on production should be followed up by efforts to make progress in arms control negotiations. Thirdly, the German government would allow the stationing of ERW on the territory of the Federal Republic only if the alliance would reach a joint decision on their introduction, if deployment were to take place not solely on German soil, and if within two years the West had not abandoned deployment because appropriate successes had meanwhile been scored in arms control negotiations.[142]

In view of the West European hesitations, President Carter unilaterally decided in April 1978 to defer the decision on producing neutron weapons. He indicated that the United States would make its final decision dependent in part on whether the Soviet Union exercised restraint in its conventional and nuclear arms programs. At the same time, Carter announced that the United States with its allies would continue to modernize NATO forces in order to guarantee their common security and the forward defense of Europe.[143]

The debate on the neutron bomb did not remain without consequence. First of all, the various reports on the effects of such weapons produced a critical sensitivity in the public that provided fertile ground for an increasingly intense debate on the difficult rationality of deterrence and defense in the nuclear age. Secondly, many European politicians, especially Chancellor Schmidt, were taken by surprise and let down by the U.S. president's decision after they had taken pains to lay the domestic political foundation for deployment in Western Europe. They had argued that the neutron weapon did not entail a qualitatively new system but rather was a particularly small battlefield weapon that used concentrated radioactive radiation, which would keep the collateral damage in any action as small as possible. Moreover, they had reasoned that in view of Soviet conventional superiority, especially in tanks, the introduction of such weapons would help keep the spectrum of deterrence intact and thus credible. Finally, the German government wanted to avoid another U.S.-German conflict and, with the approach of Brezhnev's visit to Bonn (May 1978), the suspicion that cooperation with Washington and the NATO allies might be of lesser importance to

Bonn than relations with Moscow. What remained was doubt on both sides of the Atlantic: in the Federal Republic about the leadership qualities of the U.S. president and in the United States about Bonn's readiness and resolve to make its own contribution to the common defense.

The Decision on Deployment of Eurostrategic Weapons

After the fiasco over the neutron bomb, the alliance focused its attention on how the tactical nuclear weapons stationed in Europe could be modernized or supplemented by new systems. The introduction of long-range Eurostrategic weapons was to provide NATO with additional operational means for the new "countervailing strategy"—which was a variation of the flexible response strategy directed more to military targets than to population centers. At the same time, strengthening the middle element of the NATO "triad" would help restore the credibility of deterrence. For this purpose, NATO set up in the spring of 1977 a High Level Group (HLG), which in the course of 1979 recommended the deployment of 572 new long-range theatre nuclear weapons in Europe (LRTNF).

While the United States was chiefly concerned with getting a modernization of NATO's tactical nuclear weapons potential under way, the West European interest was directed to bringing the nuclear weapons systems and forces previously not included in SALT or MBFR into a negotiating context and in this way offsetting the existing imbalance in the regional correlation of forces. At the beginning of 1979, NATO set up a Special Group charged with developing, parallel to the work of the HLG, suitable arms control options.[144]

Before the NATO Council of Ministers at its December session could make its decision on introducing the prospective Eurostrategic systems and present new proposals for arms control, General Secretary Brezhnev declared in a spectacular speech in East Berlin on October 6, 1979 that the Soviet Union was prepared to enter into negotiations on reducing nuclear weapons in the intermediate area if NATO were to forgo introducing such systems on its side. At the same time Brezhnev announced a unilateral reduction of the forces stationed in the GDR by 20,000 men and 1,000 tanks. In the following weeks Moscow intensified its propaganda campaign with the aim of preventing or at least delaying the NATO decision. In particular, the Soviet leaders warned that a decision to introduce Eurostrategic weapons could not fail to have consequences for German-Soviet relations. Nor could there be arms control negotiations if NATO clung to its present position.[145]

After intensive public debate in the countries affected, particularly in the Federal Republic, where the relationship between defense and detente, the goals and instruments of NATO strategy, and the credibility of alliance obligations were discussed at great length, the foreign and defense ministers of NATO adopted at a series of conferences on December 12, 13, and 15, 1979 an extensive modernization program for NATO's nuclear forces. Specifically, this program provided for the deployment of 108 LRTNF systems of the Pershing II type and 96 cruise missiles (GLCM) on the territory of the Federal Republic, while a further 368 cruise missiles were to be stationed in Great Britain, Italy, Belgium, and the Netherlands. In addition, the NATO ministers proposed negotiations between the United States and the Soviet Union on limiting land-based intermediate-range systems in the framework of SALT III. Further, it announced a unilateral withdrawal of 1,000 U.S. nuclear warheads from Europe as well as new initiatives for MBFR and confidence-building measures in the CSCE framework.[146]

For the Federal Republic of Germany the dual-track decision of NATO was primarily a reaffirmation of the two pillars of West German security policy as it had been understood since the end of the 1960s: a capability to deter aggression and a will to negotiate. The Federal Republic declared its readiness to undertake greater armament efforts if that were necessary for maintaining the military balance; but it also argued for new arms control efforts to restore this balance at a lower level.[147]

Against the NATO plans to deploy long-range nuclear weapons capable of reaching Soviet territory from Western Europe, Moscow reacted with pointed political threats and the full operation of its propaganda apparatus, directed primarily at the Federal Republic. With that it became clear that for Bonn in this case security and detente might not be had simultaneously.

Although the NATO modernization decision was first and foremost politically motivated, it was usually legitimated or criticized by proponents and opponents in military terms. Thus, three reasons were cited primarily for the necessity of introducing long-range theatre nuclear weapons into Western Europe:

1. The increasing vulnerability of both sides' land-based intercontinental missiles, which undermined strategic stability through the loss of escalation control (i.e., it appeared less credible that the United States would use its strategic forces in defense of Western Europe since it would thereby risk not only the destruction of its cities, but also the loss of its land-based ICBM potential);
2. The approximate parity between the United States and the Soviet Union in the realm of strategic weapons, as defined in the SALT treaties,

which gave greater political and military importance to disparities in other areas of the military balance of power;

3. And, finally, the modernization of the Soviet Union's medium-range nuclear potential by the introduction of "MIRVed" SS-20 systems, which together with the Warsaw Pact's conventional land forces in Europe represented a Soviet predominance that had to be counterbalanced.

However, from a military-strategic standpoint, substantiating the need for a modernization response in terms of the existing imbalance of forces in Europe was questionable for a number of reasons. One essential difficulty in comparing Eurostrategic forces lay in differentiating these systems from intercontinental strategic weapons on the one hand and from battlefield weapons on the other. Particularly controversial was how to count sea-based Poseidon missiles or the FB-111 aircraft stationed in the United States but assigned to SACEUR, the British and French nuclear weapons, and battlefield weapons with ranges under 100 kilometers.[148] A numerical correlation obscured qualitative criteria such as survival probability in case of conflict, capability to penetrate enemy defenses, and operational flexibility. Any comparisons fell short mainly because they did not take into account the military-strategic and political functions, but rather started from the unrealistic assumption of a "Eurostrategic" nuclear war. The political argument that NATO's LRTNF was a "response" to the Soviet deployment of the SS-20 was interpreted to mean that the nuclear weapons of NATO should cover these Soviet missiles in the event of conflict. Since they were neither suited nor requisite for this, it was then concluded that the whole NATO modernization was superfluous.

From a European point of view, the deployment of long-range theatre nuclear weapons in Western Europe could be really justified only in political terms.[149] It established a military link between the strategic nuclear potential of the United States and the land forces present in Europe, which in turn raised the credibility of the threat of escalation in the event the Warsaw Pact launched an attack with massive conventional forces. This effect would be achieved above all as a result of the fact that the Pershing II missiles could reach the territory of the Soviet Union within a few minutes and strike military targets with minimal prewarning time and great accuracy.

However, the "coupling" worked both ways, namely as a partnership in risk. While the United States was strategically bound to Europe under the threat of "counterdeterrence," the "hostage role" of Europe was reinforced in the case of a military conflict. This meant that neither could the Warsaw Pact launch a remotely promising conventional attack on Europe without having to reckon with a nuclear counterstrike, nor could the West Europeans be certain that beyond a certain threshold in an escalating conflict in other regions they were not running the same risk of a nuclear attack as the American people.[150]

Yet this very "partnership in risk" presupposed that Europeans and the United States viewed the political and military functions of LRTNF in similar terms. This, however, was not the case. In European eyes these forces were primarily a political link between the strategic potential of the United States and the alliance's forces deployed in Europe and were designed above all to act as a deterrent. A regionally limited nuclear war-fighting option was not acceptable to Western Europe. However, the strategic planning of the United States (principally the Single Integrated Operations Plan—SIOP) was based on the assumption that deterrence would be effective only if in the event of conflict an attacker were denied the attainment of his military ends by the use of all appropriate weapons systems. From this standpoint, the capability to wage a regionally limited nuclear conflict with a broad spectrum of nuclear weapons of various ranges appeared essential. This difference in defining the military purposes of tactical nuclear weapons raised a number of political problems in the European-Atlantic relationship.

Above all there was the question of whether the deployment of Pershing IIs on the soil of the Federal Republic was militarily sensible *and* politically expedient. Because of its short flight time and high accuracy the Pershing was especially threatening to the Soviet Union and invited a preemptive strike. The Pershing IIs had a destabilizing effect and constituted an additional risk for Western Europe without their being able to perform properly the task of escalation control for which they were intended. From a European standpoint, therefore, it would have been preferable to deploy them at sea. But given their political function, visibility was important. Moreover, it was in the European interest to negotiate a reduction of the nuclear battlefield weapons deployed in Europe, which by definition made a regional limited war wageable or at least conceivable. A prerequisite, of course, was that conventional forces were strengthened, as the credibility of deterrence had to remain intact.

At the same time the NATO dual-track decision contained elements of Atlantic burden sharing. Besides the military risk, the allies also shared the political costs entailed in stationing new weapons systems. This was especially true for those countries, such as the Federal Republic, that were to receive these weapons. In the debate on the deployment of Eurostrategic weapons the German government underscored the principle of "non-singularity," i.e., that it could not become the "aircraft carrier of the alliance" (Herbert Wehner). Besides the Federal Republic, other West European countries would also have to accept such weapons. Moreover, they ought to be introduced solely with units of the U.S. Army and not with the Bundeswehr under a dual-key system. The authority to decide on their use would have to reside exclusively with the United States. These conditions represented a modification of the nuclear cooperation practiced within the alliance since the 1960s. Thus, following a release authorization by the U.S. president the decision on use was to be made jointly by the allies according to NATO guidelines and operational planning.

By declining to accept Pershing IIs and GLCMs for deployment by the Bundeswehr the German government was retreating from one of the most visible elements of its nuclear collaboration in the alliance, without, however, completely giving up its desire for a say in nuclear affairs. There were two reasons for this: first, Bonn had become the prime target of the Soviet Union's campaign against the NATO modernization decision and feared a serious deterioration of German-Soviet relations if it assumed too prominent a nuclear role; secondly, the controversy over the neutron warhead had created a highly sensitized public, which circumscribed the political actions, mainly of the SPD.

Partly from political conviction, partly with an eye to the opponents of the modernization decision in the ranks of the coalition parties, the German government emphasized that the NATO dual-track decision consisted of two parts: an intention to deploy and an offer to negotiate. From Bonn's point of view it was important both to begin talks on the theater nuclear weapons in Europe and to give new impetus to the stagnating MBFR negotiations in Vienna. In the debate on the NATO decision it argued that if the Soviet Union removed its SS-20s, then a subsequent NATO deployment would become superfluous. When as a result of deteriorating East-West relations and internal U.S. developments Washington grew more reticent about entering into new arms control talks with the Soviet Union, the German government used the two elements of the NATO decision to bind its implementation to Washington's readiness to negotiate in earnest with Moscow on a reduction of Eurostrategic weapons.

Only the inflexibility of the Soviet leadership spared the West from Moscow's exploiting the ambiguity of Bonn's position and forcing the Federal Republic to show its true colors. The weakness of the German policy lay in the facts, first, that the main reasons for the NATO decision were not simply the disparities in nuclear weapons deployed in Europe and that the establishment of a numerical equilibrium as a result of arms control negotiations would not have made deterrence more credible, and secondly, that Bonn did not sit at the bargaining table and so could not decisively influence either the basic negotiating positions or the results of the talks. The German government could only articulate its interests in bilateral contacts with the U.S. government and via the appropriate NATO bodies (in particular, the Special Consultative Group established for this purpose). This reduced Bonn's emphasis on the arms control components of the NATO decision to a tactical instrument.

The domestic opposition to the dual-track decision had first been articulated within the SPD, though the critics were by no means recruited solely from the governing party's left wing and the Young Socialists. One of the first was the head of the SPD parliamentary group in the Bundestag, Herbert Wehner, who expressed his concern that the introduction of long-range theater nuclear weapons could jeopardize the continuance of detente policy. At the SPD party congress in Berlin in early December 1979 the dominant issue was whether detente would be endangered by the projected NATO decision or whether the military balance would first have to be restored before the West could arrive at arms control agreements and successfully continue its detente efforts. However, the SPD congress approved by a large majority a motion presented by the party leadership in which the NATO dual-track decision was seen as an instrument of detente policy.[151]

For the CDU/CSU, on the other hand, the dual-track decision signified the belated acknowledgement of a deteriorating military balance of power in Europe. The parties emphatically supported both parts, though they attached greater importance to the modernization part than to that of negotiation.

The vehemence of the domestic political debate on the NATO decision in the Federal Republic and the emphasis on its arms control aspects by leading SPD politicians activated among some of the allies latent doubts about Bonn's loyalty to the alliance.[152] In Washington, President Carter's national security adviser, Zbigniew Brzezinski, started circulating the nasty term of "self-finlandization" of the Federal Republic; in Paris, rumors were aired about a new "Rapallo," and in other Western capitals the question was raised whether Bonn's detente policy had not put the Federal Republic into an alliance-burdening dependence on the Soviet Union. In all of this it was often overlooked that the Federal Republic was making as great a contribution as ever to the common defense of the West. Its annual defense expenditures from 1970 to 1981—that is, in the detente era!—had more than doubled, rising from 22.6 billion DM to 52.2 billion DM. With an authorized strength of 495,000 men the Bundeswehr constituted the largest conventional army on the continent. Bonn also rendered NATO defense assistance to Turkey, Greece, and Portugal and participated in the infrastructure program of the alliance. The Host Nation Support Program, concluded with the United States and signed in 1982, represented the logistical basis for U.S. troop reinforcements in an emergency and relieved the U.S. taxpayer. Hence, it was absurd to speak of a rising tide of pacifism in the Federal Republic. However, because of its political situation at the dividing line of Europe, the Federal Republic did have a legitimate interest in preserving and not carelessly jeopardizing the results of detente policy.

Afghanistan and its Consequences for East-West Relations

The simultaneity of the Western deployment decision and the Eastern display of power in Afghanistan at the turn from 1979 to 1980 triggered a multifaceted development that was expressed in the form of criticism of the NATO dual-track decision, yet had its origins in the deterioration of East-West relations as well as the resulting fear of a military conflict, and that subsequently threw into question the political unity of security and detente that had been upheld since the Harmel Report.

Since the end of the 1960s, the foreign policy of the Federal Republic had rested on the premise that its security would be best ensured by a combination of defense capability within the Western alliance and willingness to negotiate with the Soviet Union and the other states of the Warsaw Pact. The success of Ostpolitik, which had yielded an extensive normalization of East-West relations in Europe, took away the aggressive character from Eastern military power in the public mind. As the fear of German revanchism and militarism was receding among the Eastern neighbors, so, too, was the feeling of being threatened diminishing within the Federal Republic. The argument of the Social-Liberal coalition that its detente policy had made peace in Europe more secure tallied with the Soviet assertion that the detente process was irreversible. As a result, the deterioration of East-West relations at the global level, which set in after the Yom Kippur War and the first oil crisis in the mid-1970s and which was aggravated by the breakdown of closer East-West economic cooperation,[153] was perceived only dimly or not at all in the Federal Republic.

Since in Europe the policy of conciliation and cooperation was continued, there seemed to be no question about the strength and viability of detente policy. Critical questions along those lines from the opposition could be chalked up to an "obstinate refusal to learn in matters of Ostpolitik." Until the shock of the Soviet intervention in Afghanistan in December 1979, the detente process in Europe seemed unquestioned. Then, prominent Social-Liberal politicians at first refused to accept any negative impact of the events in the distant Hindu Kush on European detente policy. In light of the virtually unanimous condemnation of the Soviet Union in the United Nations and by the non-aligned states, they interpreted these events as an East-South conflict.[154]

For the United States such an assessment was not possible. Confronted with the dual crisis of Afghanistan and Iran, where Iranian revolutionary militia had held members of the U.S. embassy in Tehran hostage since November 1979, the United States insisted on punishment of Moscow and demanded alliance solidarity. In view of the strong language coming out of Washington, many people in the Federal Republic got the impression that peace was threatened by both superpowers. Such sentiments were promoted by Chancellor Helmut Schmidt when he conjured up the danger of a new world crisis à la 1914. He told a campaign rally in Essen, "We cannot afford gestures of strength and pithy signs of staunchness. We have had it with that."[155] This was an expression of a widespread feeling among Germans. But despite its different assessment of the crisis, Bonn attempted, by finely measured acts of alliance solidarity (Olympic boycott, increases in defense expenditures, support for Turkey) not to do any irreparable damage to U.S.-German relations. It also took pains not to sever its ties with Moscow and rather to repair the broken channels of communication between East and West. This was the purpose served by Chancellor Schmidt's visits to Washington in March 1980 and to Moscow in June of that same year.[156]

At the same time, and surely not uninfluenced by the moods of the politicians, the fear of an international crisis prevalent in the West German public (and, intensified by the closeness of the city, among West Berliners) began to turn into an uneasiness with the alliance. This was expressed first within the SPD, still in concert pitch at an SPD's expert conference on security policy in April 1980 in Cologne, then in violent demonstrations at a ceremonial swearing in of recruits in the Bremen Weser Stadium commemorating the Bundeswehr's 25th anniversary. Such manifestations of brutal force against the Bundeswehr and representatives of the alliance were, of course, the exception in an increasingly critical debate within the Federal Republic on the role of military power in society. Yet they clearly showed the susceptibility of the Bundeswehr and its integration into society—an integration, in fact, vigorously promoted by the SPD—as points of attack for a radical opposition under the banner of anti-militarism.

The fear of a nuclear accident or military conflict and the discontent with a society oriented to unrestrained economic growth combined in many young people to produce a diffuse feeling of existential anxiety. This was articulated at church gatherings (characteristic was the "Fear Not" motto of the Hamburg church meeting of June 1981) and in large demonstrations for disarmament and detente in Europe (e.g., more than 250,000 participants in Bonn on October 10, 1981). The strength of this movement consisted in the common commitment to peace, conveyed in a highly ethical frame of mind bringing together Christian groups from both churches, humanistic pacifists and ecologists, undogmatic socialists and communists; its weakness was, first, the heterogeneity of its impulses and goals, secondly the remoteness from policy of its concepts, which in rejecting the NATO dual-track decision or promoting nuclear-weapons-free zones were taken from the grab bag of history.[157]

A final consequence of this crisis, which had so roughly shaken the people of the Federal Republic out of their detente euphoria, was a sense of equidistance from both great powers. Many observers wrongly interpreted this an anti-Americanism. At first the dominant concern was that relations with Moscow could be irreparably damaged and the Federal Republic possibly drawn into a military conflict if it were to go along with the policy of boycotting the Soviet Union. Concern was also expressed over the heightened display of military power by the United States, notably in the crisis areas of Southwest Asia. This engendered the question of whether the political, economic, and military interests of the Federal Republic were well looked after in the close connection with the United States or whether Bonn would not have to strive for a greater measure of political independence.

The criticism of the United States intensified following the inauguration of the Reagan administration in January 1981. The language with which the new leadership promised to return the United States to power and greatness after the humiliations of the Vietnam War and the hostage crisis in Iran and its newly initiated containment strategy vis-à-vis the Soviet Union prompted memories of the cold war; rejecting these was an attempt to maintain a limited cooperation with Moscow at the European level just as it was an act of repressing contemplation of the dangers emanating from the Soviet display of power.

The domestic political discussion of Ostpolitik and German policy had contributed to a situation in which warnings from opposition politicians about the "global aims of the Soviet Union, which rest upon an insatiable demand for security and a claim to revolutionary world leadership and which [threaten] the entire West"[158] went unheard. After the Soviet invasion of Afghanistan the CDU/CSU could see its position confirmed. To their credit the Union parties did not use the crisis in East-West relations to strike self-serving postures of "we knew all along," but rather loyally participated in the efforts to limit the damage. However, the crisis did give them the opportunity to project themselves as "party of the U.S.," i.e., as a political force which, from a similar view of the world situation, stood for a trustful partnership with the United States and for a strengthening of the "community of values" of the Western alliance. Despite doubts articulated by some of the political elite, this close connection with the Western democracies, particularly with the United States, was supported by the majority of the population. Opinion polls showed that all through the debate on the dual-track decision, German membership in NATO and even the NATO decision itself continued to be supported by a majority. The criticism was pointed at the TNF deployment, and increased as the date of their stationing approached—and abated again after the first missiles were in place. This gives the impression of a great lability—or emotionality and suggestibility—of the climate of opinion in the Federal Republic.[159]

Criticism of the NATO Dual-Track Decision

The West German debate on the NATO dual-track decision and its implementation must be seen against the background of deteriorating East-West relations and widespread domestic anxiety over the international crises. This debate had three lines of thrust in the Federal Republic:

1. A fundamental criticism as put forward by adherents of the peace movement, who argued for reversing the NATO decision and instead intensifying efforts on behalf of disarmament and arms limitation;
2. A security policy critique that did not fundamentally call into question the East-West deterrence system but rather, for a combination of military-strategic and political reasons, called for renouncing the deployment of land-based Eurostrategic systems;
3. An inherent criticism that upheld the dual-track decision as such, yet wanted to see the negotiating aspect emphasized.

Loudest and often the least based on factual knowledge was the criticism from the camp of the peace movement. The common point of departure for all groups was the thesis that deterrence and peace were mutually incompatible. The security of the Federal Republic could not be ensured by the introduction of new nuclear weapons, rather these would create new insecurities and ultimately endanger human survival in Central Europe. For these reasons the NATO modernization decision had to be prevented—some felt by means of better argumentation

(Weizsäcker), others by agitation and protest (Jo Leinen). On this common basis there were then essentially three lines of argument, though with a number of positions in between. One argued in primarily moral-pacifistic terms and called for a radical rethinking on questions of security, which could be guaranteed not by military deterrence but only through trust and political stability (Eppler). A second direction regarded a thwarting of the NATO modernization as a step toward a new European structure that would bring about a disengagement of the nuclear great powers via the establishment of nuclear-weapons-free zones (Bahro, Berlin's Alternative List). The third line argued more in strategic terms and disputed the military necessity for a modernization. It maintained that when all FBS systems were taken into account (that is, including those deployed at sea), there existed a balance of forces between NATO and Warsaw Pact. The deployment of Eurostrategic systems by NATO would, then, introduce into this region qualitatively new systems whose ability to reach Soviet territory was destabilizing. But the focus of this criticism was the fact that these systems would give the United States a war-fighting option, namely for a limited nuclear war in Europe that would result in devastating destruction while the United States itself ran no comparable risk (Mechtersheimer, Bastian, Lutz).[160]

The security policy critique of the NATO decision pursued very diverse aims depending on the political perspectives and motives of the authors. Common to all of them was that they did not expect the deployment of land-based long-range theatre nuclear weapons to make any contribution to the security of the alliance, yet were convinced that the deterrence system in the short term could not be fully replaced by cooperative structures or rendered superfluous by disarmament. The most far-reaching proposal came from four prominent U.S. political figures—McGeorge Bundy, George Kennan, Robert McNamara, and Gerard Smith—who called for a position of no first use of nuclear weapons. Their primary object was making deterrence militarily and politically credible. To that end the alliance, in their view, needed only adequate survivable and diversified second-strike forces in the nuclear domain as well as a conventional potential in Europe equal to that of the Soviet Union. Such a policy could help obviate a number of the alliance's current difficulties, not least of a financial nature. It might also clear the way for a serious reduction in nuclear weapons on both sides.[161] The European criticism of this proposal focused mainly on the fact that a policy of no first use of nuclear weapons ran counter to the NATO strategy of war prevention. The connection with the nuclear deterrence potential of the United States would be weakened and thus a conventional war in Europe again made wageable.

The proposal of the American "gang of four" found some convergence with considerations raised by the SPD's disarmament policy spokesman, Egon Bahr, in light of the Palme Commission Report on "Common Security," which Bahr coauthored. To defuse the nuclear confrontation in Europe, above all to eliminate the risk of a war limited to Europe, Bahr called for the withdrawal of all atomic weapons from those states in Europe that did not have command over them. The four nuclear-weapons states would continue to have atomic weapons at their disposal, nuclear deterrence would remain intact, and thus the danger of a conflict's escalating would remain unchanged. However, an approximate balance of conventional forces between NATO and Warsaw Pact would have to be established; and the alliance, with its obligations and guarantees, had to be maintained.[162] In addition, Bahr adopted the Palme Commission's proposal that a 150-kilometer wide nuclear-weapons-free zone be created on both sides of the iron curtain. This meant, however, that the NATO dual-track decision could be used at most as a catalyst for negotiations, but the negotiations would have to aim at a "zero option," the total elimination of all nuclear weapons in Central Europe, while the medium-range weapons of the Soviet Union (likewise the French, British, and U.S. sea-based systems) would be left untouched.

While its proponents justified the NATO decision on the ground of the parity reached at the strategic level between the world powers and the continued existence of regional disparities, the peace researcher, philosopher, and physicist Carl Friedrich von Weizsäcker questioned the underlying political structures. He diagnosed a "destabilization of the nuclear truce" as a consequence of global political instabilities, in particular the inability of the world powers to solve their own problems and, at the military level, the development of nuclear weapons for limited employment. As a result, the potential for international conflicts and the danger of a limited war in Europe had grown. The introduction of land-based long-range nuclear weapons in Europe would further increase the probability of their use and the attendant risks. Therefore, Weizsäcker called for greater efforts to achieve a mutual, balanced, and controlled disarmament. To preserve a regional balance he considered it justifiable to strengthen non-nuclear means of defense and deploy sea-based medium-range nuclear weapons.[163] However, against the idea of stationing LRTNF at sea, proponents of the NATO decision insisted that only a land deployment provided the political coupling and increased military deterrence capability.[164]

A third line of discussion argued on the basis of the dual-track decision but called for giving political priority to the arms control portion in implementing it. This would be logically consistent insofar as the NATO decision made the scope of the deployment of U.S.

intermediate-range missiles on the territory of European states dependent on the results of negotiation. The aim of negotiations would therefore have to be a complete abandonment of deployment—the so-called "zero option." The dual-track decision ought to be used primarily as a political instrument for reaching the necessary agreements not only to curb the arms race, but in the long term to create the basis for a joint "security partnership" between East and West.[165] The question emerges, however, whether the concept of "security partnership," used especially by Egon Bahr and Karsten Voigt, adequately characterized the inherent dangers of the arms race for East and West or the resulting community of interest in avoiding a military conflict. Beyond the basic goal of war prevention was there agreement between East and West on ways and means? Further, were both sides interested in the same way in implementing common security?

The German government assumed that the modernization part of the NATO decision would stand. In view of the complexity of negotiations and the widely divergent negotiating positions of the two world powers, the prospects were slight that there would be concrete results before the stationing would begin. Hence, a number of SPD politicians called for a moratorium on further deployment until the negotiations had made more headway. They also wanted to reactivate detente policy. Particular weight was to be given to nonmilitary steps, with greater efforts to initiate confidence-building measures throughout Europe and expand economic cooperation with the East European states. (In this regard, criticism was frequently leveled at the way the Foreign Office pursued an arms limitation policy that had nonpartisan and alliance-oriented aims but unimaginative results.) Under tremendous pressure from within the party, the SPD decided at its party congress in Munich in April 1982 to reserve a final decision on LRTNF deployment until the fall of 1983.[166]

The opposition to the dual-track decision on the part of the party rank-and-file weakened the credibility of the government's statements that it continued to stand by both parts of the NATO decision. Yet Bonn was able to point to its domestic political problems in more emphatically pressing Washington to resume serious negotiations with the Soviet Union. Since Chancellor Schmidt had bound his political future to the NATO decision, it might have been expected that he would prevail upon the party rank-and-file and at the end of 1983 the SPD would have agreed—most reluctantly, to be sure—to implement the decision. Moreover, as a result of the strong domestic criticism the Federal Republic had gotten into a situation where adherence to the NATO deployment decision had become the acid test of its alliance reliability.

When the SPD was relieved of government responsibility in the fall of 1982, the criticism voiced by broad sectors of the party did not actually become irrelevant, but it did lose its crucial importance for the Federal Republic's course of security policy. In its government statement the new CDU/CSU-FDP coalition was already stressing that it unreservedly stood by the NATO decision of 1979 and would carry it out: the negotiation track and—if necessary—the modernization track.[167] The accent of the negotiations on intermediate-range nuclear missiles was pared down again to "normal," i.e., to a parallelism of deployment and negotiations. Still, the German government continued on the assumption that Washington was serious in bringing about a positive negotiated outcome.

In the end the critical debate on the NATO decision generated an intensive discussion of security policy in the Federal Republic and Western Europe ranging from the question of the role of military force in international policy to reflection on the prevailing military strategy of NATO and the strength and viability of various arms control concepts.[168] This was paralleled by a similar discussion in the United States. Here the debate had two lines of thrust: first, it was a discussion among experts in search of new concepts for a credible deterrence in the face of growing U.S. vulnerability; secondly, at the beginning of the 1980s there had emerged in different parts of the country an antinuclear-weapons movement in which groups with various world views and political positions had come together to demand a stop of the arms race and above all a freeze on nuclear weapons arsenals. In the 1982 congressional elections the call for a "nuclear freeze" won a majority in eight of nine states in which such initiatives were on the ballot. Along with the pressure from the allies, this mood in the U.S. public contributed to revealing to the administration in Washington the importance of resuming the arms control dialogue with Moscow.

U.S.-Soviet Negotiations on Eurostrategic and Global Strategic Nuclear Weapons Systems (INF and START)

The way back to the negotiating table in Geneva proved to be more difficult than had been foreseen and slower than wished by the German government, which domestically had pinned its security policy to the negotiations. According to its original planning, after the U.S. Congress had ratified the SALT II Treaty and the alliance had adopted the dual-track decision the United States would begin preparations for SALT III and incorporate the issue of long-range tactical nuclear weapons into them. To involve the allies NATO had appointed a Special Consultative Group (the old Special Group that had been preparing the NATO decision with the HLG since 1979). The SCG took up its work in January 1980 and subsequently developed general negotiating principles for talks on "Intermediate Nuclear Forces"—INF.

In the fall of 1979 the Soviet Union had tried to entice the alliance with its willingness to reduce its intermediate-range missiles if in exchange NATO would give up its modernization decision; now, after the NATO decisions and the suspension of the SALT II ratification process in Congress, Moscow declared that henceforth the basis for such negotiations had ceased to exist. It demanded that first the NATO decision would have to be suspended and clarity established as to the fate of SALT II. However, during Chancellor Schmidt's visit to Moscow in late June 1980 Moscow did indicate its willingness to enter into bilateral talks with the U.S. on limiting intermediate-range nuclear missiles even before ratification of SALT II. These talks, however, would have to cover all systems in and for Europe. In a speech in Alma Ata in late August 1980 Brezhnev finally came out in favor of an "immediate" initiation of negotiations. Then, at the margins of the UN General Assembly, the foreign ministers of the Soviet Union and the United States agreed to open talks in Geneva in mid-October on limiting intermediate-range weapons stationed in Europe. An initial round of talks took place in Geneva from October 17 to November 17, 1980; these, however, did not get beyond the preliminaries, as the upcoming change in administration in the United States did not allow for meaningful negotiations.

In the Federal Republic and other West European countries one saw with consternation that the new Reagan administration was taking its time in formulating its own negotiating approach for the Eurostrategic systems, while both the preparations for the LRTNF deployment and the emplacement of new SS-20s in the Soviet Union were proceeding apace. Several times General Secretary Brezhnev proposed a moratorium for the duration of the talks, but the West rejected this, arguing that it would mean only slight interference with Soviet planning but would prevent NATO from carrying out its decision on schedule. At the same time, Moscow stressed its willingness to continue the negotiations. The West, at a meeting of the NATO Council of Ministers in Rome in May 1981, reaffirmed its adherence to both parts of the NATO decision and projected the start of negotiations on LRTNF before the end of 1981.[169]

In a speech before the National Press Club in Washington on November 18, 1981, President Reagan announced that he had written General Secretary Brezhnev a letter proposing that negotiations on limiting intermediate-range nuclear systems be initiated in Geneva on

November 30. As a first step, the United States was prepared not to deploy Pershing IIs and ground-launched cruise missiles if the Soviet Union would in turn dismantle its SS-20, SS-4, and SS-5 missiles. Thus, the U.S. government raised to its official negotiating goal the "zero option" advocated by the allies and the German government in particular. Yet it was unclear whether this was done for material reasons or whether it was designed to bolster a course of negotiation that made an agreement dependent upon drastic Soviet concessions. At the same time President Reagan announced that as soon as possible, but in any case in 1982, negotiations on strategic weapons systems would be resumed. The goal of the United States in these "Strategic Arms Reduction Talks" (START) would be to achieve a substantial reduction in strategic weapons systems.[170]

On November 30, 1981, in Geneva, the U.S. negotiator, Paul Nitze, and the Soviet delegation chief, Yuli Kvitsinsky, initiated the negotiations on intermediate-range nuclear weapons (INF). The main contours of the U.S. negotiating position had been worked out in the alliance (in the SCG) and were geared to the "zero option" mentioned by President Reagan in his speech of November 18. With its draft treaty presented on February 2, 1982, the United States wanted to achieve first a greater strategic stability and secondly a reduction in the threat to Western Europe by establishing a stable balance between East and West at the lowest possible force level. Based on the principles of equal ceilings (parity), inclusion of comparable systems (reciprocity), and a step-by-step yet comprehensive approach to negotiation, the U.S. proposed the complete dismantling (i.e., destruction) of all long-range nuclear weapons in Europe (Pershing II, GLCM, SS-20, SS-4, and SS-5) as well as a mutual ban on testing, production, and deployment of land-based missiles with ranges of 1,800-5,500 kilometers, along with appropriate non-circumvention clauses.

The Soviet Union presented on February 2, 1982 the draft of a joint statement of intent in which the reduction and ultimately the ban on all types of nuclear weapons in Europe was called for. On the same day in Moscow, General Secretary Brezhnev proposed, as a first step, extensive reductions, e.g., a reduction of intermediate-range weapons by one third on both sides, if it were not possible to come to terms right away on banning all nuclear weapons. He repeated his suggestion of a moratorium but broadened it to the effect that the Soviet Union could unilaterally withdraw a number of the SS-20s stationed in its Western region. Although both sides had agreed upon strict confidentiality, the official Soviet news agency TASS published further details of the Soviet negotiating position:

- mutual reduction of nuclear weapons with ranges over 1,000 kilometers to 600 systems by 1985 and to 300 systems by 1990;
- reduction of weapons by destroying them or withdrawing them behind commonly agreed lines of demarcation;
- no deployment of new weapons during the negotiations and a willingness to impose a qualitative and quantitative freeze on weapons already deployed. In anticipation of a subsequent negotiated solution, the Soviet Union was prepared to eliminate part of its SS-20 missiles in its European area.

At the beginning of the second round of negotiations on May 25, 1982, the Soviet Union again presented a draft treaty.[171]

To the German government it was first of all a welcome development that the dialogue on arms control had again been set in motion. This was important with respect to the internal opposition within the SPD and with a view to the peace movement, yet it was also the only way to keep intact the basic concept of security policy, founded on the correlation of defense readiness and will to negotiate. In view of the prevailing tendency with the Reagan administration to see one's own—superior—military potentials as the prime guarantor of security, Washington's turn to a course of negotiation was regarded in Bonn as a definite success for German diplomatic efforts. The Bonn government also noted with satisfaction that the Western negotiating concept took German interests into full account, though details of the Western draft treaty had not been worked out beforehand in the alliance. The following points were emphasized in the Western negotiating proposal:

- a mutual "zero-zero option" was sought for intermediate-range nuclear missiles;
- other systems were excluded initially but could be limited at a later stage;
- the geographical scope was defined broadly, in accordance with the range, mobility, and strategic significance of the systems negotiated;
- the counting unit was warheads, not launchers;
- associated measures (e.g., a freeze on the present state of nuclear missiles of lesser ranges) were to ensure that agreements could not be underrun.[172]

In assessing the progress of the negotiations, the German government's officially displayed optimism contrasted with the skepticism, if not downright pessimism, expressed by the U.S. negotiating delegation. However, in Bonn no one was disregarding the immense difficulties impeding an agreement. The two sides had entered into the talks with very different objectives: for the United States they marked an attempt to eliminate or reduce the Soviet SS-20 missiles that so disturbed the Europeans; they also took account of the need for a continuity of the negotiating dialogue with the Soviet Union. Moscow, on the other hand, wanted above all to prevent the deployment of U.S. long-range nuclear weapons in Europe, weapons that not only could reach Soviet territory but would also reinforce the strategic connection between the United States and Western Europe. This, then, gave rise to different negotiating strategies, concepts, and timetables. While the Eastern side demanded inclusion of all European systems, thus counting the British and French nuclear forces as well as all U.S. nuclear-capable aircraft stationed in Western Europe or on aircraft carriers, the Western side wanted first to negotiate only on those systems to which the modernization decision referred, and then include others, e.g., aircraft, in a later phase. As to geographic scope, the United States took the view that limitations would have to be worldwide with special deployment limitations for Europe, whereas the Soviet Union wanted to negotiate only on the systems deployed in Europe and its adjacent maritime areas, thus, e.g., to leave the SS-20s stationed in the central and Asiatic part of the Soviet Union out of consideration. Finally, both sides started from different assessments of force relations in intermediate-range nuclear weapons: Moscow maintained that there existed an approximate balance, as its count included both British and French systems and the FB-111 aircraft stationed in the United States but assigned to SACEUR, while Washington proceeded on the basis of a substantial Soviet lead in Eurostrategic weapons. This advantage appeared even larger when warheads were counted, whereas Moscow based its calculations on delivery systems as the counting unit.

The differences in the negotiating positions underscored the fact that each side was intent on maximizing its own strategic advantage. The doubts about the readiness of the United States and the Soviet Union to work toward a compromise grew even more when it became known that in July 1982 Nitze and Kvitsinsky had arrived at an interim solution according to which the United States would give up deployment of Pershing IIs and station a considerably smaller number of GLCMs, and in return Moscow would reduce its European intermediate-range missiles to 50-100 systems; yet this proposed compromise was rejected by both governments without closer examination. (In the United States, the dismissal of the head of the Arms Control and Disarmament Agency, Eugene V. Rostow, was even justified by hinting that he had exceeded his authority.)[173]

At first it was unclear how a limitation in intermediate-range systems would relate to limitations in strategic weapons. This difficulty was cleared away when President Reagan, in a speech in Eureka, Ill., on May 9, 1982, announced the opening of START negotiations for the end of June. In the following weeks the U.S. government communi-

cated further details on its negotiating concept. The most important differences from the SALT II treaties was that the United States now sought significant reductions that would establish agreed ceilings at least one-third below the present levels. Limitations and reductions would be effected primarily in land-based intercontinental missiles according to the number of warheads, but also by systems and throw weights, which Washington regarded as a particular danger not only for its own ICBM potential, but for the stability of strategic deterrence as well. The Soviet response to the U.S. initiative was not hostile; Moscow welcomed the drastic reductions proposed by President Reagan as a step in the right direction. It did, however, criticize the selection of systems for reduction and accused the United States of striving primarily for its own advantage. In the Soviet view both sides should adhere to the principles of equality and equal security as well as preserve the positive results achieved in previous negotiations. As it had done with the INF talks, Moscow also proposed a quantitative and qualitative moratorium in the realm of strategic weapons. Then on June 29, 1982, the START negotiations were opened in Geneva.[174]

Concurrently, on July 8, 1982, the West presented new proposals for the MBFR talks in Vienna. With that, the East-West dialogue begun in the 1970s on arms control and disarmament had been resumed at all three levels—the conventional, the tactical-nuclear, and the strategic. Although the objects of negotiation had remained the same and the negotiating concepts, as well as the problems, were comparable, still it could not be ignored that the fundamental objectives of the negotiations had changed. Conditioned in part by domestic politics, in part by alliance considerations, the various Western proposals had been reduced to concepts of damage limitation and diplomatic poker; they could scarcely be valued any longer as instruments of a policy that regarded negotiations with the other side as an indispensable element of one's own security. The fabric of security policy woven in the Harmel Report had worn thin.

4

Renunciation of Force as an Instrument of Ostpolitik

RENUNCIATION OF FORCE AND THE GERMAN QUESTION

In the 1950s there had emerged in Europe a situation in which the strategic stalemate between the United States and the Soviet Union had made it impossible to solve the political problems of the continent through the use of military power. The threat of force had also grown considerably less credible. Paradoxically, the concerted used of renunciation of force in pursuit of diverse political goals was becoming increasingly important.[1] The aim of such a policy was not, at least not primarily, to preclude the use of threat of military force by mutual agreement or common appeal to existing legal norms such as Article 2 of the United Nations Charter. Rather, concretizing renunciation of force by applying it to a specific dispute or a particular relationship between states, often in a formal commitment to nonaggression, served to bring about a qualitative change in intergovernmental relations and to establish a modus vivendi with regard to specific conflicts.

For the Federal Republic of Germany, renunciation of force was first and foremost an instrument of its German policy. In the Paris Treaties the Federal Republic had declared that it would conduct its policy in accordance with the principles of the United Nations Charter, in particular Article 2, and resolve its disputes by peaceful means, without recourse to force or the threat of force. Specifically, it committed itself "never to have recourse to force to achieve the reunification of Germany or the modification of the present boundaries of the Federal Republic."[2] In return, the three Western powers pledged their support for the Federal Republic's German policy and committed themselves to renunciation of force in their relations with the Federal

Republic. They declared that "the achievement. . .of a fully free unified Germany" and "a freely negotiated. . .peace settlement for the whole of Germany" remained the fundamental goals of their policy.[3] Final determination of Germany's boundaries would have to be postponed until a peace treaty had been concluded. In addition, the Western powers committed themselves to defending the security and well-being of Berlin.

In order to win concessions on the German question, the Adenauer government subsequently attempted to concretize renunciation of force toward the East as well. In a September 1956 memorandum on reunification Bonn offered the Soviet Union and "other eastern neighbors" a renunciation-of-force agreement.[4] The Eden Plan and, four years later, the Herter Plan provided for a renunciation of the use of force and a commitment to peaceful settlement of conflicts.[5] Underlying these proposals was the idea that a reunification of Germany would be more acceptable to the states of Europe if, besides military restrictions, Germany were committed to a policy strictly abjuring the use or threat of force. This, of course, overlooked the fact that the fundamental problem of Europe was not the modalities of German reunification, but the power-political competition of the Soviet Union and the United States. The resulting conflict of interests between the great powers did not allow for a political modus vivendi in the 1950s. For fear of possible stabilizing consequences, the West European allies rejected a renunciation-of-force policy or a nonaggression pact with the East, as proposed on several occasions by the Soviet Union. In view of the Federal Republic's unsatisfied demand for reunification and a new European order defined by a peace treaty, such a pact at that time might have reduced tensions in Europe.

During the Berlin negotiations in the late 1950s and early 1960s, the Western powers urged the German government to go beyond its renunciation-of-force position of 1954. To avoid a formal recognition of the Oder-Neisse line and the invalidity of the Munich Agreement, Bonn considered proposing to Poland and Czechoslovakia, possibly also to Hungary, Rumania, and Bulgaria, an agreement on renunciation of force and the establishment of diplomatic relations. Foreign Minister von Brentano made a proposal along these lines in the Western four-power working group during the preparatory talks for the Geneva Summit Conference. Still, Bonn continued to maintain that a final determination of borders could be made only in a peace treaty with a reunited Germany.[6]

However, this policy foundered on external political conditions and domestic political opposition. The Geneva conference did not take the desired course. Instead of focusing on the German problem, the foreign ministers talks concentrated more and more on maintaining the status quo in West Berlin and finally broke off without results. In the Federal Republic the League of Expellees raised loud objections to any treaty connection with Poland and Czechoslovakia, which it viewed as a recognition of the Oder-Neisse line as a final boundary. This development prompted the German government to shelve for the time being the idea of exchanging contractual declarations abdicating the use of force.[7]

Yet, in conjunction with the U.S.-Soviet probing toward a Berlin settlement in the fall of 1961 and spring of 1962, the German government once again considered a possible exchange of renunciation-of-force or nonaggression statements between NATO and the Warsaw Pact, coupled with a Berlin arrangement. Here it became very clear that the Soviet Union regarded Berlin as a lever for gaining recognition of the postwar realities in Europe. Thus, a nonaggression pact, which the Soviets conceived of as being accompanied by arms control measures such as a reduction of foreign troops and a nuclear-weapons-free zone in Central Europe, would serve as an ersatz peace treaty with Germany. The United States, however, had in mind primarily the safeguarding of Berlin. In its counterproposals, which provided for confirmation of four-power rights with regard to Germany and Berlin and establishment of an international authority for the access routes to Berlin, the United States indicated its willingness to accept an exchange on nonaggression statements between NATO and the Warsaw Pact. These declarations were to relate to all lines of demarcation in Europe, thus to the Oder-Neisse frontier and the boundary line between the Federal Republic and the GDR as well as to the Wall in Berlin.

Played up because of an indiscretion, the U.S. ideas triggered grave apprehension in the Federal Republic that Washington might set aside the Federal Republic's interests in Germany in favor of an arrangement with the Soviet Union. In Bonn there was loud complaint over the lack of consultation. In reality these ideas had been intensively discussed both in the four powers' Berlin contingency group in Washington and in the Permanent NATO Council in Paris, though not in the form of a developed proposal.[8] On both the proposed access authority and the nonaggression declarations the position of the Federal Republic was divided and ambivalent. Fundamental concerns were mixed with fear of isolation within the alliance. Especially Minister without Portfolio Krone, a close confidant of Adenauer and chairman of the newly created German Defense Council, feared that the renunciation of force statements envisaged by the U.S. would, de facto, if not de jure, confirm the status quo in Europe and thus anticipate a settlement by means of peace treaty. Foreign Minister Schröder, on the other hand, attached greater importance to the dangers of the Federal Republic's being isolated in the alliance than to the possible negative consequences of such accords for the German question. Moreover, he saw advantages in the proposed permanent four-power organ as well as in safeguards for Berlin.

Foreign Minister Schröder differed from his critics more in the methods than in the objectives of his policy. Tactically, Schröder sought to use agreement in principle with the U.S. proposals to assure the Federal Republic a hand in formulating them and thus to provide a means for modifying them toward greater consideration of Bonn's interests. His approach thus clearly differed from that of his predecessor and of the chancellor, who in critical situations tended to sound the alarm.[9]

The West German line of argument on renunciation of force in the late 1950s and early 1960s was above all concerned with the contractual aspect, the element of treaty-binding. Bonn refused to establish diplomatic relations with the East European states for fear of undermining its claim to sole representation, nor was it prepared to bind itself to these states in any other way. The creation of formal ties under international law—and not so much the instrument of renunciation of force per se—was seen as stabilizing and confirming the status quo. Moreover, a recognition or even increased international standing of the GDR was to be prevented. Above all, a nonaggression treaty, which was the focus of the discussion in the early 1960s, implied the anticipation of settlements by peace treaty. This type of agreement ran counter to a policy aimed at changing, or at least keeping open, the status quo on the German question until a final settlement, i.e., a peace treaty with a reunified Germany, could be reached. Renunciation of force, however, was more compatible with a modus vivendi. The treaty partners recognized the existence of an unsolved problem but committed themselves to a peaceful settlement without recourse to the use or threat of force.

The Soviet Union also incorporated nonaggression and renunciation of force into its strategy on European security. The many proposals for a nonaggression pact between the Warsaw Pact and NATO in the decade between 1955 and 1964 were aimed primarily at gaining a confirmation and recognition of the status quo in Europe. At the same time, proponents of such a pact saw in them a means of in fact overcoming this status quo. They speculated that the diminished orientation to "enemies" attendant upon a renunciation of force would lead to modification of the alliance systems and ultimately to their dissolution. This objective became especially clear in light of the July 1955 Soviet draft which provided for a joint consultation process for resolving disputes, in addition to a commitment by the participating states of the Warsaw Pact and the North Atlantic Treaty not to employ armed force against one another.[10]

The Soviet Union argued that the cause of tensions in Europe was the existence of two military groupings locked in hostile confrontation. If this were eliminated and a European security system established, then the German question too could be tackled. However, in the mid-1950s the Soviet Union was primarily concerned with preventing the rearmament of the Bundeswehr and weakening the cohesion of the Western alliance by seeking to arouse hopes for detente among the European peoples. The discussion on a nonaggression pact thus ran largely parallel with the concurrent debate on a disengagement in Europe and had recourse to the same arguments.

The instrumentality of the Eastern proposals on renunciation of force becomes evident in the way the argumentation changed in accordance with the international situation, while the objective, confirmation of the status quo, remained constant. In the period 1956-1958 the proposal was incorporated into the Soviet campaign for peaceful coexistence. There was no attempt to present designs for a European security system. Rather, the nonaggression pact was ranged with proposals for ending nuclear weapons testing, reducing the numbers of foreign troops in Germany, and preventing surprise attacks. These proposals added up to an impressive demonstration of the Soviet Union's peaceful intentions before the world public—which was undoubtedly one of the motives behind them.[11]

During the Berlin crisis of 1958-1962 the Soviet Union attempted to achieve its European goals by direct means, through pressure on the militarily weakest point of the West: Berlin. The proposals for nonaggression and renunciation of force had more the character of incidental music designed to lay bare the Western dilemma in Berlin. Here it would be the West that would have to resort to force if its rights were infringed. The Berlin crisis was also a way of inducing the West to recognize the GDR. East Berlin's proposal for an intra-German nonaggression pack tended in the same direction.[12]

In the post-Cuba phase, the proposal of a nonaggression pack was put forward mainly for its detente effect, though it was also aimed at upsetting Western plans for a NATO mulitlateral force (MLF). A relatively uncomplicated nonaggression treaty between NATO and the Warsaw Pact or between its members—in which for a time even some of the Federal Republic's Western allies expressed an interest—would supposedly demonstrate that the partial cooperation between competing systems manifested in the establishment of a direct communications link and the conclusion of the Test Ban Treaty could be extended to the European continent, too. The East European states argued that a nonaggression treaty could thus initiate a peaceful European development.[13] This addressed one of the fundamental problems: the divergent political conceptions of the future structure of Europe, which allowed for serious negotiations on a renunciation-of-force policy or nonaggression pact between NATO and the Warsaw Pact only after the principal European powers' blockage of interests had been—if only partially—removed.

THE GERMAN "PEACE NOTE" OF MARCH 25, 1966

Changes in the Internal and External Framework of West German Foreign Policy

The building of the Berlin Wall in August 1961 had brutally demonstrated to all Germans the failure of past German policy. They had to recognize that maintaining the status quo had become the paramount goal of the principal European powers. The outcome of the Cuban crisis had underscored this. The strategic stalemate between the superpowers and the diplomatic stalemate with regard to Europe had resulted in a political immobility that precluded East-West agreement on Western terms but at the same time entailed the risk of accidental war if the dangerous character of the military confrontation could not be mitigated through cooperative arms control. This assessment of the international situation gave rise to the U.S. efforts for arms control agreements with the other superpower and a relaxation of European tensions.

In light of these developments there was a growing awareness in the Federal Republic that a no to superpower detente would lead to political isolation of the Federal Republic. Chiefly the United States, but also France and other West European allies, urged Bonn to take initiatives of its own toward the East. The discussion over the Test Ban Treaty pointed out the narrow margins within which the Federal Republic could deviate from the detente course of its most powerful ally. And, in the West German public, the argument grew that reunification was not feasible in the foreseeable future and, therefore, a reappraisal of past positions was necessary. Already, in the fall of 1961, the Bundestag had approved a report from the SPD representative and refugee official, Wenzel Jaksch, calling for a more active policy toward the East. A policy of strengthening economic, cultural, and political contacts should lead to a normalization of relations with the East European states.[14] In various writings, such as the Tübingen memorandum of lay Protestants, the so-called "Expellees Memorandum" of the Protestant Church in Germany, and a sensational correspondence between the Catholic bishops in Poland and those in the Federal Republic, recognition of the Oder-Neisse border was advocated as a precondition for normalizing relations with the East European states.[15] The thesis of *Wandel durch Annäherung* (change through contact) formulated by Egon Bahr, then adviser to the governing mayor of Berlin and the SPD candidate for chancellor, Willy Brandt, was an argument for strengthening intra-German relations. A range of relief measures for the people and increased economic relations were to break down barriers and make coexistence bearable.[16] The arguments of Peter Bender took the same direction, advocating the consolidation of the GDR or its recognition as a prerequisite for overcoming—in the long run—the division of Europe.[17] A spirited journalistic debate, carried out mainly in periodicals such as *Die Zeit* and *Der Spiegel*, the *Süddeutsche Zeitung* and the *Frankfurter Rundschau*, the *Monat* and the *Frankfurter Hefte*, indicated that in domestic politics change was under way.

Within the German government it was primarily Foreign Minister Schröder and the FDP, led by Minister for All-German Affairs Erich Mende, who were resolved to follow a course receptive to and supportive of the Western policy of detente, even if this meant giving up the Hallstein Doctrine and, as was argued at the time, "provisionally" accepting the status quo. In this Schröder could count on support from the SPD, which had long advocated a normalization of relations with the East European states, whereas parts of his own parliamentary group, especially its chairman von Brentano and Minister without Portfolio Krone, as well as the Bavarian sister party led by Franz Josef Strauss put up vehement opposition. The critics of the Schröderian Ostpolitik regarded an increasing East European engagement as a threat both to the principles of past policy on Germany, especially the claim to sole representation and the Hallstein Doctrine derived from it, and to the close relations with the West.

Further impulses came from the Federal Republic's allies. After the Cuban crisis, the United States had begun to put its relations with the Soviet Union on a more constructive footing. Moreover, it was now calling upon the West Europeans to do their part in improving relations with the East European states—thus President Lyndon B. Johnson in his "bridge-building" speech of December 1965.[18] The public discussion in the Federal Republic was also influenced by the concept put forward by the political adviser to the administration in Washington, Zbigniew Brzezinski, of strengthening contacts with the East European states but isolating the GDR.

> To undermine the East European stake in East Germany, the West
> will have to differentiate sharply between its attitude toward East
> Germany and toward the rest of Eastern Europe. For East Germany,
> the policy must be one of isolation; for East Europe, one of peaceful
> engagement—economic, cultural, and eventually political. Only then
> will East Germany become a political anachronism on the map of Eu-
> rope, a source of continuing embarrassment to Moscow, and no
> longer a source of security to the East Europeans.[19]

However, an even greater impact was made by the efforts of Italian
and Belgian politicians in particular to normalize the relations of their
countries with the states of Eastern Europe, especially as these efforts
were also intended to tap the East European market for their domestic
industries.[20]

The establishment of trade missions in Warsaw, Bucharest,
Budapest, and Sofia in 1963 and 1964 broke the old taboo that formal
relations were not possible with states that had recognized the GDR.
They remained, however, below the threshold of diplomatic relations
and left out the GDR. Crossing that threshold appeared for the time
being impossible without giving up or modifying the Hallstein Doctrine.[21] At the same time the German government, as part of a "two-
pronged approach," was making efforts to improve relations with the
Soviet Union. A visible sign of first results was the announcement of a
visit to Bonn by Premier Khrushchev. The ouster of Khrushchev not
only prevented this visit, but for the time being severed German-Soviet
contacts. The new leadership in the Kremlin needed time to consolidate its power and review its foreign policy.

The Note of March 25, 1966

At the end of 1965 there were more and more indications that the
Soviet leadership was beginning to reactivate its foreign policy, particularly with respect to Germany. State Secretary Karl Carstens's visit to
Moscow on the occasion of a chemical exhibition in October 1965 gave
both governments an opportunity to find out how great an inclination
to negotiate there was in Moscow and Bonn. From his visit Carstens
returned home with the impression that the Soviet government was
very interested in continuing the dialogue with the German government.[22] In Bonn it was increasingly felt that a diplomatic initiative
from the German government would meet with a businesslike recep-
tion in Moscow and might well lead to further talks on improving
German-Soviet relations. The primary purpose of the note, however,
was less to initiate new talks on the German question, for which there

was still no perceptible basis given the contrary positions of East and West; rather, it was an attempt to bring new shades into policy on Germany. Bonn was tired of being constantly reviled by the East and repeatedly pressured by the West to develop its own active Ostpolitik.

The peace note was remarkable more for its style and tone than for its substance: the language was both trenchant and civil. The document was delivered to all governments with which the Federal Republic maintained diplomatic relations as well as to the East European and Arab states, though not to the GDR. Its contents were divided into six parts. In the first and second parts the German government stressed its readiness for peace and explained its—well-known—position on the German question. In the third and fourth parts it rejected the Soviet accusations that it was conducting an aggressive and revanchistic policy and espoused "both a solution to the German question and a consistent disarmament policy that contributes to preserving peace."[23]

In the final part it submitted a series of proposals on arms control and detente in Europe. Specifically, it proposed:

- The non-nuclear states should renounce, as the Federal Republic had, the production of nuclear weapons. For their part, the nuclear powers should pledge not to deliver nuclear weapons into the national control of other countries.
- The nuclear powers should also commit themselves not to increase the number of atomic weapons in Europe, but rather to reduce them progressively. In the process, the existing balance of power would have to be maintained, an effective control provided, and measures of this nature linked with progress in solving the political problems of Europe.
- Strengthening of safeguards administered by the International Atomic Energy Organization pertaining to transfer of fissionable material when the receiver countries are not members of EURATOM.
- Readiness to exchange with the governments of the Soviet Union, Poland, Czechoslovakia, and any other East European state formal declarations in which each side would renounce to the other nation the use of force in settling international disputes.
- An exchange of observers of military maneuvers with the East European states and willingness to take part in an international disarmament conference insofar as this promised success.

The document plainly bore the marks of compromise. It was supposed to demonstrate West German flexibility and readiness to negotiate, yet the German government also believed it had to uphold its basic positions on the German question. This was registered with particular clarity in the fact that the GDR was not among the recipients of the note. Vis-à-vis Poland, the German government maintained its position that Germany continued to exist in the borders of 1937 as long as other borders had not been recognized by a freely elected all-German government. As for the Munich accords of 1938, it said that they had been torn up by Hitler and no longer had any territorial significance. Thus the German government had taken a small step toward meeting the Czechoslovakian demand for a decree of nullification of Munich. Bonn's declared readiness for conciliation with the East European states was not, however, sufficient to break down the obstacles that had mounted in relations with the East European states as a result of the events of the Second World War and the long-held demand for restoration of Germany in its borders of 1937.

Except for the offer to exchange renunciation-of-force statements with the East European states, the German proposals were limited to security issues. With the measures for non-proliferation of nuclear weapons and control of fissionable material, the German government assumed first of all that other states ought to take upon themselves the same restrictions as it had in 1954. By accentuating a ban on production and a non-diffusion of atomic weapons into national control by the nuclear powers, Bonn was also trying to influence the international discussion on a non-proliferation treaty in its interest. With the proposal of freezing or reducing nuclear weapons in Europe, the German government was taking up elements of the Gomulka and Rapacki plans, combining them, however, with the demand for progress in solving the German question.[24] Finally, the proposal on exchanging observers for maneuvers originated from the Geneva disarmament talks and was primarily a gesture of good will. Bilateral accords of this sort were designed to avoid the dangers the German government associated with observation posts or inspection systems in which the GDR would have to be included.

But even the renunciation of force was viewed at that time primarily as a measure of security and detente. First, one had to counteract the real or alleged fear that the Federal Republic could contemplate solving the controversial issues in its relationship with the East European states by the use or threat of force. The problems had to be publicly and contractually set upon the road to settlement by peaceful means. Given the absence of any real foundation for an agreed solution, especially to the German question, the renunciation-of-force position was given the function of a moratorium designed to defuse the conflict but not prejudice a negotiated settlement. In the short term the German government expected a renunciation-of-force position to yield a relaxation of tensions.

The critical element of the peace note was the continued priority of the reunification claim. New was the fact that the security needs of the

East European states were explicitly acknowledged in an official document of the Federal Republic and these states were offered formal agreements going beyond the establishment of trade missions. The proposed renunciation of force was to testify "that there exists an unsettled matter of conflict without whose resolution animosity will continue and a peaceful settlement will not be possible." In this sense renunciation of force was an instrument for keeping the status quo open.[25]

The four-power conferences of the 1950s had demonstrated the futility of efforts to achieve a solution to the German question acceptable to East and West. Consequently, the efforts of the German government were geared toward not prejudicing a future settlement by "consolidating an unsatisfactory, imbalanced, not yet pacified state of affairs." The security measures it proposed were carefully selected so that none of them would cement the status quo. Where political repercussions were feared, as in the proposal for freezing or reducing nuclear weapons in Central Europe, these measures were combined with the demand for simultaneous progress on the German question. Yet the question remains whether Bonn's desired normalization of relations with the East European states would not also have tended to stabilize the status quo, not legally of course, but perhaps all the more effectively in the political-psychological realm.

The note reflected compromise not only in the adherence to previous positions on Germany combined with a striving for detente with the East European states, but also in the way the note came about. Clearly the note was not a major move, a long-planned initiative of detente policy, but rather an action taking shape out of the given situation with the paramount object of self-description. With a view to the East European states as well as the West's pressure for initiatives from the Federal Republic it was joined with practicable elements of detente.[26]

The initiative behind the note of March 1966 had come essentially from Foreign Minister Schröder. At the Paris meeting of the NATO Council of Ministers in December 1965 and with the visit of Chancellor Erhard to Washington it was clear that the allies were no longer prepared to demonstrate their solidarity with the Federal Republic's desire for reunification and to counter the Eastern attacks on Bonn if the latter did not rouse itself to its own detente measures. Added to this was the growing international discussion about a non-proliferation treaty. To protect its positions and to avoid drawing the charge that it wanted to hinder an international relaxation of tensions, the German government had considered it prudent to come forward with an initiative of its own.

Reactions at Home and Abroad

The note of March 25, 1966 was supported by a broad consensus within the Federal Republic. In an effort to win the approval of all political forces, the government had passed on the draft to the chairmen of party groups in the Bundestag—Rainer Barzel (CDU/CSU), Fritz Erler (SPD), and Knut von Kühlmann-Stumm (FDP)—with the request for suggestions or corrections. However, the time was so short that substantial changes could not be worked out or taken into account. Neither was the Foreign Affairs Committee called into the deliberations.

On March 25, 1966, Chancellor Erhard informed the Bundestag of the contents of the note. In the discussion on the chancellor's statement, speakers of all three Bundestag parties expressly assured the government of their support for the policy initiated with the peace note.[27] This was the time of a high degree of consensus on the German question among all the political forces in the Federal Republic. Criticism of Bonn's approach was voiced only by the expellee associations. Yet there were marked differences—which became more pronounced during the summer—in evaluating the effectiveness and success of the German note, in assessing Soviet policy toward Germany and Europe, and in contemplating subsequent steps down the road now taken with the diplomatic initiative in March.

The note met with very different reactions among its recipients. In official statements and in their responses the Federal Republic's allies, with the exception of France, welcomed the German initiative. A number of non-aligned states also responded favorably, but it should be noted that these countries were well disposed toward Bonn's policy and wanted to express this. It was especially disappointing that the Eastern European states did not deal with the ideas put forward in the note, though they declared their interest in improving and normalizing relations with the Federal Republic.[28] Reserved, too, was the tenor of the international press. There was positive recognition that the Federal Republic had overcome its previous immobility, but criticism that once again the borders of 1937 had been brought up and that Bonn had not committed itself to accept an unequivocal nuclear ban.

In view of the meager results of the March note, and of the prospect for an exchange of speakers with the GDR, the SPD and FDP (the opposition party and the smaller coalition partner of the CDU/CSU) pressed for continuation of efforts toward normalizing relations with the East European states. On three points they went considerably beyond the suggestions made in the March note: with respect to the invalidity of the Munich accords, on the issue of including the GDR in a renunciation-of-force agreement, and, in a cautious way, with the offer of assurances to Poland on respecting the Oder-Neisse border. But above all the SPD wanted more done in the area of arms control, namely under the twofold rubric of alliance policy and detente initiative toward Eastern Europe.[29]

The government confined itself largely to reiterating its position. It was not prepared at this time to go beyond the offers contained in its March note. Once it became clear that the exclusion of the GDR from the proposed nonaggression accord was a major impediment to negotiations with the East European states, consideration was made in the government camp also as to how the GDR could be incorporated into a renunciation-of-force arrangement without its being directly addressed and thus accorded greater international status. Meanwhile, there began in relatively inconspicuous fashion initial German-Soviet explorations into the possibility of talks,[30] as well as negotiations with Rumania on establishing diplomatic relations.[31]

The different assessments of Soviet policy toward Germany and Europe entailed not so much a question of whether Moscow was pursuing an offensive or a defensive policy, but rather a concern about the limits and conditions of Soviet willingness to negotiate. Would the Soviet Union be prepared to talk only on its set conditions—recognition of the German partition and European borders, renunciation of control over nuclear weapons, establishment of a Free City of West Berlin? Or was it realistic to assume, as leading politicians of the CDU did, that the Soviet Union could be moved to a negotiated settlement from a position of Western strength or through economic and military concessions? Or was detente in Europe and in the long run the resolution of the German question really only possible on the basis of accepting the territorial status quo, as many Social Democrats believed?[32]

In spite of all the emphasis on a will to seek common ground, the debate on the future course of Ostpolitik and detente thus also revealed the mutual blocking of interests among West Germany's political forces. The policy championed by Foreign Minister Schröder of turning the Federal Republic onto the detente course of the allies, especially that of Washington, had yielded little in the short term, as the government continued to maintain its traditional positions on the German question. But from a conservative standpoint this course had already meant a "consolidation, affirmation, and legitimation of the Soviet possessions in Europe."[33] Strong forces within the government, mainly grouped around the Bavarian CSU, regarded with mistrust the U.S. effort to achieve a partial conciliation with the Soviet Union. If the United States was no longer prepared to work actively and continuously to question the status quo, then the Federal Republic would have to join forces with France and do everything possible to achieve the unification of Western Europe and its development into an interdependent factor in international politics. In their view a solution to the German question was possible only in a European framework, only by means of stronger national activity of all European states, including those of Eastern Europe.

A third position was marked out by the Social Democrats and some of the Free Democrats. They put forward the view that the Federal Republic's strategy for foreign policy and reunification had to be actively pursued in three different fields: security policy, which at the same time was alliance and arms control policy; policy toward Eastern Europe, which ought to be primarily detent policy, and—here the SPD differed fundamentally from the other groupings—that of developing intra-German relations. For this, SPD Chairman Willy Brandt, at the Dortmund party congress, had found the formula of a "qualified, orderly, and limited-term coexistence of the two territories of Germany."[34] Leading politicians within the SPD had recognized that an isolation of the GDR would reinforce East German dependence on the Soviet Union and intensify the confrontation between the two German states, yet offer no real chance for solving the German question.

In the domestic political constellation there seemed to be scarcely any possibility of joint action; neither had the detente policy of Schröder's the necessary support in the cabinet, nor did the pro-French course indicated by the CSU offer a genuine alternative. Cooperation between the Schröder wing within the government and the opposition was also not possible without the CDU's having also crossed the Rubicon of a de facto recognition of the realities of postwar Europe.

THE GERMAN-SOVIET DIALOGUE
ON RENUNCIATION OF FORCE

Changed Domestic and International Constellations

Three mutually independent developments made possible the opening of talks with the Soviet Union on a renunciation-of-force agreement, beginning in the winter of 1966-67 and culminating in the signing of the Moscow Treaty in the summer of 1970: reorientations in Soviet policy, intensified efforts toward detente on the part of the Western allies, and changes in West German domestic politics.

Soviet policy in the 1960s pursued above all the goal of loosening the U.S. engagement in Europe and using the offer of cooperation with some of the Western states to drive a wedge between them and the others. In the mid-1960s, as the United States became absorbed in the war in Indochina and its domestic problems, the Soviet leadership tried to win over first Paris and then, as a response and counteroffensive to the West German Ostpolitik, Bonn. This explains a relatively conciliatory Soviet response to the German peace note and the pronounced readiness to improve relations with the Federal Republic. Like the Polish and Czechoslovakian regimes, the Soviet Union accused the Federal Republic of refusing to accept the facts created in Europe after the Second World War and of blocking a relaxation of tensions in Europe by its insistent claim to sole representation; however, Moscow also expressed its interest in improving relations with the Federal Republic. In so doing it mentioned a number of areas where it felt some cooperation was possible. It also took up the German government's offer of exchanging renunciation-of-force declarations, though it attached the condition "that such an agreement must not serve as a cover for aggression against a third state." With that, the road was cleared for direct talks between Moscow and Bonn.[35]

But the Federal Republic also felt compelled to intensify its Ostpolitik and detente efforts if it were not to risk isolation within the Western alliance. De Gaulle's trip to Moscow in the summer of 1966, the restrained Western response to the German peace note, and finally President Johnson's speeches of August and October 1966, in which he proclaimed detente and reconciliation between East and West to be the great common goal of the West—these events heralded very clearly that in the West all signals had been set to detente.[36]

The third factor was the formation of the Grand Coalition in December 1966. In its coalition paper the SPD had already come out in support of an exchange of legally binding declarations renouncing the use of force, which would include the GDR. Its assumption of government responsibility along with the CDU/CSU meant that its ideas on detente and Ostpolitik would now play a greater role in official government policy. The new German government proclaimed as its most important goal in foreign policy: "a consistent and effective peace policy...to remove political tensions and contain the arms race."[37]

At the same time the government announced a more independent West German detente policy, for which the Social Democrats had been pressing for several years. This became possible once Bonn had eliminated the conflict of aims between alliance policy and policy on Germany and had turned the Federal Republic onto the detente course of its allies. It had other causes also. The United States's entanglement in Vietnam and consequent domestic problems gave cause for concern that the United States would reduce its engagement in Europe. The

French policy toward the East, especially notions of a Franco-Soviet he-gemony, as expressed, e.g., in a study from the Centre d'Etudes de Politique Etrangère,[38] was perceived as a threat to German interests. In addition, there was the feeling that the economic power of the Fed-eral Republic enabled Bonn to wield a more active foreign policy as well.

The Concept of a European Order of Peace

The Grand Coalition was a tactical alliance of the Federal Repub-lic's two large political parties aimed at overcoming the economic and political stagnation of the Erhard government. This coalition, however, was made up of those political forces in West Germany that had previ-ously proceeded from divergent premises and objectives in foreign policy, and especially in detente policy. It remained to be seen whether the linking of such different approaches would lead to a new dynamic in foreign policy or rather to domestic paralysis.

For Chancellor Kiesinger and the CDU/CSU the paramount politi-cal goal was still to maintain a Western society and have the GDR—by means of internal liberalization—participate in it as much as possible. The method continued to be the demand for realization of the German people's right to self-determination. The Federal Republic's claim to sole representation was to be maintained and the legal positions in re-gard to the German question preserved until a final peace settlement. In Ostpolitik Kiesinger essentially carried on along the lines drawn by Schröder. The process of relaxation and normalization was now to in-clude the GDR, with humanitarian measures figuring prominently, but it was stressed that the government was not prepared to recognize the GDR. The concept of a European order of peace provided a conceptual framework in which policy toward the East and the West would be em-bodied. Without jeopardizing the security of the Federal Republic and without calling into question its integration in the West, German policy would work toward a European balance of interests and, in the course of European reunification, a solution to the German question.[39]

What ideas did the coalition partner associate with the concept of a European order of peace? In an essay in the Yugoslavian journal *Inter-nationale Politik*, then-Foreign Minister Brandt wrote: "Our supreme goal must be...securing peace in Europe. All other problems, includ-ing the problem of the division of Germany, must be subordinated to this goal. Components of our policy are: reduction of tensions, im-provement of relations, and preparatory contributions to a European order of peace."[40] Thus Brandt clearly set the priorities differently from Kiesinger, subordinating the resolution of the German question to realization of a European order of peace.

In Brandt's view, a European order of peace was more than a European security system that could get by with disarmament and arms control measures and possibly international guarantees. It presupposed that the military confrontation would be diminished and ultimately overcome and that the legitimate security interests of the European states would be taken into account. But a European order of peace necessarily meant also that political tensions would be reduced and cooperation and rapprochement between nations would be deepened. For Brandt this was primarily an intellectual and political framework in which the German question could be settled on the basis of a modus vivendi. A precondition was that Europe would assume a position of greater weight in world affairs, where it could have a say alongside the superpowers—in the interest of peace. This presupposed the unification of Europe, all of Europe. It was a long-term goal that could be realized only in generations. Brandt, however, made it clear that the development of the European Community, its enlargement by Great Britain and other applicants, and its progression to a political union was not in contrast to an all-European solution. On the contrary, a dynamic Western policy was seen as a prerequisite of a successful Eastern policy.

The three most important instruments of this policy were the exchange of renunciation-of-force statements, which encompassed the problems resulting from the division of Germany, the renunciation of national control over nuclear weapons, and a mutual reduction of conventional forces in Europe. This was designed above all to reduce the mistrust impeding a normalization of relations between the Federal Republic and the East European nations. At the same time the military confrontation was to be reduced in a balanced, step-by-step fashion and peaceful ways of settling conflict were to be found. Finally, the capstone of this development was to be a system of collective security, involving the United States and the Soviet Union, as the preliminary stage of a European order of peace.[41]

The First Round of German-Soviet Talks on Renunciation of Force

The reaction of the East European recipients to the Federal Republic's March 1966 peace note had shown that the exclusion of the GDR offered the Warsaw Pact states an opening for propaganda attacks against the Federal Republic. Moreover, it had been recognized, especially within the SPD, that a policy of isolating the GDR was leading up a blind alley. In the coalition negotiations the SPD had then been able to establish agreement that European detente and intra-German relaxation of tension were conditional upon each other.

In its policy statement of December 1966 the German government reiterated its willingness to exchange renunciation-of-force declarations with the Soviet Union and other East European states, whereby the coalition government of CDU/CSU and SPD explicitly included the unresolved problem of the German division. As had its predecessors, this government regarded renunciation of force as first and foremost a matter of security, but not as an isolated step, rather as one embedded in a series of proposals on disarmament and detente and the improvement of bilateral relations.[42] However, the exchange of statements formally renouncing the use of force was accorded a special importance with respect to a European order of peace. In February 1967, the German government handed the Soviet ambassador in Bonn the draft of a statement renouncing the use of force. Besides a preamble expressing the desire for detente in relations among the European states, this text contained just one operative paragraph stipulating that both states would shape their policy in accordance with the principles of the Charter of the United Nations, in particular Article 2, and that they would renounce the use of force in particular in pursuing their goals on the German question. The renunciation of force was not bound to any preconditions. Similarly, the German government expected the Soviet Union not to set any prior conditions.[43]

In the spring and summer of 1967 the talks were continued between State Secretary Klaus Schütz of the Foreign Office and Soviet Ambassador Semyoh Tsarapkin. In these discussions it was evident that the two sides had both very different assessments of the problems of Germany and Central Europe and divergent conceptions of the essence of a renunciation of force. This became abundantly clear in light of two Soviet memoranda delivered to the German government in October and November 1967. The Soviet government wished to know whether the Federal Republic would also be prepared to exchange statements renouncing the use of force with the GDR on the same terms as with the other East European states. In the second memorandum the Federal Republic was called upon, among other things, to articulate a clear position with respect to the "inalterability of the borders established in Europe, including the Oder-Neisse border and the border between the German Democratic Republic and the Federal Republic of Germany."[44]

The two drafts for renunciation-of-force declarations showed the scope of Soviet demands even more clearly. While in its projected statement the Soviet Union insisted on its rights as a victorious power, rights derived from the Potsdam Agreement, the Federal Republic for its part was supposed to:

- recognize and respect the inviolability of the existing frontiers in Europe and raise no territorial demands on other states;

- respect the status of West Berlin as a special political entity;
- declare the Munich accords null and void from the start;
- renounce the acquisition and production of nuclear weapons as well as any direct or indirect control, and
- take effective measures to prevent a development of militarism and revanchism in its territory.

Thus, it emerged from the Soviets' written proposals that Moscow did not want to confine the bilateral exchange of statements to the German-Soviet relationship, but rather wanted to encompass all unresolved issues between the Federal Republic and its Eastern neighbors and at the same time impose certain restrictions on West German policy. State Secretary Georg-Ferdinand Duckwitz, who as Schütz's successor conducted the talks from the German side as of October 1967, wrote about this: "In our view the renunciation of force is to be unconditional, to express solely the common readiness to find a modus vivendi, not to prejudice solutions, but the Soviet Union is attempting to use it as a means of gaining recognition of the 'realities' it created unilaterally in Europe after the war."[45]

For the Soviet government, renunciation of force was an instrument of its European policy. It attempted to use this as a means to gain acceptance of its political goals, i.e., a legal confirmation of the status quo and a recognition of its hegemony over the eastern half of Europe. The Federal Republic understood the renunciation of force as an attempt to concretize the already valid yet abstract international legal norms prohibiting the threat and use of force as per Article 2 of the United Nations Charter; i.e., to apply this general norm to the unsettled issues specific to the Federal Republic's relation with its Eastern neighbors. The renunciation of force according to Article 2 was also designed to deprive Articles 53 and 107, the UN Charter's so-called Enemy States Clauses, of any foundation. The German government stressed, however, that agreements on renunciation of force must not prejudice a final solution of existing disputed issues. Until a mutually acceptable peace treaty had been negotiated, they would have to counteract the fear or the claim that the Federal Republic could seek a settlement on its terms through the use or threat of force.

Despite these differences of opinion, the German government tried to keep the talks with the Soviet Union alive. In the Bundestag debate on defense in December 1967, Foreign Minister Brandt emphasized the importance that the government attached to the exchange of statements renouncing the use of force. In the USSR and the East European states it had been able to discern, besides mistrust and political presumption, objective interest as well. There should, then, be no lack of goodwill on their part to reach agreement.[46]

One day later, the Soviet government handed the German chargé d'affaires in Moscow a statement in which it claimed that revanchism and militarism were taking hold of broader and broader spheres of social and political life in the Federal Republic. It criticized especially the emergence of the National Democratic Party (NPD) and alleged that Bonn was carrying out a program of extensive preparations for war. Thus, it was characteristic that the German government set itself against "exchanging...in the appropriate constitutional form with the German Democratic Republic declarations on the non-application of force." That emphasized once again the aggressive character of West German policy.[47] In response to this the German government delivered to the Soviet ambassador in Bonn an aide-mémoire asking whether the Soviet Union was still interested in an exchange of ideas on a renunciation of force.[48] The inflation of Soviet demands—in its last memorandum the Soviet Union had for the first time called for the Federal Republic to exchange renunciation-of-force statements with the GDR on the same basis as with the other East European states—indicated that at this juncture Moscow was not interested in an agreement. Still, the German-Soviet exploratory talks continued.

In April 1968 the German government once again explained in a memorandum its views on the problems broached by the Soviet Union—the question of borders, the Munich accords, the status of Berlin, renunciation of force with the GDR, militarism, and neo-Nazism—and stressed that it considered desirable first of all an agreement on renunciation of force. Further, it noted that a number of the points made by the Soviets pertained to the interests of third states, and stated that it was prepared to meet with these governments. In this way Bonn sought to avoid recognizing Moscow as sole spokesman for East European concerns. Although the German government was well aware of the actual or claimed power position of the Soviet Union, Bonn considered it an inadmissible infringement of the sovereignty and independence of the East European states—which in theory Moscow also recognized—if the Soviets wanted to settle *inter alios* issues that concerned only these countries themselves.[49]

Many times in the summer of 1968 both the Soviet government and the German government declared that they wanted to continue the exchange of views. However, the demands and accusations raised in the Soviet aide-mémoire of July 5, 1968 reduced to a minimum the prospects for a more or less meaningful continuation of the talks.[50] Without waiting for a response, the Soviet government, in a surprise move on July 11, published part of the documents on the renunciation of force and thus forced the German government to take a similar step, although both sides had agreed on confidentiality.

The breakup of the talks came at a time when the Federal Republic was getting ready to concretize further its policy on renunciation of force, especially with regard to its relationship with the GDR. Bonn wanted to exchange renunciation-of-force declarations with East Berlin also, on the condition that this did not imply any recognition of the GDR under international law. This position was indicated in the German reply of April and explained in detail to the Western powers by Foreign Minister Brandt at the NATO Council meeting in Reykjavik.[51]

Bonn also hoped to be able soon to enter into talks with Poland on renunciation of force, once a public exchange of "signals" and indirect contacts by way of Stockholm and Brussels had prepared the climate for them.[52]

The reasons for Moscow's flagging interest in coming to terms with Bonn are to be sought in developments within Eastern Europe. The breakup of the talks occurred at the high point of tensions in Czechoslovakia, a few weeks before the intervention of Warsaw Pact troops. The publication of the notes by the Soviet Union took place on the same day that *Pravda* sharply attacked the "Manifesto of 2,000 Words" and warned Prague against further deviations, with explicit reference to the Soviet intervention in Hungary in 1956. At that point the Soviet Union was less interested in improving its relations with Western Europe than with securing its possessions in Eastern Europe. The tendencies manifested in Czechoslovakia and Rumania of striking out on independent courses of domestic and foreign policy, as well as the willingness shown in some East European states to normalize relations with the Federal Republic, threatened Soviet hegemony and led to tensions within the bloc system. It also forced the Soviet Union to break off the dialogue with the Federal Republic on renunciation of force. Not entirely without reason, it regarded Bonn's Ostpolitik as one of the causes behind the softening of bloc solidarity, without its having been able to get the West, and the Federal Republic in particular, to confirm the status quo and thus to recognize the Soviet sphere.

This development also strengthened the mutual dependence between East Berlin and Moscow. The Soviet attempt to keep a close rein again on the socialist states in its domain dispelled East Berlin's dilemma of having either to give up its goal of international recognition in favor of an arrangement with the Federal Republic or else isolate itself from its East European partners striving for detente with Western Europe. For its part the Soviet Union needed a dependent GDR as an ally in its effort to parry the divergent tendencies within the Warsaw Pact and to impose a stronger bloc discipline. To this end—as the accusations leveled at the German government showed—Moscow needed Bonn as a scapegoat, as a permanent threat for sustaining its hegemonial claim and justifying the stationing of its troops in the countries of the Warsaw Pact.[53]

With an exchange of statements renouncing the use of force the Soviet Union would have had to recognize that the Federal Republic was steering a peaceful course, and thus Moscow would have lost one of its most important political instruments within its bloc. This was all the more important for the Soviet government as Bonn denied it the possibility of acting as advocate of East European interests, bargaining a renunciation of force for the recognition of the Oder-Neisse line, the nullification of the Munich accords, the separation of West Berlin from the Federal Republic, and the recognition of the GDR.

The Inclusion of the GDR in a Renunciation of Force

How the GDR was to be incorporated into a renunciation-of-force agreement posed a special problem for the German-Soviet talks. Whereas the Erhard government's note of March 1966 had excluded the GDR, the Grand Coalition tried to incorporate "the unresolved problem of the German division" into the offer to exchange renunciation-of-force declarations. Underlying this formulation was a compromise between the governing parties. While the SPD had pressed for giving up the policy of isolating the GDR and inviting East Berlin to talks on renunciation of force, the CDU/CSU feared that such negotiations and, all the more so, an official agreement with the other German state would enhance the latter's international stature and ultimately prejudice the German question. The compromise reached by the two parties provided that a direct exchange of statements with the GDR was to be avoided, but that the GDR would be encompassed within a renunciation of force with the Soviet Union and other East European states. In this connection Foreign Minister Brandt spoke of a "network of agreements renouncing the use of force."[54]

However, in the exploratory talks the Soviet government insisted that the West German government also indicate to the GDR its willingness to enter into talks on renunciation of force. Its demand became all the more emphatic with each attempt by the Bonn government to dodge the issue. Thus, Bonn had to find a formula that accommodated the Soviet Union's demand for including the GDR in a renunciation of force, yet at the same time preserved the German position of nonrecognition. In lengthy discussions, conducted mainly in the Kressbronn Group, the two parties' most important coordinating body, the SPD prevailed with its view that the GDR would also have to be addressed in any renunciation of force. In his report on the state of the nation in March 1968, Chancellor Kiesinger then added renunciation of force to the list of matters on which the West German government was prepared to negotiate with East Berlin "if the other side agrees not to link these talks with the demand for recognition under international law."[55] Bonn's April 1968 note in response to the Soviet Union made reference to this statement. At the Reykjavik meeting of the NATO Council in 1968, Foreign Minister Brandt explained in detail the German government's ideas on an intra-German renunciation of force. With reference to the rights of the four powers regarding Germany as a whole and Berlin, both sides were to declare that they respected the unity of the nation and were striving for a peaceful reunification. They were to commit themselves to use only peaceful means in pursuing a solution to the national question, to renounce the use or threat of force in all disputes arising in intra-German relations, and to make no attempt to forcibly alter the social structure of the other side.[56]

Yet neither the GDR nor the Soviet Union accepted these proposals. This was a characteristic situation for German policy of the 1960s: the Eastern side rejected or raised its demands in response to a proposal of Bonn's that the German government had previously felt was an untenable concession. There is little to suggest that the German government had expected its offer of direct negotiations with the GDR to overcome the impasse in the German-Soviet exploratory talks. Rather, at that point it had probably tried to deprive the other side of a cheap alibi in order to move ahead, if not with Moscow and East Berlin, then still in its negotiations with the other East European states. After the establishment of diplomatic relations with Rumania, the GDR had been able, with Soviet and Polish support, to gain acceptance for its demand that before normalizing its relations with any other East European state the Federal Republic would have to accept the existence of two German states, recognize the existing borders, and renounce nuclear weapons.[57] This blockade was to be underrun by the demonstration of West German willingness to talk and East German intransigence.

Similarly, there emerged the question whether the Eastern side was interested primarily in using renunciation of force to gain a higher-level recognition of the GDR or whether it wanted to force Bonn to disclose the limits of its room for maneuver vis-à-vis East Berlin and thus to prevent a rapprochement between the Federal Republic and the East European states that were interested in establishing diplomatic relations, notably Czechoslovakia and Hungary. It is not very likely, therefore, that, in the face of the Soviet Union's paramount interest in the summer of 1968 of keeping intact or reconsolidating its dominion in Eastern Europe, an even greater accommodation on the part of Bonn would have removed the obstacles in the talks on renunciation of force.

In this regard, Bonn was faced with the special problems of Berlin. While the Soviet Union was demanding the establishment of an "independent entity of West Berlin" and the GDR was trying to hamper traffic between West Germany and the city, the German government was determined to defend and, if possible, strengthen the bonds between Berlin and the Federal Republic. This also involved the three Western powers, who were not prepared to give up the rights they had acquired as a result of Germany's defeat in the Second World War. A prime argument for a renunciation of force with the GDR was that any statement from East Berlin would also have to relate to the access routes to Berlin. However, any counterdemand from the GDR or the Soviet Union for a renunciation of the use or threat of force from West Berlin could not be met by the Federal Republic or the West Berlin municipal authorities, but only by the three Western allies, and by them not vis-à-vis the GDR but only in relation to the Soviet Union. Hence, a four-power agreement on Berlin was prerequisite to a renunciation of force encompassing Berlin, just as the insecurity of West Berlin constituted a major impediment to more extensive accords between the Federal Republic and the GDR.

Recognition of the Territorial Status Quo

The term "recognition of the realities" used by the Soviet Union in the talks on renunciation of force reflected the Soviets' paramount interest in a formal confirmation of the status quo by the West, and especially the Federal Republic of Germany. The Federal Republic was the sole West European state to conduct a policy based on the hope that this situation could in the long run be changed in favor of a reunified Germany. For this reason the German government firmly held to the thesis that Germany would continue to exist in its borders of 1937 until a peace treaty had been concluded with a reunified Germany. The Soviet Union probably at no time feared that the Federal Republic could assert the claims of its legal position through force; yet the West German insistence presented a political challenge to Moscow and entailed the danger that one day other East European states would raise their demands to Moscow, too. The Soviet Union therefore had no interest in seeing the Federal Republic renounce solely the use or the threat of force, while its claims remained intact. The German government, on the other hand, saw a renunciation of force as a means of finding a modus vivendi with the East European states without negatively prejudicing reunification or border questions.

Despite the fundamental incompatibility of the two positions, the exchange of notes on this matter showed a high degree of tactical flexibility—unlike in the question of recognizing the GDR. Thus, the Soviet memorandum of October 1967 stated that the policies of the states could proceed only from "the real situation existing on the European continent today, from the territorial integrity of the states and unconditional respect for their sovereignty and independence"[58]—a formulation that the German government could largely agree to.

In its government policy statement, the Grand Coalition had already attested to the invalidity of the Munich Agreement and declared that it had no territorial claims against anyone. Nevertheless, these statements did not imply any substantial departures from the positions of the two sides. The more circumspect Soviet formulation in the October memorandum was revoked just a month later in the draft treaties communicated to the German government. Now Bonn was expected to recognize the inviolability of the existing borders in Europe and to declare the Munich accords null and void from the start. Similarly, Chancellor Kiesinger told the Bundestag on April 25, 1969 that the German government was not prepared to negotiate with the Soviet government on the basis of recognizing the so-called realities.[59] Yet with all the contradiction in the statements and antagonism in the positions, this issue did seem amenable to compromise between the Federal Republic and the Soviet Union if both sides had the political will to use renunciation of force as a political element to govern mutual relations—a thesis confirmed by the Moscow Treaty of August 12, 1970.

It has already been pointed out that for the Soviet Union in 1968 consolidation of its power domain had priority over strengthening and normalizing relations with the Federal Republic. But during this period the German government was prepared to renounce force only if this were not linked with other political issues. Bonn's primary aim was to clear away ostensible and real fears of West Germany in Eastern Europe and thereby come to a normalization of relations with these countries. No doubt the advocates of a renunciation of force in the Federal Republic were hoping also for similarly beneficial effects on German domestic politics in terms of breaking down the anti-communist fixation. In a climate of detente there would then be a greater likelihood of finding acceptable solutions to the outstanding political questions. For the German government, then, the renunciation of force was chiefly an instrument of detente policy and less a means toward new European structures. Also, the consensus within the Grand Coalition was just sufficient for sustaining a common detente policy, but not for tackling the problems of Europe's political order in any substantive way.

The Soviet Union's Intervention Claims

The German-Soviet dialogue on renunciation of force was strained particularly by Moscow's attempt to derive from the Potsdam accords and Articles 53 and 107 of the United Nations Charter a right to intervene in the Federal Republic. In the Soviet memorandum of November 1967 it was explicitly emphasized that in the absence of a German peace treaty the exchange of statements renouncing the use of force would not affect the rights and duties of the Soviet Union resulting from the Charter of the United Nations.[60] In the view of the German government, however, such a proviso would have devalued the renunciation of force and was, therefore, unacceptable.

One of Bonn's aims in pursuing a renunciation of force was to broaden the scope for its policy. Recognition of Soviet reserved rights, however, was not compatible with this objective. Moreover, there was always the latent fear that an agreement with the Soviet Union could entail Soviet interference in the political and social life of West Germany. Yet such views often failed to take into account the instrumentality of a renunciation of force, that its object was not just a guarantee against the use or threat of force, but a qualitative change in the relations of the treaty partners. Of course, the intent behind this policy was to rule out force as a means of resolving conflict. However, the policy was carried out in the knowledge that the security of the Federal Republic was guaranteed primarily by the Atlantic alliance.

Various motives can be attributed to the Soviet approach. It is not well known that the Soviet Union did not disclaim its rights from the enemy states clauses even vis-à-vis the GDR—as the Western powers had done upon accepting the Federal Republic into the Western defense system.[61] Thus, basing a renunciation of force exclusively on Article 2 of the United Nations Charter would have accorded the Federal Republic a privileged position, legally, in relation to the GDR. By referring to the Potsdam Agreement the Soviet Union wanted to stress that it adhered to its four-power rights in relation to Germany. Neither was it in the West German interest to call into question the four-power rights and obligations based upon the Potsdam accords, as the security of Berlin was based upon them, too; nor could Bonn concede to the Soviet Union an intervention proviso derived from them and thus the right to meddle in its internal affairs.

It was, therefore, principally political reasons that moved the German government to deny the Soviet government recourse to the enemy states clauses. In the negotiations on renunciation of force Bonn took pains to ensure that these were conducted solely on the basis of Article 2 of the UN Charter, which did not contain terms of exception. Further, in public statements and legal opinions it sought to demonstrate that none of the victorious powers of the Second World War had a right to armed intervention in the Federal Republic of Germany. In its view,

> interventions by force and appealing to alleged victors' rights and Articles 53/107 would constitute aggression in violation of international law and therefore, given the right to individual or collective self-defense, would trigger the alliance contingency according to Article 5 of the NATO Treaty.[62]

At its bidding, the governments of the three Western powers issued press statements in September 1968 rejecting the Soviet intervention claim.

Renunciation of Force and Renunciation of Nuclear Weapons

The Conference of Non-nuclear Powers in September 1968 afforded the German government the opportunity to continue its renunciation-of-force policy in another context. Since the security guarantees given the non-nuclear states by the nuclear powers were felt to be inadequate, and yet the non-nuclear states were unable to find a universally acceptable formula for a total or partial proscription of atomic war, the German government proposed a general resolution on renunciation of force. This resolution stressed the indivisibility of the UN Charter's ban on the use of force, the right of every state to equality, sovereignty, and territorial integrity, and the principles of self-determination and nonintervention in internal affairs. It reaffirmed also the principle of individual and collective self-defense.[63]

The formulation that the renunciation of force was indivisible and could not be applied selectively, and that every state had an equal and inalienable right to invoke this principle, was directed both against the Soviet provisos for intervention in the Federal Republic and against the thesis of the limited sovereignty of the socialist states, which Moscow had given as justification for its intervention in Czechoslovakia.

The German government's approach was intended politically as a continuation of its renunciation-of-force policy in a multilateral framework, and it was viewed in this way by many states. However, in arguing for its draft resolution the West German delegation in Geneva cited the security problems of the non-nuclear states in light of their unequal defense potentials compared to the nuclear powers. The resolution on the renunciation of force of the Conference of Non-nuclear States was a model of an "abstract" renunciation of force without preconditions, as German diplomacy was striving for with the East European states. In the form of a resolution binding on no one it was little more than a demonstration of goodwill without political commitment—aside from the public relations success it afforded the Federal Republic in that, for the first time since the Second World War, Bonn had gained acceptance for its ideas at a major international conference.

Building Domestic and Foreign Support
for the Policy of Renunciation of Force

It has been pointed out that the renunciation-of-force policy being pressed mainly by Foreign Minister Brandt and his adviser, Egon Bahr, head of the planning staff in the Foreign Office, had a narrow domestic political basis on which to operate. The difficulties in finding a common line within the coalition restricted the government's room for maneuver. Thus it took more than four months before, in April 1968, a response could be given to the Soviet memoranda of October and November 1967. Not infrequently the West German public or the East European parties were irritated by statements on the renunciation of force that did not tally with the official position. One example of this was Bahr's response, in a television discussion, to a question about the status quo: "But we have accepted it. When the German government says 'renunciation of force'—well, what else is this?"[64] Likewise, the German government's offer to include the GDR in a renunciation-of-force agreement was bound to lack credibility if at the same time the chairman of the CDU/CSU group in the Bundestag, Rainer Barzel, was stating that the communists throughout the world would have to be played off against the Ulbricht system, which was "a Soviet foreign domination on German soil." Barzel also stressed that the legal, moral, and historical positions remained unchanged and only the methods could and must change.[65]

These were the sensitive points upon which the views of the coalition partners diverged. Should the Federal Republic insist upon an "abstract" renunciation of force, i.e., without reference to the outstanding political issues in Europe, should it make a renunciation of force a prerequisite for talks on the political problems, or should other substantial issues be included in the exploratory phase? In its exploratory talks with the Soviet Union and other East European states, how far could the German government go toward recognizing the status quo, and how could adherence to the legal positions on the German question be made consistent with a de facto acceptance of the political realities of the European situation? The Federal Republic's relationship with the GDR was a critical point. All the parties were united in their rejection of recognition under international law, yet it remained a point of contention among them whether the claim of sole representation ought to be asserted vis-à-vis East Berlin or whether the German government should name authorized representatives to negotiate an intra-German renunciation of force on the basis of equality.

It was not always possible to distract from the differences in position by making subtle distinctions, as Kiesinger and Brandt were wont to do outside of party congress and campaign speeches, or to bridge them by compromise formulas, which was done by government policy statements and diplomatic documents. These contradictions, of which the Soviet position statements on renunciation of force were not free either, necessarily weakened the credibility and hence the negotiating position of the German government.

The paralysis in Ostpolitik in the summer of 1968 was without doubt a bitter disappointment for the West German government; but the foreign political stagnation did ease matters as it spared the coalition a test of its cohesion over issues of renunciation of force. The Non-proliferation Treaty had brought the parties to the brink of just such an ordeal. A commentary by Heinz Murmann in the *Handelsblatt* described the mood within the coalition. Murmann wrote that Ostpolitik and the Non-proliferation Treaty had shown

> how diverse are the temperaments in the coalition and how varied the limits of how far each side is prepared to go. In the SPD one still hears, with some justification, the view that the CDU/CSU really lacked a clear concept for foreign policy; it had only reluctantly let itself be taken in tow by its coalition partner and was trying its best to apply the brakes. In the CDU, on the other hand, the word is that the SPD was too rash, that it was too ready to accept positions that would not be honored, it paid too little heed to the legal positions from which one simply must not budge.[66]

In contrast, the FDP, following internal struggles over direction and leadership, had moved closer to the SPD in its foreign policy objectives. It had even overtaken it "to the left" on points of German policy relevant to a renunciation of force.[67] But foreign policy cooperation between SPD and FDP comparable to that between the Schröder wing of the CDU and the SPD in the mid-1960s was not yet possible politically. For the SPD, in contrast to Schröder, it was not a matter of mustering support in relation to forces of differing orientation in one's own party, but of moving the stronger coalition partner to embrace decisions from which it was shying away. Not until after the Bundestag elections of 1969 would there be a *renversement des alliances* to replace the common cause of CDU/CSU and SPD, an alliance that had emerged from the stagnation in domestic and economic policy, with an SPD-FDP coalition united on issues of foreign policy.

The allies were kept informed of the German-Soviet talks by the German government within the Western four-power consultative group. Their reactions fluctuated between endorsement of further initiatives along the road taken and skepticism as to their prospects for success. The skepticism, coming above all from the United States, was expressed with marked clarity in a speech by U.S. Deputy Secretary of State Nicholas Katzenbach in which he warned the European governments not to undertake any independent ventures in Moscow.[68] In Western capitals there was satisfaction over the Federal Republic's having left the brakeman's cabin, but there was no desire for Bonn to board the detente train's locomotive, where the United States and France were already arguing over who was to be driver and who stoker.

The Resumption of the Dialogue on Renunciation of Force in 1969

In the summer of 1969 the domestic political basis for the Grand Coalition to conduct a common foreign policy, particularly to continue detente policy, had become even narrower. The Social Democrats had continued on the course charted at their Nuremberg party congress, namely toward a recognition of the territorial status quo in Europe; Chancellor Kiesinger and the CDU/CSU, once the government's initial initiative in Ostpolitik had run aground, had retreated to the positions laid down by Schröder in the mid-1960s. The discussion on the Nuclear Non-proliferation Treaty had revealed the polarization of the political forces before a broad public at home and abroad.

It, therefore, had to come as a surprise when in July 1969 the German government took a new initiative to reopen the talks on a mutual renunciation of force broken off the previous year by the Soviet Union. Together with a note expressing its readiness to negotiate, Bonn conveyed to the Soviet government new draft declarations renouncing the use of force. In substance these maintained the well-known positions but in their formulation made concessions to Moscow.[69] This had been preceded in the spring of 1969 by talks between Foreign Minister Brandt as well as State Secretary Duckwitz and the Soviet ambassador, Tsarapkin, from which the German government had received the impression that the Soviet Union was interested in a continuation of the exploratory talks.

One reason for the Soviet readiness to talk was surely Moscow's eagerness to reestablish the contacts with the West that had been severed following the intervention in Czechoslovakia. And, in Brandt's view, for the Federal Republic there were no alternatives to the detente policy already begun. The methods would perhaps have to be reviewed, but nothing had changed as far as the goal was concerned. The occupation of Czechoslovakia in August 1968 had indeed focused attention on the fact that cutting off or at least reducing the military, political, and legal potential for intervention represented one of the critical problems for a European order of peace. Without a comprehensive renunciation of force covering the controversial enemy states' clauses in the relationship of the Soviet Union with the Federal Republic there could be no talk of an "order of peace" or even simply a normalization of relations with the Eastern superpower. For the Soviet Union, on the other hand, the foremost concern was consolidating its sphere of influence; a renunciation of force was a means toward solidifying the "real situation" in Europe.

Three sets of motivations were at work in the German government's approach in the summer of 1969. In the spring the Soviet Union had resumed its efforts to strengthen contacts with the West; in particular, with the Budapest Appeal of March 1969 it had revived its campaign for a European security conference. There is much to suggest that the conference project afforded Moscow primarily a vehicle for ensuring bloc-conformity in policy toward the West without there being a full consensus within the Eastern alliance on objectives and specific stages. In any case, the proposal was once again on the European agenda and was taken up with varying degrees of enthusiasm by Eastern, Western, and neutral states. The Federal Republic had to consider how the conference project could be used to further German interests. Very early on Foreign Minister Brandt became convinced that it would not be in the German interest either to hamper the proposed conference or to make it a forum for discussion of the German question. The bilateral negotiations on a renunciation of force with the Soviet Union and the related intra-German talks offered possibilities for arriving at a modus vivendi on the outstanding issues in relations with these countries and for creating a more favorable starting position for the Federal Republic in the event the conference came to pass.[70]

The German-Polish relationship presented another vantage point. For the reasons just described the German government also wanted to reach a settlement with Poland. Both sides had probed informally and proclaimed publicly their readiness to negotiate. After the intervention in Czechoslovakia, however, both Warsaw and Bonn seemed to have adopted the view that it would be unwise to move ahead in German-Polish relations without German-Soviet negotiations having been first or simultaneously set in motion with some prospect of success.

Economic considerations also played a role. In view of Italian, French, and British advances into the East European market, German industry was pressing for similar possibilities. In relation to the Soviet Union it desired above all a new trade agreement, which in 1964 had foundered on the Berlin proviso. Thus, a normalization of relations with the East European states opened up promising perspectives for an extension of Eastern trade and joint economic projects.[71]

Of course, another factor was that for the Federal Republic there was no alternative to a policy of conciliation with Eastern Europe. Perhaps one conceivable approach might have been to achieve a functional detente with Eastern Europe by way of a political arrangement with the GDR. Yet at that time this option was as closed to East Berlin as it was to Bonn. Hence, the conditions setting the internal and external political frame of reference for West German policy indicated a continuation of the dialogue on renunciation of force, in the hope that this dialogue could be carried on with more conviction after the elections in the fall of 1969.

OSTPOLITIK AS A RENUNCIATION-OF-FORCE POLICY

The formation of the Social-Liberal coalition in the fall of 1969 removed the domestic political blockage impeding the conduct of a promising but as yet unfulfilled policy of renunciation of force with the Soviet Union and the other East European states. In his statement of government policy on October 28, 1969, Chancellor Brandt stressed that his government would continue the policy initiated by the Grand Coalition, but also made it clear where it would go beyond the policy of its predecessor: the Social-Liberal coalition's policy of renunciation of force would proceed on the basis of the realities created in Europe by the Second World War and would take into account the territorial integrity of its neighbors. This would apply to the GDR as well.[72]

The first crucial point was to declare a renunciation of force in relation to the Soviet Union and the East European states and to establish a modus vivendi for the currently unresolvable disputes, particularly with respect to European borders. Foreign Minister Scheel summarized this as follows:

> The renunciation of force...starts with the situation as it is. It does not prescribe it but describes it, without attaching value judgments. It does not say whether something is good or not, just or unjust...It starts from the geographic status quo and offers a political modus vivendi within the limits of this status quo. It respects and accepts

reality. It does not undertake to recognize it in international law and thereby to legalize it. These realities include the present course of frontiers in Europe, the actual territorial possession of the European states. Both sides commit themselves in the knowledge that there will continue to be problems between them. Were there no problems—in fact grave and at present seemingly unresolvable problems—a renunciation of force would be superfluous.[73]

The renunciation of force, however, was designed to defuse the problems politically and thus make them more amenable to a long-term solution.

The second essential correction of course consisted in a readiness to enter into negotiations with the GDR at the government level without discrimination and without preconditions, though the Federal Republic's recognition of the GDR under international law was not under consideration. "Even if there exist two states in Germany, still they are not foreign territory for one another. Their mutual relations can only be of a special kind."[74] The formula of "two states in Germany" took into account as much the constitutional injunction on preserving the unity of the nation as it did the postwar realities in Central Europe. The normalization of relations between the two parts of Germany was to release them from their clinch and integrate them into the East-West detente process, but at the same time lay the foundation for a long-term solution to the German question. Once German-German relations had been settled, the Bonn government would then give up its veto position with regard to international recognition of the GDR. It made this conditional on East Berlin's willingness to normalize relations between the two German states.

Renunciation of Force and Modus Vivendi with the Soviet Union

The renunciation-of-force policy of the Social-Liberal coalition had four main objectives:

1. To break down the dangerous confrontation from the days of the cold war and make possible an interest-based cooperation between the Federal Republic and the states of Eastern and Central Europe including the GDR. Thus, the Federal Republic was prepared to accept a modus vivendi on the postwar problems of Europe if in return the Soviet Union and the other East European states respected West Berlin's ties with the Federal Republic;
2. To avoid an isolation of the Federal Republic from its partners in the West, who were not about to have their detente efforts constantly constrained by Bonn and in particular were not prepared to respect the Fed-

eral Republic's claim of sole representation for an unlimited period of time. In this sense its policy had the purpose of a relief action;

3. To initiate a normalization of relations with the states of Eastern Europe and the GDR so as to prevent the *querelles allemandes* from becoming the predominant theme of the planned Conference on Security and Cooperation in Europe. In this sense the renunciation of force was a prerequisite and purpose of European detente policy;

4. To lay a political foundation for stronger trade and economic relations with the East European states. Access to the East European markets was to be opened up to West German industry; the national economies of COMECON were held out the promise of modern technology and Western capital.

Leading politicians of the Social-Liberal coalition conceived of the normalization of relations with the socialist states of Eastern Europe as an historic mission—comparable to the reconciliation with France brought about by Adenauer. With it the German government hoped to make a decisive contribution to East-West detente and the stabilization of the situation in Europe. If Bonn could rid itself of its past scapegoat function for the socialist states, such a policy promised a greater scope and flexibility in dealing with the East, the West, and the third world. Domestically the international stabilization would facilitate the "policy of internal reform," under which dictum the Brandt/Scheel cabinet had come to office (among other things, it would permit shifts in the national budget, e.g., from defense to social reforms).

Political relief was also afforded by the Federal Republic's signing of the Non-proliferation Treaty. This was consummated on November 28, 1969, after Bonn had obtained further clarification on its rights and obligations as a party to the treaty. This cleared away one more obstacle that had strained the credibility of its detente policy in the preceding years.

A week later, on December 8, 1969, the Federal Republic's ambassador in Moscow, Helmut Allardt, began initial negotiations with Foreign Minister Gromyko on a renunciation of force. This date had been agreed upon by Bonn and Moscow through an exchange of notes of November 15 and December 7, 1969. For the Federal Republic the talks were conducted on the basis of instructions devised by Ambassador Allardt and State Secretary Bahr from the Chancellor's Office as well as experts from the Foreign Office. Here the German government could return to designs for a negotiating concept that had been worked out by the Foreign Office planning staff under the direction of Egon Bahr during the Grand Coalition.

After a full three meetings the initial round of German-Soviet talks came to an end shortly before Christmas; they were confined to the presentation of maximum positions. Foreign Minister Gromyko put forward a comprehensive negotiating package in which the Soviet side demanded that the Federal Republic formally recognize the status quo in Europe, including recognition of the GDR under international law and of the inalterability of existing borders, before the signing of a renunciation-of-force agreement. Ambassador Allardt, on the other hand, started from the July 3, 1969 draft statements formulated by the government of the Grand Coalition. But primarily both sides wanted to find out in this first round of talks whether and on what basis negotiations on a renunciation of force were possible.[75] Moscow wanted to know whether the Federal Republic was prepared to recognize formally the status quo in Eastern and Central Europe, while Bonn was searching for ways and means to achieve a modus vivendi that would allow a normalization of relations notwithstanding its fundamental positions on the German question: unity of the nation, four-power responsibility for Germany as a whole and Berlin, integration in the West.

New initiatives toward the East—on November 25, 1969, Bonn had also invited Poland to enter into talks on renunciation of force and in late January had agreed to a personal meeting between the heads of government of the two German states—were linked with a lively diplomatic activity with the West. Prior to the public announcement of its aggressive Ostpolitik and German policy, Chancellor Brandt had sent his political confidant and future state secretary in the Chancellor's office, Egon Bahr, to Washington to explain Bonn's intentions, particularly to President Nixon's national security adviser, Henry Kissinger, and thus to ensure the backing of Bonn's most important ally. Brandt was aware of the Western allies' skepticism and mistrust toward an independent Ostpolitik and he knew that the resulting tensions could weaken the Federal Republic's negotiating position in Moscow. The allies needed time to adjust to what they saw as an abrupt change of course by Bonn. Precisely those who had for years advised the Federal Republic to exercise more flexibility in its relations with Eastern Europe now feared the dynamic of an active Ostpolitik that could exert a pull on the other partners, too. They were anxious about the increased power of the Federal Republic following normalization of its relations with the East European states, or they even conjured up the danger of a new "Rapallo."

In this regard, the United States assumed a central importance. Upon his visit to Washington in April 1970 Chancellor Brandt was assured by Kissinger that the U.S. basically supported his Ostpolitik.

There would be no attempt to change his basic course. We would not encourage any particualr negotiating strategy. Nor would we comment on specific terms of his negotiation. For this he would have to take responsibility; we would not participate in the German domestic debate, on either side. We would support Brandt's objectives, stay silent on his methods, urge closer consultation with his allies, warn against raising excessive expectations. And we would give him sense of partnership, which was the best assurance against the latent dangers of purely national policy.[76]

These assurances from Kissinger had become necessary as critical commentary by various politicians had raised some doubt about the U.S. position. To some extent German politicking was also being carried out in Washington as members of the CDU/CSU looked there for ways to keep on being right. For the German government, however, alliance backing for its policy was essential to its success. It therefore welcomed the action by the NATO Council at its December 1969 session and at its meeting in Rome in May 1970 adopting Bonn's political views and goals.[77]

The most important coordinating body on these matters was the Bonn group,[78] in which the representative of the German government kept the three Western powers informed about its negotiations with Moscow and they in turn watched that the rights and responsibilities of the four powers for Germany as a whole and Berlin were not infringed upon. This central hinge on German policy between the Federal Republic and its Western allies subsequently developed into the most important Western coordinating body for questions of East-West relations.

"Bahr Paper" and Moscow Treaty

In their coalition talks the SPD and FDP had agreed that State Secretary Bahr would at some point lead the talks with the Soviet Union. By 1970, the internal Western consultations had assured Bonn the support of its allies, and, though there had as yet been no material convergence of positions, the initial probes in Moscow had demonstrated the genuineness of the Soviet will to negotiate—especially in light of the fact that these negotiations would be conducted by Foreign Minister Gromyko himself. In late January 1970, then, the German government entrusted Bahr with the preparations for the negotiations. This raised the level of the talks and accelerated the negotiating process, since Bahr, as architect of Ostpolitik and close confidant of Brandt, could negotiate in Moscow with greater flexibility and authority than Ambassador Allardt.

In the talks with the Soviet Union it was first a matter of breaking down mutual mistrust, then of finding out which interests were negotiable and how much room there was for bargaining and compromise. The main difficulties were presented by the borders issue, recognition of the GDR, the rights and responsibilities of the four powers, and West Berlin's integration into the Federal Republic. On the question of borders a satisfactory formulation was found with "inviolability" of frontiers, instead of the "inalterability" originally demanded by the Soviet Union. Moreover, the primacy of the renunciation of force took away from the agreement the quality of a border treaty. This formulation was compatible with the traditional legal provisos inasmuch as a later reunification was viewed not as a territorial annexation but as a unification of two independent political systems. Regarding the Soviet demand of a recognition of the GDR under international law, Bahr argued that an unqualified recognition of the GDR by the Federal Republic was not possible as this would violate the rights of the four powers—thus also rights of the Soviet Union. Bahr later termed this issue the most difficult point of the negotiations:

> The international recognition of the GDR that the Soviet Union demanded from us was just not acceptable. This was the crux of the matter...If this crucial point had not been enforceable or become acceptable to the Soviet Union, then I would have had to leave, and would have left, without success.[79]

The inclusion of Berlin in the planned treaty instruments took place only indirectly in that the normalization of relations was to proceed "on the basis of the actual situation existing in Europe."[80]

After a full three rounds of negotiation from January to May 1970, Bahr was able to come to terms with Gromyko, or, as it were, the responsible section head in the Soviet Foreign Ministry, Valentin Falin, on a preliminary agreement, the so-called "Bahr Paper." This document, through indiscretion, came to light prematurely and set off an extremely acrimonious discussion in the West German public.[81] It already contained the central points of the future treaty. In it the Federal Republic and the Soviet Union espoused the development of peaceful relations among the European states on the basis of the actual situation existing in Europe. The renunciation of force was concretized by the Federal Republic's commitment to respect "today and in the future" the territorial integrity of all European states and the inviolability of their frontiers, including the Oder-Neisse line and the demarcation line between the Federal Republic and the GDR. In addition, the Federal Republic renounced any and all territorial claims. In return, the Soviet side renounced the raising of intervention claims according to the UN Charter's "enemy states clauses" in that both sides agreed to be guided in their mutual relations by the renunciation of force set forth by Article 2 of the Charter.

Besides this, Bahr and Gromyko had agreed upon a number of supplementary declarations of intent. In them the Federal Republic declared its readiness to conclude analogous treaties with Poland, Czechoslovakia, and the GDR. These would then form a unified whole with the Moscow Treaty. Bonn assented to an agreement with the GDR that was binding under international law and regularized their relations on the basis of equality, non-discrimination, and noninterference in the internal affairs of the other state. This was something other than the international recognition of the GDR originally demanded by Moscow, a recognition for which East Berlin had pressed and against whose "tempering" it had put up vehement opposition. The treaty with Czechoslovakia was to settle the questions connected with the invalidity of the Munich Agreement—there was no longer any word of a nullification decree "from the start." Finally, Bonn committed itself to support "in the course of the detente in Europe" the admission of the two German states into the United Nations. This meant that Bonn would give up its veto over international recognition of the GDR if progress had been made in normalizing relations between the two German states. Finally the Federal Republic and the Soviet Union declared their fundamental support for the planned European security conference and their will to achieve an all-around development of their mutual relations.[82]

The leaking of the Bahr Paper in the Federal Republic against the government's intent provoked a fierce controversy:

> Misunderstandings and intentional misinterpretations aside, it became clear for the first time to substantial sectors of the public that this was no less a matter than the liquidation of the 20-year special German conflict with the Soviet bloc—a matter of recognizing the GDR as a state among states and of renouncing border demands for all time. The legal distinction that this renunciation could not be binding on a reunified Germany was in fact politically immaterial insofar as the coming into being of this all-Germany in the indefinitely distant future would in no way be tolerated by the superpowers and its neighbors without prior stipulation of its external borders. The disclaimers demanded affected nothing that belonged to the Federal Republic and contained nothing more than a "recognition of the realities." Yet anyone could imagine what they meant, whereas the simultaneous gains in security, freedom of movement, and intra-

German contact were for many much harder to imagine and at this moment were by no means assured on the critical question of Berlin.[83]

The opposition charged that the government's negotiator, State Secretary Bahr, had bargained too quickly and too much on his own; a greater measure of "professionalism," it was opined, would have spared the Federal Republic many a concession.[84] The criticism is surely correct in the sense that the way the negotiations were conducted and the time perspective indicated by Chancellor Brandt for concluding an agreement—the summer of 1970—had put a certain pressure on the German government to get results. But the Soviet Union had solid interests in reaching an agreement, as Bonn held a key role in bringing about the European security conference desired by the Soviet Union and was not prepared to clear the way for it without satisfactory results in the negotiations. It is not correct that Bahr had negotiated in Moscow without backing and coordination by the chancellor and the foreign minister; however, not all parts of the Foreign Office were informed of all the steps in the negotiations. To allow the exploratory talks to run as undisturbed as possible, State Secretary Duckwitz of the Foreign Office had given instructions that reports were to be directed to the head of the house. After every meeting, Bahr and Allardt sent detailed reports to Bonn; moreover, between the negotiating rounds Bahr made a practice of intensive consultations with members of the cabinet and the Foreign Office and each time received new instructions. The allies were informed within the Bonn group and in bilateral consultations. The foreign affairs committees of the Bundestag and Bundesrat as well as leading politicians of the three party groups were similarly informed.[85]

The weight of the decisions and the intricacy of the ongoing negotiations with Moscow, Warsaw, and East Berlin meant, of course, that there would be varying assessments of what had been achieved in Moscow, both within the German government and in the coalition parties. The fundamental differences of opinion between government and opposition became particularly evident in the Bundestag debates on May 27 and June 17, 1970, initiated by a major interpellation of the CDU/CSU concerning policy on Germany, the East, and Europe.[86] It was, therefore, not surprising that the public was also disconcerted, and the coalition parties had to take some losses in the Landtag elections in North-Rhine Westphalia, Lower Saxony, and the Saarland on June 14, 1970.

The cabinet in Bonn decided, therefore, not to rush the actual treaty negotiations, which would be conducted by Foreign Minister Scheel, and rather use the time to do more informal sounding out of the Soviet side about a reunification proviso to be pronounced by the German side when the treaty was signed. At the same time the cabinet, the coalition parties, and the foreign affairs committees of the Bundestag and Bundesrat were to be thoroughly informed of the content of the treaty and the obligations to be undertaken by the Federal Republic, and the public was to be educated about the political significance.

To make it clear that the Bahr Paper was not an already agreed upon treaty text, the cabinet on June 7, 1970 adopted guidelines for the German-Soviet treaty negotiations that once again affirmed the basic position of the German government on the renunciation of force, the Berlin question, the right to self-determination, the normalization of relations with the GDR, and the continued validity of existing treaties. After further internal clarifications—in particular of the constitutional aspects of the planned treaty—as well as intensive international consultations, the cabinet on June 23, 1970 empowered Foreign Minister Scheel to enter negotiations. At the same time it declared that progress in European detente was inseparably linked with a satisfactory Berlin settlement and announced that a treaty renouncing the use of force could not be put into effect until a similar agreement had been achieved on Berlin.[87]

On July 27, 1970, Foreign Minister Scheel arrived in Moscow together with State Secretaries Egon Bahr of the Chancellor's Office and Paul Frank of the Foreign Office, plus a large delegation. With respect to the operative parts of the treaty, the prior publication of the Bahr Paper had greatly limited the foreign minister's latitude for bargaining, since any alteration would affect not only the material interests of the Soviet Union, but its prestige as well. Hence, the German delegation concentrated on attaching a preamble to the treaty, which was to make it clear that this agreement was a bilateral treaty of cooperation and not a premature settlement by peace treaty. At the same time the "German option" was to be at least implicitly anchored in the treaty by the mention of the German-Soviet Agreement of 1955 on the establishment of diplomatic relations. This German claim to self-determination as set forth in the Basic Law was also the subject of a "Letter on German Unity," which was to be presented to the Soviet Union at the signing of the treaty and was to clarify that sustaining this claim was not in contradiction to the aims of the treaty. Further, the Soviet Union was officially notified that the German government would not submit the German-Soviet Treaty to the Bundestag for ratification until the four-power negotiations on Berlin had yielded satisfactory results. On this basis the German-Soviet Treaty was initialed on August 7, 1970 by Foreign Ministers Scheel and Gromyko and, following deliberations in the German cabinet and informing of the allies, signed on August 12, 1970 by Chancellor Brandt and Prime Minister Kosygin in the presence of General Secretary Brezhnev.[88]

The significance of the Moscow Treaty for German-Soviet relations can best be gauged by comparison with the seemingly unbridgeable positions of just a few years before. In place of nonbinding renunciation-of-force statements or Soviet maximal demands that amounted to unconditional recognition of European borders, there was now a treaty in which both sides declared their readiness to normalize their relations and create a modus vivendi in the interest of peace in Europe. Part of this modus vivendi was a commitment to be guided by the principles of renunciation of force both in mutual relations and in questions of European and international security and to respect the postwar realities of Europe: the existence of the GDR and the postwar borders of Europe as well as the integration of West Berlin into the Federal Republic.

For a generation that had lived in the hope of reunification—if possible in the borders of 1937—facing the necessity of this step was no doubt bitter. Yet, in the words of Chancellor Brandt, "Nothing is lost with this treaty that was not gambled away long ago."[89] At the same time, this step gave the Federal Republic the possibility of normalizing its relations with the states of Eastern Europe. In some sense, as it made possible the kind of reconciliation with Poland that had been achieved with France and Israel, it made a final break with the crimes committed by Germans in the Second World War.

However, the political value of the Moscow Treaty, which essentially consisted of declarations of intent, remained to be proven. First of all, it remained to be seen whether a normalization of relations with Poland, Czechoslovakia, and especially with the GDR, could be built upon the foundation laid in Moscow. Secondly, the Soviets had yet to deliver on the Berlin question, and thirdly, it would take at least ten to fifteen years before there could be reliable judgments as to whether the treaty had really normalized German-Soviet relations and proven its durability in difficult times.

Negotiations with Poland

A few days after the offer of talks had been made to Moscow, the head of the West German trade mission in Warsaw, Minister Heinrich Böx, presented to the Polish Foreign Ministry a note from the German government proposing talks on matters of common interest. The note made reference to remarks by the Polish party chief Wladyslaw

Gomulka, who at a campaign rally in Warsaw on May 17, 1969 had indicated a willingness to enter into talks with the Federal Republic without precondition. Besides that there had been a range of informal contacts between leading SPD figures and representatives of the United Polish Workers Party (UPWP).

The central problem in German-Polish relations and hence for the prospective talks was that Poland demanded a final recognition of its western border by the Federal Republic of Germany, while the German government placed the border question under the peace treaty proviso. Bonn did not want to commit a future all-German government, nor was it about to encroach upon the rights and responsibilities of the four powers for Germany as a whole. Added to this were questions of indemnification for crimes of National Socialism on the one hand, and, on the other, steps to allow Germans remaining in Poland to emigrate and reunite their families.

The talks between Warsaw and Bonn were opened on February 4, 1970. The German negotiating delegation was led by State Secretary Duckwitz; his counterpart was Deputy Foreign Minister Josef Winiewicz. While the Polish government demanded—just as Gomulka had in his speech of May 1969—a final and unequivocal recognition of the Oder-Neisse border, Bonn's negotiators were initially sounding out the other side on the "Nuremberg formula," the "recognition or the respecting of the Oder-Neisse Line until a peace settlement is reached."[90] The German government was striving for a broadly based, general improvement in German-Polish relations. It was prepared to take the Polish interest in secure borders into account within the framework of a renunciation-of-force agreement, which would also contain a renunciation of territorial claims by the Federal Republic. But the respecting of existing borders would have to be subject to the peace treaty proviso and must not prejudice the existing rights of the allies. With seemingly little room for compromise the positions were set forth in memoranda that the two delegations exchanged on March 1 and 3 and that presented the two sides' views in the form of proposed formulations for the next round of negotiations.

An agreement on this basis, however, was not possible. For political and psychological reasons, the Polish government regarded as insufficient a border guarantee by Bonn as part of a renunciation-of-force agreement; it could point to the fact that despite the 1925 declarations renouncing the use of force (in the Locarno Treaties) and those of 1934 (in the German-Polish Nonaggression Pact) Germany had invaded Poland in 1939. Duckwitz, on the other hand, argued that the allies' reserved rights prevented the Federal Republic from reaching a final border settlement with Poland.

A convergence of the positions did not come about until the German side submitted at the end of April a formulation that met the Polish desire for a definite determination of borders. The border question, in fact, illustrated how the various negotiating levels constituted a system of communicating tubes. The progress made by State Secretary Bahr in the Moscow negotiations generated a need to make concessions in the Warsaw negotiations in order to prevent their failure. The formulations accepted in Warsaw could then be introduced into the Moscow negotiations. Once the Soviet Union had in the Bahr Paper forgone an explicit recognition of borders and expressed its satisfaction with their being respected, the German side proposed a formulation according to which the two treaty partners would declare "that the Oder-Neisse line is Poland's western frontier. The Federal Republic of Germany will respect the integrity of Polish territory now and in future. Existing treaties will not be affected by this."[91]

Assisted by Bahr, Chancellor Brandt several times took a personal hand in the negotiations. The negotiating atmosphere in Warsaw was particularly benefited by a letter that Brandt sent to Gomulka on April 20, 1970, assuring the latter "that we are entirely in earnest in desiring a conciliation and practical settlement...The German government understands Poland's desire to live within guaranteed borders and does not question the integrity of Polish territory."[92] This letter was, however, not conducive to a good coalition climate in Bonn, as Foreign Minister Scheel had not been informed of it and the negotiating delegation from the Foreign Office saw itself placed in the role of an agent for policy conceived in the Chancellor's Office. The consequence was a shake-up at the top of the Foreign Office that meant replacement of Duckwitz as official state secretary—not, however, as chief negotiator in the German-Polish talks—as well as a greater distance of the Foreign Office from the chancellor's office in day-to-day affairs.

The Polish desire for stronger economic and technological cooperation with the Federal Republic had a positive impact on the treaty talks. The economic negotiations, which had begun back in 1969 but broken off several times, culminated in June 1970 in a long-term agreement between the two countries on trade and economic-technological cooperation for the period 1970—74. Within the scope of this agreement the Federal Republic's exports to Poland increased from 658 million marks to 3.61 billion marks and its imports rose from 744 million to 1.42 billion marks. Altogether, the Federal Republic's share of Poland's trade with the West grew to over 30 percent. At the same time, however, Poland's debt in the West was also increasing—the seed of future problems.

Still, the Federal Republic's proposed border formula did not surmount all the difficulties. The Polish delegation was trying to establish a considerably stronger form of recognition of frontiers. It did not give in until it had learned of the accords reached by Bahr in Moscow and become aware of the importance of the Bahr Paper's general clause on the "actual situation existing in Europe" as the basis for the normalization process. However, the publication of the Bahr Paper in the Federal Republic put a strain on relations between Warsaw and Bonn. The stipulation of a formula for the Oder-Neisse frontier by State Secretary Bahr and Foreign Minister Gromyko not only prejudiced the latitude for bargaining in the German-Polish negotiations, but also negated the political sovereignty of Poland and thus reaffirmed the controversial "Brezhnev Doctrine." In Bonn, there had, in fact, been consideration as to whether it would not be preferable to give priority to negotiations with Poland and Czechoslovakia. But the German government had realized that the key to normalization of relations with the East European countries was in Moscow. Moreover, the negotiations with Warsaw, and later with Prague, too, turned out to be a great deal more difficult than those with Moscow, for each of them wanted to achieve special, exceptionally airtight solutions to their distinct conflicts, whereas the Soviet Union was satisfied with a de facto recognition of the status quo. Hence, the negotiations with Poland lasted until late fall 1970.

As quid pro quo for Moscow's and also Warsaw's acknowledgement of the continued validity of existing treaties and the rights of the four powers (and thus of the peace treaty proviso) Bonn was supposed to commit itself to supporting, even as part of an all-German government in any peace treaty negotiations, the maintenance of the Oder-Neisse line as the Polish western frontier. But the German government could not agree to this if it did not want to risk losing the treaty for want of the two-thirds majority required for ratification. Another problem was the demand that persons of German origin in Poland be allowed to emigrate and reunite with their families. The Polish side rejected this with the argument that there was no "German minority" in their country; besides, the wishes of Polish citizens to emigrate to the Federal Republic could not be the subject of an international agreement.

The concluding negotiations in Warsaw in November 1970 thus still afforded sufficient matter for conflict. As in Moscow, they were conducted by Foreign Minister Scheel. At the beginning of the negotiations, Scheel made it clear that the German government could enter into commitments only for the Federal Republic of Germany and could neither anticipate a settlement by peace treaty nor replace it with bilateral accords. Likewise, it would have to take into account the rights and responsibilities of the four powers for Germany as a whole and Berlin. At the same time Scheel recognized—as other leading politicians in the Federal Republic had done before him—Poland's moral right to live within secure borders permanently. Ultimately, a treaty settlement was arrived at on this basis. For the difficult problem of reuniting families the Polish government declared its willingness to authorize the Polish Red Cross to settle these humanitarian questions with the aid of "publically usable information."

Finally, on November 18, 1970 Foreign Ministers Scheel and Stefan Jedrychowski could affix their initials to the agreed treaty text. In the preamble it was recalled that Poland had been the first victim of the Second World War, which had inflicted great suffering on the nations of Europe; it was noted, however, that in both countries there had grown up a new generation, whose future was to be made secure through the inviolability of frontiers and respect for the territorial integrity and sovereignty of all states in Europe. In Article 1 it was stated that the Oder-Neisse line laid down in the Potsdam Agreement "shall constitute the western State frontier of the People's Republic of Poland." As in the Moscow Treaty, the two states reaffirmed the inviolability of their frontiers now and in future, committed themselves to respect each other's territorial integrity without restriction, and renounced any territorial claims. The readiness expressed in Article 3 to take steps toward full normalization of relations and a broadening of cooperation implied the readiness to establish diplomatic relations and exchange ambassadors following ratification of the treaty. Finally, as in the Moscow Treaty, it was stated that existing agreement would remain in force.

In correspondence between the Federal Republic of Germany and the three Western powers the rights and responsibilities of the four powers were reaffirmed and it was stated that the German government had acted solely in the name of the Federal Republic of Germany. In an information, which was also part of the treaty instruments, the People's Republic of Poland informed the German government of its readiness to facilitate the emigration of Polish citizens of German origin.[93] Then, on December 7, 1970, the Warsaw Treaty was signed by Chancellor Brandt and Prime Minister Józef Cyrankiewicz and Foreign Ministers Scheel and Jedrychowski. During this visit Brandt symbolically fell to his knees at the monument to those killed in the Warsaw ghetto uprising.

Just as with the Moscow Treaty, Bonn had kept its allies abreast of the progress of the negotiations in Warsaw. In its endeavor to reach a compromise with Poland it could be sure of the support of its partners in the West. Upon his trip to Poland back in September 1967 President de Gaulle had spoken of "Poland's clearly defined borders." When Chancellor Brandt had visited Washington, President Nixon had told him that the United States would be understanding if the Federal Republic were to decide on recognition of the Oder-Neisse border.[94] Still, the Federal Republic had to show particular consideration for preserving the allies' reserved rights with regard to Germany as a whole and Berlin. When the Paris and Bonn Treaties had been concluded in 1954, these rights had first of all the function of committing France, Great Britain, and the United States to the goal of German reunification and a border settlement in the framework of a peace treaty. Since then this role had shrunk to a kind of reassurance clause. But above all, these rights were designed to give the four powers a formal say in the structural reorganization of Central Europe, and the allies did make use of this authority in the context of bilateral and multilateral Ostpolitik, most visibly in the four-power negotiations on Berlin. The linchpin of German and allied coordination was again the Bonn Group, supplemented by bilateral contacts with Chancellor Brandt's visit to Washington in April 1970 and Foreign Minister Scheel's meeting with his French counterpart Maurice Schuman in May 1970 in Paris. Also, the NATO meeting in Rome in May 1970 afforded the opportunity for a joint stock-taking of policy toward the East and detente.

In the case of the Warsaw Treaty the domestic debate was carried on in a somewhat less hectic atmosphere than with the Moscow Treaty. Throughout the negotiating process the government had taken pains not only to inform the foreign affairs committees of the Bundestag and Bundesrat as well as the heads of the coalition parties, but also to take the leadership of the League of Expellees and various refugee associations into its confidence. The Committee for an Indivisible Germany also played a helpful role, providing a framework for largely unemotional discussions between leading politicians of the coalition and opposition parties. Finally, CDU and CSU deputies had visited Poland several times and had occasion to become acquainted with the Polish attitude on the border question, and, conversely, to apprise the Poles of the fact that the opposition, despite its insistence on legal positions, likewise desired a reconciliation with the Polish people. Nevertheless, the treaty's explicit renunciation of the former German eastern territories precluded the CDU/CSU's parliamentary approval of the Warsaw Treaty.[95]

An appraisal of the Warsaw Treaty has to take into account the difficulties that had accumulated between Poland and Germany as a result of a calamitous past, which necessitated laborious detail work to produce solutions that were at once politically and morally convincing as well as legally viable. A comparison with the Moscow Treaty shows that in accepting the Oder-Neisse frontier the Federal Republic had gone further in order to oblige the Polish people in their understandable demand to live within secure borders. By its nature, therefore, the Warsaw Treaty was primarily a border treaty and only secondarily a renunciation-of-force agreement like the Moscow Treaty. Though the German government could not enunciate an explicit and unconditional recognition without jeopardizing ratification of the treaty by the Bundestag and Bundesrat, still it believed that with the accords it had laid the foundation for a lasting reconciliation between the German and the Polish peoples.

A number of political developments in Poland and the Federal Republic came together and made it necessary to "touch up" the Warsaw Treaty in 1975—76. In the Federal Republic there were episodes during the ratification process—e.g., the March 1972 joint resolution of the Bundestag on foreign policy and policy on Germany—which the Polish side interpreted as an "abandonment" of statements in the Warsaw Treaty. But two other factors were even more serious. In Poland the economic problems were coming more and more into the open, leading to strikes and, following their violent suppression, to the removal of the party chief, Gomulka. The economic and technological cooperation between the Federal Republic and Poland had indeed multiplied on the basis of the 1970 trade agreement and grown further as a result of a new ten-year agreement concluded in 1974, yet Polish indebtedness in the West had assumed alarming dimensions. What Poland needed was credits on favorable terms. At the same time there were growing numbers of those of German origin who wanted to emigrate to the Federal Republic on the basis of the treaty "information" of December 1970. Most prominent among those wishing to leave were well-trained skilled workers, whose departure threatened to aggravate even further the labor shortage in Poland. Because of the economic situation, therefore, the Polish government came to see a material connection between German compensatory financial assistance and a more generous granting of emigration permits, a connection that in the course of time knotted into a solid linkage.

In October 1973 an agreement seemed to be in the works when Foreign Minister Scheel on a visit to Warsaw promised that the German government would examine the possibility of a credit for Poland on favorable terms. For its part, the Polish side stated its readiness to seek a comprehensive solution in the next three to five years to the issue of Poles of German origin leaving the country in accordance with the "information." Upon his reciprocal visit to Bonn in December 1973 the Polish foreign minister cited a figure of 50,000 persons each year.

Yet at the same time the Polish government raised indemnification demands for victims of the German concentration camps and occupation regime. The German government flatly rejected this, for it feared that such a course would prompt similar demands from other states. After that, the resettlement stream dwindled.

On the basis of bilateral talks between State Secretary Walther Gehlhoff from the Foreign Office and Polish Ambassador Waclaw Piatkowski, Chancellor Schmidt was able to reach an agreement with the Polish party chief, Edward Gierek, attendant to the signing of the Helsinki Final Act in August 1975. The Federal Republic agreed to a compensation of 1.3 billion marks for Polish pension claims and a loan of 1 billion marks; in return, Poland promised exit permits for another 120,000 to 125,000 persons. Two months later Foreign Ministers Hans-Dietrich Genscher and Stefan Olszowski signed a five-part package:

1. An agreement in which each state undertook to assume payments of pension and state accident insurance even when citizens of one had acquired claims against the insurance carriers of the other;
2. An agreement on a global settlement of pension claims by the Federal Republic providing a onetime compensatory payment of 1.3 billion marks to the People's Republic of Poland (since only 700 million marks had been originally budgeted, the additional 600 million marks were evidently to enable the Polish state to provide pension payments to victims of concentration camps as well);
3. A loan of 1 billion marks from the German Development Loan Corporation with a 2.5 percent annual rate of interest, several years' deferral of repayment, and long-term repayment schedule;
4. A protocol in which the Polish side stated that it would be able to grant approval for 120,000 to 125,000 persons of German origin to emigrate to the Federal Republic in the course of the next four years;
5. An agreement establishing a long-term program for the development of economic, industrial, and technical cooperation.[96]

These agreements and understandings required various forms of ratification and approval. In the ensuing debate the discussion flared over the issue of what binding effect the resettlement protocol attained. To ensure ratification—now in doubt in the Bundesrat since a change in government in Lower Saxony had altered the majority ratio—another touch-up was necessary. This was done in the form of a supplementary exchange of letters promising that citizens of German origin would still be able to emigrate after the protocol's term had expired.

The Treaty with Prague

The remaining normalization of relations with Czechoslovakia could not be effected until the summer of 1973. The Treaty on Mutual

Relations was initialed on the day that State Secretary Bahr and State Secretary Kohl exchanged the ratification documents to the Basic Treaty (June 20, 1973)—over a year after the Treaties of Moscow and Warsaw and the Berlin Agreement had come into force. This late date is all the more surprising as Chancellor Kiesinger's policy statement of 1966 (like the Erhard government's peace note of the same year) had expressed the view "that the Munich Agreement which had come about under the threat of force, is no longer valid."[97] Moreover, exploratory talks with Prague were initiated shortly after negotiations on the Warsaw Treaty had been concluded. Yet it took eight rounds of talks to arrive at a formulation acceptable to both sides concerning the invalidity of the Munich accords. Actual treaty negotiations between Bonn and Prague did not begin until May 1973.

Why was it that Prague came to bring up the rear of the detente convoy? One reason lay in the political and legal complexity of the issue. Thus, from what point (from the very beginning or later) was the Munich Agreement of 1938 to be considered null and void? Or would it be at all necessary to make a formal statement about the point in time? Ultimately, the legal consequences of a decree of nullification would have to be determined. The Bahr Paper—which in a sense constituted a German-Soviet skeleton agreement on the problems issuing from the European status quo—did not go beyond a statement of intent, that those questions pertaining to the invalidity of the Munich Agreement were to be settled in a form acceptable to both sides. What such a settlement might look like, however, remained open. Also, the Czechoslovakian leadership was constrained to proceed cautiously since the consolidation process following the Warsaw Pact intervention of August 1968 was not yet finished. For its part, the Federal Republic hesitated to make legally binding statements on the invalidity of the Munich Agreement if it were not sure that this would not give rise to new legal uncertainties (e.g., on questions of citizenship). Opposition from the Association of Sudeten Germans also had to be taken into account, at least as an opinion factor. Finally, there were problems with respect to the inclusion of West Berlin in the Prague agreement; these would have to be settled at a higher level (in an understanding that Foreign Minister Scheel concluded with the Soviet government in November 1973) before the treaty between the Federal Republic and Czechoslovakia could be signed on December 11, 1973.[98]

The question of the invalidity of the Munich Agreement was so complicated because it entailed a confluence of historical, political, and legal problems. The "diktat of Munich" had been the work, besides the Reich, of France, Great Britain, and Italy; each of these countries had found its own way of distancing itself from the Munich Agreement. Then, the cession of the Sudetenland had not been effected in a single legal act; the agreement itself was preceded by an exchange of notes between London, Paris, and Prague (September 19–21, 1938) in which self-determination for the Sudetenland and its union with the Reich had already been agreed to in principle. This was followed by a series of agreements between the German Reich and Czechoslovakia arranging the details, e.g., the determination of the new borders. And finally, all of these arrangements were invalidated by the Wehrmacht's invasion of the rest of Czechoslovakia on March 15, 1939 and the establishment of a "Protectorate of Bohemia and Moravia." Thus, it was a matter of reaching settlements on a whole bundle of legal acts and political developments. On top of this there were the political-psychological strains: on the Czechoslovakian side the trauma of the forced consent to territorial cession brought about under pressure from one's own allies; on the part of the Federal Republic the distress of the Sudeten Germans' expulsion in 1945. Thus it was that the negotiations required considerable time, although the matter itself—the invalidity of the agreement of 1938—was not in dispute.

The Czechoslovakian demand that the Munich Agreement be declared null and void from the start aimed essentially at recognition of the wrongfulness of the forced territorial cession of 1938. The opinion in Bonn was that the Munich Agreement had been "torn up" by Hitler with the German invasion in March 1939, and had become invalid at the latest with its denunciation by the Czechoslovakian government in exile in 1940 or by the Western powers in 1942. These views reflected the German legalistic tradition combined with the fear of possible negative legal consequences from a decree of nullification *ex tunc*.

Once Bonn had formally normalized relations with the other East European states and the GDR, Czechoslovakia became increasingly concerned that it could be left out of the European detente process. In various speeches and statements in early 1973 the leadership in Prague signaled its readiness to end the "pause for reflection" taken upon German request in the summer of 1972 and to seek a compromise solution. This consisted in declaring the Munich Agreement of 1938 null and void, but specifying no date for it, and in making additional determinations to preclude legal uncertainties arising from the decree of nullification.[99] Thus, in Article 2 it was stated that the treaty did not affect the legal effects of the law as applied in the period between September 30, 1938 and May 9, 1945, that the nationality of the persons concerned was not affected, and that the treaty did not constitute a legal basis for material claims on the part of Czechoslovakia. Further, both sides committed themselves, as in the Warsaw Treaty, to a renunciation of force in accordance with Article 2 of the UN Charter, to the inviolability of common borders, and to respect for territorial integrity. In addition, they declared that they "have no territorial claims whatsoever against each other and that they will not assert any such claims in the future." Finally, the Federal Republic and Czechoslovakia announced "further steps for the comprehensive development of their mutual relations." The most important step was the establishment of diplomatic relations, which took place on December 11, 1973, the same day as the signing of the Prague Treaty. In a supplementary exchange of letters it was agreed that West Berlin would be included in the most relevant provisions of the treaty. Also, the Czechoslovakian government clarified that punishable acts perpetrated in the period 1938–45, with the exception of war crimes and crimes against humanity, fell under the statute of limitations. Finally, Prague assured the Federal Republic that the emigration of Czechoslovakian citizens of German origin to the Federal Republic would be facilitated and that the tourist and visitor traffic between the two countries would be improved.

The Prague Treaty was certainly the most difficult of the Eastern treaties from a legal standpoint, yet it was also the most justifiable politically, for here it was a matter of rectifying a piece of clear-cut National Socialist power politics. It is regrettable that it was concluded so late—and that subsequently it could not serve as a basis for developing that measure of neighborly cooperation projected in the treaty. The treaty came too late for a reconciliation between the two nations—by five and a half years for Czechoslovakia, three years for the Federal Republic—as both had meanwhile recovered the normality of everyday life in different social systems and blocs.

With the Prague Treaty the last obstacles had been removed to the establishment of diplomatic relations with Bulgaria and Hungary. Out of regard for East Berlin and Prague, both countries had made a normalization of relations with the Federal Republic (and the creation of embassies out of the trade missions in existence since the early 1960s) dependent on prior recognition of the status quo in Europe by the Federal Republic. This did not call for special treaties since there were no unresolved political problems in the German-Bulgarian or German-Hungarian relationships. On December 21, 1973, it was announced in Bonn, Sofia, and Budapest in almost identically worded communiqués that the Federal Republic and Bulgaria and the Federal Republic and Hungary had resolved to develop further the relations between their countries and to establish diplomatic relations.[100]

THE QUADRIPARTITE AGREEMENT ON BERLIN

A satisfactory settlement on Berlin was central to the efforts to set in motion a normalization of relations between the Federal Republic and the Eastern and Central European states. The four-power responsibility for Berlin and the ties of West Berlin to the Federal Republic were among the accomplished facts in Europe after the Second World War—the "actual situation existing in this region," as it was put in the Bahr Paper and likewise in the Moscow Treaty. If Bonn were to respect the territorial integrity of the European states in the framework of a treaty-based modus vivendi, then it expected the equivalent from the Soviet Union and its East European allies in relation to Berlin. To make it clear that these were two sides of the same coin, the Federal Republic had already declared upon signing the Moscow Treaty that this treaty could not come into force until there was "a satisfactory settlement of the situation in and around Berlin."[101]

An agreement on Berlin—which, in recognition of the rights reserved to the four powers for Berlin and Germany as a whole, could be made only by or in collaboration with these powers—was in turn the prerequisite for a settlement of relations between the two German states. Once the GDR was recognized as a state of equal standing in Germany, it would be even more difficult for the Federal Republic or the Western powers to deny the GDR rights and attributes of sovereignty over the access routes to and from Berlin. Thus, a transit arrangement guaranteeing unimpeded access had to be worked out first. If both German states were one day to be members of the United Nations it would have to be settled who could represent Berlin to the outside world without this issue becoming a constant source of intra-German wrangling. The postwar development had clearly shown how any change in East-West relations inevitably had an impact on Berlin, the most sensitive point in Central Europe. Hence, it was inherent in the logic of the Social-Liberal coalition's Ostpolitik—but also in that of U.S.-Soviet detente—to seek to stabilize the latent crisis center.

In 1968 and 1969, access restrictions and obstructions on the connecting routes to Berlin as well as Soviet protests against the meeting of the Federal Convention in Berlin once again directed attention to the unsatisfactory situation of the city. Addressing employees of the Siemens works during his visit to Berlin in February 1969, President Nixon proposed four-power negotiations on Berlin. The Soviet Union also indicated that it was interested in talks. Moscow was mainly intent upon restricting the presence of the Federal Republic in Berlin. The Western powers, on the other hand, wanted to talk about improving access to Berlin and indicated Bonn's reciprocal readiness to enter into talks with the GDR on traffic problems and to compromise on its Berlin presence. In August of that year the Soviet Union officially proposed the initiation of negotiations.[102]

For a number of years Foreign Minister Brandt had pressed for negotiations to stabilize the situation of the city and dispel its ever-present state of crisis. In 1967 Klaus Schütz, then parliamentary state secretary in the Foreign Office, had developed elements for a Berlin settlement. While the United States viewed negotiations on Berlin skeptically in light of the West's narrow margins for bargaining, Brandt realized early on that a satisfactory Berlin settlement had a central role to play in detente policy. Without it a recognition of the GDR would not be possible.

The Western powers gave up their reticence about negotiations on Berlin only as the contours of the Social-Liberal coalition's Ostpolitik began to emerge. There was now the possibility of a quid pro quo that could be used to improve the situation in and around Berlin; at the same time, the four-power negotiations offered a subtle instrument with which the dynamic of the Social-Liberals' Ostpolitik could be monitored and, if need be, held in check.[103]

The negotiating levels and organs developed for the Berlin talks corresponded to the complex structure of interests. Formally the talks took place between the four powers responsible for Berlin and Germany as a whole, represented by the British, French, and U.S. ambassadors in Bonn along with the Soviet representative in East Berlin. The Western negotiating position was substantially worked out in the Bonn Group with the participation of the Federal Republic and the West Berlin Senate. On the Eastern side there was naturally close coordination between Moscow and East Berlin. Especially on the Berlin question the Soviet leadership could not afford to act contrary to the will of the GDR, which was directly affected by an agreement; rather, they coerced Ulbricht into stepping down in favor of Honecker. Ulbricht's resignation, allegedly for reasons of health, was announced on May 3, 1971. Around the Berlin talks there were also many informal negotiating contacts, e.g., between President Nixon's national security adviser, Kissinger, and the Soviet ambassador in Washington, Dobrynin. Kissinger and Dobrynin gave instructions for informal talks between the U.S. and Soviet ambassadors Kenneth Rush and Pjotr Abrassimov, while State Secretary Bahr met with Foreign Minister Gromyko and the Soviet ambassador in Bonn, Falin. There were also contacts between Bonn and East Berlin's State Secretary Michael Kohl.

However, in light of the results of the negotiations the most important procedural arrangement was the "back channel" instituted by Kissinger in April 1971: direct negotiating contacts between Rush, Falin, and Bahr, who on the Western side got their directives from Kissinger and Brandt, sometimes bypassing the foreign ministries. To be able to circumvent the diplomatic apparatus, a special communications link was set up via a U.S. Naval officer in Frankfurt. A series of complications resulted from the difference in tempo between the "front channel" negotiations, i.e., the four-power talks, and the "back channel" contacts. Thus in the critical final stage Secretary of State Rogers summoned Ambassador Rush to break off the negotiations immediately and report to Washington, as Rush seemed to have exceeded his negotiating instructions—a conflict that was cleared up only through a certain degree of obstinacy on the part of the ambassador and by the personal intervention of President Nixon.[104] On the other hand, the behind-the-scenes connection, because of the small number of negotiators involved and the support that all three obtained from the heads of their governments, made for smoother negotiations with less frictional loss—and they brought the government in Bonn directly into the search for a Berlin settlement acceptable to all sides.

The Berlin negotiations entailed a wealth of problems, which Schütz had described with the expression *zustand, zugang und zutritt*. This formulation went beyond the three "essentials" set forth by President Kennedy in late July 1961, or rather represented their German equivalent: (1) the right of the three Western powers to a "presence in West Berlin," (2) the right of "access through East Germany," (3) the obligation "to guarantee in West Berlin the self-determination of its future and the free choice of its way of life."[105] *Zustand* concerned the status of Berlin: the rights of the four powers for Berlin as a whole and the rights of the three powers in West Berlin, the inclusion of West Berlin in the judicial and economic system of the Federal Republic, as well as West Berlin's ties to the Federal Republic, including foreign political representation by the Federation. *Zugang* to West Berlin and beyond comprised the entire military and civilian traffic between West German territory and West Berlin and was the touchiest point, for here the viability of the city was decided and here the interests of the West were most vulnerable because of Berlin's geographical situation. *Zutritt* meant more possibilities for West Berliners to visit East Berlin, as had existed before the building of the Wall and then trickled down to limited agreements on frontier-crossing permits.

In preparing for the Berlin negotiations the three Western powers and the Federal Republic had concentrated on coming up with provisions by which the Berlin access routes would be freed of impediments and harassment. Besides a satisfactory settlement on access the Federal Republic also wanted a recognition of the Federal Republic and West Berlin's belonging together and of Bonn's right to represent the city abroad.

Negotiations of the Four Powers

In the first phase of the talks, which were opened on March 26, 1970 in the former Allied Control Council building in West Berlin, each side confined itself to setting forth its position with no indication of compromise. The Soviet position became more flexible as the German government—most directly Bahr in his talks with Gromyko in Moscow—made it clear that Bonn could undertake far-reaching obligations to respect the status quo in Europe, as demanded by Moscow, only if the Soviet Union for its part guaranteed unimpeded access to Berlin. The Soviet leadership refused to make any direct promises to the German government because this would have weakened the four-power responsibility, which it also claimed, and besides would have provoked conflicts with the East Berlin government. Yet Moscow did recognize that without a Berlin settlement the prospects for ratification of the Eastern Treaties were virtually nil, especially in light of the opposition criticism in the Federal Republic that the obligations were unbalanced. Thus, after the Moscow Treaty had been signed there was growing Soviet interest in an agreement; at the same time the West recognized that there was now the prospect of reaching a more comprehensive settlement on Berlin.

However, 18 months of tough talks and negotiations were needed before an agreement on Berlin was ready. At first, Moscow held firm to its maximum demands, which culminated in the removal of any West German presence and the transformation of West Berlin into a "free city." On the issue of access it declared it had no jurisdiction, as this was a matter for the GDR. The Western powers, on the other hand, wanted a Soviet guarantee for not only unimpeded, but facilitated access to Berlin as well as a recognition of the political ties between the Federal Republic and Berlin. On the latter point the West was prepared to remove some of the more demonstrative aspects of the West German presence (e.g., meetings of the Federal Convention). The prime concern was to deprive the Soviet Union and the GDR of the pretext for harassment of West Berlin.[106] But since neither side was prepared to give up its legal positions the four powers decided at the beginning of 1971, at the suggestion of Egon Bahr, to exclude the juridical and status question from the negotiations. At the same time, Moscow indicated possibilities for compromise on the disputed question of access: the Soviet Union would pronounce a general guarantee for unimpeded access, but details would have to be arranged between the two German states. It also showed a willingness to compromise on the matter of West German presence: the Soviet Union was prepared to accept a certain measure of West German presence if, in turn, it were allowed a presence in West Berlin, say in the form of a consulate.

On this basis a compromise settlement on Berlin emerged as a possibility in early 1971 and then slowly began to take shape in the following weeks and months. Its foundation was the Four-Power Agreement. Building upon this, the West German government and the Berlin Senate on the one hand and the GDR government on the other would negotiate the modalities of a settlement on access and entry; finally, the whole of it would be sealed and put into force by a final Quadripartite Protocol. This procedure underscored how closely bilateral Ostpolitik and allied policy on Germany and Berlin were interlinked: "The four powers could not do without the Germans and the Germans could not do without the four powers" (Egon Bahr).[107] Yet the negotiations between the four powers on the various details still took the entire summer before the Quadripartite Agreement, which then constituted the basis for the subsequent German-German negotiations, could be signed on September 3, 1971.

In accordance with the understanding arrived at in early 1971, the text of this agreement left open the object of negotiation, rather circumscribing it by reference to the "relevant area" and to the four-power rights and responsibilities stemming from the war and postwar periods. Notwithstanding the differences in legal views, the situation as it had developed in this area was not to be altered unilaterally (Part I, Article 4). In the operative part of the Quadripartite Agreement the western sectors of Berlin were explicitly mentioned. The Soviet Union agreed that the transit traffic of civilian persons and goods between the western sectors of Berlin and the Federal Republic by road, rail, and waterways through the territory of the GDR would be unimpeded. Moreover, this traffic would be facilitated in that it would "take place in the most simple and expeditious manner" (Part II, A). The three Western powers declared that the ties between the western sectors of Berlin and the Federal Republic of Germany would be maintained and developed, whereby they recognized that these sectors would continue not to be a constituent part of the Federal Republic and not be governed by it (Part II, B).

A supplementary exchange of letters clarified how this stipulation was to be interpreted—e.g., that the established provisions concerning the applicability of West German legislation in West Berlin would remain unchanged. In the agreement the Soviet Union also stated that the visits and communications between West Berlin and East Berlin and with the rest of the GDR were to be improved, while the problems of the enclaves, including Steinstücken, might be solved by exchange of territory (Part II, C). Detailed arrangements were to be agreed upon between the respective German authorities. The modalities of these were described in detail in various annexes. Here the Soviet Union indicated that the arrangement was made "after consultation and agreement with the government of the German Democratic Republic." This upheld the legal standpoint of the Eastern side that transit traffic through the territory of the GDR and visiting possibilities were matters falling within the jurisdiction and sovereignty of the GDR. The three Western powers mentioned consultation with the Federal Republic but did not refer to its approval, as this would have contradicted the legal position that Berlin was not a state of the Federal Republic. The reference to the two German states, however, did make it clear that the Quadripartite Agreement had come into being with their participation.

Further, the Quadripartite Agreement indicated that the representation of West Berlin's interests could be exercised by the Federal Republic (Part II, D and Annex IV), in a sense acting on a mandate from the three Western allies. The agreement also contained a passage on the establishment of a Soviet consulate general in West Berlin (Annex IV). On the questions of *zugang* and *zutritt* the West had largely been able to realize its demands on a legal foundation. On the matter of *zustand* an airtight arrangement had not been achieved—this is shown by the dispute over the ways in which West Berlin's ties to the Federal Republic could be further developed—yet substantial improvement had been made, especially in that West Berlin's representation abroad by the Federal Republic had for the first time been recognized by treaty.

Before the Quadripartite Agreement could be signed there remained the problem of a binding German version upon which the German-German talks would be based. Since the United States in particular had made its signature to the agreement dependent on the existence of such a text, a German agreement was worked out under great time pressure by the delegations of the Federal Republic and the GDR, which at that point were already conducting talks on traffic questions. In this, several key concepts were controversial (e.g., "ties": *bindungen* or *verbindungen*; "constituent part": *bestandteil* or *konstitutiver teil*). Following intercession by the ambassadors of the four powers, agreement was reached on a German text. With it the signing was carried out, though the GDR immediately distanced itself from the text. The translation of the above-mentioned concepts continues to be in dispute.[108]

German-German Negotiations

The ensuing German-German negotiations first yielded a protocol on postal and telecommunication traffic, whose items 6 and 7 pertaining to West Berlin were introduced into the four-power accords. However, the most important German executory agreement was the transit agreement governing all civilian traffic between the Federal Republic and West Berlin. The transit traffic was to use designated border-crossing points and transit routes; also, it would be subject to the laws and regulations of the GDR. The provision on misuse was especially significant, for here the Federal Republic's interests in legal security on the transit routes confronted the GDR's interest in political security. Only in the event of a misuse of the transit routes should a traveler have to reckon with being searched, turned back, or actually detained. These actions could not be predicated on his belonging to a particular category of persons, on account of his political activity in the Federal Republic or West Berlin, or because of previously committed acts punishable under the law of the GDR. The visa procedures were simplified, but neither the Western powers nor the Federal Republic were able to do away with the visa requirement altogether. The modalities of traffic in goods were also regulated. In negotiations between the Berlin Senate and the GDR an agreement was reached on extending possibilities for permanent residents of Berlin (West) to visit in East Berlin and the GDR, and on an exchange of various enclaves and plots of land on the borders.[109]

These executory agreements worked out between the Federal Republic or the Berlin Senate and the GDR were in place on December 17 and 21, 1971. Prior to the signing, they were communicated to the Western powers for approval and designated by them as in accord with the quadrilateral agreement. The final Quadripartite Protocol, which brought the entire settlement into force and, besides, provided for four-power consultations in the event of difficulties in its application or a violation of commitments undertaken, could not, however, be signed until June 3, 1972, as the Soviet Union—in a reversal of the West German government's Berlin linkage—now made the Berlin settlement's coming into force dependent upon the Federal Republic's prior ratification of the Eastern Treaties.

The Berlin settlement produced three main results: the confirmation of the three Western powers' presence in West Berlin on the basis of original rights, the recognition of the essential unity of West Berlin and the Federal Republic, and the guarantee of unimpeded access to and from the city. Though not all Western negotiating goals were achieved and the differing legal standpoints had to be covered over by compromise formulas, the agreement did stabilize the situation in and around Berlin politically and legally. Above all, it decisively increased the viability of the city and improved the quality of life for its inhabitants—by obviating the constant calling into question of its status, by making secure the access routes, and by improving freedom of movement for West Berliners. This betterment has been reflected in the city's economic upsurge since the Berlin Agreement.

Main points of criticism included the recognition of the East's legal standpoint that West Berlin was not a constituent part of the Federal Republic, as well as the reduction of the West German presence, e.g., the ban on sessions of the Federal Convention or the Bundestag in Berlin and on constitutional or official acts by the West German president, chancellor or other federal ministers. Since these were more demonstrative aspects of the Berlin presence (and were conceived of as such in the past), the discussion here tended toward mere shadow boxing; the recognition of West Berlin as a federal state of the Federal Republic *and* the continued validity of the allied rights and responsibilities in relation to all of Berlin were not to be achieved simultaneously. The interpretation that Berlin was a state of the Federal Republic could in fact be supported by several decisions of the Federal Constitutional Court,[110] yet stood in contradiction to the position of the allies, who, with the suspension of Article 23 of the Basic Law and Articles 1 and 2 of the Berlin constitution, had always maintained that a special status applied to West Berlin. Bonn, then, was mainly concerned with reaching a practicable settlement by which the West German presence would be confirmed in principle and the viability of the city ensured for an unlimited period of time. Here it could count on a high degree of agreement in principle with large parts of the CDU/CSU opposition.

Still, the Berlin agreements had weak points in some of the consciously ambivalent formulations pertaining to the status of the city. The extension of international treaties to Berlin was settled with the aid of the so-called "Frank-Falin formula," which explicitly referred to the Quadripartite Agreement of September 3, 1971.[111] Yet controversy remained over how to interpret the Berlin agreements' stipulation that the ties between Berlin (West) and the Federal Republic would be developed. Did this passage relate solely to traffic and postal connections, as Moscow initially argued, or did it comprise the totality of political, economic, and legal ties, as the West maintained? And finally, did it cover augmenting or only strengthening of existing ties? This issue was inflamed at the end of 1973 by Bonn's plans to establish a Federal Environmental Agency in Berlin. The Soviet Union also objected to the rotational election of the governing mayor of Berlin as president of the Bundesrat (and thus deputy of the West German president) and to the delegation of members to the directly elected European Parliament. Clarification could not be agreed upon. While the Bonn government emphasized the right to "development of ties," the Soviet Union could rely on the stipulation that the situation in Berlin may not be changed unilaterally. Moscow repeatedly professed its "strict observance and full application of the agreement,"[112] but made no secret of the fact that it was interested primarily in the "observance" and regarded an extension of the links between West Berlin and the Federal Republic as not conforming to the treaty.

Hence, Berlin continued to be a seismograph registering the state of East-West detente. This became particularly clear when in October 1980 the GDR government unilaterally raised the minimum exchange requirements for visits to East Berlin and the GDR. In so doing it did not contravene the letter of the provisions on visitor traffic or the traffic agreements, but it did, de facto, impair intracity communication and thus the spirit of the Berlin settlement. Nonetheless, the potential for applying pressure in and with Berlin had been substantially reduced. Above all, the Quadripartite Agreement had brought a considerable improvement in the quality of life in Berlin; together with the intra-German agreements on transit to and from Berlin, on improved postal and telephone traffic, as well as travel and visitor traffic, it had substantially ameliorated the lot of the people in the divided city.

> To this extent the Berlin settlement was typical of the settlement of the German question as a whole: for the sake of a pragmatic policy of conciliation and understanding, one set aside legal positions that were not to be realized anyway, without however fully abandoning them. This policy helped clear the way for detente in Europe and remove...the obstacles to convening the Conference on Security and Cooperation in Europe. A satisfactory Berlin settlement had been the prerequisite for the West's agreement to undertake more far-reaching talks on East-West relations in Europe.[113]

It was likewise the prerequisite for ratification of the Treaties of Moscow and Warsaw, which was initiated by the German government immediately following the settlement and consummated—after sharp domestic controversy—on May 17, 1972. Finally, the Berlin settlement opened up the possibility for a normalization of intra-German relations.

THE NORMALIZATION OF RELATIONS
BETWEEN THE TWO GERMAN STATES

The heart of Ostpolitik was the settling of relations between the two German states. In his policy statement of October 28, 1969, Chancellor Brandt had declared that it was the political aim of the Social-Liberal coalition "to preserve the unity of the nation by releasing the relationship of the two parts of Germany from its cramped rigidity." He offered the GDR negotiations designed to yield formal cooperation below the threshold of recognition under international law. In this connection he used the formula of "two states in Germany" that could not be foreign territory to each other.[114] Translating into practical policy the concept of *wandel durch anaäherung* developed by Egon Bahr in the 1960s was an attempt to pass from a regulated coexistence *(nebeneinander)* to mutual cooperation *(miteinander)* without losing sight of the unity of the nation.[115]

The offer to conduct negotiations with the GDR on normalizing their mutual relations also entailed a revision of Bonn's previous policy of non-recognition. Bonn opened up the prospect of clearing recognition of the GDR by third states if "East Berlin joins in our efforts to establish a modus vivendi." Specifically, a Foreign Office circular distributed to the Federal Republic's representation abroad on the day of the policy statement indicated:

> Treaty agreements with the GDR should contribute to overcoming the division of our nation. Therefore, our position on the foreign relations of the GDR is conditioned by the extent to which East Berlin joins in our efforts to go from regulated coexistence to mutual cooperation. From other states we expect that until this relationship has been settled they will not prejudice the issue of the GDR's international standing and thus not hamper the intra-German efforts.[116]

The question of the GDR's external relations was thus used as a means of promoting an intra-German modus vivendi.

The Beginning of Dialogue: Erfurt and Kassel

Correctly assessing the European balance of power, the West German government had given priority to negotiations with Moscow over a comprehensive modus vivendi in Central Europe; Bonn initially confined itself to setting forth its aims and objectives in this area. Whether the GDR wanted to present its position on the outstanding issues or simply to regain the negotiating initiative, in any case, on December 17, 1969 Ulbricht, in his capacity as chairman of the GDR's Council of State, proposed to President Heinemann "the establishment of relations between the two German states on the basis of equality under international law, in accordance with the principles of peaceful coexistence." To this letter was attached a "Draft Treaty Concerning the Establishment of Equal Relations between the German Democratic Republic and the Federal Republic of Germany." This nine-article draft treaty proposed inter alia the "establishment of normal equal relations...free of any discrimination...on the basis of generally recognized principles and norms of international law," the exchange of ambassadors, and the immediate admission of both German states to the United Nations. Further, the draft contained statements on recognizing the existing European frontiers, renouncing the use of force, and respecting West Berlin as an independent political entity.[117]

Chancellor Brandt used his "Report on the State of the Nation" on January 14, 1970 to discuss Ulbricht's proposals. He declared the West German government's willingness to carry on with the GDR a wide-ranging exchange of views on all matters that could be of importance for a regulation of relations between the two German states, but without committing itself on specifics at that point. In view of the fact that the exploratory talks with Moscow were still in their initial stage, Bonn did not want to bind itself in any way; at the same time it felt that with the offer of general negotiations it would be able to circumvent Ulbricht's tactics. Brandt formulated six principles by which the government would be guided in negotiations with the GDR:

1. Commitment to preserving the unity of the nation: the two German states could not be foreign territory to each other;
2. Applicability of the principles of international law: no discrimination of any kind, respect for territorial integrity and borders;
3. Commitment to the peaceful resolution of all disputes;
4. No forcible alteration of the social structure of the negotiating partner;
5. Provision for cooperation as good neighbors, especially in the area of science and technology, as well as humanitarian measures;
6. Respect for the rights and responsibilities of the four powers with regard to Germany as a whole and Berlin;
7. Support for the four-power negotiations for improving the situation in and around Berlin.[118]

A few days following Brandt's statement, Ulbricht responded with an international press conference in East Berlin. The East German leader repeated the GDR's demand for "normal and equal relations based on international law" but no longer depicted the GDR's draft treaty of December as the only basis for talks. Moreover, the GDR wanted to wait and see the outcome of negotiations between the Federal Republic and the Soviet Union.[119] This, then, gave the initiative back to the Bonn government, which proposed to East Berlin negotiations on an exchange of statements renouncing the use of force. It named as its chief negotiator Minister for Intra-German Relations Egon Franke—a choice scarcely acceptable to the GDR as it had always called into question the existence of special intra-German relations. The GDR, instead, demanded normal diplomatic relations.

In response, the chairman of the GDR Council of Ministers, Willi Stoph, criticized the West German government for not having addressed the GDR's draft treaty, though he carefully avoided designating it as the sole basis for negotiations. "In the interests of bringing about peaceful coexistence and establishing by treaty normal relations between the German Democratic Republic and the Federal Republic of Germany on the basis of the generally accepted norms of international law," he proposed instead a meeting between him and Chancellor Brandt for February 1970 in East Berlin. On February 11 Chancellor Brandt accepted the invitation but requested that the date be moved back; at the same time he made it clear that the meeting would have to be conducted without preconditions.[120] A number of sensitive status questions, especially respecting Berlin, had to be clarified before it was agreed that the two heads of government would meet in Erfurt on March 19 and that this encounter would be followed by a second in the Federal Republic.

The meeting between Brandt and Stoph in Erfurt had chiefly a political-psychological significance. It was demonstrated, for all the world to see, that German and German could talk with each other. At the same time it became clear—unintentionally—how strong a feeling of togetherness remained among Germans after 25 year of division. On matters of substance the meeting did not yield any progress. Brandt repeated the six principles that he had mentioned in his State of the Nation address in early January as guiding principles for intra-German negotiations, and Stoph once again submitted the GDR's demand that the two German states establish mutual relations based on the principle of equality and conforming to the norms of international law. He summarized his government's demands in seven points: (1) Establishment of normal relations between the GDR and the FRG based on the principle of equality and conforming to international law; the FRG to give up its claim of sole representation in any form; (2) Nonintervention in the foreign relations of the other state, renunciation of the "Hallstein Doctrine"; (3) Renunciation of force in accordance with Article 2 of the UN Charter; (4) Membership of the GDR and the FRG in the United Nations; (5) Renunciation of possession of or control over nuclear weapons; (6) Renunciation of B and C weapons, reduction of military spending; (7) Removal of all vestiges of the Second World War; (8) Settlement of all debts vis-à-vis the GDR and a commitment to pay reparations.[121]

The only concrete result of this meeting was that both sides agreed to reconvene for another talk on May 21, 1970 in Kassel.

In Kassel, Stoph again made the settlement of concrete issues in relations between the two German states dependent upon prior recognition of the GDR under international law. As a response to the GDR's draft treaty of December 1969, Brandt presented a 20-point memorandum, the so-called "Twenty Points of Kassel," containing the principles and treaty elements for the establishment of equal relations between the Federal Republic of Germany and the German Democratic Republic. Its most important elements included the Federal Republic's intention of concluding with the GDR a fully valid treaty to regularize the relations between the two states in Germany and improve the contacts among the people. This treaty would have the same binding effect as other treaties between sovereign states and would contain commitments to renounce the use of force, to respect territorial integrity and borders, and not to interfere in internal affairs. In particular, "neither of the two German states can act on behalf of or represent the other." But the treaty would have to take into account the special situation in Germany and of the Germans, "who live in two states and yet regard themselves as belonging to one nation." This would be done first by respecting the rights and responsibilities of the four powers and the arrangements made by them as well as by respecting the ties between West Berlin and the Federal Republic. Secondly, the treaty should provide settlements for the problems that had emerged from the division and facilitate cooperation in all areas, in trade as in travel.[122] Thus, giving up the claim of sole representation was closely connected with steps toward normalization of mutual relations.

The meeting in Kassel brought the realization that it would be pointless to continue public talks, that the disputed issues would, instead, first have to be clarified by specialists before any more top-level meetings could be held with any prospect of success. Although at this point Bonn and Moscow had reached an agreement in principle in the form of the Bahr Paper—upon which the Twenty Points were based—the GDR was not prepared to drop its demand for recognition under international law and to take into account the special situation between the two German states. Rather, its attitude had stiffened since Erfurt. This may also have been a reaction to the domestic developments occasioned by the meeting of the two heads of government. In any event, in Kassel, Stoph suggested a "pause for reflection"—with a willingness in principle not to let the lines of communication be broken. However, there was not yet any sign of a basis for a compromise.

At the end of October 1970 it was announced in Bonn and East Berlin that the exchange of views was to be continued. The initiative for the talks came from the GDR; faced with the progress at the other levels of East-West negotiation, East Berlin was afraid of losing touch with the detente dialogue. On November 27, 1970 a first confidential discussion was held in East Berlin between State Secretaries Bahr and Kohl. Since neither side was prepared to retreat from its fundamental positions, the contacts between Bonn and East Berlin concentrated on practical questions of traffic. There were two reasons for this: first, practical improvements in this area were within range, and secondly, the Berlin negotiations indicated that while the four powers would effect a general settlement, the two German states would still have to come to terms on concrete details. Here, of course, there was the danger that intra-German arrangements could prejudice a four-power settlement. The GDR was fostering such endeavors, e.g., by offering the governing mayor of Berlin direct negotiations with the East Berlin government on questions of West Berliners' visiting in East Berlin and the GDR. Neither was Bonn entirely immune to the temptation of making direct agreements with the GDR so as to accelerate the Berlin talks.[123] On the other hand, the Federal Republic also recognized the danger that intra-German accords could undermine a four-power settlement. Thus the talks between Bahr and Kohl concentrated on general traffic questions, from which the Berlin traffic was excluded. These talks gradually developed into a regular direct line between Bonn and East Berlin, capable of bearing the numerous setbacks in mutual relations.

When in early September 1971 the Quadripartite Agreement was in place and the Western powers called upon the Federal Republic—just as the Soviet Union did the GDR—to begin transit negotiations in fulfillment of the agreement, there already existed the nucleus of a functioning negotiating body that could go to work without time-consuming exploratory talks. Parallel to this, the Berlin Senate was negotiating with the GDR on matters of intracity communication, visits by West Berliners in the GDR, and an exchange of territory. Shortly before Christmas supplementary arrangements were completed between the GDR and the Federal Republic and Senate.[124] Ulbricht's fall from power in May 1971 might have contributed to the progress made in intra-German relations; in any case, at roughly the same time the GDR dropped its precondition of recognition under international law. Parallel to the intensification of negotiating contacts with Bonn, the GDR did continue its policy of ideological demarcation from the Federal Republic. At a press conference in January 1970, Ulbricht had rejected the thesis of the unity of the nation; he referred to the two German states' different lines of historical development after the Second World War, resulting in the two states' belonging to qualitatively different political and social systems.[125] The demarcation campaign reached a peak with the speech by the first secretary of the SED's central committee, Erich Honecker, in early January 1972 before members of the National People's Army on Rügen Island. Treaties and agreements between the socialist states and the Federal Republic, he said, won the GDR a greater international authority. At the same time they had helped more clearly differentiate the GDR from the FRG. "Between the socialist German Democratic Republic and the imperialist FRG there is no unity and can be no unity. That is as certain and as clear as the fact that the rain falls to the ground and does not flow up to the clouds. Incessant talk about 'unity of the nation' does not change this in the least."[126] Along with this demarcation campaign, the GDR was making preparations for a constitutional reform, which took place at the end of 1974 and entailed a dropping of all references to one German nation.

Fourteen days after Honecker's "demarcation speech," State Secretaries Bahr and Kohl began confidential negotiations on a traffic treaty between the Federal Republic and the GDR. Until early May the two negotiators met on a biweekly basis, alternating between Bonn and East Berlin. Following settlement of the traffic questions pertaining to Berlin it was natural to turn at that point to the German-German traffic. While Bonn wanted mainly to ease conditions for visitor and tourist traffic, the GDR's intent was to mute the force of occupation law on the Berlin traffic by including it with general traffic settlement freely worked out with the Federal Republic. The Soviet Union also had an interest in a successful outcome to the talks. It hoped that the projected easing of the traffic situation would create a more amicable climate for the ratification of the Eastern Treaties by the Bundestag. When the traffic treaty was initialed on May 12, 1972—five days before the crucial vote in the Bundestag—State Secretary Kohl indicated that the treaty and the related measures to alleviate traffic conditions were contingent on ratification of the Treaties of Moscow and Warsaw. The traffic treaty, which included a series of protocol notes, exchanges of letters, and oral statements, laid a legal foundation for cross-border road, rail, and waterway traffic. For the GDR it marked the first state treaty concluded with the Federal Republic and thus a step up in political stature; for the Federal Republic it was a vehicle for limited easing of travel restrictions between the two states, which certainly left much to be desired on the Western side yet did poke holes in the GDR's demarcation policy.[127]

The preamble, stating that the treaty was concluded in the desire to develop normal, good-neighborly relations between the two states, opened up the perspective of a more comprehensive settlement between the two German states. In an after-dinner speech during a goodwill visit to Bulgaria, Honecker declared the GDR ready to enter into a discussion with the Federal Republic

> on the establishment of normal relations between the German Democratic Republic and the Federal Republic of Germany and to make the necessary arrangements for this according to international law. A development could be initiated...leading to a peaceful coex-

istence between the GDR and the FRG, to normal, good-neighborly relations with the prospect of cooperation in the interests of peace, in the interests of the citizens of both countries.[128]

This normalization would have to take place on the basis of the norms and principles of international law, whereby Honecker explicitly referred to the statements in the Bahr Paper. Moreover, since it was a matter of regularizing relations between states of different social orders, the principles of peaceful coexistence would have to apply.

The Basic Treaty

One month after initialing the traffic treaty, negotiators Bahr and Kohl began the talks on contractual foundations for relations between the two states (June 15, 1972); by early August Bahr had received detailed instructions and cabinet authorization to commence official negotiations, which then opened in East Berlin on August 16. The West German government had already outlined its negotiating aims in the six points of Chancellor Brandt's "State of the Nation" message and in the "Twenty Points of Kassel." Specifically, the treaty was to:

- take into consideration in the strongest possible way the special quality of German-German relations and to uphold the four-power rights with regard to Germany as a whole;
- arrange humanitarian measures facilitating contacts and visits;
- recognize West Berlin's ties to the Federal Republic and its representation abroad by Bonn;
- unblock the Federal Republic's relations with a number of socialist states adhering to the position of East Berlin.[129]

Prior to the cabinet go-ahead Bonn had provided detailed information on negotiating goals and strategies to the three Western powers within the Bonn Group and to the CDU/CSU opposition via its chairman, Barzel. The inclusion of the opposition in the government's decision-making process was designed not least to ensure the ratification of the traffic treaty. The measure was still pending before the Bundestag, which had adjourned for the new elections precipitated by the coalition's loss of a governing majority. However, this also accorded with the intention of the CDU/CSU not to let Ostpolitik become a campaign issue.

In the case of the Basic Treaty, the West German government was essentially the *demandeur*. Bonn wanted a durable solution to defuse the *quérelles allemandes* and a viable normalization of relations with the GDR. On this basis specific problems could be settled, human contacts between the two German states strengthened, and so a growing apart of the two parts of Germany prevented. The recognition of the GDR as second German state did not mean, either politically or legally, the dissolution of the common nationality; thus the Federal Republic and the GDR could not be "foreign territory for each other." The relations between Bonn and East Berlin would, therefore, be special relations, even though the treaty would have the same binding character under international law as agreements with other states. It was not just the abstract reunification injunction in the Basic Law, or considerations of public opinion and majority-building, that led the Social-Liberal coalition's architects of Ostpolitik to uphold the "unity of the nation." This was not an objective to be attained in the short- or medium-term, but rather a compass point for a policy of perseverance.

The policy of "special relations between the two German states" could be founded on the rights of the four powers with respect to Germany as a whole and Berlin, rights firmly established not just with the West in the Paris and Bonn Treaties of 1955, but also reaffirmed in the Quadripartite Agreement on Berlin. Appealing to these four-power rights did implicitly concede a sovereignty gap; yet this was also an instrument of Bonn's policy on Germany. These rights were not only a vestige of all-Germany, but also, beyond mere wishful thinking, concrete evidence to support the claim that the Federal Republic and the GDR shared a closer relationship than the other states. Invoking the four-power rights could help ensure the support of the three Western powers, who, like the Soviet Union—though not so brazenly—had an interest in keeping a "finger in the German pie."[130] Just as the FRG and the GDR had been active behind the scenes and from the prompt box in the four-power negotiations on Berlin, so, too, were the four powers involved in the German-German negotiations.

Yet the GDR's primary aim was recognition under international law by the Federal Republic; East Berlin wanted normal diplomatic relations and rejected any right by Bonn to construe a special relationship between the two German states. Hence, would it be willing to content itself with relations below the threshold of full diplomatic recognition? And what could Bonn offer it in return? Blocking international recognition of the GDR could not be sustained much longer. If a satisfactory intra-German settlement were not in place in the foreseeable future, then the "Scheel Doctrine" limiting Western relations with the GDR would have no ground to stand on. Because of their treaty obligations toward the Federal Republic, the Western powers would refrain from recognizing the GDR against Bonn's will; but this had long since ceased to hinder them from cooperating with the GDR below the threshold of diplomatic relations. Bonn's only trump card was admission to the United Nations, where the three Western powers could veto an application for admission by the GDR. (Similarly, the Soviet Union could block admission of the Federal Republic.) But this joker no longer worked in the case of the UN's specialized agencies, where the great powers did not have a veto power. Moreover, the Federal Republic came under a very tangible time pressure with respect to the Conference on Security and Cooperation in Europe (CSCE). The preparatory conference had begun in the fall of 1972 with the GDR's participation; to all involved it was clear that the GDR would take part as a member of equal standing in the main conference scheduled for the summer of 1973.

Bonn, then, had to offer not only its own recognition of the GDR—in qualified form—but also the possibility of admission to the United Nations as well as diplomatic relations with the Western powers and other states on friendly terms with the Federal Republic. However, the latter would also place their demands on the GDR; Bonn certainly did not have sole control over these trumps. A not unimportant factor in this regard was the "China card" which Bonn held following the establishment of diplomatic relations with the People's Republic of China in mid-October 1972. With it Bonn could exercise a certain influence on China's stance in voting on acceptance of the two German states into the world organization and, e.g., prevent a veto of the GDR's application for admission into the Security Council.

Besides the international trend toward recognition of the GDR and the pending East-West conferences, the dissolution of the Bundestag at the end of September 1972 and the early elections set for November 17 put added time pressure on the Bonn government. With the election outcome wide open, the negotiators had little time to bring the Ostpolitik initiated in 1969 to its logical conclusion in a treaty between the two German states. But the GDR was similarly faced with a pressure for results. In view of the opposition parties' rhetoric on German policy, East Berlin had to fear that with a CDU/CSU-led government it would reach no agreement at all and risk a deterioration in the climate of German-German relations.

The negotiations were extremely difficult in view of the fundamental contradiction in negotiating objectives. While Bonn had given up any claim to sole representation in the Bahr Paper and later again explicitly in the Twenty Points, East Berlin had, not least under the impact of the Moscow-Bonn accords, modified its demand for international recognition with the formula that it was seeking to establish normal relations with the Federal Republic and was prepared "to make the necessary arrangements for this under international law" ("Sofia formula").[131] This still did not prevent East Berlin from first demanding recognition under international law, but it did leave a position to fall back on in the negotiations. A sticking point here was Bonn's refusal to exchange ambassadors with East Berlin. Contrary positions also marked the issue of citizenship and that of extending the treaty to West Berlin. Such an extension was limited not only by the GDR's refusal to recognize formally West Berlin's ties with the Federal Republic, but also by the terms of the Berlin Agreement, according to which questions of status did not fall within the jurisdiction of the Federal Republic.[132]

Despite the different starting positions, an agreement was still possible before the Bundestag elections on November 17, 1972, perhaps precisely because of this event. On November 6 the negotiations between the delegations led by Bahr and Kohl were concluded, on November 7 the West German cabinet approved the negotiated settlement, and on November 8 the treaty instruments were initialed and publicized.

In the Basic Treaty the two German states agreed to develop normal good-neighborly relations with each other on the basis of equal rights and to this end to exchange permanent missions. However, a full year and half would pass before the missions could take up their work in Bonn and East Berlin. Too many difficult questions of legal status had to be clarified. In the treaty the two states further committed themselves to be guided by the purposes and principles of the UN Charter, to refrain from the threat or use of force, and to respect the inviolability of the existing border between them. Further, they would proceed on the assumption that neither of the two German states could represent the other internationally or act in its name. They declared that they would respect the independence and autonomy of the other in its internal and external affairs.

The Federal Republic and the German Democratic Republic stated their readiness to settle practical and humanitarian questions in the process of normalizing their relations and to conclude a number of agreements on developing and promoting cooperation in various areas. The Basic Treaty was supplemented by a series of protocols, exchanges of letters, and statements governing specific issues such as reuniting of families, facilitation of travel, border traffic, and working conditions for journalists. The projected arrangements were then to be subject to extension to West Berlin on a case-by-case basis. In conformity with the Quadripartite Agreement on Berlin, the permanent mission of the Federal Republic could represent the interests of West Berlin vis-à-vis the GDR. Both sides also agreed to apply for membership in the United Nations at roughly the same time. Beyond this, they expressed the desire to consult on matters of mutual interest, particularly with respect to preserving peace in Europe.[133]

One important treaty stipulation was the continued validity of the bilateral or multilateral international treaties and agreements previously concluded by, or affecting the treaty partners. In identically worded notes to the three Western powers and the Soviet Union, which formed part of the exchange of letters on the treaty, both sides explicitly stated "that the rights and responsibilities of the four powers and the corresponding, related quadripartite agreements, decisions, and practices cannot be affected by this treaty." Even before the treaty negotiations had been concluded, the ambassadors of Great Britain, France, the United States, and the Soviet Union had exchanged views on the rights and responsibilities of the four powers in conjunction with the intention of the two German states to apply for admission to the United Nations, and had published a joint declaration.[134]

On the question of the unity of the nation and, deriving from it, special German-German relations, the mention of "historical facts" and "two German states" in the preamble turned out to be the largest common denominator. The two sides further declared that they wished to put their relations on a formal basis "without prejudice to the differing views...on questions of principle, including the national question." Upon signing the treaty, the West German government also presented to the GDR a "Letter on German Unity," which, analogous to the document presented to the Soviet Union, stated "that this treaty does not conflict with the political aim of the Federal Republic of Germany to work for a state of peace in Europe in which the German nation will regain its unity through free self-determination."[135] This letter was received without contradiction by the government of the GDR and is part and parcel of the treaty instruments, though it is not included in East Berlin's showpieces.

In appraising the Basic Treaty, Chancellor Brandt stated that notwithstanding all the antagonisms the treaty would end the period of hostility between the two states and inaugurate a period of cooperation.[136] The opposition, however, rejected the treaty with the argument that it confirmed the German division before the world. Here it could refer to a report in the London *Times* where it was said that the treaty sealed the dissolution of the Bismarckian Reich 101 years after its founding.[137] In harmony with this view Honecker declared that history had rendered its verdict: On German soil there had emerged two German states with different social systems, states which despite their irreconcilable social differences could have normal relations with each other in the sense of peaceful coexistence. The ideological antagonism, however, made demarcation, and not reconciliation or convergence between them, the order of the day.[138] Spokesmen for the Bonn government, on the other hand, maintained that the treaty had in no way altered the legal situation in Germany. The German question remained open until it was possible for the German people to regain their unity in peace and self-determination. Foreign Minister Scheel stated: "The Treaty is a treaty for the people and for the future in Germany. We want to strengthen the bonds between the two parts of Germany and we want to make possible again contacts between the people."[139]

Praise and criticism of the Basic Treaty illuminated the Federal Republic's fundamental dilemma in attempting to regularize its relations with the East and Central European states, including the GDR, on the basis of the status quo and to find a modus vivendi for the outstanding questions. Bonn had to recognize de facto the emergence of two German states on German soil, belonging moreover to differing social orders and alliance systems, and at the same time to keep open de jure the German question by means of a number of compromise formulations, if it wanted to avoid risking a challenge on constitutional grounds and a parliamentary rejection of the treaty. There is much to support the contention of Benno Zündorf that the treaty, worked out just in time before the Bundestag election, constituted an optimal negotiating result under the given conditions. Its substantial merits made up for the odium of raising the international standing of the GDR, and it contained a maximum in Eastern concessions, not least because the GDR (and with it the Soviet Union) wanted to contribute to the reelection of the Brandt/Scheel government.[140]

THE DOMESTIC ACCEPTANCE OF THE EASTERN TREATIES

West German Ostpolitik has been characterized by elements of continuity as much as by new departures. Adenauer's proposal of a "truce" with the Soviet Union and Schröder's "policy of small steps" were attempts to overcome cold war confrontation for a time or in specific areas, such as trade. The Grand Coalition's policy of renunciation of force went one step further. In spite of the fundamental discord on the German question it attempted to normalize relations with the Soviet Union and the East European states. The Ostpolitik of the Brandt/Scheel government, however, was something qualitatively new. It was prepared explicitly to accept the facts of postwar Europe— including the existence of the GDR—and, in return for agreements safeguarding Berlin, to recognize the statehood of the GDR and establish treaty-based relations with it. Despite all the formal legal reservations this meant de facto acceptance of the division of Europe. This marked departure from the position of previous governments was then bound to generate domestic political conflicts.

The domestic controversy over Ostpolitik not only entailed substantive issues, e.g., whether the government had abandoned basic interests of the Federal Republic, whether it had made unwarranted concessions or negotiated too quickly; it also reflected the conflict encountered in any parliamentary system over method and substance of government policy, as opposition and government criticize and present alternatives so as to win a mandate to govern from the voters. And finally, intraparty processes played a role: struggles over direction within a party or coalition, pressures for outward political unity, personal rivalries, and struggles for leadership.

In contrast to other Western states the Federal Republic does not have a tradition of bipartisan foreign policy. For just a little under ten years—from the Wehner speech in June 1960 to the policy statement of the Social-Liberal coalition in October 1969—there was something like a basic consensus on foreign policy in the Federal Republic; it was motivated by domestic politics and designed to enhance the credibility of the SPD as a party capable of governing. Hence, it lasted only as long as the domestic situation required it, until for the first time in the history of the Federal Republic a Social Democratic chancellor was laying down the guidelines of policy. The inability of the Grand Coalition to act on all the critical issues of foreign policy had already demonstrated the shakiness of this consensus.

The reason why the political conflict would necessarily erupt with such vehemence upon the change in power in 1969 was domestic. For one, the CDU/CSU, which had remained the strongest political force in the West German party system, was not prepared fully to accept an opposition role after 21 years of uninterrupted responsibility. Thus its goal was to regain governing power as soon as possible. It also had to cope with an unresolved leadership question. Then, the SPD, and especially its strategist Herbert Wehner, likewise set itself for confrontation: in order to realize the whole of Social-Liberal policy—which at first was essentially a Brandt/Bahr policy—and to preserve the unity of party and coalition.

When it appeared that its high tack could not withstand the winds on its starboard, the government hove to and attempted—e.g., with the aid of a joint resolution of the Bundestag on foreign and German policy—to bring about a limited cooperation with the opposition and save its Ostpolitik from capsizing in parliament. But the CDU/CSU also had an unresolved leadership question and a split in various foreign policy groupings, which set narrow limits on any cooperation with the government. Positions on Ostpolitik were thus as much instruments of intraparty struggle as they were elements of parliamentary conflict.

Elsewhere in society, the churches had been advocating reconciliation with the East European states since the mid-1960s. The trade unions also supported this policy, which was not surprising in view of their proximity to the SPD. The attitude of the business associations was marked by reticence and ambivalence. Their economic interests were geared to normalization of relations with the Soviet Union and the other East European states, their political orientations directed them to the camp of the treaty opponents.

The Debate on the Treaties of Moscow, Warsaw, and Prague

The essence of the CDU/CSU criticism leveled at the Eastern treaties was that the German government had given up positions and options without adequate compensation from the other side. In tone they varied from an uncompromising no to Ostpolitik, as set forth by the CSU and Franz Josef Strauss as well as the conservative group in the CDU around the former chancellor, Kurt-Georg Kiesinger, the party's foreign policy expert, Werner Marx, and the expellee leader, Heinrich Windelen, to moderate reservations and desires for greater specificity, for which the "progressive group" around Walther Leisler Kiep and Norbert Blüm were arguing. These different positions clearly emerged in the Bundestag, particularly in the debate prompted by the CDU/CSU's May 1970 major interpellation on policy concerning Germany, Europe, and the East.[141] On the Moscow Treaty a middle position was marked out by the August 1970 resolution of the parliamentary group and executive board of the CDU, which expressed the following concerns:

> The right of the Germans to self-determination is jeopardized by the Moscow Treaty;
> the determination of borders must remain reserved for a peace treaty;
> the Moscow Treaty does not yield concrete improvements in intra-German relations; freedom of movement for people, ideas, and opinions has yet to be guaranteed;
> the Moscow Treaty does not contain any constructive elements paving the way to a better order of peace in Europe;
> the German government's policy underlying this treaty threatens the foundations of Western integration and alliance policy;
> the Moscow Treaty has the effect of raising the international status of the GDR toward recognition under international law;
> the treaty commitments are imbalanced, with one-sided consideration given to the interests of the Soviet Union;
> the Moscow Treaty fails to clarify the issue of preserving a free Berlin.[142]

However, the final position on the treaties was made conditional on examination of the protocols of the Moscow negotiations and on future results in Ostpolitik and policy on Germany. This meant in particular a satisfactory outcome from the four-power negotiations on Berlin and an "improvement of relations, a reduction of tensions, and improvements for the people."[143]

The opposition found it even more difficult to arrive at a uniform stance on the Warsaw Treaty. A number of liberal Union deputies had long been advocating a reconciliation with Poland and were prepared to concede the Polish people guarantees on the border question. Others were calling for massive opposition to a treaty that would violate the right to self-determination of Germans and Poles alike and retroactively legalize the expulsions after 1945. However, the positions articulated by the CDU/CSU parliamentary group on the German-Polish treaty were dominated by the desire for understanding and reconciliation, and no demands were raised against Poland. Of the treaty, the CDU/CSU demanded:

- creation of a modus vivendi based on the Oder-Neisse line and subject to a settlement by peace treaty for all of Germany;
- renunciation of the threat or use of force;
- binding and concrete arrangements for safeguarding the human rights of persons and groups, in particular the right to free movement and unimpeded contacts with relatives;
- creation of a German-Polish youth organization;
- greater exchange in the economic, cultural, and scientific fields;
- institution of a German-Polish chamber of commerce;
- establishment of full diplomatic relations with the inclusion of West Berlin.[144]

Once the Berlin accords had been concluded the CDU/CSU modified its reservations toward the Eastern Treaties. The involvement of the three Western powers in the Berlin Agreement had made it abundantly clear that the Social-Liberal coalition's course of Ostpolitik, despite some differences of opinion on matters of substance and procedure, did have the support of the Federal Republic's allies. With its no to the treaties, therefore, the opposition was running the risk of isolation in foreign policy. One of its main themes, that the government's Ostpolitik was endangering the cohesion of the Western alliance, was turned into its opposite. Added to this were shifts in public opinion. Opinion polls showed that two-thirds of those polled supported the Brandt/Scheel Ostpolitik.[145] Yet in the April 1972 Landtag elections in

Baden-Württemberg the sympathy for Ostpolitik had scarcely any influence on voting behavior—on the contrary, the CDU was able to make sizable gains on the coalition parties. With the crumbling of the government's Bundestag majority through party defections over Ostpolitik, there developed yet another danger: that the CDU/CSU would come to hold the balance of power over the Eastern Treaties, being in a position to approve them or bring them down.

From then on the CDU/CSU made consent to the treaties dependent on inclusion of the right to self-determination in the treaty instruments themselves and, further, on agreement with the GDR on concrete humanitarian measures and greater freedom of movement for people, goods, and information.[146] On the right to self-determination, the government could point to the "Letter on German Unity" presented at the signing of the Moscow Treaty; also, Moscow had agreed to include this letter in the Soviet ratification process.[147] On the matter of humanitarian measures, the government could refer to the transit agreement to the Berlin Treaty and to the German-German negotiations on a traffic treaty, talks which in the spring of 1972 were on the verge of completion (the traffic treaty was initialed on May 12, 1972). Moreover, the coalition offered the opposition a joint parliamentary resolution on the Eastern Treaties that would once again accentuate the element of a modus vivendi. The Social-Liberal coalition had staked its word with its negotiating partners in Eastern Europe; at this point Ostpolitik was incomplete, lacking the regularization of relations with the GDR as its final piece. The government tried, therefore, through a combination of additional procedural concessions from the Soviet Union—which were obtained in intensive talks with Falin, Moscow's ambassador in Bonn—and verbal nods in the direction of its domestic opponents' views, to save the treaties and get them past the parliamentary hurdles of the ratification process without changes in the treaty texts themselves.

In April 1972 events began to follow in rapid succession. One day after the Landtag elections in Baden-Württemberg, which had given the CDU an absolute majority, the Union resolved to bring down Chancellor Brandt by a vote of no confidence in the Bundestag. But on the no-confidence motion on April 27, the Union parties' candidate for chancellor, Rainer Barzel, fell two votes shy of the required absolute majority. One day later the Bundestag rejected the chancellor's budget on a tie vote (247 to 247). Meanwhile the Springer press and the magazine *Quick* had heated up the domestic climate with publication of more secret treaty documents. A few days before the elections in Baden-Württemberg they published selected parts of the Moscow negotiation protocols.[148] Under the stress of the stalemate, government and opposition reached agreement on the text of a joint resolution on the Eastern treaties reaffirming the right to self-determination, confirming the peace treaty proviso with respect to borders, and asserting the goal of restoring national unity in a European framework.[149]

The stalemate in the Bundestag was mirrored by a similar impasse within the Union parties. On April 10, 1972 the CDU's executive board called for a setting aside of the treaties and renegotiating. But on May 9 representatives of the parliamentary groups of SPD, FDP and CDU/CSU agreed on a joint resolution on the Eastern Treaties designed to make these acceptable to Union deputies, and on May 15 the CDU board recommended acceptance of the treaties in the Bundestag. In its view not all doubts about the treaties had been removed, yet acceptance of the joint resolution and rejection of the treaties was contrary to political logic. The CSU was opposed to this, and the conservative group in the Union tended to go along with the Bavarian sister party's negative stand. To preserve party unity the Union's parliamentary leadership then recommended abstention. On May 17, 1972 the Moscow Treaty passed the Bundestag by 248 votes to 10, with 238 abstentions; the Warsaw Treaty by 248 votes to 17, with 231 abstentions. Two days later the Bundesrat passed the treaties with the vote evenly split between the states governed by the SPD/FDP and those by the CDU/CSU. The treaties went into effect on May 24, 1972.[150]

On the treaty with Czechoslovakia the CDU/CSU could develop its position without regard to relative strengths in the Bundestag, as the government now enjoyed a comfortable majority following the elections in the fall of 1972—which had been a kind of referendum on Ostpolitik. Also, the election of Carstens as parliamentary group leader and Kohl as party chairman had, for the time being, solved the CDU/CSU's internal question of leadership. Although some of the knowledgeable politicians of the CDU characterized the Prague Treaty as carefully negotiated, the Union unanimously rejected it in the Bundesrat vote in March 1974 and in the Bundestag in June 1974. The decisive factors were the reservations of the expellee associations, especially those of the Sudeten Germans, and after the Berlin settlement the difficulties in applying the Berlin clause; thus the treaty was viewed as affording inadequate safeguards for expellees' basic rights and proprietary interests and insufficient considerations for Berlin.[151] Upon closer examination of the material provisions and the Union parties' objections, the negative vote by the Union against the Prague Treaty seems even more dubious than its attitude toward the Treaties of Moscow and Warsaw.

The Union practiced this strategy of "acceptance despite rejection" once more when it voted on the pensions agreement supplemental to the Warsaw Treaty. In the Bundestag the October 9, 1975 agreements with Poland were never in danger as the coalition parties had a solid majority and 11 Union deputies voted with the majority. The stumbling block this time was the Bundesrat, where a 21:20 ratio in the spring of 1976 became 26:15 for the Union-governed *länder* following the change in government in Lower Saxony. In a tense poker game down to the last minute the Union obtained additional binding assurances from the Polish side on the issue of emigration for Polish citizens of German origin. Though all the CDU/CSU-governed *länder*—with the exception of the Saarland, which abstained—had initially voted for rejection, one day later, on March 11, 1976, the German-Polish pensions agreement passed the Bundesrat with the votes of all states. Once again domestic political considerations had been the decisive impulse for the Union's parliamentary decision on Ostpolitik.[152]

Agreement in Principle between Government and Opposition with Regard to Berlin

In its original arguments against the Moscow Treaty the CDU/CSU opposition had asserted that the Soviet Union's readiness for detente would have to be demonstrated by whether it was prepared to respect the actual situation with regard to Berlin. In early 1970 the CDU/CSU set forth its stance in a confidential position paper:

- West Berlin is part of the democratic order of the Federal Republic;
- West Berlin is an inseparable part of the legal, economic, and financial system of the Federal Republic;
- West Berlin and every individual West Berliner are represented abroad by the Federal Republic;
- the connecting routes between West Berlin and the rest of Federal German territory are secured by binding agreement against disruption, contentious harassment, blocking, or other impediments to the traffic of goods and persons;
- the inhabitants of West Berlin are freed of the discriminatory measures that make it impossible for them to visit East Berlin and East Germany;
- the Federal Republic has the same right to a political presence in West Berlin as the GDR claims in East Berlin;
- a satisfactory settlement on Berlin must, like the Moscow Treaty, be good for an unlimited period of time.[153]

With that, the Union's stance essentially coincided with the views of the government. If it nevertheless became a controversial issue, culminating in charges that the government was undermining the Western negotiating position, this was primarily for reasons of domestic politics. Because the Union had made a satisfactory settlement on Berlin the touchstone for the Eastern Treaties and then in mid-1971 such an agreement was in place, it now was forced to make a move. It would have either to acknowledge this outcome and draw the consequences for its position on the Treaties of Moscow and Warsaw or else to declare the Berlin settlement inadequate and/or construct new reservations about the Treaties of Moscow and Warsaw. If it wanted to do the latter, then it would have to take into account that the Berlin settlement had been approved by the Western allies as a central element of East-West detente and judged by the people of West Berlin and by public opinion in the Federal Republic as predominantly positive.

Within the CDU/CSU there were a number of deputies, such as Walther Leisler Kiep and Johann Baptist Gradl, who saw in the Berlin Agreement a distinct improvement of the situation. So as not to discredit the work of the Western allies, but also not to have to raise its own reservations about the coalition's Ostpolitik, the Union decided in favor of a positive assessment of the Berlin Agreement. In so doing it emphasized that essential measures for facilitating access to and from Berlin, for eliminating discrimination against West Berliners and for Bonn's representation of West Berlin originated in CDU/CSU proposals; on the other hand, it criticized the West for having made concessions, at Bonn's urging, in the establishment of a Soviet consulate in West Berlin, the reduction of the West German presence, and the way the relations between West Berlin and the Federal Republic were recognized. It made no further mention of the status question, which it had emphasized in its original statements of position, but which had been excluded from the Berlin negotiations in view of the irreconcilable differences of opinion. Thus it argued by way of "what is good goes down the opposition's craw, what looks bad is thrown to the government."[154]

The Discussion on the Basic Treaty and Admission to the United Nations

The negotiations with the GDR on the Basic Treaty were concluded during the heated phase of the 1972 election campaign; so it is not surprising that the initial positions taken by the political parties were conditioned by campaign perspectives. Government and coalition parties presented the accords with the GDR as the result of their policy for peace and detente, while they dismissed the Union parties' policy on Germany and Ostpolitik as lacking credibility in view of their contradictory position on ratification of the Moscow and Warsaw Treaties.[155]

The leadership of the Union parties, on the other hand, was anxious to avoid getting pinned down. First, it had to keep the Basic Treaty from becoming the decisive issue of the campaign; moreover, it wanted to ensure the greatest possible latitude for its own policy options on Germany and the East after the hoped-for electoral victory. It therefore argued that examination of the negotiated treaty text must not be influenced by the "time pressure and hurly-burly of the campaign" but then raised the prospect of improving the treaty through renewed negotiations in the period between initialing and signing.[156] This tentative stance largely reflected consideration for intraparty differences, as had emerged in the struggle over ratification of the Eastern Treaties. Given the different conceptions within the Union, especially between CDU and CSU, a full discussion of the Basic Treaty could have jeopardized the unity of the Union in the election campaign.

In assessing the Basic Treaty the Union had to weigh the treaty's raising the international standing of the GDR and the Federal Republic's relinquishing the claim of sole representation against the humanitarian promises of the treaty. The majority of the parliamentary party as well as the state governments led by the CDU/CSU arrived at a negative judgment, based on the following concerns:

- the treaty did not yield sufficient contractually safeguarded measures of humanitarian relief and improvements in freedom of movement for people, opinions, and information. There were still orders to shoot at the Wall;
- the treaty lent support to the two-states theory through the recognition of the GDR as an autonomous and independent state and by the concurrent admission of the FRG and the GDR to the United Nations on an equal footing; in political practice this could be equated with a recognition of the GDR under international law;
- the treaty contained no agreement between the two states on the unity of the nation; it hampered realization of the Germans' right to self-determination;
- the treaty did not mention the rights and responsibilities of the four powers for Germany as a whole and Berlin; it undermined the spirit and the letter of the Paris and Bonn Treaties and the related declaration in which the three Western powers committed themselves to the reunification of Germany in freedom;
- the treaty did not encompass Berlin; the application to Berlin of the agreements and arrangements that were in the future to be concluded on the basis of the treaty depended on the consent of the GDR in every instance;
- with the treaty the West German government had met longstanding demands of the GDR but had received nothing commensurate in return. It had acted under the pressure of getting results under time constraints.[157]

The debate on the Basic Treaty, which took place in the Bundestag May 9-11, 1973, concentrated mainly on the question of whether this treaty kept the German question open, or at least did not make it more difficult to overcome the division of Germany. While opposition deputies spoke of a "partition treaty" that would necessarily give the rest of the world the impression that the Germans freely acquiesced in their divided existence, government spokesmen stressed that the Basic Treaty was the product of sober insight into the necessity for finally taking action and defusing the current state of division as a source of conflict in the heart of Europe. It would enable greater contact and communication among the people in Germany and create the preconditions for cooperation between the two German states.

Regarding admission to the United Nations, a strong group of Union deputies insisted that the Federal Republic's admission at the same time and with the same status as the GDR was equivalent to an international recognition of the GDR. The government, on the other hand, argued that the Federal Republic's continued absence from the United Nations was no longer consistent with its role and responsibility in the community of nations.

The law ratifying the Basic Treaty was passed by the Bundestag on May 11, 1973 by a vote of 268 (SPD, FDP, and 4 CDU votes) to 217 (CDU/CSU); the bill on the Federal Republic's admission to the United Nations was carried with a 364-to-121 margin. The Bundesrat, which had rejected the Basic Treaty on its first reading with the votes of the CDU/CSU-led states, decided upon second reading on May 25, 1973 against a motion by Bavaria to refer the treaty to conference committee; with that the treaty was also approved by the assembly of *länder*. In that same session the Bundesrat majority voted in favor of admission to the United Nations.[158] Despite Bavaria's appeal to the Federal Constitutional Court, the Federal Republic and the GDR put the Basic Treaty into force on June 21, 1973; on the following day the United Nations Security Council recommended the admission of the two German states into the world organization.

The Verdict of the Federal Constitutional Court

The debate on the Social-Liberal coalition's Ostpolitik and German policy peaked again in the summer of 1973 in the wake of Bavaria's appeal to the Federal Constitutional Court. On May 28, 1973 the Bavarian government petitioned to have the Basic Treaty declared "incompatible with the Basic Law and therefore null and void." Two days before the vote in the Bundesrat Bavaria had already sued for an interim court order to stop the treaty from entering into force until its constitutionality had been determined. On June 4, 1973 the court rejected this suit as "presently not imperative." Then on June 13 Bavaria again filed for a court order to prevent the June 20 exchange of notes with the GDR and thus the Basic Treaty's entering into force, but this also was rejected by the court on June 18. In a closed oral pleading the federal government had explained that it could temporarily defer the Basic Treaty's coming into force as well as its own application for admission to the United Nations, but that it could no longer influence the fate of the GDR's application, which the four powers had expressly committed themselves to support by their declaration of November 1972. With the breach of linkage between UN admission and Basic Treaty, including the humanitarian measures connected with it, the Federal Republic might jeopardize the greatest part of what it had achieved through negotiation.[159]

The proceedings to determine the constitutionality of the Basic Treaty were accompanied by a series of procedural skirmishes aimed at radically altering the composition of the bench and gaining time. Thus, Bavaria twice charged that Judge Dr. Joachim Rottmann was biased because he was said to have already publicly expressed decided views on the legal situation in Germany. In its first decision on May 29 the court ruled this suit unfounded; however, after more documentation was submitted, a second decision on June 16 found it justified. This procedural issue had an extraordinary political importance. For when the first decision was made on Bavaria's suit for an interim injunction, it had become clear that of the eight judges a group of four (including Rottmann) considered it fairly unlikely that on the basis of the grounds adduced up to that point the court would find the treaty law unconstitutional, while the other judges did consider this a possibility. Though in their second rejection the judges had invoked the principle of "judicial self-restraint," which prohibits the court from interfering in the political responsibility of the executive, still the matter was obviously a highly political one. The Bavarian government as petitioner, the Federal government as a party to the suit, and the court itself (whose composition is the product of a hard-fought process of proportional party representation) are political organs that in this case had to pass judgment on a highly political matter.

The Bavarian government had argued its appeal on the grounds that the Basic Treaty

- contravened the constitutional mandate on preserving the political unity of Germany;
- violated the injunction on reunification;
- precluded the right of the other part of Germany to accede to the jurisdiction of the Federal Republic's constitution, the Basic Law;

- was incompatible with the provisions of the Basic Law pertaining to Berlin;
- contravened the obligation to render protection and assistance to all Germans including those in the GDR.[160]

The federal government, in turn, petitioned to have the treaty law on the Basic Treaty declared compatible with the Basic Law. It argued that the treaty

- served the constitutional goals of advancing peace and humanity by bringing practical benefits to the people;
- in concurrence with the legislature, adhered to the continued existence of Germany and left the German question open;
- did not contradict the mandate on reunification, for the three Western powers remained bound to relate the four-power proviso to Germany as a whole;
- adhered to the continued existence of Germany as a legal subject and avoided any qualification of the GDR as a foreign entity;
- adhered to the unity of the German nation and German nationality;
- did not imply any recognition of the GDR under international law;
- left the status of Berlin untouched as it had been set by the Quadripartite Agreement.[161]

In its position statement the federal government emphasized that the treaty did not obstruct reunification either legally or practically, no matter what form of realization this might one day take. Further, the treaty did bring improvements of both a political and humanitarian nature and did keep the situation open for future progress. In short, there was no alternative to this treaty.

Following the oral pleading on June 19, the judgment on the main issue was rendered on July 31, 1973. The Federal Constitutional Court recognized the law ratifying the Basic Treaty of December 12, 1972 as compatible with the Basic Law "in the interpretation following from the given reasons."[162] The opinion of the court, which in this case acquired the force of law besides the verdict itself, represented a compromise of considerable political significance. The majority of the judges let pass a treaty against which they harbored political misgivings; the minority that was positively disposed toward the treaty tolerated the sometimes downright willful interpretation of the majority; all the judges faced the censure this political compromise brought upon them.

On the central question, the compatibility of the Basic Treaty with the constitutional mandate on reunification, the court upheld its judgment in the decision banning the Communist Party of Germany. Thus, the reunification mandate in the preamble of the Basic Law had constitutional status; therefore, no constitutional organ of the Federal Republic of Germany might give up the restoration of national unity as a political goal. However, it was left to the discretion of the federal government to decide with what political means and by what political ways it sought to achieve or approach this goal. Here the court did not raise criticism or express its views on the prospects for this policy. However, the constitution did enjoin the federal government not to relinquish any legal title founded on the Basic Law by means of which it could effectively work toward the realization of reunification and self-determination. The court concluded that the treaty could be interpreted in such a way as not to conflict with the Basic Law.

To reach such conclusions the federal judges considered it necessary to take a position on the legal status of Germany. In the contest of theories on the continued existence of the German Reich[163] they created a new variant by combining the "roof" and "nucleus" theories into a "partial identity theory." According to this, the German Reich continued to exist, possessing as before a legal capacity, but for want of institutional organs lacked the capacity to act. As a state the Federal Republic of Germany was identical with the German Reich, but with regard to its territorial extent was only partly identical. Its sovereignty was limited under constitutional law to the jurisdiction of the Basic Law, but it considered itself responsible for all of Germany. Because the GDR belonged to Germany, it could not be regarded as a foreign entity in relation to the Federal Republic.[164] This construction of legal theory is in itself not very conclusive and is politically questionable, as it denies the evident political reality of the GDR's statehood and autonomy.

One can fully agree with the court's opinion that the treaty was a "seriously intended, new foundation for determining the relationship of the two states...notwithstanding the fact that the contracting parties are legally free to agree at any time to alter or amend the treaty in accordance with the legal principles applicable to it"; but this was scarcely consistent with the statement contained in the same paragraph that the treaty was not an "agreed modus vivendi." Equally problematic was the interpretation that the treaty had a dual character; "by its nature it is a treaty in international law, by its specific content a treaty governing mainly *inter se* relations." These *inter se* relations were to be governed by international law "in the absence of a constitutional legal order, as here because of the disorganization of the comprehensive state." The treaty was also "not a treaty of partition precluding today or for the future that the federal government at all times does whatever it can to ensure that the German people can again organize its political unity." The statements on the German-German border were also oriented to the orthodox thesis of a still-existing state of

"Germany as a whole." From this the court concluded that it was to be treated as "a constitutional border similar to those between the states of the Federal Republic of Germany."[165]

A glaring breach of the principle of "judicial self-restraint"—and a contradiction of the prior formulation about the political responsibility of the executive—was the detailed commentary on how the federal government had to render protection and assistance to all Germans according to Articles 116(1) and 16 of the Basic Law. This was the stipulation that every treaty and agreement concluded with the GDR had to be extended to Berlin unless the reserved rights of the allies precluded it. The judges also noted the demand that all subsequent treaties and agreements as provided for in Article 7 of the Basic Treaty must conform to the norms of the Basic Law. A guarantee of secrecy in the postal and telecommunications systems was given as an example. Furthermore, with reference to the Basic Treaty, the court called upon the federal government to work toward eliminating the Wall, the barbed wire, death strips, and the order to fire. Thus the court judges not only needlessly constricted the scope of practical policy, but they also deprived themselves, by their remoteness from reality, of a bit of credibility.

Viewed as a whole the judgment did in fact leave the Basic Treaty intact, yet the interpretation given it by the Federal Constitutional Court and particularly the binding of future West German governments to the principles set forth in the court's opinion did damage Ostpolitik, whose culmination the treaty was supposed to be. While the commitment to restoring the national unity of Germany was noted with uneasiness in the West, the judgment was understood in the East European states as a turning away from a policy of detente proceeding "from the real situation," especially since the federal government could not distance itself from the judgment.[166] It is probably no coincidence that the position of the East European states on the Berlin question began to harden at precisely this time. Yet much more fateful was the fact that an outdated image of Germany was invested with the aura of the Constitutional Court's *benedictio* and the policy of future German governments was saddled with concepts from the 1950s. The critics of the Social-Liberal coalition's Ostpolitik and German policy could feel vindicated, and its supporters were not to kick about it.

SETBACKS IN DETENTE POLICY

One of the architects of the Social-Liberal policy on Germany and Ostpolitik, Egon Bahr, remarked after the Basic Treaty had been concluded that previously the Federal Republic had had no relations with the GDR, now it would have bad ones, and this was a measure of progress. It would take a long time before it got any better.[167] This prognosis was to prove correct.

Intra-German Relations Between Demarcation and Cooperation

In mid-1973 the GDR raised the minimum exchange requirement for visits to East Berlin and the GDR from 5 to 10 and 20 marks respectively; it forbade so-called "bearers of confidential information" any Western contacts, and it resorted to turning back traffic on the transit routes as a protest against the establishment of a Federal Environmental Agency in West Berlin. This went hand in hand with an intensified campaign of ideological demarcation on the part of the leadership of the Socialist Unity Party (SED). Concerned that greater contacts with the West as a result of the Basic Treaty could destabilize its political system, the GDR leadership used ideology and purse to curb these contacts and keep their deleterious effects as slight as possible.

Yet the negotiations between Bonn and East Berlin were meanwhile moving ahead. Between 1974 and 1980 these negotiations resulted in more than a dozen agreements and protocols in various fields, e.g., on the improvement of travel and transit traffic, including the stipulation of lump sum payments in lieu of visa fees and road tolls, improvement of the postal and telecommunications systems, the public health systems, environmental protection, and the marking of borders. In late October 1974 the GDR relented on the minimum exchange requirements and reduced the figures to 6.50 and 13 marks; at the end of November pensioners were fully exempted from the compulsory exchange, and further measures to facilitate travel were announced.

These pledges were the prerequisite for concluding a new arrangement between the Federal Republic and the GDR on the swing in intra-German trade. The interest-free credit line was set at 850 million clearing units for the period up to the end of 1981. At the same time East Berlin submitted to the Federal Republic extensive proposals for expanding and improving the traffic routes to and from Berlin, e.g., two-rail expansion of the most important railway lines from Berlin to West Germany, building of an autobahn from Berlin to Hamburg, and repair of some existing stretches of autobahn. The costs for these measures were to be assumed by the Federal Republic. The GDR offered the Berlin Senat, among other things, negotiations on a reopening of the Teltow Canal as well as on sewage and waste disposal. It expressed an interest also in obtaining machinery, equipment, and industrial facilities from firms in the Federal Republic and Berlin.[168]

The international recognition of the GDR, its membership in the United Nations, and its equal participation in the CSCE provided an element of domestic political consolidation of the GDR, just as the continuous growth of the national economy at a rate of 5 percent led to an improved supply of housing and consumer goods for the people.[169] The "stabilization through economic prosperity" also strengthened popular consent to the East German system and thereby made contacts with the West less risky. In this way there developed a close correlation between the Federal Republic's increased supply of goods and capital to the GDR (by the end of 1980 this amounted to 20 percent of the GDR's gross national product) and the reciprocal measures of facilitating travel and visitor traffic (in 1980 visits by Westerners to the GDR and East Berlin numbered 8 million—in a population of 17 million). Just as the normalization between the two German states was a function of the modus vivendi with the Soviet Union and the East European states, so too this process stood in a symbiotic relationship to general East-West detente, depending and in turn reacting upon it.

However, giving Ostpolitik a treaty foundation, particularly in the Berlin Agreement, was possible only with the support of the Western allies. Brandt made this very clear when he referred to the foundation of Ostpolitik in the Western alliance.

> Our Ostpolitik is based on our Westpolitik. This is a fact and not a matter of doubt. Our efforts toward reconciliation and cooperation with the East are geared toward achieving greater peace and security for Europe. Thus, they also benefit Western cooperation. Here and there suspicions and fears have surfaced that there is a contradiction between the treaty with the Soviet Union and our active participation in the work of West European unification and in the Atlantic alliance. This is an assessment proceeding from false premises. I want to say this here once again with complete clarity: the Federal Republic of Germany conducts its Ostpolitik not as a wanderer between two worlds, but from a position firmly established in Western cooperation. Atlantic alliance and West European partnership are for us essential prerequisites for the success of conciliation with the East.[170]

Multilateralization of Detente Policy

The policy of renunciation of force initially conducted on a bilateral basis—more or less to make up the historical ground the Federal Republic had lost by its adherence to outmoded positions on the German question—converged with the multilateral detente and arms control policy of the Western alliance in the years 1972-73. The Conference on Security and Cooperation in Europe (CSCE)[171] assumed a special significance in this regard. From Bonn's viewpoint this conference, which took place in several phases from July 3, 1973 to August 1, 1975 in Helsinki, Geneva, and again Helsinki, had three main functions: first, the Soviet conference proposal was used as leverage for bringing about, preliminary to the conference, a satisfactory settlement of the German question inclusive of West Berlin; at the same time this was to undercut the Soviet strategy of playing up the results of the all-European conference as a kind of substitute peace treaty with Germany. Secondly, the conference project seemed to offer the possibility of dealing with European detente in conjunction with military security, two sets of issues that previously had been handled separately. Thus the preconditions for a durable European security system, or as Brandt had termed it, a "European order of peace," seemed to be at hand. And finally, the conference offered the Federal Republic a framework in which it could pursue its objectives in Ostpolitik and detente jointly with its partners in the group of the Nine and the Fifteen. This multilateral approach would shield it from the accusation voiced among the allies during the active phase of Ostpolitik that Bonn was risking the continuance and cohesion of the alliance for the sake of transient successes.[172]

Western, and particularly West German, diplomacy was able to utilize the conference project to the advantage of its own Ostpolitik, as in fact both sides, by way of a "mutual linkage," made the convening of the conference contingent on a satisfactory settlement of outstanding questions, particularly on Berlin. On the other hand, the expectation that CSCE negotiations could mute the military confrontation went unfulfilled. Only after a long tug-of-war did the Soviet Union agree to conduct talks on troop reductions, though at a separate conference, the Vienna MBFR negotiations.[173] Several of the Western allies were also in favor of the tactical separation in negotiations: the U.S. because it did not want to negotiate on military questions at a large European conference involving countries of varying security status, and France because it would accept no interference whatsoever in its military policy. The CSCE was limited to modest confidence-building measures such as advance notification of major military maneuvers and exchange of observers.

Other results of the CSCE, to which the 35 participating states committed themselves in signing the Final Act in August 1975, included a declaration on principles governing international conduct. Of particular importance for the Federal Republic were the principles of renunciation of force, the possibility of peaceful alteration of borders, the right to self-determination, and respect for human rights pertaining to the individual. Bonn had agreed to recognize the inviolability of borders as an autonomous principle only after the Eastern side had made concessions on measures concerning humanitarian questions and increased cultural and informational exchange. These included provisions to facilitate the reuniting of families and remove obstacles to unrestricted journalistic reporting. Reaching agreement on greater East-West economic cooperation was relatively unproblematic. Politically, Bonn and its partners were intent upon underscoring the competency of the European Community for the common foreign trade of the Nine and having the EC recognized as a factor in international policy. This was symbolized by the Italian prime minister's signing of the Final Act on behalf of the EC in his capacity as incumbent chairman.[174]

The outcome of the CSCE can best be described as a joint interim balance sheet on the detente process in Europe. Whereas in Soviet eyes the Final Act constituted international recognition of the territorial status quo in Europe, to the West it contained the promise of improving the political status quo by making borders more permeable to goods, information, and people, and thus raising the quality of life in Europe. Yet neither side had any legal title; translating the results of the CSCE into practical policy largely depended on the goodwill of the parties involved. Periodic follow-up conferences were to assess progress in implementing the CSCE results and take constructive steps toward further development.

The human rights issue developed into an indicator of the progress of the detente process—or rather of its problems. A fundamental misunderstanding arose as the majority of Western leaders had signed the CSCE Final Act in the expectation that Moscow and the other East European leaders would be prepared to accept a liberalization of their regimes so as not to forfeit the fruits of detente. But the party leaders in the East assumed that they would be able either to insulate their systems from the impact of Helsinki or at least readily keep its negative consequences under control. Hence, the emergence of the civil rights movement in the socialist states took them by surprise and forced them to take harsh countermeasures if they did not want to risk the stability of their regimes. The developments in Poland were one illustration of this. For very different reasons on the part of both President Carter and his national security adviser, Brzezinski, the United States felt it could play the human rights issue against the Soviet Union, as a form of containment, by demonstratively insisting on Soviet compliance. Bonn was no less interested in this but attempted primarily through diplomacy and money to ameliorate conditions for people in the other part of Germany. The conflict was carried out at a CSCE follow-up conference in Belgrade, which met from October 1977 to March 1978. A deadlock ensued and the conference broke up without tangible results.[175]

However, the human rights issue was more a symptom than a cause of the fact that the essential conditions of international policy had changed and an isolated detente in Europe was no longer possible. Conflicts in the third world had demonstrated the futility of Kissinger's attempt to bind Moscow to a U.S.-Soviet control arrangement for managing international crises, while the Jackson-Vanik amendment to the U.S.-Soviet trade agreement had reduced the credibility of Washington as a reliable detente partner for Moscow. Following the Soviet intervention in Afghanistan the prospects for success at a second CSCE follow-up conference in Madrid declined even further. This conference lasted nearly three years (from November 1980 to September 1983) instead of the originally planned three months. One of the main topics in Madrid was the French proposal for a European disarmament conference to discuss mainly confidence-building measures, a proposal taken up by Poland and the states of the Warsaw Pact as well as a number of non-aligned countries.[176]

Still in the summer of 1983 agreement was reached on a concluding CSCE document and a mandate for a Conference on Disarmament in Europe.[177] There were various reasons for this, indicative of the CSCE's different functions in national foreign policies. Of foremost concern for Moscow was its ability to project itself as standard-bearer for detente and thereby break out of the isolation imposed chiefly by the United States following the events in Afghanistan and Poland. From the standpoint of the neutral and non-aligned states, their policy's autonomy and room for maneuver were largely dependent on a more fluid relationship between East and West, where neither side would give pretexts for exerting pressure and urging loyalty. In the West, France set itself at the head of detente advocacy with its project of a European disarmament conference, in fact with a concrete security proposal (however lacking in substance). This was the role that Bonn had filled in the 1970s. The policy of "benign neglect" that the United States brought to broad areas of the CSCE largely accorded with Bonn's interests. Only in a multilateral context could the Federal Republic hope to continue a limited detente and Ostpolitik without coming into conflict with its security interests, which implied as undisturbed a relationship with the U.S. as possible.

Stagnation in Intra-German Relations

With the close coupling of Ostpolitik and East-West detente the Federal Republic was running the risk that changes in the general climate of international relations would have repercussions on Bonn's Ostpolitik and policy on Germany, directly or with a certain time lag. This became especially evident as the Soviet intervention in Afghanistan in late 1979 and the U.S. reaction to it seemed to spread a hoarfrost over European hopes for detente. To many political figures in the Federal Republic this turn of events was a shock. Many tried at first to insulate Central Europe from the deteriorating East-West relations and wanted to exert an influence on the dominant powers to keep them from breaking off the lines of communication entirely. Others were calling for the Europeans to decouple their detente policy from the superpowers. Yet those who argued for a "Europeanization of Europe"[178] underestimated the intertwining of the European situation with global East-West relations, while others who wanted to press the superpowers toward more cooperative behavior failed to recognize how deep the gulf between Washington and Moscow had already become.

After what it regarded as discriminatory treatment on the question of trade relations, especially after the Jackson-Vanik amendment had linked trade with the emigration of Soviet Jews, Moscow had come to the conclusion that a continuation of East-West detente with the United States had but a very limited potential for Soviet profit. Following the Middle East war of 1973 and the establishment of Soviet footholds in Angola, Ethiopia, and Yemen, but especially in the wake of the Soviet Union's forced arms build-up in the realm of medium-range nuclear weapons, Washington came to the view that Moscow would take one-sided advantage of continuing detente policy if Washington did not make clear that it would firmly oppose any further increase in Soviet power.[179]

On top of this came the developments in Poland. The workers revolts in August 1980 and the challenge to state power from the independent trade union "Solidarity" unsettled the Eastern-bloc states. The widespread sympathy in the West for the Polish workers showed that recognition of the status quo related primarily to European borders and did not give the authoritarian regimes of Eastern Europe a blank check. For fear that the bacillus of rebelliousness could spread and threaten the stability of the GDR, the East German leadership sought to contain the danger of contagion by a renewed increase in the minimum exchange requirement for citizens from the Federal Republic and Berlin—this time to 25 marks in each case, with no exemptions for pensioners—and by administrative measures against Polish citizens.

At the same time the GDR intensified its campaign of ideological demarcation. In a speech in Gera in mid-October 1980 Honecker demanded as a prerequisite for a comprehensive normalization of relations between the Federal Republic and the GDR the unconditional recognition of the existence of two sovereign, mutually independent states with different social orders as well as respect for the principle of nonintervention. He demanded that the Federal Republic "finally" be prepared to recognize a separate nationality of the GDR, to transform the permanent missions into embassies, and to bring about "a settlement on the course of the border on the Elbe according to international law."[180]

However, with this dual strategy, designed primarily to stabilize the domestic political situation, perhaps also to send a signal to the East, the GDR was running the risk of disrupting, if not reversing, the normalization process in German-German relations. With its status demands it was hammering on stakes that had become rotten in the course of history, but which had also been driven deeper still by the ruling of the Federal Constitutional Court, thus distinctly limiting Bonn's room for maneuver with the GDR for the foreseeable future. Raising the compulsory exchange, or "entrance fee," also struck at a core concern of Bonn's policy on Germany, where a special significance was attached to "humanitarian measures." The West German government therefore made it clear that it considered a "drastic change" in the compulsory exchange as a prerequisite for negotiations on the GDR's proposed large-scale projects in the areas of energy and transportation. Though in view of the financial predicament with the federal budget it was to be expected that in the next few years Bonn would be able to muster only very limited funds for large, cost-intensive projects—regardless of the GDR's attitude.

The Polish crisis and the raising of the compulsory exchange put a persistent strain on German-German relations; yet neither side wanted to see the lines of communication severed completely. In December 1981 the twice-postponed meeting between Chancellor Schmidt and Chairman Honecker was held at Lake Werbellin in the GDR. The talks did not bring any progress in German-German relations, let alone the secretly hoped for reduction of the compulsory exchange. As in the visit of the Soviet party leader, Brezhnev, to Bonn three weeks before, the talks at Werbellinsee devoted considerable attention to questions of security and arms control. There were a number of reasons for this new accent in German-German relations—despite the extraordinarily limited room for maneuver in this area, particularly on the part of the GDR. For one thing, East Berlin was taking its place in the Moscow-led "peace campaign," which was directed above all at the Federal Republic and whose aim it was to prevent the deployment of new U.S. intermediate-range missiles in Western Europe. Secondly, the GDR could in this way give evidence of having a say in matters of international security, and finally, the SED leadership was also responding to the growing war-fears among the people in the GDR. This was reflected in the communiqué, in the formulation "that war must never again originate from German soil" and that the two German states were aware of their great responsibility for safeguarding peace in Europe.[181]

But the Schmidt-Honecker meeting also illustrated how little latitude the two German states had for shaping the development of intra-German relations. In an interview with the SED's central organ *Neues Deutschland*, Honecker left no doubt about this when he spoke of the "interrelation between the bilateral and the international sides of our relations" and underscored their importance for peace and detente. "On the other hand, neither of the two states can decouple itself from international politics. They cannot remain unaffected by a general deterioration of the world situation."[182] While the SED general secretary was referring here mainly to the NATO modernization decision, the proclamation of martial law in Poland on the last day of the Schmidt visit (December 13, 1981) clearly pointed to the narrow limits of Western detente policy.

The deterioration of the situation in Poland confronted the Federal Republic with a twofold dilemma: a way out of the Polish crisis seemed possible only by way of economic and political stabilization of a repressive regime and thus ran counter to Western values, while the policy pursued by the United States of isolating Poland and "punishing" the Soviet Union would assuredly not bring about any liberalization in Poland, but would in fact subject East-West relations to an unbearable strain. The middle road taken by the Bonn government—political condemnation of the military regime but continuation of limited economic cooperation—brought the Federal Republic into contradiciton with the hard line of Washington's policy, yet was unable to revive detente policy.

This came out very clearly in the controversy over the gas pipeline deal concluded by a consortium of West European firms with the Soviet Union in 1981. This involved delivery of equipment for the Trans-Siberian pipeline in exchange for later deliveries of gas to Western Europe, with German firms and banks having a sizable share in the business. After the imposition of martial law in Poland the administration in Washington issued an embargo on the supply of capital goods to the Soviet Union, including licenses and deliveries for the pipeline deal; this produced a strain on U.S.-European relations when most of the West European firms, with active support from their governments, ignored the restrictions decreed by Washington.[183] Only after protracted negotiations between the United States and the Europeans, in part in the European Political Cooperation (EPC) framework, in part in the

Bonn Group, did the United States relent in November 1982 and lift the sanctions imposed on West European firms, while the Europeans agreed to exercise greater restraint in trading with the East.

Yet another case showed the practical limits of using economic means to effect political changes. At the end of 1981 and, after a six-month extension, again in mid-1982, the West German government was unable to use the review and extension of the swing in intra-German trade to induce the GDR to reduce the minimum exchange requirement. For the GDR swing and intra-German trade were of immense economic importance since it was economically dependent upon the imports from the Federal Republic and the credits connected with them (for the Federal Republic, on the other hand, the intra-German commerce constituted less than 2 percent of its total foreign trade). But from Bonn's standpoint the political benefits were paramount. This was made clear once again in the summer of 1983 when the Kohl government—with the active participation of Franz Josef Strauss, one of the strongest critics of previous detente policy—used state-guaranteed private bank credits amounting to 1 billion marks to keep the connection to East Berlin intact during a period of possible further deterioration of the East-West relations as a result of the deployment of Pershing IIs and GLCMs in the Federal Republic.

In all these years the Federal Republic and the GDR indicated repeatedly that they considered the efforts to bring about a conciliation of interests as unfinished. "Whether," in the words of the Federal Republic's retiring permanent representative in East Berlin, Günter Gaus, "this mutual interest can be translated into concrete results at present depends least of all on the two German states."[184] This does not release them from their responsibility to continue seeking possibilities for a policy of conciliation and detente.[185] However, such a policy reaches its limits at the reality that the GDR is the westernmost state of the Eastern military bloc and that the Federal Republic of Germany sees its security guaranteed only in the framework of NATO and by its close link with the United States.

5

Security and Detente: A Conflict of Priorities in German Foreign Policy?

The foreign policy of the Federal Republic of Germany has been very much a product of the conditions under which it originated and of the international system in which it has evolved. Bonn has had only limited autonomy in defining the issues of its foreign policy. With the fundamental decision to forge close links with the Western democracies, a decision formalized in 1952 and 1954 in the Bonn and Paris Treaties, the Federal Republic also accepted the consequent order of priorities for its foreign policy: security through close ties with Western Europe and the United States, economic prosperity through integration with the West, and a deferred solution to the German question. In the 35 years of the Federal Republic's existence this order has remained unchanged although the significance and methods of achieving the objectives themselves have undergone substantial transformations. The greatest change has occurred in the Federal Republic's position on the German question, which has run the gamut from active hope for reunification as a result of the Soviet Union's relinquishing its zone of occupation, to simply keeping the German question open, to achieving a modus vivendi with the East on the basis of the territorial status quo and officially recognizing the German Democratic Republic. At the present time the Federal Republic's policy on the German question has reached a new phase of emphasis on German identity.[1]

Until the mid-1960s Bonn's changes of position in foreign policy were belated adaptations to new directions in its allies' positions and to changed international structures. The first significant change of position that was indigenous and not guided by prior actions of its allies occurred in 1969, following a shift in power in the Federal

Republic's domestic politics. This was the decision to embark upon a policy of detente with the Soviet Union, the East European countries, and the German Democratic Republic on the basis of the status quo. The architects of this policy, foremost among them Brandt and Bahr, hoped in this way to be able to bring about at some time in the future a change of this status quo. They hoped that the existing alliance systems would be superseded by a European order of peace with a solution to the German question—German unity in whatever form might be possible. The Federal Constitutional Court supported the goals of this policy for other, conservative motives, elevating change of the status quo in Europe to a political mandate. Nevertheless, the successors of Brandt and Scheel, above all Helmut Schmidt, but also Helmut Kohl, wanted to conduct their policy on the basis of the existing realities and directed their efforts toward stabilization of the status quo. In consequence of this reorientation of policy, they found themselves faced with a debate about German national identity and Germany's political future, a debate nourished by disappointed hopes and growing fear of war.

THE 1980s AND THE POLICY OF EQUILIBRIUM

Security and detente, the preeminent objectives of West German foreign policy, have always been pursued on the basis of the Federal Republic's integration in the West and usually with a high degree of consensus, harmony, and cooperation in West European and Atlantic relations. Yet, as our survey of this policy has shown, at various junctures the latent conflict of priorities between Bonn's defense and alliance policy with the West and its detente policy toward the East has surfaced in various ways and forms, forcing the Federal Republic to try to reconcile differing views of the East-West antagonism and the requisite approaches to resolving it. This has sometimes posed seemingly irreconcilable alternatives and raised the necessity of potentially divisive choices. Such conflicts were of minimal significance as long as the Federal Republic's limited autonomy allowed it only to follow the path dictated by the Western powers, and particularly by the United States, especially as it agreed with its direction and goals, and there were no viable alternatives. This was certainly the case with the Federal Republic's reaction to the Stalin notes of 1952 offering reunification of Germany in exchange for German neutrality. The first serious conflict of priorities occurred in the latter half of the 1950s when the Western powers made their first attempts to reach agreement with the Soviet Union despite the continuing political and ideological competition over the center of Europe. There was conflict again in the 1960s when the United States gave agreements with the Soviet Union precedence over settlements within NATO. Areas of contention were the Berlin problem and the Non-proliferation Treaty. The tensions were primarily a consequence of the difficulties the Bonn government had in adapting itself to the changing positions of its allies. It testifies to the high degree of external control of the Federal Republic's political system that the fundamental change in its Ostpolitik and detente, i.e., the acceptance of the status quo as the basis for its approach to the German question, took place without being accompanied by serious conflicts of priorities in its foreign relations.

A conflict of priorities in the Federal Republic's foreign relations did emerge, however, when at the end of the 1970s and beginning of the 1980s the United States turned away from the policy of limited cooperation with the Soviet Union and reverted to a strategy of containment, while the Federal Republic tried to cling to its policy of detente. The outstanding issues of contention were economic, notably the Yamal gas pipeline deal with the Soviet Union. Differing U.S. and European attitudes toward East-West trade indicated fundamentally different concepts of economic security. The United States subordinated economic benefits (excepting its own shipments of grain to the Soviet Union) and consideration of its allies' interests to political and military opposition to the Soviet Union. The West Europeans believed they could separate economic from military interests. They viewed the natural gas pipeline—besides its salutary impact on employment and trade—as an effective way of enhancing their economic security by diversifying their supply of energy and thus making it less vulnerable to crises.[2] The Federal Republic's dependence on imported raw materials and its orientation to export, plus the importance attached to reciprocal cooperation in maintaining detente with the Soviet Union, were compelling arguments for Bonn not to abandon the deal. Yet, because of the close linkage of its defense policy with that of the United States, the Federal Republic was sensitive to pressure from Washington and, in light of its assessed security needs, was anxious not to elicit negative U.S. responses such as a reduction of U.S. military forces stationed on its territory.

The disagreement about the construction of the natural gas pipeline reflected a growing disjunction between the goals and substance of detente policy on the one hand and defense policy on the other, and in the relative importance Washington and Bonn attached to each. Since the Yom Kippur war doubts had grown in the United States as to whether the policy of detente was really inducing the Soviet Union to exercise restraint in crisis situations and to curb its arms programs as the architects of detente policy had expected. Moreover, in the United States the policy of detente was being increasingly drawn into the play of domestic interests, as when Congress with the Jackson-Vanik amendment effectively killed the U.S.-Soviet trade agreement by linking it to the question of Jewish emigration from the Soviet Union. The U.S. assessment of the possibilities of cooperation with the Soviet Union had gradually changed without Europe's fully registering the magnitude of the change. Against the background of U.S. humiliation over the hostage crisis, the Soviet invasion of Afghanistan was enough to cause the United States to turn about and embark on a renewed policy of containment toward the Soviet Union.[3]

For the United States the first order of business was to increase its military efforts. This had a double function: it was intended to close gaps in the spectrum of U.S. deterrent and defense capability, in particular the "window of vulnerability" (i.e., of land-based ICBMs) stressed by the incoming Reagan administration, and to provide the United States with a political instrument that would permit it effectively to oppose Soviet advances in different parts of the world and conduct negotiations with Moscow from a position of strength. Former Secretary of State Kissinger was enlisted to frighten the Europeans out of their carping complacency and exhort them to increase their military efforts, above all in the area of theater nuclear weapons. In a widely reported speech on the thirtieth anniversary of NATO, Kissinger proclaimed: "Deterrence is dead!"[4]

The Reagan administration distinguished itself from its predecessors principally in two ways: by its strong rhetoric, designed to assuage wounded national pride and restore the self-respect lost in Vietnam, Watergate, and Teheran, and by directing its foreign policy almost exclusively to the East-West conflict. The new administration expected its allies to share its views on world affairs and to support its efforts to contain Soviet influence. They were to fall in step behind Washington; if they did not, the United States would proceed unilaterally. Only gradually did the Reagan administration come to understand that in many cases it simply did not have the coercive power to make its partners march again to the sound of the American drum, and that cooperation with its allies was actually in its own best interests. On the pipeline deal it relented its opposition, in exchange for European promises to curb high tech exports and to act with more discretion on credits to COMECON countries. In the meantime, the administration had encountered increasing domestic opposition to its conduct of foreign policy. Above all, it was unable to increase the defense budget to the amount it wanted or to obtain congressional approval for the MX program it had expected. These setbacks and the accompanying reversal in public opinion were attributable in large part to the country's economic difficulties, primarily the recession and the budget deficit, and the emergence of the nuclear freeze movement. In response to this development President Reagan ultimately reestablished the connection between armament decisions and disarmament efforts.[5]

The changes in East-West relations at the global level had a profound impact on the Federal Republic. Bonn reacted to the Soviet intervention in Afghanistan by attempting to downplay its significance and to portray it as an East-South rather than East-West conflict, while the United States used the Soviet intervention as an occasion for doing what it would have liked to do vis-à-vis Iran: show the flag and demonstrate its strength. For the sake of preserving detente, Bonn sought to continue its cooperation with the countries of Central and Eastern Europe, especially with the GDR, as long as the situation in Poland permitted. The proclamation of martial law in Poland in December 1981 as well as the increase of the minimum exchange rate for visitors to East Berlin and the GDR made it clear, however, that detente was not "separable," that developments in Europe were intertwined in many ways with global East-West relations.

The deterioration of East-West relations came as shock to many in the Federal Republic. Some expressed resentful, I-told-you-so disparagement; they had, they said, warned again and again against having any illusions about East-West rapprochement. Others reacted with dismay or criticism of the two superpowers, who were held responsible for the deterioration of East-West relations. From this turn of events they drew the conclusion that the Federal Republic should extricate itself to some degree from the web of superpower relations and pursue a more independent, European foreign policy.[6] Thus the conflict of priorities between Bonn's detente policy and its policy of alliance solidarity became a matter of urgency.

Could Bonn mediate between the apparently increasingly irreconcilable goals of Western defense policy and detente? The NATO dual-track decision of December 1979 had marked a successful attempt to do just that. The NATO allies had resolved to counter the growing Soviet threat from medium-range ballistic missiles and strengthen the credibility of the U.S. deterrent, but they also called on Moscow to enter into negotiations on arms limitation in the INF area and offered not to implement the deployment decision if the Soviet Union would dismantle its medium-range missile systems aimed at Western Europe, in particular its new SS-20s. However, given the multitude of pressures on both sides, the INF negotiations did not yield results and were finally broken off by Moscow in November 1983. Considering the implementation of the deployment decision a serious political setback, the Soviet

Union threatened that a new "ice age" would descend on East-West relations.

The NATO decision, signaling the West's determination to counter the Soviet arms build-up as well as its willingness to agree to arms limitation, coincided with the crisis in East-West relations stemming from events in Afghanistan, with a shift to the right in the United States that brought a new administration with Reagan in the White House, and with the emergence of a peace movement in Western Europe. These circumstances cast doubts on the seriousness and credibility on the NATO decision on deployment and its offer to negotiate. The Federal Republic, whose first priority had been negotiations leading to the removal of Soviet medium-range weapons, found itself in the paradoxical situation of having to champion the NATO decision and hold fast to it at all costs in order to demonstrate its readiness to participate in NATO's defense of Western Europe. The United States, whose primary interest lay in modernizing its theater nuclear weapons, had to yield to pressure from its allies and declare its willingness to negotiate with the Soviet Union on a "zero solution" for medium-range weapons and significant reductions in strategic weapons systems. This dynamic and the necessity to take into consideration NATO's interests exerted strong pressure on both the Federal Republic and the United States to conform to their allies' collective wishes.[7]

The crisis in European-American relations over the policy of detente indicated to the Federal Republic the limits of its freedom of action. Bonn did not, promptly or belatedly, adapt to its chief ally's change in policy as it had done in the past, but its attempt to bridge the widening gap between the two superpowers prompted the suspicion in the West that, as a result of Soviet attempts to both intimidate and court it, Bonn wanted to loosen its connection with NATO and play a more independent role with respect to the United States. These suspicions, which President Carter's national security adviser, Zbigniew Brzezinski, had summed up in the term "self-Finlandization," were further fed by a thriving peace movement in Germany which slowly eroded the political support for this two-track policy, at least within the majority party, Helmut Schmidt's SPD.

If the Europeans had expressed doubts about the credibility of the strategic protection afforded by the United States, which they saw jeopardized by political vulnerability and lack of political leadership, it was now the Americans' turn to express uncertainty as to whether the Europeans would fully live up to their obligations in the North Atlantic Alliance. But the Federal Republic's main interest was to ensure that NATO, vitally important for its military security, not be weakened, and that the fruits of detente achieved by Ostpolitik in Central Europe not be jeopardized. Bonn tried to keep the link between the two goals of the Harmel formula of 1967 intact and urged its partners to follow suit. Capability to defend Western Europe and willingness to negotiate with the Soviet Union and its allies continued to be the two pillars of the Western alliance. To pursue these two goals simultaneously had become both a foreign policy objective and a domestic necessity.

To be sure, the interpretation of these principles had changed in the course of time. At the beginning of the 1970s their meaning was expanded to a very broad concept of security and detente; then years later this was modified to military security and "realistic" detente, the latter to be achieved primarily through negotiations on arms control and disarmament. NATO, too, now saw its role as a more modest one. Instead of trying to attain a "just and lasting peace in Europe," it pursued a less ambitious goal: reestablishing international stability and, on the basis of this stability, building a constructive relationship between East and West.[8]

Little noticed by the public, the political leadership of the Federal Republic had already begun in the mid-1970s, with the changeover from Brandt to Schmidt, to draw back from the broad goal of a "European order of peace" in favor of a policy of equilibrium between the opposing sides. Peace was no longer seen as a result of a change in the existing security structures but, on the contrary, in their stabilization. This policy did not presuppose courage and imagination as much as credibility and reliability. Of course, this change took into account the reduced expectations regarding the development of East-West relations, which would continue to bear the imprint of the political and ideological antagonism between the superpowers. But it was also an expression of Helmut Schmidt's different political perspectives, in which the notion of balance had long played a central role.[9]

The policy of equilibrium had the advantage of being fully compatible with the requirements of military security; it could encompass a countervailing strategy and the political demand for maintaining or reestablishing a balanced relation of military forces. The policy itself caused no conflict of goals with the Federal Republic's allies; rather, it aimed at avoiding such a conflict. (The debate in NATO about the alliance's security policy should, therefore, not be blamed on the policy of equilibrium propounded by Schmidt.) More so, and little noticed abroad, it represented a bipartisan domestic consensus. The weakness of this relatively static conception of security was that it could be used as a pretext for not taking any political initiatives and that it provided no answers for the German question. It was, then, certainly no accident that men like Bahr and Gaus were not satisfied with this pedestrian policy of equilibrium and instead began to reflect on alternative strategies for achieving security that would explicitly allow for resolving the German question.[10] The critics of Schmidt's policy often overlooked the fact that equilibrium was not in itself a final goal but rather a way of preserving peace in Europe during a difficult period of transition. The maxims of this policy could, therefore, provide an appropriate strategy for a "major second-tier power" whose range of action was restricted by historical conditions, geographical situation, and political constraints.[11]

This policy of equilibrium did not prevent the CDU/CSU—in power again after the FDP had switched sides in October 1982, thus unseating the Schmidt government—from fully embracing a renewed warming of German-German relations in spite of the missile frost. Out front was Franz Josef Strauss, once one of the most outspoken critics of Ostpolitik, now channelling a billion-mark private bank loan into the East Berlin state coffers. The GDR, in turn, relaxed some restrictions on emigration to the Federal Republic, thereby diffusing domestic discontent. And it really sounded like a new melody of German togetherness when both Kohl and Honecker talked of a common German responsibility to see to it that no future war would start from German soil.

AUTONOMY AND FOREIGN POLICY OPTIONS OF THE FEDERAL REPUBLIC OF GERMANY

Conflicts of priorities in West German foreign policy have been, from Bonn's point of view, primarily differences of opinion within the Western alliance, mainly between the Federal Republic and the United States, about the function and importance of detente policy toward the East. The Federal Republic's ability to pursue detente and other goals of its foreign policy has been greatest when this policy was in accord with that of its allies. This was evident in the process of bilateral coordination between Bonn and Washington during the active phase of detente in the early 1970s. This process was notable in two respects. First, the Federal Republic's Ostpolitik was not a "solitary journey to Moscow," as some critics claimed. Rather, the architects of this policy had precisely calculated in advance what they could hope to achieve with it. Within the existing system of alliances there was room for a modus vivendi with the East, but there was no room for a European security system that would replace or overarch the alliance systems. The architects of the Federal Republic's Ostpolitik had also developed consultation processes, both formal and informal, that guaranteed the indispensable consent of Bonn's allies. Secondly, within this framework it was Bonn that determined the direction and the pace of negotiations with Moscow and Warsaw, and later with East Berlin. Only at great cost to its relations with the Federal Republic would it have been possible for Washington to slow down or bring to a halt this dynamic; consequently, it did not even try but instead enclosed these negotiations in a framework of multilateral coordinating processes and otherwise pursued a policy of "damage control."

Thus the Federal Republic succeeded in replacing unilateral political and economic dependence with reciprocal interdependence. While in matters of security the Federal Republic's obvious necessity to rely on the strategic protection provided by the United States had kept its capacity for autonomous action small, the policy of detente dramatically expanded its political room for maneuver. The recognition of the territorial status quo in Europe had freed the Federal Republic from the necessity of pursuing—with instruments that were becoming increasingly blunt and risked international isolation—a policy toward the Soviet Union and the East European states that was intended to be offensive, although implemented defensively, and that was, moreover, ineffectual. The policy of detente made it possible for Bonn to be much more flexible in the formulation and execution not only of its Ostpolitik but also of its policy toward the West, as well as in the development of its relations with the countries of the third world. However, because of the great value attached to the continuation of East-West detente, the Federal Republic entered into a new dependence with the Soviet Union, which had the power to make a continuation of detente conditional on what it regarded as satisfactory behavior on the part of the Federal Republic. The policy of equilibrium stipulated that the interests of security and the interests of detente be balanced. Rapprochement vis-à-vis Moscow could not exceed the point at which the Federal Republic risked its protection by the United States, at least as long as it perceived itself as being deficient in security, and the United States the only credible net exporter of security.

In the domestic debate the hierarchy of values and priorities was challenged whenever the Federal Republic had arrived at a crossroads and was, in fact or apparently, faced with decisions about its future direction with regard to security and/or the German question. This was the case from 1952 to 1955 before the Federal Republic's association with the West had been formalized and when there still seemed to be a possibility of reunification; from 1970 to 1972 when the conclusion of the Eastern Treaties seemed to consolidate Germany's division and its postwar borders while at the same time endangering the Federal Republic's connection with its Atlantic allies; and again, from 1980 to 1983 when the implementation of the NATO double-track decision seemed only possible at the risk of new East-West confrontation. In retrospect it is evident that in all three cases it was a matter of pseudo-alternatives. In the 1950s the Federal Republic did not have the freedom of action necessary for actively pursuing a policy of reunification based on the Soviet proposals, against the interests of the Western powers. In the early 1970s it was only a matter of time before pressure from its allies would have forced the Federal Republic to accept the territorial status quo in Europe under conditions more unfavorable than those prevailing at the time. If this had happened the consequence probably would have been a greater strain on the Federal Republic's relations in NATO than was caused by the irritations resulting from the dynamics of Bonn's Ostpolitik. In each case the policy of the German government kindled fierce domestic controversy that seemed to shake the political system to its foundation. The end result, however, was a strengthening of the coalition then in control of the government. In 1957 the coalition of Christian Democratic Union and Christian Social Union was able to win an absolute majority in the parliamentary elections in which the central issues were rearmament and equipping the Bundeswehr with nuclear launchers. In the elections of 1972 the Social Democratic Party carried the day with its arguments in favor of the treaties with the Soviet Union and other East European countries. In 1983 the Kohl/Genscher government was challenged by the SPD on the missile issue, but won by a handsome margin, in spite of widespread anxiety and misgivings about INF deployment.

Since the beginning of the 1980s a new debate has been in progress, one ignited by the NATO dual-track decision and fueled by a mixture of fear of war and concern for humanity's future. Guided by the slogan "peace without weapons," the new peace movement, or at least some groups within its heterogeneous spectrum, is taking a stand in opposition to the precedence of military security over other considerations and is thereby calling into question the Federal Republic's relations with its allies and restoring urgency to the question of Germany's future. It is not clear, however, whether this debate is a dispute over the priorities of the Federal Republic's foreign policy and particularly security policy or whether it is basically a social and generational conflict such as occurred at the time of the extra-parliamentary opposition and the student revolt (in other forms and with other goals, of course). Nor is it yet clear what the effects of this foreign policy debate will be.

A number of feedback processes connect foreign relations and domestic politics. These connections become most clear when, as a consequence of crises in domestic politics, a government is more or less paralyzed in its foreign relations, as in 1966 when the Erhard government was too weak to undertake the adaptation of its foreign policy demanded by the nuclear question, and again in 1982 when the chairman of the Free Democratic Party and minister of foreign affairs, Hans-Dietrich Genscher, was more concerned with the survival of his party than with initiative in security policy. Even if the change of government following such periods of coalition weakness resulted from the dynamics of domestic politics and for essentially economic reasons, nevertheless such change has generally been accompanied by a redefinition of priorities in foreign affairs.

The dominance of security concerns and the corresponding value attached to relations with the United States and membership in NATO has affected the structures of the Federal Republic's foreign policy in several ways. First, this dominance of security concerns has resulted in a high degree of continuity in Bonn's foreign policy, with the Western alliance functioning as a kind of control instrument whenever Bonn seemed about to stray from the consensus within the alliance. In this way the limits of Bonn's room for maneuver in foreign affairs were set, limits within which it could pursue its policy on detente and the German question.

A further result of the Federal Republic's close association with the West has been the consolidation of its democratic system. German democracy has achieved an unexpected stability and has so far been able to withstand extremism of the right and of the left. Two factors have contributed decisively to this stability: the Federal Republic's continued economic growth and the popular acceptance of its fundamental decision to align itself with the West.

Because of the Federal Republic's economic and political success the German question has been pushed into the background and the German Democratic Republic has not become, in the minds of the West Germans, that part of the German nation in need of redemption. Rather, the Germans have come to understand that maintaining security and association with the West (association with the East from the GDR's viewpoint) *and* reunification are mutually exclusive under the prevailing international conditions. Because the Adenauer government, mindful of its limited options, did not actively pursue a policy of reunification, it contributed to the legend that it had consciously rejected German national unity, especially by not giving greater consideration to the Stalin notes of 1952 and by readily accepting the Berlin Wall in 1961. The propagators of this legend did not understand that it was not in this government's power to realize German unity. In the first half of the 1970s the governing coalition of Social Democrats and Free Democrats achieved as much as was possible: a well-regulated coexistence of the two German states that made cooperation possible when the international conditions permitted. It is not inconceivable, however, that in the two German states a new generation is growing up that might, in its efforts to find a political identity of its own or in its criticism of the prevailing primacy of military security, pose anew the question of German national unity.

Raising the German question again, however, means not only reappraising the priorities of West German foreign policy, but also calling into question the structures that have shaped the postwar European order: the division of Europe, the emergence of two opposing alliance systems, and the establishment of the nuclear superpowers as the guarantors of this order. A change in these structures appears possible only if both the Soviet Union and the United States withdraw from Europe. Hence a number of writers have argued for "Europeanizing Europe," as Peter Bender put it, and have called on the Europeans to have confidence in themselves and willingness to stand their ground, and to create the preconditions for overcoming the division of Europe. But in view of global military, economic, and political interdependence, is a European regionalism still possible today except at the price of irrelevance in world politics? Would the United States and the Soviet Union be content simply to look on as the region that was the basis for their status as world powers in the postwar period pulls back from their influence? Would not such a change of the structures in Europe create new security problems, the solution of which would be comparable to squaring the circle, as it would still be a matter of guaranteeing security both for and from Germany? Peter Bender writes that the division of Germany into two separate states has become a constitutive element of European detente.[12] But must one not go further and ask whether the division of Europe might not have become a stabilizing element of world politics and, therefore, a factor in the Federal Republic's security? At least as long as the Federal Republic does not throw itself into confrontation but instead draws from Germany's division incentive and commitment to cooperate with its sister state and the East European nations.

And so there are no easy outs, no clear-cut departures for German foreign policy. Security and detente remain foremost among the goals of the Federal Republic's foreign policy: security as an obligation to be fulfilled through its participation in the North Atlantic alliance and its collaboration with the United States; detente as its responsibility to Europe arising from the division of this continent. Its *staatskunst* lies in keeping these two goals mutually compatible.

Notes

CHAPTER 1

1. For an overview of European history, and Germany's role in Europe, see Gordon A. Craig, *Europe since 1815.* Alternate Edition (New York: Holt & Winston, 1974); Anton W. DePorte, *Europe Between the Superpowers: The Enduring Balance* (New Haven and London: Yale University Press, 1979); Gordon A. Craig, *Germany 1866-1945* (New York and Oxford: Oxford University Press, 1980).

2. On the genesis of the Federal Republic of Germany see Peter H. Merkl, *The Origin of the West German Republic* (New York: Oxford University Press, 1963); Hans-Peter Schwarz, *Vom Reich zur Bundesrepublik: Deutschland im Widerstreit der aussenpolitischen Konzeptionen in den Jahren der Besatzungsherrschaft 1945-1949* (Neuwied: Luchterhand, 1966); Theodor Eschenburg, *Jahre der Besatzung 1945-1949* (Stuttgart: Deutsche Verlags-Anstalt, 1983).

3. This concern was shared by both Chancellor Adenauer and opposition leader Schumacher, though both drew different conclusions. See Konrad Adenauer, *Memoirs, 1945-53* (Chicago: Regnery, 1965). Only the first volume of Adenauer's memoirs has been translated into English; for his whole oeuvre see *Erinnerungen*, 4 vols. (Stuttgart: Deutsche Verlags-Anstalt, 1965, 1966, 1967, 1968); also see Klaus Gotto, ed. *Konrad Adenauer: Seine Deutschland- und Aussenpolitik 1945-1963* (Munich: Deutscher Taschenbuch Verlag, 1971). For Schumacher, see Arno Scholz and Walter G. Oschilewski, eds. *Turmwächter der Demokratie: Ein Lebensbild von Kurt Schumacher. Vol. 2: Reden und Schriften* (Berlin-Grunewald: Arani 1953); also see Lewis J. Edinger, *Kurt Schumacher: A Study in Personality and Political Behaviour* (Stanford, Calif.: Stanford University Press, 1965).

4. See also Josef Joffe, "The Foreign Policy of the German Federal Republic," in *Foreign Policy in World Politics*, ed. by Roy C. Macridis, 5th ed., (Englewood Cliffs, N.J.: Prentice-Hall, 1976), pp. 117-151.

5. See The Future Tasks of the Alliance (Harmel Report). Report of the NATO Council, December 14, 1967, *The North Atlantic Treaty Organization: Facts and Figures* (Brussels: NATO Information Service, 1981), pp. 288-90; also see Communiqué on the Special Meeting of Foreign and Defense Ministers, December 12, 1979, Texts of *NATO Final Communiqués. (Vol. II 1975-1980)* (Brussels: NATO Information Service, 1982), pp. 121-123; Communiqué on the NATO Council Meeting, December 13-14, 1979, ibid., pp. 124-129.

6. On the partition of Europe and the origins of the cold war see John Lewis Gaddis, *Strategies of Containment: A Critical Appraisal of Postwar American Security Policy* (New York and Oxford: Oxford University Press, 1982); Thomas H. Etzold and John Lewis Gaddis, eds. *Containment: Documents on American Policy and Strategy, 1945-1950* (New York: Columbia University Press, 1978); John H. Backer, *The Decision to Divide Germany: American Foreign Policy in Transition* (Durham, N.C.: Duke University Press, 1978). On Soviet policy see Thomas W. Wolfe, *Soviet Power and Europe 1945-1970* (Baltimore and London: The Johns Hopkins Press, 1970). For a German point of view, see Wilfried Loth, *Die Teilung der Welt: Geschichte des Kalten Krieges 1941-1955* (Munich: Deutscher Taschenbuch Verlag, 1980).

7. See Convention on Relations Between the Three Powers and the Federal Republic of Germany, May 26, 1952, As Amended by Schedule I of the Protocol on Termination of the Occupation Regime in Germany, Signed at Paris, October 23, 1954, in *Documents on*

Germany, 1944-1970, U.S. Senate, Committee on Foreign Relations, 92nd Cong., 1st sess. (Washington, D.C.: Government Printing Office, 1971), pp. 248-53.

8. On the evolution of the European post-war system, see F. Roy Willis, *France, Germany and the New Europe, 1945-1963* (Stanford, Calif.: Stanford University Press, 1965); Robert E. Osgood, *NATO: The Entangling Alliance* (Chicago: University of Chicago Press, 1962); Robin Alison Remington, *The Warsaw Pact: Case Studies in Communist Conflict Resolution* (Cambridge, Mass. and London: The MIT Press, 1971); Alfred Grosser, *The Western Alliance: European-American Relations Since 1945* (New York: Continuum, 1980).

9. See Catherine McArdle Kelleher, "Germany and NATO: The Enduring Bargain," in *West German Foreign Policy: 1949-1979,* ed. by Wolfram F. Hanrieder (Boulder, Colo., Westview, 1980), pp. 43-60.

10. For the Geneva Summit Conference and the various arms control and disarmament initiatives of the 1950s see U.S. Department of State, ed., *Documents on Disarmament 1945-1959,* 2 vols. (Washington, D.C.: Government Printing Office, 1960).

11. See Adenauer, *Erinnerungen 1953-1955,* pp. 471 ff.

12. See British Memorandum Submitted at the Geneva Conference of Heads of Government: Joint Inspection in Europe, July 21, 1955, *Documents on Disarmament 1945-1959,* pp. 488-89; address by First Secretary Khrushchev to a mass rally in East Berlin, July 26, 1955, *Pravda,* July 27, 1955.

13. Hanrieder has coined the phrase "penetrated system" for the early period of the Federal Republic; see Wolfram F. Hanrieder, *West German Foreign Policy 1949-1963: International Pressure and Domestic Response* (Stanford: Stanford University Press, 1967), pp. 227-45.

14. For the integration of the Federal Republic into the Western alliance see Militärgeschichtliches Forschungsamt, ed. *Verteidigung im Bündnis: Aufbau und Bewährung der Bundeswehr* (Munich: Bernhard & Graefe, 1975); Karl Carstens and Dieter Mahncke, eds. *Westeuropäishe Verteidigungskooperation* (Munich: Oldenbourg, 1972).

15. On the political dimension of the European Communities, see Werner J. Feld, *The European Community in World Affairs: Economic Power and Political Influence* (Port Washington, N.Y.: Alfred Publishing Co., 1976); Helen Wallace, William Wallace and Carole Webb, eds. *Policy-Making in the European Communities* (Chichester & New York: John Wiley & Sons, 1977); Werner J. Feld, ed. *Western Europe's Global Reach: Regional Cooperation and Worldwide Aspirations* (New York: Pergamon Press, 1979).

16. See address by National Security Adviser Henry A. Kissinger at the Associated Press annual dinner in New York, April 23, 1973, *U.S. Department of State Bulletin 1973,* May 14, 1973, pp. 593-98; Communique of the European Community Summit Meeting at Copenhagen, December 14-15, 1973, reprinted in *The New Europe and the United States,* ed. by Gerhard Mally (Lexington, Mass.: D.C. Heath and Co., 1974), pp. 377-84; Declaration on Atlantic Relations, adopted by the NATO Council in Ottawa, June 19, 1974, and signed by the Heads of NATO Governments in Brussels, June 26, 1974, *Texts of Final Communiqués* (Brussels: NATO Information Service, 1975), pp. 318-21.

17. See the Genscher-Colombo initiative for the political development of the European Communities, *Bulletin of the European Communities,* 1981: 3.4.1.

18. For the most recent data on the integration of the German economy into the international economy, see the annual *Statistisches Jahrbuch* (Wiesbaden: Statistisches Bundesamt); the monthly report *Monatsberichte der Deutschen Bundesbank* (Frankfurt: Deutsche Bundesbank); and the weekly *Wochenberichte des DIW* (Berlin: Deutsches Institut für Wirtschaftsforschung).

19. For an in-depth analysis of Germany's trade policy vis-à-vis the Soviet Union, see Angela Stent, *From Embargo to Ostpolitik: The Political Economy of West German-Soviet*

Relations, 1955-1980 (Cambridge: Cambridge University Press, 1981); on the Yamal pipeline issues, see Angela E. Stent, *Soviet Energy and Western Europe* (New York: Praeger, 1982).

20. For an (early) overview, see Ulrich Scheuner and Beate Lindemann, eds. *Die Vereinten Nationen und die Mitarbeit der Bundesrepublik Deutschland* (Munich and Vienna: Oldenbourg, 1973).

21. This phrase has been coined by the French economist François Perroux. A journalistic treatment of this theme is given by Edwin Hartrich, *The Fourth and Richest Reich* (New York: Macmillan, 1980); various analyses, more scholarly though debatable, are presented in *The Political Economy of West Germany: Modell Deutschland*, ed. by Andrei S. Markovits (New York: Praeger, 1982).

22. See Hans-Peter Schwarz, "Das aussenpolitische Konzept Konrad Adenauers," in *Konrad Adenauer*, ed. by Gotto, pp. 97-155; Adenauer, *Erinnerungen 1955-1959*, p. 377.

23. See Arnulf Baring, *Aussenpolitik in Adenauers Kanzlerdemokratie* (Munich: Oldenbourg, 1969); Arnulf Baring, *Sehr verehrter Herr Bundeskanzler! Heinrich von Brentano im Briefwechsel mit Konrad Adenauer 1949-1964* (Hamburg: Hoffman & Campe, 1974); Wilhelm G. Grewe, *Rückblenden: Aufzeichnungen eines Augenzeugen deutscher Aussenpolitik von Adenauer bis Schmidt* (Frankfurt: Propyläen, 1979); Herbert Blankenhorn, *Verständnis und Verständigung: Blätter eines politischen Tagebuches 1949-1979* (Frankfurt: Propyläen, 1980).

24. See statement by Herbert Wehner in the Bundestag on June 30, 1960, *Verhandlungen des Deutschen Bundestages*, 3. Sitzungsperiode, June 30, 60, pp.7052-61; for the reorientation of the SPD, also see Abraham Ashkenasi, *Reformpartei und Aussenpolitik: Die Aussenpolitik der SPD Berlin-Bonn* (Cologne and Opladen: Westdeutscher Verlag, 1968); Hartmut Soell, *Fritz Erler. Eine politische Biographie* (Bonn-Bad Godesberg: J.H.W. Dietz Nachf., 1976), 2 vols.

25. For an excellent interpretation of the persons and forces bringing about the "changing of guards" in 1969, see Arnulf Baring, *Machtwechsel: Die Ära Brandt-Scheel* (Stuttgart: Deutsche Verlags-Anstalt, 1982).

26. See Willy Brandt, *Aussenpolitik, Deutschlandpolitik, Europapolitik: Grundsätzliche Erklärungen während des ersten Jahres im Auswärtigen Amt,* (Berlin: Berlin Verlag, 1968); Willy Brandt, *A Peace Policy for Europe* (New York: Holt, Rinehart & Winston, 1969); Willy Brandt, *Begegnungen und Einsichten: Die Jahre 1960-1975* (Hamburg: Hoffman & Campe, 1976).

27. See Helmut Schmidt, *The Balance of Power: Germany's Peace Policy and the Powers* (London: Kimber, 1971); Wolfram F. Hanrieder, ed. *Helmut Schmidt: Perspectives on Politics* (Boulder, Colo.: Westview, 1982). Also see Marion Dönhoff, *Foe into Friend: The Makers of the New Germany from Adenauer to Helmut Schmidt* (London: Weidenfeld & Nicholson, 1982).

28. See Wolf-Dieter Karl and Joachim Krause, "Aussenpolitischer Strukturwandel und parlamentarischer Entscheidungsprozess," in *Verwaltete Aussenpolitik. Sicherheits- und entspannungspolitische Entscheidungsprozesse in Bonn*, ed. by Helga Haftendorn et al. (Cologne: Wissenschaft und Politik, 1978), pp. 55-82; on German parliamentarism see Gerhard Loewenberg, *Parliament in the German Political System* (Ithaca, N.Y.: Cornell University Press, 1966).

29. On foreign policy decision-making in the Federal Republic, see Renate Mayntz and Fritz W. Scharpf, *Policy-Making in the German Federal Bureaucracy* (Amsterdam: Elsevier, 1975); Helga Haftendorn, "West Germany and the Management of Security Relations," in *The Foreign Policy of West Germany*, ed. by Ekkehart Krippendorff and Volker Rittberger (London and Beverly Hills, Calif: Sage Publications, 1980), pp. 7-31; Joachim Krause and Lothar Wilker, "Bureaucracy and Foreign Policy in the Federal Republic of

Germany," ibid., pp. 147-70; Nevil Johnson, *Government in the Federal Republic of Germany: The Executive at Work* (Oxford: Pergamon Press, 1973); David P. Conradt, *The German Policy* (New York and London: Longman, 1978).

CHAPTER 2

1. See Hans-Peter Schwarz, "Die Politik der Westbindung oder die Staatsraison der Bundesrepublik," *Zeitschrift für Politik*, 22 (1975): 307-37.

2. For the Paris Treaties of October 23, 1954, see U.S. Senate, Committee on Foreign Relations, *Documents on Germany 1944-1970*, 92nd Cong., 1st sess., 1971 (Washington, D.C.: Government Printing Office, 1971); pp. 248-53. For an interpretation of the decisive events of 1955 and their historical basis, see Hans-Peter Schwarz, *Die Ära Adenauer: Gründerjahre der Republik 1949-1957* (Stuttgart: Deutsche Verlags-Anstalt, 1981).

3. Upon invitation of the Soviet leadership, Adenauer traveled to Moscow, September 9-13, 1954, with the purpose of establishing a direct relationship with the Kremlin. For a detailed account of this trip, see Konrad Adenauer, *Erinnerungen 1953-1955* (Stuttgart: Deutsche Verlags-Anstalt, 1966), pp. 487-556; Wilhelm Grewe, *Rückblenden, Aufzeichnungen eines Augenzeugen deutscher Aussenpolitik von Adenauer bis Schmidt* (Frankfurt: Propyläen, 1980), pp. 232-55; Carlo Schmid, *Errinnerungen* (Bern: Scherz, 1979), pp. 564-85.

4. See Geneva Conference of Heads of Government, July 18-23, 1955 (Washington, D.C.: Government Printing Office, 1955).

5. On the disarmament negotiations of the 1950s, see Department of State, ed. *Documents on Disarmament 1945-1959*, 2 vols. (Washington, D.C.: Government Printing Office, 1960), also see Charles R. Plank, *Sicherheit in Europa: Die Vorschläge für Rüstungsbeschränkung und Abrüstung 1955-1965* (Munich: Oldenbourg, 1968).

6. The dominant role played by Adenauer in the formulation of German foreign policy is most clearly revealed through his close relationship with the High Commissioners. After the Foreign Office was reopened, he assumed its direction and was supported in this effort by such important officials as Hallstein, Grewe, Blankenhorn and others. When Heinrich von Brentano was named foreign minister in June 1955, Adenauer retained explicit control over specific areas of foreign policy, particularly those questions concerning the situation of Germany as a whole and the Federal Republic's relationship to the Four Powers. See Konrad Adenauer, *Erinnerungen 1955-1959* (Stuttgart: Deutsche Verlags-Anstalt, 1967) P. 121. For further information concerning the decision-making process in foreign policy during the "Adenauer Era," see Arnulf Baring, *Aussenpolitik in Adenauers Kanzlerdemokratie: Bonns Beitrag zur Europäischen Verteidigungsgemeinschaft* (Munich: Oldenbourg, 1969). Additional insights may be gained from numerous memoirs, for example, Arnulf Baring, *Sehr verehrter Herr Bundeskanzler! Heinrich von Brentano im Briefwechsel mit Konrad Adenauer 1949-1964.* (Hamburg: Hoffman & Campe, 1974); Grewe, *Rückblenden*; Anneliese Poppinga, *Meine Erinnerungen an Konrad Adenauer* (Munich: Deutscher Taschenbuch Verlag, 1972); Herbert Blankenhorn, *Verständnis und Verständigung: Blätter eines politischen Tagebuches 1949-1979* (Frankfurt: Propyläen, 1980).

7. Important sources for Adenauer's thinking are the four volumes of his memoirs, *Erinnerungen* (Stuttgart: Deutsche Verlags-Anstalt, 1965-68). Also see Konrad Adenauer, *Reden 1917-1967: Eine Auswahl*, ed. by Hans-Peter Schwarz (Stuttgart: Deutsche Verlags-Anstalt, 1975). For an interpretation of his thoughts on foreign policy see Hans-Peter Schwarz, "Das aussenpolitische Konzept Adenauers," *Konrad Adenauer: Seine Deutschland- und Aussenpolitik 1945-1963*, ed. by Klaus Gotto (Munich: Deutscher

Taschenbuch Verlag, 1975) pp. 97-155; Klaus Gotto, "Adenauers Deutschland- und Ostpolitik 1954-1963," ibid., pp. 156-286; Bruno Bandulet, *Adenauer zwischen West und Ost: Alternativen der deutschen Aussenpolitik* (Munich: Weltforum Verlag, 1970); Anneliese Poppinga, *Konrad Adenauer: Geschichtsverständnis, Weltanschauung und politische Praxis* (Stuttgart: Deutsche Verlags-Anstalt, 1975).

8. Adenauer, *Erinnerungen 1953-1955*, p. 304. For a discussion of Adenauer's security politics see Hans-Gert Pöttering, *Adenauers Sicherheitspolitik 1956-63: Ein Beitrag zum deutsch-amerikanischen Verhältnis* (Düsseldorf: Droste, 1975)

9. Adenauer, *Erinnerungen 1955-1959*, p. 226; also see Poppinga, *Konrad Adenauer*, p. 63ff. and p. 129ff.

10. Adenauer, *Erinnerungen 1955-1959*, p. 273.

11. ibid., p. 18f.

12. For the various proposals see *Documents on Disarmament 1945-1959*, and the synopsis in Eugene Hinterhoff, *Disengagement* (London: Stevens & Sons Ltd., 1959).

13. Jakob Kaiser, from 1945-47 chairman of the CDU in the Soviet Zone, had hoped for a reunified and neutral Germany as a bridge between East and West; see Hans-Peter Schwarz, *Vom Reich zur Bundesrepublik: Deutschland im Widerstreit der aussenpolitischen Konzeptionen in den Jahren der Besatzungsherrschaft 1945-1949* (Neuwied and Berlin: Luchterhand, 1966), p. 299ff.

14. Schwarz, "Das aussenpolitische Konzept Adenauers," in *Konrad Adenauer: Seine Deutschland- und Aussenpolitik 1945-1963*, p. 143; also see Adenauer, *Erinnerungen 1949-1953*, p. 457.

15. See Adenauer, *Erinnerungen 1955-1959*, p. 266; Adenauer, *Erinnerungen 1949-1953*, p. 301ff. Also see Poppinga, *Konrad Adenauer*, p. 80ff.

16. Adenauer, *Erinnerungen 1945-1953*, p. 496.

17. Adenauer, *Erinnerungen 1953-1955*, p. 217.

18. Here I neither agree with Gotto's nor with Poppinga's interpretation. Gotto maintains that reunification was one of the three main goals of Adenauer's foreign policy while Poppinga feels that the goal of reunification was inseparable for Adenauer from his policy of western integration. See Gotto, "Adenauer's Deutschland- und Ostpolitik," in *Konrad Adenauer: Seine Deutschland- und Aussenpolitik 1945-1963*, p. 9; Poppinga, *Konrad Adenauer*, p. 43.

19. See Adenauer, *Erinnerungen 1955-1959*, p. 377f. and 383. Also see Poppinga, *Konrad Adenauer*, p. 92ff. On the proposal of a "Burgfrieden" (truce) with the Soviet Union, see interview of Adenauer with the *Second German Television*, October 5, 1963, cited in *Konrad Adenauer: Seine Deutschland- und Aussenpolitik 1945-1963*, p. 233. Also see Bandulet, *Adenauer zwischen West und Ost: Alternativen der deutschen Aussenpolitik*, p. 232ff.

20. See Karl Jaspers, *Freiheit und Wiedervereinigung: Über Aufgaben deutscher Politik* (Munich: Piper, 1960).

21. The so-called "Globke Plan," drawn up by the chancellor's aide, Hans Globke, is reprinted in *Adenauer-Studien*, ed. by Rudolf Morsey and Konrad Repgen, p. 202ff., vol. 3 (Mainz: Mathias-Grünewald, 1974).

22. Of course Adenauer never said this directly, but the tenor of his memoirs surely lends itself to such conjecture.

23. Adenauer, *Erinnerungen 1953-1955*, p. 216.

24. See Schwarz, *Das aussenpolitische Konzept*, p. 112f. Adenauer himself writes about his "Potsdam nightmare" in *Erinnerungen 1953-1955*, p. 216.

25. See Adenauer, *Erinnerungen 1953-1955*, p. 244ff. On Adenauer's skepticism with regard to four-power conferences, also see Felix von Eckhardt, *Ein unordentliches Leben: Lebenserinnerungen* (Frankfurt: Ullstein, 1971), p. 237; Blankenhorn, *Verständnis und Verständigung*, p. 158ff.

26. Adenauer, *Erinnerungen 1953-1955,* p. 216.

27. Adenauer in a speech in Bochum on June 15, 1954, cited in Poppinga, *Konrad Adenauer,* p. 127.

28. Adenauer, *Erinnerungen 1955-1959,* p. 384.

29. Adenauer, *Erinnerungen 1953-1955,* p. 454.

30. The high priority accorded to the guarantee of freedom should not be interpreted as if Adenauer placed little value on securing peace. On the contrary, his memoirs reveal that his policies were to avoid a military conflict on German soil whenever possible.

31. See the remarks made by Chancellor Adenauer on June 5, 1957 at a press conference in Vienna, *Dokumente zur Deutschlandpolitik,* ser. 3, vol. 3.2, ed. by Bundesministerium für innerdeutsche Beziehungen (Frankfurt: Alfred Metzner, 1961ff.), p. 1174ff.; on May 31, 1957 at government press conference, *Dokumente zur Deutschlandpolitik,* ser. 3, vol. 3.2, p. 1190f., and on August 3, 1957 in an interview with *Radio Saarland, Bulletin des Presse- und Informationsamtes der Bundesregierung,* 43, 8/31/57: 1352f.; also see Adenauer, *Erinnerungen 1955-1959,* p. 35ff. and p. 283f.

32. Adenauer, *Erinnerungen 1955-1959,* p. 284.

33. See Adenauer, *Erinnerungen 1953-1955,* p. 224ff.; Adenauer also saw in the abortive EDC a point of departure for a system of arms limitations in Europe. See Adenauer's statement before the Bundestag in *Verhandlungen des Deutschen Bundestages,* 2. Sitzungsperiode, 3. Sitzung (DBT/II/3), October 20, 1953, 11-22.

34. See the so-called "Molotov Plan for Withdrawal of Occupation Forces and Neutralization of Germany Pending a Peace Treaty and German Reunification," *Documents on Germany,* p. 238. Also see President Eisenhower's proposal of May 18, 1955, *The New York Times,* May 19, 1955.

35. Adenauer, *Erinnerungen 1953-1955,* p. 441ff.

36. Ibid., p. 446.

37. See Helga Haftendorn, "Adenauer und die Europäische Sicherheit," *Konrad Adenauer und seine Zeit: Politik und Persönlichkeit des ersten Bundeskanzlers,* ed. by Dieter Blumenwitz (Stuttgart: Deutsche Verlags-Anstalt, 1975), pp. 92-110 (here p. 98ff.).

38. See Hinterhoff, *Disengagement,* Appendix; also see Paul van Zeeland, *Les Fondements de la Paix* (Brussels, 1957).

39. For the text of the second and third Eden Plan, see *The Geneva Conference of Heads of Government, 1955* p. 31ff., p. 59.

40. See *Newsweek,* May 16, 1955. On Adenauer's reaction see his *Erinnerungen 1955-1959,* p. 35ff. and 39f.

41. "Outline of Terms of Treaty of Assurance on the Reunification of Germany," October 27, 1955, *Documents on Germany,* p. 281f.

42. See Baring, *Sehr verehrter Herr Bundeskanzler!,* p. 239ff.

43. This tendency has been indicated by Heinrich Krone in his journal notes, published in *Adenauer-Studien,* vol. 2, pp. 148-201.

44. In June 1947 Kurt Schumacher wrote: "Europe will either find a common economic and political base for its development or it will be ground between two huge millstones...And the Russians must recognize that Europe must be democratic if it wants to be European and the United States must recognize that Europe must have socialism if it does not want to lie under dictatorship." See his "Europa—demokratisch und sozialistisch," in *Turmwächter der Demokratie: Ein Lebensbild von Kurt Schumacher. Vol. 2: Reden und Schriften,* ed. by Arno Scholz and Walther G. Oschilewski (Berlin-Grunewald: Arani, 1953, pp. 424-35 (here p. 425); *Vol. 1: Sein Weg durch die Zeit,* 1954). An important political biography of Schumacher is Lewis J. Edinger, *Kurt Schumacher: A Study in Personality and Political Behavior* (Stanford: Stanford University Press, 1965); for an interpretation of his concept of security and national politics, see Ulrich Buczylowski,

Kurt Schumacher und die deutsche Frage: Sicherheitspolitik und strategische Offensivkonzeption vom August 1950 bis September 1951 (Stuttgart: Seewald, 1973); Udo F. Löwke, *Für den Fall, dass... Die Haltung der SPD zur Wehrfrage 1949-1955* (Hannover: Verlag für Literatur und Zeitgeschehen, 1969).

45. See Kurt Schumacher, "Die Sozialdemokratie im Kampf für Freiheit und Sozialismus," *Protokoll des Düsseldorfer Parteitages der SPD*, September 11-14, 1948; Schumacher, "Demokratie und Sozialismus zwischen Osten und Westen," in *Turmwächter der Demokratie*, vol. 2, pp. 51-70.

46. See Buczylowski, *Kurt Schumacher und die deutsche Frage*, pp. 50ff.

47. Löwke, *Für den Fall, dass...* p. 61.

48. See Kurt Schumacher, *Deutschlands Beitrag für Frieden und Freiheit. Die Politik der Sozialdemokratie in der gegenwärtigen Situation* (Dortmund: Sozialdemokratische Partei Deutschlands, 1950). Also see Löwke, *Für den Fall, dass...*, p. 64.

49. Kurt Schumacher, *Deutschlands Forderung: Gleiches Risiko, gleiches Opfer, gleiche Chancen!* (Dortmund: Sozialdemokratische Partei Deutschlands, 1950). Also see Löwke, *Für den Fall, dass...*, p. 67.

50. Here I am guided by Buczylowski's opinion; see *Kurt Schumacher und die deutsche Frage*, p. 95ff.

51. Regarding the East's German policy which reached its high point with the Soviet note of March 1952 and the proposal of neutralization as a precondition for reunification see Gert Meyer, *Die sowjetische Deutschland-Politik im Jahre 1952* (Tübingen: Böhlau, 1970).

52. See resolution of the SPD party group in the Bundestag, March 12, 1952, *Acht Jahre sozialdemokratischer Kampf um Einheit, Frieden und Freiheit: Ein dokumentarischer Nachweis der gesamtdeutschen Haltung der Sozialdemokratie und ihrer Initiativen* (Bonn: Vorstand der SPD, 1954).

53. See Hartmut Soell, *Fritz Erler Eine politische Biographie*, vol. 1 (Bonn-Bad Godesberg: J.H.W. Dietz Nachf., 1960) p. 160ff. This biography of Erler gives presently the most important interpretation of Social Democratic foreign and security policies for the period from approximately 1952 to Erler's death in 1966.

54. With the proposals for a collective European security system ideas from the League of Nations period were taken up and discussed; for example, Churchill spoke in the British House of Commons of an "East Locarno" in May 1953. See *The Times*, May 12, 1953. In the Parliamentary Council 1948-49 similar ideas had been discussed by Erich Kordt and Carlo Schmid; see Gerhard Wettig, *Entmilitarisierung und Wiederbewaffnung in Deutschland 1943-1955: Internationale Auseinandersetzungen um die Rolle der Deutschen in Europa* (Munich: Oldenbourg, 1967), p. 238 ff. Thoughts of this kind were next taken up by Erler and Schmid in 1952. These proposals were an alternative to the EDC in two ways: first, such a security system would assure Germany's security through a collective guarantee system; secondly, it would give the Soviet Union the assurance that a reunified Germany would not serve as a deployment area for the Western bloc. See Soell, *Fritz Erler*, p. 152ff.

55. This formula has been a constant theme of Fritz Erler's; as one example among many, see his speech in the Bundestag on January 25, 1955, DBT/II/70, January 25, 1955, pp. 3722-35.

56. See Carlo Schmid's and Fritz Erler's statements in the foreign policy debates in the Bundestag on October 7, 1954 and on February 25, 1955, DBT/II/47, October 7, 1954, pp. 2269-74 and pp. 2287-94, and DBT/II/70, February 25, 1955, pp. 3722-35. Also see Soell, *Fritz Erler*, p. 166ff.

57. Soell, *Fritz Erler*, p. 172f.

58. See "Aktionsprogramm der SPD in der vom Berliner Parteitag der SPD verabschiedeten erweiterten Fassung," *Jahrbuch der Sozialdemokratischen Partei*

Deutschlands 1954/55 (Hannover: Neuer Vorwärts Verlag, 1956), pp. 285-317.

59. Sponsored by the SPD and the Unions in January 1955, a large meeting of predominantly left-wing intellectuals gathered in the Frankfurt Paulskirche, historic site of the first German Parliament (The Paulskirche Assembly, 1848-49). It called for a stop of all rearmament plans, and expressed its concern that German integration into the Western alliance would create a major obstacle for future reunification. See "Deutsches Manifest," in *Die Linke und die nationale Frage. Dokumente zur deutschen Einheit seit 1945*, ed. by Peter Brandt and Herbert Ammon (Reinbek bei Hamburg: Rowohlt, 1981), p. 128ff., January 29, 1955.

60. "Programm der SPD zu den bevorstehenden Vier-Mächte-Verhandlungen über die deutsche Wiedervereinigung der SPD 1954/55," May 9, 1955, *Jahrbuch der SPD 1954/55*, pp. 340-47.

61. See "Ollenhauer-Plan für Sicherheit und Wiedervereinigung," *Pressemitteilung der SPD-Fraktion*, May 23, 1957. Also see *Jahrbuch der SPD 1956/57* (Bonn and Hannover: Neuer Vorwärts Verlag, 1958), p. 13f. For further reference, see Lothar Wilker, *Die Sicherheitspolitik der SPD 1955-1966: Zwischen Wiedervereinigungs- und Bündnisorientierung* (Bonn-Bad Godesberg: Neue Gesellschaft, 1977), p. 29ff.

62. See Erler's speech before the Bundestag on July 4, 1956, DBT/II/157, April 7, 1956, pp. 8585-88.

63. See Vorstand der SPD, "Deutschlandplan der SPD: Kommentare, Argumente, Begründungen, Bonn 1959," *Dokumente zur Deutschlandpolitik*, ser. 4, vol. 1, pp. 1207-22. Also see Fritz Erler, "Disengagement und die Wiedervereinigung Deutschlands," *Europa-Archiv* (EA) 14 (1959): 291-300.

64. See below, p. 69ff.

65. Soell therefore speaks of the "Erler line" and the "Wehner line" in the SPD's "German plan;" see his *Fritz Erler*, p. 376ff. At about the same time the FDP proposed a "German Plan," which was based on a concept of parallelism between the establishment of a security system and steps towards reunification.

66. See Herbert Wehner, "Vor einem Jahr," *Vorwärts*, March 17, 1960. Regarding the reorientation of the SPD's foreign policy, see Hartmut Soell, "Die deutschlandpolitischen Konzeptionen der SPD-Opposition 1949-1961," in *Deutschlandpolitik der Nachkriegsjahre*, ed. by Erich Kosthorst, Klaus Gotto, Hartmut Soell (Paderborn: Schöningh, 1976), pp. 41-61.

67. See Hugh Gaitskell, *The Challenge of Coexistence* (London: Methuen, 1957); Gaitskell, "Disengagement: Why? How?", *Foreign Affairs* 36 (Summer 1958): 539-56; Dennis Healey, *A Neutral Belt in Europe* (London: Fabian Society, 1958).

68. See Erler's statement on the SPD party group's parliamentary inquiry concerning atomic weapons and the debate in the Bundestag on May 5, 1957, DBT/II/209, May 10, 1957, pp. 12051-137.

69. See the address by Polish Foreign Minister Adam Rapacki before the United Nations General Assembly on October 2, 1957, *Documents on Germany*, p. 323; note from Rapacki to the American ambassador in Warsaw on the establishment of a denuclearized zone in Central Europe, February 14, 1958, *Documents on Germany*, pp. 328-31.

70. Entschliessung des Vorstandes der SPD, November 20, 1957, *Jahrbuch der SPD 1956/57*, p. 356.

71. In support of negotiations based on the Rapacki Plan, see Ollenhauer's address before the Bundestag on January 21, 1958, DBT/III/9, January 23, 1958, pp. 312-21; Carlo Schmid's speech, ibid., pp. 354-63, and Erler's speech of the same day, ibid., pp. 368-75, and of March 20, 1958, DBT/III/18, March 20, 1958, pp. 880-93. Also see Erler's "Disengagement: Solution in Europe?", *News from Germany*, October 1958.

72. In a letter to his boyhood friend, Erich Schmidt, dated June 23, 1959, Erler wrote:

"Herr Ulbricht sits on Soviet bayonets. It is only possible to overcome his regime when one withdraws this support...," (Soell, *Fritz Erler*, p. 382).

73. Fritz Erler, *Ein Volk sucht seine Sicherheit: Bemerkungen zur deutschen Sicherheitspolitik* (Frankfurt: Europäische Verlags-Anstalt, 1961), p. 31.

74. Ibid., p. 31 and p. 41.

75. See Helmut Schmidt's speech on November 5, 1959 before the Bundestag, DBT/III/87, November 5, 1959, pp. 4758-67. Schmidt presented and explained these proposals in his book, Helmut Schmidt, *Defense or Retaliation: A German View* (New York: Praeger, 1962). Later Schmidt claimed that, with this speech, he had been the first one to call for negotiations on troop reductions on both sides in Europe. This was later realized in the MBFR negotiations.

76. *Aufgaben einer neuen Bundesregierung: Acht-Punkte-Programm der SPD Bundestagsfraktion als Grundlage der Koalitionsverhandlungen*, November 1966 (Bonn: Vorstand der SPD, 1966).

77. "Joint statement by the Governments of United States of America, United Kindom and France," October 23, 1954, *Selected Documents on Germany and the Question of Berlin 1944-1961*, ed. by the Foreign Office (London: Her Majesty's Printing Office, 1961), p. 189.

78. Regarding the evolution and use of this linkage in the years 1955-56, see Thomas Jansen, *Abrüstung und Deutschland-Frage: Die Abrüstungsfrage als Problem der deutschen Aussenpolitik* (Mainz: Von Hase & Koehler, 1968).

79. For the text of the Franco-British phased plan of March 19, 1956, see *Documents on Disarmament 1945-1959*, vol. 1, pp. 595-99; the text of the Gromyko Plan of March 27, 1956 is reprinted ibid., pp. 603-7; for the United States' memorandum addressing partial disarmament of January 12, 1957, see ibid., pp. 731-34; for the "Western Working Paper: Proposals for Partial Measures of Disarmament," August 29, 1957, see ibid., pp. 868-74.

80. "Declaration on German Reunification by France, the Federal Republic of Germany, the United Kingdom and the United States, signed at Berlin," July 29, 1957, *Documents on Germany*, pp. 321-23 (here p. 322).

81. The most meaningful proposals were those by Dennis Healey, the defense expert of the British Labor Party, and Hugh Gaitskell, its chairman. Gaitskell's proposals were similar to those of the SPD. He favored the establishment of a European guarantee system with a united bloc-free Germany at its center. Healey's thoughts focused on a "neutral belt" between the two alliance systems that would encompass Germany, Poland, Czechoslovakia, and Hungary as well as other states to the north and south of this zone. For information on the "Gaitskell Plan, see Gaitskell's speech before the House of Parliament on December 19, 1956, *Parliamentary Debates*, DLXII, pp. 1329-37.

82. For the text of the Reith Lectures see George F. Kennan, *Russia, the Atom, and the West* (New York: Harper 1958).

83. See address by Rapacki to the United Nations General Assembly on October 2, 1957, *Documents on Disarmament* 1945-59, pp. 889-92; note and memorandum from the Polish foreign minister submitted to the governments of the United States, Great Britain, France, Canada, Belgium, Denmark, the Soviet Union, Czechoslovakia and the German Democratic Republic (as well as to the Federal Republic through an arrangement with Sweden), February 14, 1958, *Documents on Disarmament 1945-1959*, vol. 2, pp. 944-48 (here p. 946).

84. See Rapacki's press conference in Warsaw, November 4, 1958, *Documents on Disarmament 1945-1959*, vol. 2, pp. 1217-19; Memorandum from the Polish Government, March 28, 1962, *Documents on Disarmament 1962*, pp. 201-5.

85. For the Gromyko Plan, see *Documents on Disarmament 1945-1959*, vol. 1, pp. 603-7; for the letter from Premier Bulganin to Chancellor Adenauer on the equipping of the

Bundeswehr with nuclear weapons, December 10, 1957, see *Dokumente zur Deutschlandpolitik*, ser. 3, vol. 4.3, pp. 1859-1960. Similar letters were sent to the heads of government of the other NATO countries. See letter sent to President Eisenhower, *Documents on Disarmament 1945-1959*, vol. 2, pp. 918-26. Also see the Soviet memorandum of December 12, 1957, to all members of the United Nations and Switzerland, *Pravda*, December 13, 1957; Bulganin's second letter to Adenauer and the enclosed memorandum concerning proposals for a reduction of international tensions, August 1, 1958, *Current Digest of the Soviet Press*, 10 (1958):20 and ibid., 10: 22-24. This memorandum was sent to all members of the United Nations and Switzerland. The three Western powers also received a note in which a summit conference was proposed. See Aide-Mémoire from the Soviet Union to the United States, February 28, 1958, *Documents on Germany*, pp. 331-33.

86. See "Declaration and Communiqué by the NATO Heads of Government," December 19, 1957, *Texts of Final Communiqués 1949-1974* (Brussels: NATO Information Service), pp. 108-116.

87. See Adenauer, *Erinnerungen 1955-1959*, p. 331f; Soell, *Fritz Erler*, p. 340-51.

88. See letter from Bulganin to Adenauer, August 1, 1958, *Current Digest 1958*, 10 (1958):20-24; and Declaration by the Government of the German Democratic Republic, July 27, 1957, *Documents on International Affairs 1957* (London: Royal Institute of International Affairs, 1960), pp. 92-96.

89. See the letter from Chancellor Adenauer to Chairman Bulganin of January 21, 1958, *Documents on Germany*, pp. 326-28.

90. For an assessment of the Rapacki Plan by Defense Minister Franz Josef Strauss see Franz Josef Strauss, "Der Weg zum Frieden," *Bulletin*, February 27, 1958: 329-30.

91. See Adenauer's meeting with Secretary of State Dulles on the eve of the NATO Conference in May 1957, *Erinnerungen 1955-1959*, pp. 303-7; his visit to the United States and his discussion with Dulles on May 27, 1957, ibid., pp. 307-9; his conversation with French State Secretary Maurice Faure, ibid., pp. 324-32.

92. See letter from MinisterPresident Felix Gaillard to Chairman Bulganin of January 14, 1958, *La Documentation Francaise. Articles et Documents*, No. 0.610, January 28, 1958.

93. See Adenauer, *Erinnerungen 1955-1959*, pp. 377 ff. and 384. Adenauer's suggestion for an Austrian solution for the GDR to some extent is a reaction to the Soviet memorandum of March 19, 1958, in which the Soviet Union declined to put the German question on the agenda of a summit meeting and instead proposed the conclusion of a peace treaty with Germany; see Aide-mémoire from the Soviet Union to the Government of the Federal Republic, March 19, 1958, *Pravda*, March 21, 1958. A similar note was sent to the United States on March 24, 1958; see *Documents on Germany*, pp. 336-37.

94. See Aide-mémoire from the Federal Republic to the Government of the Polish People's Republic, February 24, 1958, *Dokumente zur Deutschlandpolitik*, ser. 3, vol. 4.1, pp. 582-83, which was not published at that time. An unofficial government statement was reported by *Die Welt*, February 22, 1958, and reprinted in *Dokumente zur Deutschlandpolitik*, ser. 3, vol. 4.1, pp. 581-582.

95. For the position of the SPD on the Rapacki Plan see Entschliessung des Vorstands der SPD zur internationalen Lage of November 20, 1957, *Dokumente zur Deutschlandpolitik*, ser. 3, vol. 3.3, p. 1912; radio and T.V. and/statement by SPD chairman Erich Ollenhauer on January 31, 1958, *Dokumente zur Deutschlandpolitik*, ser. 3, vol. 4.1, pp. 471-474.

96. See motion by SPD party group on the efforts of the Federal Republic regarding an international relaxation of tensions and a discontinuation of the arms race, January 21, 1958, DBT, Drucksache III/54. Also see parliamentary inquiry by the FDP regarding the Federal Republic's position at the forthcoming NATO Conference, November 12, 1957, DBT, Drucksache III/82; also see the supporting speech by FDP Chairman Erich Mende

on January 23, 1958 before the Bundestag, DBT/III/9, January 23, 1958, pp. 304-10.

97. For the debate on January 23, 19, 58, see DBT/III/9, January 23, 1958, pp. 297-419; for that on March 20-25, 1958, DBT/III/18-21, pp. 823-1171.

98. DBT/III/9, January 23, 1958, p. 303.

99. Ibid., p. 369.

100. See Strauss, "Der Weg zum Frieden," *Bulletin,* February 27, 1958, pp. 329-30. His so-called "Five-point plan for an arms control and arms reduction zone in Europe" contained the following elements:

- Expansion of the nuclear-free zone to include all of Eastern Europe;
- Gradual reduction of conventional forces of East and West within the reduced zone to match the strength of forces stationed in West Germany;
- A thorough verification system, which would also cover areas outside of the zone of arms reductions;
- Development of a guarantee system which would ensure that no bombardment of the zone with nuclear weapons would occur;
- Linkage of disarmament measures with concrete steps for the reunification of Germany.

101. The federal government's negative view of disarmament and the Rapacki Plan was explained not only in the Bundestag but also in a series of interviews and commentaries in the official *Bulletin.* See "The Rapacki Plan: Ausgangsstellung zur Spaltung der Einheitlichkeit und Stärke des westlichen Freiheits- und Widerstandswillens," part 1, *Bulletin,* May 6, 1958; 816-17 parts 2 and 3, *Bulletin,* May 7, 1957: 826-29; part 4, *Bulletin,* May 8, 1958; 842-43; Wilhelm Grewe, "Disengagement—Voraussetzungen und Konsequenzen," *Bulletin,* August 23, 1958: 1577-80; "Die neue Version des Rapacki-Planes. Neutralisierung Deutschlands wäre der Anfang der Neutralisierung Europas und des amerikanischen Isolationismus," parts 1 and 2, *Bulletin,* March 11, 1959: 449-51; parts 3 and 4, *Bulletin,* March 13, 1959: 463-65. Also see Adenauer, *Erinnerungen 1955-1959,* pp. 284-85.

102. See Aufruf zum Kampf gegen den Atomtod, March 10, 1958, *Dokumente zur Deutschlandpolitik,* ser. 3, vol. 4.1, p. 629; also see Hans-Karl Rupp, *Ausserparlamentarische Opposition in der Ära Adenauer: Der Kampf gegen die Atombewaffnung in den fünfziger Jahren* (Cologne: Pahl-Rugenstein, 1970).

103. See address by Chairman Khrushchev November 10, 1958, *Documents on Germany,* pp. 350-54; note from the Soviet Union to the United States, November 27, 1958, ibid., pp. 360-66; note from the Soviet Union to the Federal Republic and the GDR from the same day, *Dokumente zur Deutschlandpolitik,* ser. 4, vol. 1.1, pp. 178-201; note from the Soviet Union to the Western powers and proposal for a peace treaty with Germany, January 10, 1958, *U.S. Department of State Bulletin,* 40:333-443. This proposal was sent to all nations that had been at war with Germany. For the notes from the Soviet Union to the Federal Republic and to the GDR see *Dokumente zur Deutschlandpolitik,* ser. 4, vol. 1.1, pp. 566-77. Also see speech by Premier Khrushchev in Tula, February 19, 1959, *Current Digest,* 11 (1959):17-18.

104. Grewe, *Rückblenden,* p. 389. We also owe Grewe for a detailed account of the preparations for the 1959 Geneva Foreign Ministers conference, ibid., p. 362ff.

105. See Gotto, "Adenauers Deutschland- und Ostpolitik 1954-1963," pp. 203-11. The Globke Plan is reprinted in *Adenauer-Studien,* pp. 202-9, vol. 2; also see Heinrich Krone's journal notes on Ostpolitik and German policy 1959-1969, ibid., pp. 134-201.

106. For an evaluation of the Berlin crisis by the federal government, see Adenauer,

Erinnerungen 1955-1959, p. 446ff.; Bandulet, *Adenauer zwischen West und Ost*, p. 154ff.; Grewe, *Rückblenden*, p. 362ff. For Walter Lippmann's proposals, see his "The Two Germanies and Berlin," *New York Herald Tribune*, April 6, 7, 8, and 9, 1959. On the French position see Alfred Grosser, *The Western Alliance: European-American relations since 1945*, (New York: Continuum, 1980).

107. See Baring, *Sehr verehrter Herr Bundeskanzler!*, p. 242.

108. See "Western Peace Plan for Germany (Herter Plan)," submitted to the Geneva Foreign Ministers Meeting, May 11, 1959; *Documents on Germany*, pp. 427-31.

109. See Department of State, ed. *Foreign Ministers Meeting*, Geneva, May-August 1959 (Washington: Government Printing Office, 1959).

110. Address by Premier Khrushchev to the party organizations of the Party High School at the Social Science Academy and Institute for Marxism-Leninism of the Central Committee, Moscow, January 6, 1961, *Documents on Disarmament 1961*, pp. 1-15 (here p. 12).

111. See the Soviet "Aide-Mémoire" to the Federal Republic concerning a German peace treaty and related matters, February 17, 1961, *Documents on Germany*, pp. 518-22.

112. See the account of Walther Stützle, *Kennedy und Adenauer in der Berlin-Krise 1961-1962* (Bonn-Bad Godesberg: Neue Gesellschaft, 1973), p. 80ff. and 97ff.; and Honoré M. Catudal, *Kennedy and the Berlin Wall Crisis: A Case Study in U.S. Decision-Making* (Berlin: Berlin-Verlag, 1980), p. 62ff. and 90ff.; Arthur Schlesinger, *A Thousand Days: John Kennedy in the White House* (Boston: Houghton Mifflin, 1965), p. 319ff.

113. In 1960 almost 200,000 persons fled from the GDR to the Federal Republic. By July 1961 the number had reached 30,000 per month.

114. Aide-Mémoire from the Soviet Union to the United States on the German question, *Documents on Germany*, pp. 523-27 (Here p. 524).

115. See Kennedy's radio and television address on July 25, 1961, *Public Papers of the Presidents of the United States, 1961* (Washington: Government Printing Office, 1962), p. 533. In this speech the President also announced a strengthening of U.S. conventional troops in Europe and an increase in their level of military alert. See Stützle, *Kennedy und Adenauer in der Berlin-Krise*, p. 119ff.; also Catudal, *Kennedy and the Berlin Wall Crisis*, p. 191ff.

116. See e.g., the declaration of the NATO ministers on Berlin, December 16, 1958, *Texts of Final Communiqués 1949-1974*, pp. 121f. The Kennedy administration, on the other hand, differentiated between the four power status of "greater Berlin," (which, for example, gave the U.S. the right of freedom of movement within the entire city) and the Western authority over the Western sectors of the city.

117. See the Communiqué on the special session of the West Berlin Senat on July 12, 1961, *Dokumente zur Deutschlandpolitik*, ser. 4, vol. 6.2, p. 1231.

118. See Communiqué on the meeting of the Permanent NATO Council on the Berlin question, August 8, 1961, *U.S. Department of State Bulletin*, 45:361.

119. "Memorandum from the Federal Republic of Germany to the Soviet Union Concerning a German Peace Treaty and the Right of Self-Determination," July 12, 1961, *Documents on Germany*, p. 544ff.

120. The building of the Wall was ordered by the GDR in a declaration of August 12, 1961, which was based on a resolution of the same day by the Warsaw Pact, see U.S. Department of State Bulletin, 45:400f. The Western Powers protested against this action in a note to the Soviet Union on August 17, 1961, ibid., p. 397; the Soviet Union countered with a note of its own on August 18, 1961, ibid., pp. 397-400.

121. See the communiqué on the talks between Chancellor Adenauer and President Kennedy on November 22, 1961, *U.S. Department of State Bulletin*, 45:967.

122. See Hans Kroll, *Botschafter in Belgrad, Tokio und Moskau* (Munich: Deutscher Taschenbuch Verlag, 1969), p. 301ff.

123. See Stützle, *Kennedy und Adenauer in der Berlin-Krise,* p. 213, and Julius Epstein, "Die Quelle des Übels: Eine Dokumentation zur Genesis der deutsch-amerikanischen Verstimmung," *Rheinischer Merkur,* August 31, 1961 (this article, inspired by Adenauer, examines in detail the various American proposals and reactions).

124. See Stützle, *Kennedy und Adenauer in der Berlin Krise,* p. 223ff.

CHAPTER 3

1. A complete interpretation of German security policy has so far been lacking. An overview is presented by Josef Joffe, "German Defense Policy: Novel Solutions and Enduring Dilemmas," in *The International Fabric of Western Security,* ed. by Gregory Flynn (Montclair, N.J.: Allenheld, Osmun, 1981), pp. 63-96. The most helpful source is Klaus von Schubert's documentation, *Sicherheitspolitik der Bundesrepublik Deutschland: Dokumentation 1945-1977,* 2 vols. (Cologne; Verlag Wissenschaft und Politik 1979). For a historically accurate organizational summary, see Militärgeschichtliches Forschungsamt, ed. *Verteidigung im Bündnis: Planung, Aufbau und Bewährung der Bundeswehr 1950-1972* (Munich; Bernard & Graefe, 1975).

2. See the memorandum from Chancellor Adenauer concerning the security of the Federal Republic both from outside and within, August 29, 1950, *Sicherheitspolitik der Bundesrepublik Deutschland* vol. 1, pp. 79-83. Regarding the debate over the rearmament of the Federal Republic, see Robert McGeehan, *The German Rearmament Question: American Diplomacy and European Defense After World War II* (Urbana, Ill.: University of Illinois Press, 1971); Gerhard Wettig, *Entmilitarisierung und Wiederbewaffnung in Deutschland 1943-1955: Internationale Auseinandersetzungen über die Rolle der Deutschen in Europa* (Munich: Oldenbourg, 1967); Norbert Wiggershaus, "Die Entscheidung für einen westdeutschen Verteidigungsbeitrag 1950" in Militärgeschichtliches Forschungsamt, ed. *Anfänge westdeutscher Sicherheitspolitik 1945-1956: Von der Kapitulation bis zum Pleven-Plan,* vol. 1 (Munich, Vienna: Oldenbourg, 1982), pp. 325-402.

3. See "Communiqué by the Western Foreign Ministers Conference on Germany," September 19, 1950, *Documents on Germany 1944-1970,* ed. by U.S. Senate , Committee on Foreign Relations, 92nd Cong., 1st sess. Washington D.C.,: Government Printing Office, 1971, pp. 183-85.

4. See Hans-Peter Schwarz, "Das aussenpolitische Konzept Konrad Adenauers" in *Konrad Adenauer: Seine Deutschland- und Aussenpolitik 1943-1963,* ed. by Klaus Gotto (Munich: Deutscher Taschenbuch Verlag, 1975), pp. 97-155.

5. On Adenauer's views on European unification, see ibid., p. 146ff.; also see Hans-Peter Schwarz, "Adenauer und Europa," *Vierteljahreshefte für Zeitgeschichte* 4 (1979):471-523; regarding Kurt Schumacher's views, see his speech in Frankfurt on June 1, 1947, entitled "Europa—demokratisch und sozialistisch" in *Turmwächter der Demokratie: Ein Lebensbild von Kurt Schumacher: Reden und Schriften,* ed. by Arno Scholz and Walter G. Oschilewski, vol. 2 (Berlin-Grunewald: Arani, 1953), pp. 424-35. Also see above, pp. 36–39 and 48–50.

6. The Soviet Union reacted to the acceptance of the Federal Republic into NATO by establishing a counter-alliance of its own, the Warsaw Pact. The character of the counter-alliance is made clear in the preamble of the Warsaw Treaty; see Robin Alison Remington, *The Warsaw Pact: Case Studies in Communist Conflict Resolution* (Cambridge: MIT Press,

1971), p. 201; regarding the role played by the GDR in the pact, see N. Edwina Moreton, *East Germany and the Warsaw Alliance: The Politics of Detente* (Boulder, Colo.: Westview Press, 1978).

7. See "The Future Tasks of the Alliance (Harmel Report). Report of the NATO Council," December 14, 1967, *The North Atlantic Treaty Organization: Facts and Figures* (Brussels: NATO Information Service, 1981), pp. 288-90.

8. The first official use of the doctrine of peaceful coexistence between antagonistic states and social systems occurred, as far as I know, in the Declaration of the Moscow Communist and Workers' Party of December 6, 1960; see *The Current Digest of the Soviet Press*, 48 (December 28, 1960), and ibid., 49 (January 4, 1961).

9. These arms limitations are part of the Brussels Treaty October 23, 1954; see U.S. Senate, Committee on Foreign Relations, *Documents on Germany*, pp. 245-46. Regarding the motivations and circumstances surrounding Adenauer's renunciation of ABC weapons, see Konrad Adenauer, *Erinnerungen 1953-1955* (Stuttgart; Deutsche Verlags-Anstalt, 1966) p. 347. Here Adenauer implied that his decision to renounce ABC weapons was spontaneous, made in order to win over French resistance against German membership in NATO and to prevent a failure of the London Nine-Power Conference. This implication does not agree with the established facts. As early as 1952 the Federal Republic had made it known to the three Western powers that it would renounce the production of ABC weapons, missiles, and other heavy armaments. See Catherine McArdle Kelleher, *Germany and the Politics of Nuclear Weapons* (New York: Columbia University Press, 1975), pp. 21-29.

10. The alliance's military strategy was first spelled out as "NATO Strategic Guidance" by the NATO Military Committee as MC 14/1 in 1952. On the evolution of military strategy see Samuel P. Huntington, *The Common Defense: Strategic Programs in National Politics* (New York: Columbia University Press, 1969[3]); Lawrence Freedman, *The Evolution of Nuclear Strategy* (London: Macmillan 1981).

11. See above, pp. 53–54.

12. The concept has been used by Hans-Peter Schwarz to characterize the dependence of the Federal Republic's security policy on the U.S.; see Hans-Peter Schwarz, "The Roles of the Federal Republic in the Community of States," *Britain and West Germany: Changing Societies and the Role of Foreign Policy*, ed. by Karl Kaiser and Roger Morgan, (London: Oxford University Press 1971) pp. 219-59.

13. On the building of the Bundeswehr, see Hans-Peter Schwarz, *Die Ära Adenauer 1949-1957* (Stuttgart: Deutsche Verlags-Anstalt, 1981), pp. 287-302; and Theo Sommer, "Wiederbewaffnung und Verteidigungspolitik," in *Die zweite Republik: 25 Jahre Bundesrepublik Deutschland. Eine Bilanz*, ed. by Richard Löwenthal and Hans-Peter Schwarz (Stuttgart: Seewald, 1974), pp. 580-602. On the position of the SPD, see Hartmut Soell, *Fritz Erler—Eine politische Biographie* (Bonn-Bad Godesberg: J.H.W. Dietz nachf., 1976), p. 195ff. Regarding the domestic debate on rearmament, see also Hans Speier, *German Rearmament and the Atomic War: The Views of German Military and Political Leaders* (New York: Row & Peterson, 1957), p. 10; Gordon A. Craig, "NATO and the New German Army," in *Military Policy and National Security*, ed. by William W. Kaufmann (Princeton: Princeton University Press, 1956), p. 218ff.

14. See Wolf Graf von Baudissin, "The New German Army," *Foreign Affairs*, 34 (October 1955):1-13; also see his *Soldat für den Frieden: Entwürfe für eine zeitgemässe Bundeswehr* (Munich; Piper, 1969).

15. See Erler's speech in the Bundestag debate on the conscription law, *Verhandlungen des Deutschen Bundestages*, 2. Sitzungsperiode, 179. Sitzung (DBT/II/179) July 6, 1956, pp. 8772-77; also the recommendations of the SPD's military committee of April 11, 1956, cited in Lothar Wilker, *Die Sicherheitspolitik der SPD 1956-1966: Zwischen*

Wiedervereinigungs- und Bündnisorientierung (Bonn-Bad Godesberg: Neue Gesellschaft, 1977), pp. 103-11 and p. 273.

16. At the NATO Conference in Lisbon in February 1952 the NATO force goals were set at 96 divisions by the end of 1954 of which 50 divisions were to be deployed by the end of 1952; see "Lisbon Communiqué by the North Atlantic Council," February 24, 1952; *Texts of Final Communiqués 1949-1974* (Brussels: NATO Information Service, 1974), pp. 68-70.

17. See *Verteidigung im Bündnis*, pp. 82-83; also see Robert E. Osgood, *NATO: The Entangling Alliance*, (Chicago: University of Chicago Press, 1962), p. 114ff.; regarding the strategic reorientation of the United States, see Huntington, *The Common Defense*, p. 64ff.; Samuel F. Wells, Jr., "The Origins of Massive Retaliation," *Political Science Quarterly*, 96 (Spring 1981):31-52.

18. See Secretary of State John Foster Dulles's address to the Council on Foreign Relations, January 12, 1954, *U.S. Department of State Bulletin*, January 25, 1954, p. 107ff.; also see Huntington, *The Common Defense*, p. 64ff.; Osgood, *NATO: The Entangling Alliance*, p. 102ff.

19. See "Überholt wie Pfeil und Bogen," *Der Spiegel*, July 13, 1955, pp. 7-11; also see Kelleher, *Germany and the Politics of Nuclear Weapons*, p. 35ff.

20. See remarks by Ollenhauer, Erler, and Blachstein in the Bundestag debate on voluntary military service and the arguments presented by the CDU-led coalition, DBT/II/100, July 16, 1955, pp. 5598-5602.

21. See speech by Strauss in the Bundestag, July 16, 1955, DBT/II/100, July 16, 1955, pp. 5603-10; also see the interpretation given by Kelleher, *Germany and the Politics of Nuclear Weapons*, p. 39ff. and p. 64ff.

22. See the communiqué by the NATO Council, December 16, 1955, *Texts of Final Communiqués* (Brussels: NATO Information Service, 1975), pp. 110-16.

23. See Anthony Leviero, "Radford Seeking 800,000-Man Cut: 3 Services Resist," *New York Times*, July 18, 1956; also the accounts by Hans-Gert Pöttering, *Adenauers Sicherheitspolitik 1955-63: Ein Beitrag zum deutsch-amerikanischen Verhältnis* (Düsseldorf: Droste Verlag, 1975), p. 62ff.; Kelleher, *Germany and the Politics of Nuclear Weapons*, p. 43ff.

24. See the text of Secretary of State Dulles's press conference, July 18, 1956, *U.S. Department of State Bulletin*, July 30, 1956, pp. 181-87; similarly, Prime Minister Anthony Eden before the House of Commons, *Parliamentary Debates: Official Reports*, 557, p. 37ff.

25. See Konrad Adenauer, *Erinnerungen 1955-1959* (Stuttgart: Deutsche Verlags-Anstalt, 1967), p. 197ff.; also see Pöttering, *Adenauers Sicherheitspolitik*, p. 62ff.; Kelleher, *Germany and the Politics of Nuclear Weapons*, p. 43ff.; Adenauer also articulated his concern in an article in the *Westdeutsche Rundschau*, July 27, 1955, "Lohnt sich der Aufbau der Bundeswehr noch?" (Is it still worth to form a Bundeswehr?), reprinted in *Bulletin der Bundesregierung*, August 21, 1956:1491.

26. See above, pp. 60-61.

27. This refers to the visit to Bonn by Allen Dulles, head of the CIA and brother of the secretary of state, and the announcement in November 1957 that the U.S. would withdraw no additional troops from Europe, as well as to the decision of the NATO Council on the basis of the "Report of the Three Wise Men" to strengthen political consultations within NATO; see "Report of the Committee of Three," *Texts of Final Communiqués*, pp. 101-5.

28. See "Strauss: Wehrpläne nicht unantastbar," *Frankfurter Allgemeine Zeitung*, October 18, 1956; "West Germany's Failure on N.A.T.O.," *The Times*, October 18, 1956.

29. See interview with NATO Supreme Commander (SACEUR), General Lauris Norstad, with German television network (ARD), February 20, 1958, reprinted in James

L. Richardson, *Germany and the Atlantic Alliance: The Interaction of Strategy and Politics* (Cambridge, Mass.: Harvard University Press, 1966), p. 50-51.

30. See communiqué by the NATO Council, December 14, 1956, *Texts of Final Communiqués* pp. 101-104.

31. See Adenauer's address to the Bundestag on March 20, 1958, DBT/III/18, March 20, 1958, pp. 840-47. Regarding Adenauer's fear of international isolation and his position on the nuclear question, see Schwarz, *Das aussenpolitische Konzept Konrad Adenauers*, pp. 97-155.

32. See Franz Josef Strauss, "Einheit und Freiheit" *Politisch-Soziale Korrespondenz*, December 15, 1957; Franz Josef Strauss, "Verteidigungskonzeption im atomaren Zeitalter," *Politisches Jahrbuch der CDU/CSU* (1960), pp. 51-55; Franz Josef Strauss, *Challenge and Response: A Program for Europe* (New York: Atheneum, 1970), also Detlef Bischoff, *Franz Josef Strauss, die CSU und die Aussenpolitik* (Meisenheim am Glan: Hain, 1973), p. 104ff.

33. See Adenauer, *Erinnerungen 1955-1959*, pp. 300-1.

34. See Kelleher, *Germany and the Politics of Nuclear Weapons*, as well as the opinion of a Bonn observer cited here: "You can almost never accept Strauss' public statements at face value. The basic themes—such as they are—remain the same. But to really understand them, you have to know what was in the wind at the moment. What was the SPD doing? Was there a state election coming up? Did Strauss need to stress how valuable he was as defense minister to ward off the criticism in another area? Was he trying to force the cabinet's hand? What was going on in the ministry?" (Ibid., p. 71).

35. In January 1958 Eisenhower had asked Congress for a major revision to atomic energy legislation to permit a greater degree of nuclear cooperation with the U.S. allies; see William B. Bader, *The United States and the Spread of Nuclear Weapons* (New York: Pegasus, 1968), p. 26ff.

36. See, e.g., the talks between Strauss and French Defense Minister Bourgès-Maunoury in January 1967, see Edmund Taylor, "The Powerhouse of German Defense," *The Reporter*, April 18, 1957, pp. 25-27. About a year later, talks between France, Italy, and the Federal Republic were initiated by the French on the topic of a common development and production of "modern weapons." Although Strauss at the time denied that questions of nuclear weapons had been discussed in these talks, Erler was able to prove that Strauss and Jacques Chaban-Delmas had envisioned the creation of some sort of European nuclear pool; see Soell, *Fritz Erler*, p. 342ff. and p. 348f. The de Gaulle government, however, relinquished these initial efforts of German-French nuclear cooperation, and instead acquired a national nuclear force.

37. Regarding the various proposals for a common European nuclear force with participation of the Federal Republic, see Dieter Mahncke, *Nukleare Mitwirkung: Die Bundesrepublik Deutschland in der Atlantischen Allianz 1954-1970* (Berlin and New York: Walter de Gruyter, 1972), p. 56ff. An excellent overview of the different nuclear-sharing options, their military implications, their political requirements and their financial costs as well as the views of the most important European states is given in reports of the West European Union on the State of European Security, see WEU/A/215, November 10, 1961; WEU/A/251, October 16, 1962; WEU/A/268, April 26, 1963; WEU/A/290, October 30, 1963; WEU/A/293, October 30, 1963; WEU/A/320, October 20, 1964; WEU/A/III,354, October 25, 1965.

38. See Kelleher, *Germany and the Politics of Nuclear Weapons*, p. 74. Similar conclusions are reached by Mahncke, *Nukleare Mitwirkung*, p. 43ff.; and Leonard Beaton and John Maddox, "Die Bundesrepublik und die Frage der Atomrüstung," *Europa-Archiv*, 17, (1962): 732-40. His former associates, Generals Heusinger and Schmückle, also maintain that Strauss had been much too clever to ask for national control of nuclear weapons without, however, excluding this possibility for all time.

39. First indications were given in various press reports in the fall of 1956, see Hans Karl Rupp, *Ausserparlamentarische Opposition in der Ära Adenauer: Der Kampf gegen die Atombewaffnung in den fünfziger Jahren* (Cologne: Pahl-Rugenstein, 1980²), p. 36. While Rupp maintains that the Federal Republic already had plans to equip the Bundeswehr with nuclear weapons by the fall of 1955 this cannot be verified. The decision first came in connection with the replacement of Blank by Strauss. Strauss, however, never doubted that the Bundeswehr would be armed with tactical nuclear weapons; see the interview with the Hesse Radio and Television network, April 8, 1957, *Dokumente zur Deutschlandpolitik*, ed. by Bundesministerium für Innerdeutsche Beziehungen, ser. 3, vol. 3.1 (Frankfurt: Alfred Metzner, 1967), pp. 577-581.

40. On the domestic political discussion regarding the equipment of the Bundeswehr with nuclear delivery systems see Pöttering, *Adenauers Sicherheitspolitik*, p. 91ff.; Wilker, *Die Sicherheitspolitik der SPD*, p. 70ff.; Soell, *Fritz Erler*, p. 340ff.; Rupp, *Ausserparlamentarische Opposition in der Ära Adenauer;* on the major interpellation (Grosse Anfrage) regarding nuclear weapons, submitted by the SPD on April 2, 1957 and the discussion of it in the Bundestag on May 10, 1957 see DBT/II/Drucksache 3347 and DBT/II/209, May 20, 1957, pp. 12051-12137; the declaration of the German nuclear scientists, April 12, 1957, is reprinted in *Dokumente zur Deutschlandpolitik*, ser. 3, vol. 3.1, pp. 594-96.

41. See remarks by Defense Minister Strauss and Chancellor Adenauer in the Bundestag debate, May 10, 1957, DBT/II/209, pp. 12129-31 and 12065-73, resp.

42. See motion submitted by the CDU/CSU and FDP parliamentary groups, May 25, 1958, DBT/III/21, p. 1169.

43. See the interpretations given by Rupp, *Ausserparlamentarische Opposition;* and Theo Pirker, *Die SPD nach Hitler: Die Geschichte der Sozialdemokratischen Partei Deutschlands 1945-1964* (Munich: Rütten & Loening, 1965), p. 238ff.

44. See remarks by Strauss and Adenauer in the "nuclear debate" of the Bundestag, DBT/II/209, May 10, 1957, pp. 12129-31 and 12065-73. Regarding the debate on the Rapacki Plan and disengagement proposals, see above, pp. 61-64.

45. On the strategic discussion in the U.S. and in NATO see Osgood, *NATO: The Entangling Alliance*, p. 147ff.; Huntington, *The Common Defense*, p. 88ff.; Michael Mandelbaum, *The Nuclear Question: The United States and Nuclear Weapons 1946-1976* (Cambridge: Cambridge University Press, 1979), p. 54ff.

46. See Adenauer, *Erinnerungen 1955-1959*, p. 351ff. and p. 377f.; and above, pp. 64-68.

47. See Uwe Nerlich, "Die nuklearen Dilemmas der Bundesrepublik Deutschland," *Europa-Archiv*, 20 (1965):637-652; Kelleher, *Germany and the Politics of Nuclear Weapons*, p. 179ff. and p. 228ff.; Mahncke, *Nukleare Mitwirkung;* John D. Steinbrunner, *The Cybernetic Theory of Decision: New Dimensions of Political Analysis* (Princeton: Princeton University Press, 1974), p. 153ff.; Osgood, *NATO: The Entangling Alliance*, p. 212ff.; Thomas C. Wiegele, "The Origins of the MLF Concept," *Orbis* 12 (Summer 1968):465-89.

48. For the reaction in the Federal Republic, see Wilhelm Cornides, "Berlin—und was dann? Zum Stand der Deutschland-Frage im Sommer 1961," *Europa-Archiv*, 16 (1961):369-78; also see above, pp. 68-81.

49. For the strategy of flexible response, see William W. Kaufmann, *The McNamara Strategy* (New York: Harper & Row, 1964); on the connection between military strategy and arms control see Thomas C. Schelling and Morton H. Halperin, *Strategy and Arms Control* (New York: The Twentieth Century Fund, 1961).

50. The articles by Gerd Schmückle, "Die Wandlung der Apokalypse," *Christ und Welt*, March 4, 1962, and Richard Jaeger, "Eine neue Strategie für die Nordatlantik-Staaten?" *Rheinischer Merkur*, December 14, 1962, were exemplary in criticism found in the Federal Republic. As had already been the case during the Radford crisis, the SPD recognized the writing on the wall earlier than the government did, see Fritz Erler's

speech in the defense debate of the Bundestag on April 6, 1962, DBT/IV/24, pp. 916-25.

51. See Defense Minister Strauss in the Bundestag, April 6, 1962, DBT/IV/24, pp. 933-43; also Adelbert Weinstein, "Militärpolitik ist Aussenpolitik: Das Verhältnis der Bundesrepublik zur NATO" in Deutschlands Aussenpolitik seit 1955, ed. by Helmut Reuther, (Stuttgart: Seewald, 1965) pp. 109-20.

52. Regarding the "Strauss plan" and the idea of a nuclear steering committee, see Kelleher, Germany and the Politics of Nuclear Weapons, p. 184ff.; the text of Strauss' speech before Georgetown University on November 27, 1961 is reprinted in Bulletin des Presse- und Informationsamtes der Bundesregierung, December 1, 1961.

53. See address by Secretary of Defense, Robert M. McNamara, at the University of Michigan, June 16, 1962, U.S. Department of State Bulletin, July 9, 1962: pp. 64-69; also see the interpretations given by Mahncke, Nukleare Mitwirkung, p. 138ff.; and Kelleher, Germany and the Politics of Nuclear Weapons, p. 228ff. For an interpretation of the U.S. position, also see Robert E. Osgood, The Case for the MLF: A Critical Evaluation (Washington: The Washington Center of Foreign Policy Research, 1964).

54. See speeches by Erler and Strauss in the defense debate of the Bundestag, April 6, 1962, DBT/IV/24, pp. 916-25 and 933-43; also Fritz Erler, "Westeuropa und die Vereinigten Staaten in der strategischen Weltsituation," Europa-Archiv, 18 (1963):887-98.

55. See Uwe Nerlich, "Die nuklearen Dilemmas der Bundesrepublik," Europa-Archiv, 20 (1965):646f. Contrary to Nerlich, Kelleher refers to the ambivalence of Strauss' position, who not only vehemently supported a NATO nuclear force but also celebrated the Athens guidelines as a diplomatic breakthrough; see Kelleher, Germany and the Politics of Nuclear Weapons, p. 199f. Foreign Minister Schröder repeatedly made his preference for a joint nuclear consultation known although he was later one of the most vigorous advocates of the MLF; see Schröder's speech before the NATO Council in Paris on December 15, 1964, Bulletin, December 19, 1964, pp. 1727-29. The one weakness in Kelleher's otherwise excellent work is that she does not go into enough detail on the considerations within the Foreign Ministry.

56. Nerlich, "Die nuklearen Dilemmas der Bundesrepublik," p. 647; see also Wilhelm Cornides, "Eine Strategie der Geduld: Das Allianz-system des Westens nach dem amerikanisch-britischen Polaris Arrangement," Europa-Archiv 18 (1963):39-50.

57. Regarding the circumstances surrounding the shelving of the MLF, see Philip Geyelin, Lyndon B. Johnson and the World (London: Praeger, 1966), p. 159ff.; also Uwe Nerlich, Der NV-Vertrag in der Politik der BRD: Zur Struktur eines aussenpolitischen Prioritätenkonflikts (Ebenhausen: Stiftung Wissenschaft und Politik, 1973), p. 37ff.

58. On the work of the Nuclear Planning Group, see Mahncke, Nukleare Mitwirkung, p. 242ff.; Paul Buteux, The Politics of Nuclear Consultation in NATO, 1965-1980 (New York: Cambridge University Press, 1983).

59. On the strategy of flexible response see Kaufmann, The McNamara Strategy; for a European perspective see Freedmann, The Evolution of Nuclear Strategy.

60. The Special Issue "Arms Control, Disarmament, and National Security" of Daedalus (Fall 1960):681-705ff. was translated into German (Donald G. Brennan, ed. Strategie der Abrüstung. 28 Problemanalysen, Gütersloh: C. Bertelsmann, 1962), and widely discussed. The German point of view is expressed in a concluding chapter by Wilhelm Cornides, "Das amerikanische Sicherheitsdenken und die Friedenspolitik der Freien Welt," ibid., pp. 462-74. A special problem in comprehending the concept of arms control has been the fact that the German language has no adequate term for "arms control." There have been various efforts to translate it; one such attempt being "Kooperative Rüstungssteuerung" (cooperative arms management), see Wolf Graf von Baudissin, "Kooperative Rüstungssteuerung als Mittel der Entspannungspolitik," Information für die Truppe, 1972: 13-40.

61. See Chancellor Adenauer's press conference in Bonn, May 7, 1962; also Julius Epstein, "Die Quelle des Übels: Eine Dokumentation zur Genesis der deutsch-amerikanischen Verstimmung," *Rheinischer Merkur*, August 31, 1962; as well as the analysis by Wolfgang Wagner, "Das geteilte Deutschland" in *Die Internationale Politik 1962*, ed. by Wilhelm Cornides and Dietrich Mende (Munich and Vienna: Oldenbourg, 1968), pp. 210-40.

62. See interview with Franz Josef Strauss in *Frankfurter Allgemeine Zeitung*, May 13, 1961. The spokesman for the Ministry of Defense expressed similar views; see Gerd Schmückle, "Eine Betrachtung über das Kriegsbild in Europa: Die Wandlung der Apokalypse," *Christ und Welt*, March 4, 1962. The article in *Christ und Welt* by Schmückle led to a controversy in the Bundestag between the SPD defense expert, Fritz Erler, and Defense Minister Strauss, see DBT/IV/24, April 6, 1962, pp. 919-20 and pp. 938-42. Regarding Strauss' concept of security, see especially "Die klare Konzeption," *Bulletin*, October 27, 1960, pp. 1954-56; "Verteidigung stärken, um zu verhandeln," *Aussenpolitik*, 12 (1961):77-81; "Strategie der Freiheit und des Friedens," *Bulletin*, April 7, 1962, pp. 573-74.

63. For Secretary of Defense McNamara's commencement address at the University of Michigan, June 6, 1962, see *U.S. Department of State Bulletin*, July 9, 1962, pp. 64-69; this summarized the information given at the NATO conference in Athens a month before.

64. The early replacement of Norstad by General Lemnitzer as SACEUR occurred to make the latter's position as chairman of the Joint Chief of Staffs available for General Taylor. The retirement of Norstad and the appointment of the "father" of flexible response was seen in Bonn as a sure sign of the reorientation of U.S. security and European policy. See interview with Defense Minister Strauss on the Bavarian Radio and Television network, July 25, 1962; *Bulletin*, July 27, 1962, pp. 1169-70.

65. See speech by Defense Minister Strauss at the University of Bonn, *Archiv der Gegenwart*, 1962, p. 10016.

66. See remarks by President Kennedy at a press conference on August 1, 1962, The *New York Times*, August 2, 1962; as well as the assurances given by a Pentagon spokesperson that the U.S. would not reduce their nuclear commitment in Europe, ibid.

67. See statement by State Secretary von Hase at a press conference, August 10, 1962, *Bulletin*, August 14, 1962:1264.

68. See Adelbert Weinstein, "Nur die abgestufte Abschreckung kann den Krieg verhindern: Ein Gespräch mit Verteidigungsminister Strauss," *Frankfurter Allgemeine Zeitung*, August 3, 1962. NATO adopted the strategy of flexible response as late as 1967 with its document MC 14/3; see communiqué of the NATO Ministerial Meeting, December 14, 1967, *Texts of Final Communiqués*, pp. 195-98.

69. See statement issued by the spokesperson for the Ministry of Defense, Major von Raven, and the statement by the Federal Press Office, August 10, 1962, *Bulletin*, July 14, 1962:1264; also interview with Defense Minister Strauss, *Frankfurter Allgemeine Zeitung*, August 9, 1962. Also see the interview with Defense Minister Strauss in *Welt am Sonntag*, August 13, 1962, reprinted in *Bulletin*, August 14, 1962:1265.

70. The extension of the length of compulsory military service was explained by Defense Minister Strauss in terms of the alliance commitments of the Federal Republic. He managed to do this without mentioning the connected strategic problems: see remarks by Defense Minister Strauss in the Bundestag as the compulsory military service amendment was introduced, DBT/IV/11, January 19, 1962, pp. 261-68 (here p. 261).

71. Erler and Schmidt took up such thoughts as they were developed in the so-called "Staff Study No. 8" by the Washington Center of Foreign Policy Research, John Hopkins University, *Possible Developments in Military Technology, Their Influence on Strategic*

Doctrine, and the Impact of Such Developments on U.S. Foreign Policy (Washington: Government Printing Office, 1959). Erler and Schmidt were the first politicians in the Federal Republic to publish on strategic questions; see Helmut Schmidt, *Defense or Retaliation: A German View* (New York: Praeger, 1962); Erler, *Ein Volk sucht seine Sicherheit.*

72. See, for example, Fritz Erler, "Abschreckung muss glaubwürdig sein," *Christ und Welt*, December 12, 1962; Fritz Erler, "Westeuropa und die Vereinigten Staaten in der strategischen Weltsituation," *Europa-Archiv*, 18 (1963):887-98; Helmut Schmidt, "Die unvermeidbare neue Strategie," *Die Zeit*, August 17 and 24, 1962, reprinted in Helmut Schmidt, *Beiträge* (Stuttgart: Seewald, 1967), pp. 504-28.

73. See the remarks made by Erler at the first and second readings of the amendment to the conscription law, DBT/IV/11, January 19, 1962, p. 269 and DBT/IV/16, February 22, 1962, p. 508; also Soell, *Fritz Erler*, p. 431.

74. The conclusion of the Test Ban Treaty in 1963, and even more so the Nonproliferation Treaty in 1968, strained German-American relations as Bonn suspected Washington was giving priority to an arrangement with the adversary rather than strengthening alliance relations. This suspicion was enhanced by an article from the director of the U.S. Arms Control and Disarmament Agency, William C. Foster, "New Directions in Arms Control and Disarmament," *Foreign Affairs* 43 (Summer 1965):587-601. For a detailed account of Bonn's position on the nuclear issue, see Helga Haftendorn, *Sicherheit und Entspannung: Zur Aussenpolitik der Bundesrepublik Deutschland 1955-1982* (Baden-Baden: Nomos, 1983), p. 613 ff.

75. Regarding the European and German position on arms control policies, see especially Alastair Buchan and Philip Windsor, *Arms and Stability in Europe* (London: Chatto and Windus, 1963). This book has been the result of a joint British-French-German study group.

76. See statement by Vice-Chancellor Erhard, November 29, 1961, DBT/II/5, November 29, 1961, pp. 22-33 (here p. 32); statement by Chancellor Erhard, October 18, 1963, DBT/IV/90, October 18, 1963, pp. 4192-4208 (here p. 4194f); as well as interview with Foreign Minister Schröder, *Düsseldorfer Nachrichten*, July 3, 1965; reprinted in *Europa-Archiv* 20 (1965): D 384-86.

77. Christliche Demokratische Union Deutschlands, *ABC der CDU: Kleines Handbuch der CDU-Politik* (Bonn: Bundesgeschäftsstelle der CDU, 1963), p. 9f.

78. See *Godesberg Program of the Social Democratic Party*, November 15, 1959 (Bonn: Vorstand der SPD, 1959); also see address by Herbert Wehner to the Bundestag on June 30, 1960, DBT/III/122, pp. 7052-61.

79. "Deutschland und Europas Sicherheit: Entschliessung des Karlsruher Parteitages," *Parteitag der Sozialdemokratischen Partei Deutschlands in Karlsruhe 1964* (Bonn: Neuer Vorwärts Verlag, 1965), pp. 972-76 (here 972).

80. "Entschliessung zur Sicherheitspolitik," *Parteitag der Sozialdemokratischen Partei Deutschlands in Hannover 1960*, (Bonn: Neuer Vorwärts Verlag, 1960), pp. 715-16 (here p. 715). Also see Fritz Erler, *Ein Volk sucht seine Sicherheit: Bemerkungen zur deutschen Sicherheitspolitik* (Frankfurt: Europäische Verlags-Anstalt, 1961), p. 27f.

81. See Fritz Erler, "Das Ringen um die deutsche Einheit" in *Sicherheit und Rüstung*, pp. 31-43 (here p. 42).

82. The debate on nuclear-sharing was initiated within the SPD by its defense expert, Fritz Erler, in July 1960 with a paper for the Board (Präsidium) of the SPD in which he referred to the American point of view. See also the statement by Willy Brandt, in which he didn't exclude nuclear sharing, *Parteitag in Hannover 1960*, pp. 555-58 (here p. 557); further see "Deutschland und Europas Sicherheit," *Parteitag in Karlsruhe 1964*, p. 973; as well as the interpretation given by Soell, *Fritz Erler*, p. 452ff.

83. See Fritz Erler, "Zur strategisch-politischen Lage: Arbeitspapier für die Deutsch-

Amerikanische Konferenz vom November 1964," in his *Politik für Deutschland: Eine Dokumentation* (Stuttgart: Seewald, 1968); pp. 582-95 (here 591f.).

84. See Willy Brandt's speech before the Federal Convention of the Seliger Gemeinde on June 5, 1964, excerpted in Fritz Sänger und Eugen Selbmann, eds. *Politik für Deutschland: Sozialdemokratische Beiträge 1962-1964* (Bonn: Neuer Vorwärts Verlag 1965), p. 14.

85. Motion submitted by the SPD regarding the third reading of the 1964 budget, DBT/IV/123, April 16, 1964, pp. 5941-42.

86. See report by the Committee on Foreign Affairs regarding the motion by the SPD on the third reading of the 1964 budget, DBT, Drucksache IV/2936; as well as the resolution by the Bundestag, Janaury 21, 1965, DBT/IV/157, pp. 7759-61.

87. See speech by President de Gaulle on the occasion of his trip to Poland in September 1967 and joint Polish-French declaration of September 12, 1967, *Le Monde*, September 12, 1967; also see paper by the Centre d'Etudes de Politique Etrangère, Paris, "Modèles de securité européenne," *Politique Etrangère*, 32 (1967):519-41.

88. See "United States Working Paper Submitted to the Eighteen-Nation Disarmament Committee: Reduction of the Risk of War Through Accident, Miscalculation or Failure of Communication," December 12, 1962, ENDC/70, *Documents on Disarmament 1962*, ed. by U.S. Arms Control and Disarmament Agency (Washington: Government Printing Office, 1963), vol. 2, pp. 1214-25.

89. See "Memorandum of Understanding between the United States and the Soviet Union Regarding the Establishment of a Direct Communications Link," June 20, 1963, *Documents on Disarmament 1963*, pp. 236-38.

90. See "Soviet Memorandum on Measures for Slowing Down the Armaments Race and Relaxing International Tension," January 28, 1964, ENDC/123, *Documents on Disarmament 1964*, pp. 12-17.

91. See "Soviet Memorandum on Measures for Slowing Down the Armaments Race and Relaxing International Tension," January 28, 1964, ibid; and statement by Polish Party Secretary Gomulka on a freeze of nuclear armaments in Central Europe, December 28, 1963, *Documents on Disarmament 1963*, pp. 651-52.

92. See interviews of Foreign Minister Schröder with the German Radio and Television network on October 6, 1963 and with the Northern German Radio on November 4, 1963, *Bulletin*, October 8, 1963:1543-45, and *Bulletin*, November 7, 1963:1736-39. Also see Schröder's address to the Western European Assembly, December 5, 1963, *Bulletin*, 1899-1902.

93. Statement by Chancellor Erhard on October 18, 1963, in DBT/IV/90, pp. 4192-4208 (here p. 4194).

94. See Theo Wieser, "Schröder über die Entspannungspolitik," *Neue Zürcher Zeitung*, October 8, 1963; also see Waldemar Besson, *Die Aussenpolitik der Bundesrepublik: Erfahrungen und Masstäbe* (Munich: Piper, 1970); p. 329ff.

95. Characteristic of such differences were the speeches to be given by Brandt, Wehner and Erler in the GDR during a planned speakers exchange (which, however, fell through); see Brandt's speech, in *Wiedervereinigung und Sicherheit Deutschlands: Eine dokumentarische Diskussionsgrundlage*, ed. by Heinrich von Siegler, vol. 2 (Bonn: Siegler, 1968) pp. 175-76; for Brandt also see his *A Peace Policy for Europe* (New York: Holt, Rinehart & Winston, 1969); Wehner's speech in *Herbert Wehner, Wandel und Bewährung: Ausgewählte Schriften 1930-1967*, ed. by Hans-Werner Graf Finckenstein and Gerhard Jahn, (Frankfurt: Ullstein, 1968), pp. 370-72; Erler's speech in his *Politik für Deutschland*, pp. 626-31.

96. Strauss had left the government by the end of 1962 due to the "Spiegel Affair." Until the formation of the Grand Coalition he had to limit himself to the role of chairman

of the Bavarian CSU which, however, did not prevent him from using the media for his purposes. In the Kiesinger Government Strauss was minister of finance and focused on monetary problems.

97. Since spring 1959 the Federal Republic attempted to become a member of the Geneva Eighteen-Nation Disarmament Conference. The Soviet Union and the Eastern European countries would have agreed to admit the Federal Republic under the condition that the GDR became a member of this conference too. This was not acceptable to Bonn. See "Bonn Seeks Seat At Geneva Talks," New York *Times*, March 20, 1969.

98. See below, chapter IV, 59ff.

99. "The Future Tasks of the Alliance," Report of the NATO Council, December 1967, *NATO: Facts and Figures* (Brussels: NATO Information Service, 1978), pp. 338-41.

100. See communiqué on the meeting of the NATO Council, December 15-16, 1966, and the resolution to study the future tasks of the Alliance, *Texts of Final Communiqúes*, pp. 177-84. Also see report on "The Future Tasks of the Alliance."

101. See President Lyndon B. Johnson's address to a conference newspaper editorialists in New York on October 7, 1966, *Department of State Bulletin*, October 24, 1966: 622-25. In this speech Johnson named three tasks which faced both the United States and Europe: (1) the strengthening and modernization of NATO; (2) the encouragement of West European integration; and (3) progress in East-West relations so as to overcome the division of Europe by peaceful means.

102. See "Modèles de sécurité européenne"; also joint French-Soviet declaration of June 30, 1966, on the occasion of de Gaulle's visit to the Soviet Union, *Le Monde*, July 2, 1966.

103. See address by Foreign Minister Brandt to the Western European Union Assembly, December 14, 1966, in Willy Brandt, *Aussenpolitik—Deutschlandpolitik—Europapolitik: Grundsätzliche Erklärungen während des ersten Jahres im Auswärtigen Amt* (Berlin: Berlin-Verlag, 1968), pp. 12-19; also, interview with Brandt on the German Radio and Television network on July 2, 1967, ibid., pp. 80-89 (here p. 85f.).

104. See declaration on European Security by the Political Consultative Committee of the Warsaw Pact States, July 5, 1966, *Documents on Disarmament 1966*, pp. 407-20.

105. See Circular Note on German Peace Policy ("Friedensnote"), March 25, 1966, *Documents on Disarmament 1966*, pp. 168-74.

106. See speeches given by Herbert Wehner, Willy Brandt and Helmut Schmidt at the Dortmund SPD Party Convention, *Protokoll der Verhandlungen und Anträge vom Parteitag der Sozialdemokratischen Partei Deutschlands vom Juni 1-5, 1966 in Dortmund* (Bonn: Neuer Vorwärts Verlag, 1966), pp. 15-17, pp. 60-89, pp. 448-450; also "Entschliessung zur Deutschlandpolitik unter sich ändernden weltpolitischen Bedingungen," ibid., pp. 1049-58.

107. See Aufgaben einer neuen Bundesregierung: Grundlage für die Koalitionsverhandlungen zur Bildung einer neuen Bundesregierung, November 1966 (Bonn: Vorstand der SPD, 1970).

108. See statement by Chancellor Kurt-Georg Kiesinger at the Bundestag, December 13, 1966, *Bulletin*, December 14, 1966, pp. 1268-70 and 1273-75. The "change of course" in the Federal Republic's security and detente policy has been accented by Theo Sommer, "Bonn Changes Course," *Foreign Affairs* 45 (Spring 1967) 477-91.

109. Egon Bahr, "Renunciation of Force and the Alliance," *Aussenpolitik*, 24 (1973) 243-254. Bahr referred in this article to the U.S.-USSR Treaty on the Prevention of Nuclear War.

110. See Gregory F. Treverton, *"The Dollar Drain" and American Forces in Germany: Managing the Political Economics of Alliance* (Athens, Ohio: Ohio University Press, 1978), pp. 37-39. Also see John Newhouse et al., *U.S. Troops in Europe: Issues, Costs and Choices* (Washington, D.C.: Brookings Institution, 1971); Elke Thiel, *Dollar-Dominanz, Lasten-*

teilung und amerikanische Truppenpräsenz in Europa: Zur Frage kritischer Verknüpfungen währungs- und stationierungspolitischer Zielsetzungen in den deutsch-amerikanischen Beziehungen (Baden-Baden: Nomos 1979).

111. See Brandt, *Begegnungen und Einsichten*, p. 320.

112. See, e.g., Hedley Bull, "The Scope for Soviet-American Agreement," in *Soviet-American Relations and World Order: Arms Limitation and Policy* (London: International Institute for Strategic Studies, 1970), pp. 1-15; Johan Jörgen Holst, "Parity, Superiority or Sufficiency? Some Remarks on the Nature and Future of the Soviet-American Strategic Relationship," ibid., pp. 25-39.

113. See ABM-Treaty and "Interim Agreement between the United States of American and the Union of Soviet Socialist Republics on Certain Measures with Respect to the Limitation of Strategic Offensive Arms," May 20, 1972, *Documents on Disarmament 1972*, pp. 197-203. Also see Declaration on Basic Principles of Relations between the United States of America and the Union of Soviet Socialist Republics, May 29, 1972, ibid., pp. 237-40. On SALT I also see Roger P. Labrie, ed. *SALT Handbook: Key Documents and Issues 1972-1979* (Washington, D.C.: American Enterprise Institute, 1979); Thomas W. Wolfe, *The SALT Experience* (Cambridge, Mass.: Ballinger, 1979); Mason Willrich and John B. Rhinelander, eds., *SALT: The Moscow Agreements and Beyond* (New York and London: Free Press, 1974); Morton A. Kaplan, ed. *SALT: Problems and Prospects* (Morristown, N.J.: General Learning Press, 1973); William R. Kintner and Robert L. Pfaltzgraff, Jr., eds. *SALT: Implications for Arms Control in the 1970's* (Pittsburgh: University of Pittsburgh Press, 1973). The negotiations on various levels which led to SALT I have been described by John Newhouse, *Cold Dawn: The Story of SALT* (New York: Holt, Rinehart & Winston, 1973); and Gerard Smith, *Double-Talk: The Story of the First Strategic Arms Limitation Talks* (New York: Doubleday, 1980).

114. See Report by Secretary of State Rogers to President Nixon on the Strategic Arms Limitation Agreements, June 10, 1972, *Documents on Disarmament 1972*, pp. 267-86.

115. See "Congressional Joint Resolution on the Interim Strategic Offensive Arms Limitation Agreement," September 30, 1972, ibid., pp. 681-83; and "American-Soviet Basic Principles of Negotiations on the Further Limitation of Strategic Offensive Arms," June 21, 1973. *Documents on Disarmament 1973*, pp. 271-73.

116. In 1972, the United Kingdom had 72 nuclear-capable V-bombers and 4 Polaris submarines; France had some 18 S-2 medium-range missiles, 36 Mirage IV bombers and one nuclear submarine. The U.S. maintained approximately 500-600 F-4, F-111, A-6 and A-7 airplanes, i.e., forward based and nuclear-capable systems which could reach Soviet territory. In the SALT I treaty not only all FBS were excluded, but also all airplanes. See *Military Balance 1972-73* (London: International Institute for Strategic Studies, 1972), p. 65f. and p. 84f.

117. See address by National Security Adviser Henry Kissinger on U.S.-European policy at the Associated Press annual dinner in New York on April 23, 1973, *U.S. Department of State Bulletin*, May 14, 1973, pp. 593-98; and Andrew J. Pierre, "Can Europe's Security be 'Decoupled' from America?" *Foreign Affairs*, 51 (July 1973): 761-77.

118. See "American-Soviet Agreement on the Prevention of Nuclear War," June 22, 1973, in *Documents on Disarmament*, 1973, pp. 283-85; on the motives for this treaty see the interpretation given by Henry Kissinger, *Years of Upheaval* (Boston: Little, Brown, 1982), p. 274ff.

119. See Uwe Nerlich, "Die Einhegung des Nuklearkrieges: Zur politischen Bedeutung des amerikanisch-sowjetischen Grundsatzabkommens über die Verhütung von Nuklearkriegen," *Europa-Archiv* 28 (1973): 669-78, for the first line of argumentation; also Minister Egon Bahr in a speech at the Tutzing Academy on July 11, 1973, see *Texte zur Deutschland-politik*, ser. 2, vol. 1 (Bonn: Bundesministerium für innerdeutsche Beziehungen, 1975), pp. 47-61.

120. See Kissinger's account in *Years of Upheaval*, p. 1151ff.

121. See "Joint American-Soviet Statement on Limitation of Strategic Offensive Arms," November 24, 1974, *Documents on Disarmament 1974*, pp. 746-47, as well as the news conference remarks by Secretary of State Kissinger, November 24, 1974, ibid., pp. 750-61; and December 7, 1974, ibid., pp. 779-84.

122. On the history of the SALT II negotiations and particularly the Vance mission, see Wolfe, *The SALT Experience*, pp. 221-26; Labrie, *SALT Handbook*, pp. 443-52; Strobe Talbott, *Endgame: The Inside Story of SALT II* (New York: Harper & Row, 1979), pp. 68-75. For a survey of the problems involved, also see Richard Burt, "Scope and Limits of SALT," *Foreign Affairs*, 56 (Summer 1978):751-70.

123. Secretary of State Kissinger has directed pointed criticism at the deterioration of the military balance, see his "NATO: The Next Thirty Years" (speech in Brussels, September 1, 1979), *Survival*, 1973: 264-68. On the opposition to SALT II, see *Does the Official Case for the SALT II Treaty Hold up under Analysis?* (Washington: Committee on the Present Danger, 1978). For an overview of the various pro-SALT arguments, see Paul C. Warnke, *The SALT Process—Why and How* (Washington: U.S. Arms Control and Disarmament Agency, 1978) U.S. Congress, Senate Committee on Foreign Relations, *The SALT II Treaty: Hearings Before the Committee on Foreign Relations* (Washington: Government Printing Office, 1979).

124. U.S. Congress, *Treaty on the Limitation of Strategic Offensive Arms and Protocol Thereto (SALT II Treaty). Message from the President of the United States Transmitting the Treaty Between the United States of America and the Union of Soviet Socialist Republics on the Limitation of Strategic Offensive Arms and the Protocol Thereto, Together Referred to as the SALT II Treaty, Both Signed at Vienna, Austria, on June 18, 1979. and Related Documents*, June 25, 1979 (Washington: Government Printing Office, 1979). For a European perspective of SALT II, see on Christopher Makins, "Bringing in the Allies," *Foreign Policy* (Summer 1979):91-108; François de Rose, "The Future of SALT and Western Security in Europe," *Foreign Affairs*, 57 (Summer 1979):1065-74.

125. See the announcement by President Reagan of the resumption of such talks and the goals of negotiations in his address to the National Press Club on November 18, 1981, *Public Papers of the Presidents of the United States, 1981* (Washington: Government Printing Office, 1982), pp. 1062-67; and at Eureka College on May 9, 1982; *U.S. Department of State Bulletin*, June 1982:34-37.

126. See above, pp. 03 ff.

127. Falk Bomsdorf, "Sicherheitsinteressen Westeuropas in den SALT-II-Anhörungen," *Europa-Archiv*, 35 (1980)49-62 (here p. 53). Also see David S. Yost, *European Security and the SALT Process* (Beverly Hills, Calif.: Sage, 1981).

128. *White Paper 1979: The Security of the Federal Republic of Germany and the Development of Federal Armed Forces* (Bonn: Federal Minister of Defense, 1979), p. 70; also see statement by the Federal Government at the occasion of the conclusion of the SALT II treaty, *Bulletin*, June 17, 1979, pp. 725-27.

129. These concerns were expressed, above all in France, see Jean-Luis Gergorin, "Les negotiations SALT et la défense de l'Europe," *Defense Nationale* (June 1978)43-56; Pierre Lellouche, "La France, les SALT et la sécurité de l'Europe, *Politique Etrangère*, 44 (1979):249-71; François de Rose, "Atlantic Solidarity and the Defense of the West: A New Strategic Equation," *Trialogue* (Fall 1979)13-15. In the Federal Republic similar thoughts were expressed by Uwe Nerlich, see Uwe Nerlich, ed *Soviet Asset: Military Power in the Competition over Europe*, vol. 1 of *Soviet Power and Western Negotiating Policies* (Cambridge, Mass.: Ballinger, 1983).

130. See Helmut Schmidt, "The 1977 Alastair Buchan Memorial Lecture," *Survival*, 1978:2-10.

131. On the NATO dual-track decision see below, pp. 36 ff.

132. See statement by Secretary of State Cyrus A. Vance as well as the State Department's "Responses to Additional Questions Submitted for the Record by Senator Biden" in the SALT II Treaty hearings, July 10, 1979, *The SALT II Treaty*, part 1, p. 181f. and p. 611ff.

133. See e.g., statement by the CDU/CSU at the conclusion of the SALT II treaty, *CDU-Dokumentation*, June 21, 1979, p. 6f.

134. A good summary of the West German position on the SALT II treaties is Peter Corterier, *MdB* (SPD) in his role as rapporteur for the Defense Committee of the North Atlantic Assembly in a hearing before the U.S. House of Representatives, September 12, 1979, U.S. Congress, House of Representatives, *Western Security Issues: European Perspectives: Hearings before the Subcommittees on International Security and Scientific Affairs and on Europe and the Middle East* (Washington: Government Printing Office, 1979), pp.14-18.

135. MBFR—Mutual Balanced Force Reductions. The acronym originally stood for a specific form of troop reductions as proposed by the West. For a summary of the MBFR negotiations see Lothar Ruehl, *MBFR: Lessons and Problems* (London: International Institute for Strategic Studies, 1982); Reinhard Mutz, *Die Wiener Verhandlungen über Truppenreduzierungen in Mitteleuropa (MBFR): Chronic, Dokumentation, Bibliographie 1973-1982* (Baden-Baden: Nomos, 1983); Reinhard Mutz, *Konventionelle Abrüstung in Europa: Die Bundesrepublik Deutschland und MBFR* (Baden-Baden: Nomos, 1984); Jeffrey Record, *Force Reductions in Europe: Starting Over* (Cambridge, Mass., and Washington: Institute of Foreign Policy Analysis, 1980); John G. Keliher, *The Negotiations on Mutual and Balanced Force Reductions. The Search for Arms Control in Central Europe* (New York: Pergamon Press, 1980).

136. See Haftendorn, *Sicherheit und Entspannung*, p. 545ff. Also see Hans-Georg Wieck, "Perspectives on MBFR in Europe," *Aussenpolitik*, 23:36-48. As director of the policy planning staff in the Ministry of Defense, Wieck has been one of the architects of the German MBFR policy.

137. See U.S. Congress, Senate Committee on Foreign Relations, *Prospects for the Vienna Force Reduction Talks*, Committee Print (Washington: Government Printing Office, 1978), pp. 6-8; also see Ruehl, *MBFR: Lessons and Problems*.

138. Schmidt, "The 1977 Alastair Buchan Memorial Lecture."

139. See Walter Slocombe, "The Countervailing Strategy," *International Security*, 5 (Spring 1981):18-27.

140. See President Jimmy Carter's press conference, July 12, 1977, *Public Papers of the Presidents of the United States, 1977* (Washington: Government Printing Office, 1978), pp. 1231-39.

141. Egon Bahr "Ist die Menschheit dabei, verrückt zu werden?", *Vorwärts*, July 21, 1977.

142. See statement by Chancellor Helmut Schmidt at the Bundestag, DBT/VIII/83, April 13, 1978, pp. 6499-6504.

143. See statement by President Carter on the development and production of enhanced radiation weapons, April 7, 1978, *U.S. Department of State Bulletin*, May 1978:31-33. On the resulting controversy, see "The Neutron Bomb Furor: A Mishandled Power Play Produces International Confusion," *Time*, April 17, 1978. On the West German debate, see Sherri L. Wasserman, *The Neutron Bomb Controversy: A Study in Alliance Politics* (New York: Praeger, 1983), pp. 65-75.

144. See Richard Burt, "Plan for New Missiles In Europe is Backed: Support by NATO Group," *International Herald Tribune*, July 6, 1979.

145. See speech by General Secretary Leonid Brezhnev at a commemoration of the thirtieth anniversary of the GDR in East Berlin, October 5, 1979, *Current Digest*, 40:1-4.

146. See the Communiqué on the Special Meeting of Foreign and Defense Ministers, *Texts of Final Communiqués*, vol. II, 1975-1979 (Brussels: NATO Information Service, 1982), pp. 121-123.; and Communiqué on the North Atlantic Council Meeting, ibid., pp. 124-129. For a helpful documentation of how the NATO decision was arrived at, see U.S. House of Representatives, Subcommittee on Europe and the Middle East, ed. *The Modernization of NATO's Long Range Theater Nuclear Forces*, Report by the Congressional Research Service, Library of Congress (Washington: Government Printing Office, 1980).

147. Statement by the federal government on the NATO dual-track decision, December 14, 1979, DBT/VIII/194, December 14, 1979, pp. 15465-68.

148. On the problems of force comparison see K.-Peter Stratmann, "Das 'euro-strategische' Kräfteverhältnis: Zweifelhafte Bewertungen als Folge der Anwendung unterschiedlicher Kriterien," *Europa-Archiv*, 36 (1981):387-98, which argues with the assessments given by the *Military Balance 1979-80*, pp. 111-119; *Military Balance 1980-81*, pp. 116-19; *World Armaments and Disarmament, SIPRI Yearbook 1980* (Stockholm: Stockholm International Peace Research Institute, 1980), pp. 175-86; ibid., 1982, pp. 3-50; *White Paper 1979*, p. 104ff; Dieter S. Lutz, "Das militärische Kräfteverhältnis im Bereich der Nuklearstreitkräfte in und für Europa," in *Nuklearrüstung im Ost-West-Konflikt: Potentiale, Doktrinen, Rüstungssteuerung* ed. by Gert Krell and Dieter S. Lutz, (Baden-Baden: Nomos, 1980), pp. 14-89.

149. On the political motives for the NATO dual-track decision from the perspective of the Federal Republic, see Karsten D. Voigt, "Das Risiko eines begrenzten Nuklearkrieges in Europa: Zur Diskussion über die westliche Militärdoktrin und den NATO-Doppelbeschluss vom Dezember 1979," *Europa-Archiv*, 37 (1982):151-60; Eckhard Lübkemeier, *PD 59 und LRTNF-Modernisierung: Militärstrategische und sicherheitspolitische Implikationen der erweiterten Abschreckung für die Bundesrepublik Deutschland* (Bonn: Friedrich-Ebert-Stiftung, 1981). For an analysis of the different European and American explanations on the deployment of LRTNF, see Michael Higgins and Christopher J. Makins, "Theater Nuclear Forces and 'Gray Area' Arms Control," in *Arms Control and Defense Postures in the 1980's* ed. by Richard Burt (Boulder, Colo.: Westview, 1982), pp. 75-96; also see *David N. Schwartz, NATO's Nuclear Dilemmas* (Washington: Brookings Institution, 1981).

150. See Karl Kaiser, Georg Leber, Alois Mertes and Franz-Joseph Schulze, "Nuclear Weapons and the Preservation of Peace," *Foreign Affairs*, 60 (Summer 1982):1157-70. This article is a reply to the one by McGeorge Bundy, George F. Kennan, Robert S. McNamara and Gerard Smith, in which the American authors pleaded for a "no first use" of nuclear weapons; see their "Nuclear Weapons and the Atlantic Alliance," *Foreign Affairs*, 60 (Spring 1982):753-68.

151. See resolution by the SPD party convention in Berlin, "Sicherheitspolitik im Rahmen der Friedenspolitik," *SPD Parteitag Berlin '79: Protokoll des Parteitages in Berlin, 3.-7. Dezember 1979* (Bonn: Vorstand der SPD, 1980) pp. 1228-44. The SPD had intended to use disarmament and detente as the main issues of its 1980 campaign. For this purpose an expert commission under the chairmanship of Alfons Pawelczyk (formerly SPD spokesman for arms control and disarmament) had prepared various position papers. Just before the publication of the motion based on them, the SPD Executive Committee included a few paragraphs in which reference was made to the disparity in TNF and a combination of military and arms control options for their removal was proposed.

152. For the many notions of crisis in the alliance with particular relevance to the debate in Germany, see Catherine M. Kelleher, "The Present as Prologue: Europe and Theater Nuclear Modernization," *International Security*, 5 (Spring 1981):150-68; Josef Joffe, "European-American Relations: The Enduring Crisis," *Foreign Affairs*, 59 (Spring 1981):835-51; Stanley Hoffmann "The Crisis in the West," *New York Review of Books*, July 17, 1980, pp. 41-50.

153. On the decline of detente from an American perspective, see Kissinger, *Years of Upheaval*, p. 228ff. and p. 979ff.; also Schweigler, *Von Kissinger zu Carter*, p. 163ff.

154. This has been repeatedly emphasized, for example, by SPD Secretary General Egon Bahr, see Gunther Hoffmann, "...ob wir an einem Krieg vorbeikommen: SPD-Bundesgeschäftsführer Egon Bahr und die Zukunft der Entspannung," *Die Zeit*, January 18, 1980; Theo Sommer, "Die Spannung muss teilbar bleiben," *Die Zeit*, January 11, 1980; Richard Löwenthal, "Die Rote Armee in Kabul: Ende der Entspannung?" *Die Zeit*, January 11, 1981.

155. See "Angst, dass die Sicherungen durchbrennen," *Spiegel*, April 21, 1980, pp. 21-27. Schmidt took his historical comparison from an article by Miles Kahler, "Rumors of War: The 1914 Analogy," *Foreign Affairs*, 58 (Winter 1979-80):374-96.

156. See Joint Communiqué on the visit of Chancellor Schmidt to the United States, *U.S. Department of State Bulletin*, May 1980:33-34; and joint communiqué on his visit to the Soviet Union, *Bulletin*, July 3, 1980:664-665; "Breschnjew ist doch kein Abenteurer: Bundeskanzler Helmut Schmidt über die Ergebnisse seiner Moskau-Reise," *Spiegel*, July 7, 1980:25-31.

157. On the German peace movement and its goals, see Hans A. Pestalozzi, Ralf Schlegel, Adolf Bachmann, eds. *Frieden in Deutschland: Die Friedensbewegung—wie sie wurde, was sie werden kann* (Munich: Goldmann, 1982); Kim R. Holmes, *The West German Peace Movement and the National Question* (Cambridge, Mass., and Washington: Institute for Foreign Policy Analysis, 1984).

158. Alois Mertes (foreign policy spokesman of the CDU/CSU in the Bundestag), "Der Western braucht eine geschlossene Strategie" *Deutchland Union Dienst*, No. 232, Dec. 8, 1980, p. 3. For similar statements by opposition politicians see Bundestag debate on January 17, 1980, in DBT/VIII/198, pp. 15584-15593 and pp. 15630-15636.

159. See Gebhard Schweigler, *West German Foreign Policy: The Domestic Setting* (New York: Praeger, 1984); also see Elisabeth Noelle-Neumann, "Ein grosser Teil der Bevölkerung bleibt standfest: Der Krieg der Meinungen über Amerika und Nachrüstung," *Frankfurter Allgemeine Zeitung*, October 30, 1981; Elisabeth Noelle-Neumann, "Drei Viertel gegen die Raketenstationierung? Die Wirklichkeit sieht differenzierter aus," *Frankfurter Allgemeine Zeitung*, September 16, 1983.

160. The various positions of the peace movement are represented in *Sicherheitspolitik contra Frieden? Ein Forum zur Friedensbewegung* (Bonn: J.H.W. Dietz Nachf., 1981); Studiengruppe Militärpolitik, ed. *Aufrüsten, um abzurüsten? Informationen zur Lage* (Reinbek: Rowohlt Taschenbuch Verlag, 1980). Ulrich Albrecht, Johan Galtung, Michael Gumbert, Reimar Stuckenbrock, eds. *Stationierung—und was dann? Friedensbewegung gegen Apokalypse* (Berlin: Europäische Perspektiven, 1983); Alfred Mechtersheimer, ed. *Nachrüsten? Dokumente und Positionen zum NATO-Doppelbeschluss* (Reinbek: Rowohlt Taschenbuch Verlag, 1981).

161. See Bundy, Kennan, McNamara, and Smith, "Nuclear Weapons and the Atlantic Alliance," and the response by Kaiser, Leber, Mertes and Schulze, "Nuclear Weapons and the Preservation of Peace." Also see John D. Steinbrunner and Leon V. Sigal, eds. *Alliance Security: NATO and the No-First-Use Question* (Washington: Brookings Institution, 1983).

162. See The Independent Commission On Disarmament and Security Issues, *Common Security: A Blueprint for Survival* (New York: Simon & Schuster, 1982); also see Egon Bahr, "Answer is Common Security," *The German Tribune*, August 29, 1982 (originally published as "Gemeinsame Sicherheit. Gedanken zur Entschärfung der nuklearen Konfrontation in Europa," *Europa-Archiv*, 37 (1982):421-30).

163. See Carl Friedrich von Weizsäcker, *Der bedrohte Friede. Politische Aufsätze 1945-1981* (Munich and Vienna: Carl Hanser, 1981); C.F. von Weizsäcker, "Die neuen Raketen gehören auf See," *Die Zeit*, May 22, 1981.

164. See Uwe Nerlich, "Die Stationierung landgestützter Mittelstreckenrakten in Europa," *Europäische Wehrkunde*, 1981:337-41.

165. See Egon Bahr, "Answer is Common Security"; Karsten D. Voigt, "Sicherheitspartnerschaft—von der Doktrin der Abschreckung zur gemeinsamen Sicherheit," *Themen der praktischen Theologie*, 1983, pp. 118-28; also see Karsten D. Voigt, "Nuclear Weapons in Europe. A German Social Democrat's Perspective," in *Nuclear Weapons in Europe*, ed. by Andrew J. Pierre, (New York: Council on Foreign Relations, 1984), pp. 98-118.

166. See resolution adopted by the 1982 Munich SPD Party Congress, "Die Friedens- und Sicherheitspolitk der SPD," *SPD Parteitag München '82. Protokoll des Parteitages in München, 19.-23. April 1982* (Bonn: Vorstand der SPD, 1982), pp. 907-11.

167. See statement by Chancellor Kohl before the German Bundestag, October 13, 1982, DBT/IX/121, pp. 7213-29 (here p. 7225).

168. See "Kriegsverhinderung im Atomzeitalter. Bericht der Arbeitsgruppe 'Neue Strategien' beim SPD-Parteivorstand," *Politik*, July 1983, pp. 1-7; *Stellungnahme der Bundesregierung zur Bundestagsdrucksache 10/51* (Alternative Strategien und Verteidigungspolitik), (Bonn: Der Bundesminister der Verteidigung, 1983); Wilhelm Bruns, Christian Krause and Eckhard Lübkemeier, *Sicherheit durch Abrüstung, Orientierende Beiträge zum Imperativ unserer Zeit* (Bonn: Neue Gesellschaft, 1984); also see John Newhouse, "Limited War, Unlimited Protest," *Orbis*, 26 (Spring 1982):89-103.

169. On the Soviet position regarding the initiation of INF talks see address by General Secretary Brezhnev to the 26th Congress of the CPSU, February 23, 1981, *Current Digest*, 33:3-21; Interview with Brezhnev with *Spiegel*, reprinted in *Current Digest*, 33:1-7; for the NATO decision see communiqué of the North Atlantic Council Meeting in Rome, May 4 and 5, 1981, *NATO Final Communiqués* (Brussels: NATO Information Service, 1982).

170. See address by President Reagan to the National Press Club in Washington, November 18, 1981, *Public Papers of the Presidents*, 1981, pp. 1062-67.

171. See U.S. Congress, Senate Committee on Foreign Relations, *Post-Deployment Nuclear Arms Control in Europe: A Staff Report* (Washington: Government Printing Office, 1984); Charles R. Gellner, *U.S.-Soviet Negotiations to Limit Intermediate-Range Nuclear Weapons* (Washington: Congressional Research Service, 1982).

172. See Friedrich Ruth, "Sicherheitspolitik der NATO: Abschreckung und Rüstungskontrolle," *Europa-Archiv* 37 (1982):135-144.

173. On the famous "walk in the woods," see Bernard Gwertzman, "U.S. Aide Reached Agreement Later Ruled Out. Tie to Ouster of Rostow," The *New York Times*, January 16, 1983.

174. See address by President Reagan at the Eureka College commencement ceremonies, May 9, 1982, *U.S. Department of State Bulletin*, June 10, 82:34-37; address by General Secretary Brezhnev to the 19th Congress of Komsomol in Moscow, May 18, 1982, *Current Digest*, 34:1-3, 23; also see Leslie H. Gelb, "Nuclear Bargaining: The President's Options," New York *Times Magazine*, June 27, 1982.

CHAPTER 4

1. In its policy, the Federal Republic has distinguished between the general principle of refraining from the threat or use of force, as in Article 2, paragraph 4 of the UN Charter, and the application of this principle to specific—usually contested—cases. It has further differentiated between renunciation of force, and nonaggression, the latter implying

"not going to attack" a country or an alliance. On the instrumental use of the principle of renunciation of force, see Thomas Oppermann, "Renunciation of Force in International Law," *Aussenpolitik,* 21 (1970):253-71; Dietrich Schwarzkopf, "Die Idee des Gewaltverzichts: Ein Element der neuen Ostpolitik der Bundesrepublik," *Europa-Archiv,* 22 (1967):893-900; Egon Bahr, "Renunciation of Force and the Alliance," *Aussenpolitik,* 24 (1973):243-54.

2. "Declaration by the German Federal Government and Joint Declaration by the Governments of France, United Kingdom, and the United States of America," Part V of the Final Act of the Nine-Power Conference, London, October 3, 1954, *Documents on Germany, 1944-1970,* ed. by U.S. Senate, Committee on Foreign Relations, 92d Cong., 1st sess. (Washington: Government Printing Office, 1971), pp. 243-48 (here p. 246); also see "Convention on Relations Between the three Powers and the Federal Republic of Germany, May 26, 1952. As amended by Schedule I of the Protocol on Termination of the Occupation Regime in Germany," signed at Paris, October 23, 1954, ibid., pp. 248-53.

3. Ibid., p. 247.

4. See "Memorandum From the Federal Republic of Germany to the Soviet Union Urging Reunification of Germany Through Free Elections," September 2, 1956, ibid., pp. 288-98.

5. See "Proposals for Solution of the German Problem Made by Prime Minister Eden at the Heads of Government Conference," (Eden Plan), Geneva, July 18, 1955, ibid., pp. 264-67; and "Western Peace Plan for Germany Submitted to the Foreign Ministers Meeting," (Herter Plan), Geneva, May 14, 1959, ibid., pp. 427-31.

6. See The *New York Times,* May 21, 1959.

7. Within the federal government, various proposals on improving relations with the Eastern European countries have been considered. In July 1959 and again in March 1961, the cabinet discussed the exchange of formal renunciation-of-force declarations with Poland and the CSSR. Each time the League of Expellees (*Bund der Vertriebenen*) protested violently. Within the administration their spokesman was the minister of communication, Hans Seebohm. See Schwarzkopf, "Die Idee des Gewaltverzichts"; also the following quasi-official statement in the government bulletin, "Nichtangriffspakte?", *Bulletin des Presse und Information-Samtes der Bundesregierung,* July 31, 1959, p. 1395.

8. The American proposals were leaked—probably by Adenauer himself—to the Bonn correspondent and subsequently published by The *New York Times,* April 14, 1962; in turn reprinted in sensational form by German papers. See Julius Epstein, "Die Quelle des Übels: Eine Dokumentation der deutsch-amerikanischen Verstimmung," *Rheinischer Merkur,* August 31, 1962; "Die Leute in Washington leben auf dem Mond: Eine Dokumentation der deutsch-amerikanischen Differenzen über Berlin", *Der Spiegel,* September 12, 1962. Also see Wilhelm Grewe, *Rückblenden: Aufzeichnungen eines Augenzeugen deutscher Aussenpolitik von Adenauer bis Schmidt* (Frankfurt: Propyläen, 1979, p. 545 ff. For the Soviet demands, see "Aide-Mémoire on the German Question," handed by Chairman Khrushchev to President Kennedy at Vienna, June 4, 1961, *Documents on Germany,* pp. 523-27.

9. At the NATO Conference in Athens, Foreign Minister Schröder remarked that the Federal Republic could agree with the proposed exchange of declarations on nonaggression between NATO and the Warsaw Pact, provided that these by no means implied a recognition of the GDR. Bonn would also agree with the exchange of declarations on a renunciation of force with respect to modifications of the existing borders and demarcation lines. See *Bulletin,* May 8, 1962; also see "Das Atlantik-Bündnis gestärkt", *Bulletin,* May 11, 1962. See p. 493.

10. On the various Soviet and other Eastern proposals for a nonaggression pact, see Charles R. Planck, *Sicherheit in Europa: Die Vorschläge für Rüstungsbeschränkung und Ab-*

rüstung 1955-1965 (Munich: Oldenbourg, 1968). The most important proposals are reprinted in U.S. Department of State, ed. *Documents on Disarmament 1945-1959*, 2 vols. (Washington: Government Printing Office, 1960.) For the "Draft Treaty on European Security," submitted by the Soviet Union at the Heads of Government Conference in Geneva, July 20, 1955, see *Documents on Germany*, pp. 267-70.

11. See e.g., "Soviet Memorandum on Questions to be Considered at a Heads of Governments' Conference," May 5, 1958, *U.S. Department of State Bulletin*, July 7, 1958, pp. 17-22; "Draft for a Nonaggression Agreement Between the NATO and Warsaw Pact Powers," May 24, 1958, *Pravda*, May 27, 1958; "Draft Treaty on Friendship and Cooperation Among the European States," July 15, 1958, *U.S. Department of State Bulletin*, September 22, 1958, pp. 465-66. One purpose of this intensive "publicity campaign" might have been to improve the negative image of the Soviet Union as a result of its bloody crushing of the Hungarian revolt in the fall of 1956.

12. On the Berlin crisis see above, pp. 68-81 (120-135). For the draft treaty on a nonaggression pact between the two German states, submitted by the GDR July 19, 1959, see *Dokumente zur Aussenpolitik der Regierung der Deutschen Demokratischen Republik*, vol. 7 (1959), (Berlin: Staatsverlag der DDR, 1960), pp. 188-90.

13. See e.g., Soviet draft on a nonaggression pact between Warsaw Treaty and NATO countries, February 20, 1963, *Documents on Disarmament 1963*, pp. 57-58; "Tripartite Communiqué on the Conclusion of the Moscow Test Ban Negotiations," July 25, 1963, ibid., 249-50; "Message by Premier Khrushchev to World Leaders: Peaceful Settlement of Territorial Disputes," December 31, 1963, ibid., pp. 654-65.

14. See the report of the Bundestag Committee on Foreign Relations, given by Wenzel Jaksch, *Verhandlungen des Deutschen Bundestages* (DBT), 3d sess., calendar 2740 and 2807; reprinted as Wenzel Jaksch, *Germany and Eastern Europe: Two Documents of the Third German Bundestag* (Bonn: Atlantik Forum, 1962). Also see "Entschliessung des Deutschen Bundestages zur deutschen Ostpolitik," June 14, 1961, DBT/III/162, pp. 9364-65.

15. For the Tübingen memorandum of lay Protestants, see *Die Welt*, February 27, 1962; the memorandum of the Protestant Church, October 1, 1965, and the correspondence by the Catholic bishops, November-December 1965, are reprinted in *Europa-Archiv* 21 (1966): 1-19.

16. For the text of Bahr's presentation at Tutzing, July 15, 1963, see Boris Meissner, ed. *Die deutsche Ostpolitik 1961-1970: Kontinuität und Wandel* (Cologne: Wissenschaft und Politik, 1970), pp. 45-48. Also see Karl Kaiser, *German Foreign Policy in Transition. Bonn Between East and West* (London: Oxford University Press, 1968), pp. 90-95.

17. See Peter Bender, *Offensive Entspannung, Möglichkeit für Deutschland* (Cologne: Kiepenheuer & Witsch, 1964).

18. See address by President Lyndon B. Johnson to a conference of newspaper editorialists in New York, October 7, 1966, *U.S. Department of State Bulletin*, October 24, 1966, pp. 622-25.

19. Zbigniew Brzezinski, *Alternative To Partition: For a Broader Conception of America's Role in Europe* (New York: McGraw-Hill, 1965), p. 139. Brzezinski's ideas of isolating the GDR were countered by Peter Bender, "Die DDR nicht isolieren," in *Denken an Deutschland*, ed. by Theo Sommer (Hamburg: Nanne, 1966), pp. 121-32.

20. See Gerhard Schröder (then foreign minister), "Germany Looks at Eastern Europe," *Foreign Affairs*, 44 (October 1965):15-25. On the connection between Eastern policy and trade also see Angela Stent, *From Embargo to Ostpolitik, The Political Economy of West German-Soviet Relations 1955-1980* (Cambridge: Cambridge University Press, 1981).

21. The so-called Hallstein Doctrine was developed by Adenauer aides Wilhelm Grewe and Walter Hallstein after the Federal Republic had established diplomatic relations with the Soviet Union in 1955. It said that any international, especially diplomatic

recognition of the GDR by a third country would be considered as an unfriendly act; its purpose was to keep Bonn's claim intact that the Federal Republic of Germany was the only democratically legitimate spokesman of the German people. For a number of years it served its purpose. When Yugoslavia established diplomatic relations with East Berlin in October 1955, the Federal Republic broke off its relations. The establishment of trade missions in Poland and other East European countries was to provide for a relationship below the threshold of diplomatic relations. When diplomatic relations with Rumania were agreed upon in early 1967, Bonn defended these with the argument that Moscow's allies in Eastern Europe didn't recognize the GDR out of their choosing. This was called the "birth defect theory." Also see Hansjürgen Schierbaum, *Intra-German Relations: Development—Problems—Facts* (Munich: tuduv), 1979, p. 4.

22. See radio interview of State Secretary Carstens with *Deutsche Welle*, reprinted in *Bulletin*, September 22, 1965 pp. 1257-58. Already, in December 1963, the Soviet government, in a message to all heads of state and of government, had proposed the exchange of renunciation-of-force declarations. See message from Premier Khrushchev to Chancellor Erhard, December 31, 1963, *U.S. State Department Bulletin*, January 20, 1964, pp. 158-63.

23. "Circular Note on German Peace Policy," aide-mèmoire of the Federal Republic of Germany addressed to all countries with which it had diplomatic relations as well as to Eastern European and Arab countries (not the GDR, Albania, PRC, North Korea, North Vietnam and Cuba), March 25, 1966 ("Peace Note"), *U.S. Department of State Bulletin*, April 25, 1966, pp. 654-57.

24. The linkage between arms control proposals and demands on the German question indicates the dilemma the German government faced. With the so-called "peace note," it tried at the same time to safeguard the status quo *and* to keep it open.

25. For an interpretation of the note by two of its architects, see Swidbert Schippenkoetter, "Gewaltandrohung und Gewaltverzicht als Probleme der internationalen Politik," in *Bedrohungsvorstellungen als Faktor der internationalen Politik*, ed. by Karl Kaiser (Düsseldorf: Bertelsmann, 1971) pp. 67-81 (here p. 78); Karl Carstens, "Die deutsche Friedensnote vom März 1966," in *Ludwig Erhard: Festschrift zum fünfundsiebzigsten Geburtstag*, (Berlin: Propyläen, 1971), pp. 383-92.

26. In an address to the NATO Council in June 1966, Foreign Minister Schröder listed the following four motives for the German initiative:

- to initiate an exchange of views on questions of arms control and security;
- to officially inform the governments of Eastern Europe on our views on questions of arms control and security;
- to make concrete proposals directed at them;
- to counter the communist propaganda which continuously portrays us as warmongers. *Bulletin*, June 21, 1966, p. 643.

27. See statement by Chancellor Erhard in the Bundestag on March 25, 1966, and the debate on the government statement, DBT/V/34, pp. 1605-11.

28. See *Texte der bisher eingegangenen Antwortnoten auf die Note der Bundesregierung vom 25. März 1966 zur deutschen Friedenspolitik* (Bonn: Presse- und Informationsamt der Bundesregierung, 1966). The most important Eastern European replies have been reprinted in *Europa-Archiv*, 21 (1966):277-302; for the U.S. note see *U.S. Department of State Bulletin*, April 25, 1966, p. 654.

29. See Helmut Schmidt's speech at the 1966 Dortmund party convention, reprinted as "Deutschlandpolitik im Wandel der weltpolitischen Bedingungen," in his *Beiträge* (Stuttgart: Seewald, 1967), pp. 545-78; also see the SPD's parliamentary interpellation

regarding proposals on arms control and safeguarding peace, calendar 5/775; and its introduction by Schmidt, September 23, 1966, DBT/V/59, pp. 2882-91. Also see the remarks by Foreign Minister Schröder in the same debate, p. 2908.

30. Already in 1966 confidential talks between Soviet and German diplomats were initiated, see Carl-Werner Sanne, "Zur Vorgeschichte des Vertrages," in *Der Vertrag vom 12. August 1970 zwischen der Bundesrepublik Deutschland und der Union der Sozialistischen Sowjetrepubliken* (Engl.: *The Treaty of August 12, 1970 Between the Federal Republic of Germany and the Union of Soviet Socialist Republics*). (Bonn: Press and Information Office, 1970), pp. 74-81.

31. Upon an initiative of Minister of Economics Schmücker, the Erhard government had begun talks with Rumania on the establishment of diplomatic relations. However, it took a change in administration to overcome concerns regarding its possible negative impact on the German question and to make the arrangements final. In January 1967 the Federal Republic, now the Grand Coalition, established diplomatic relations with Rumania.

32. Regarding the debate on Soviet intentions, see the controversy between Schmidt and Baron von Guttenberg in the Bundestag debate on September 23, 1966, DBT/V/59, p. 2884 and p. 2914; also the address by the chairman of the CSU, Franz Josef Strauss, to the Royal Institute of International Affairs in London, June 17, 1966, *Europa-Archiv* 21 (1966): D 396-403; also see his *The Grand Design: A European Solution to German Reunification* (New York: Praeger, 1966); Also see address by the chairman of the CDU/CSU party group in the Bundestag, Rainer Barzel, to the Council on Germany in Washington, June 17, 1966, *Europa-Archiv* 21 (1966): D 404-412, reprinted as "The German Question Remains Paramount," *Atlantic Community Quarterly*, 4 (Fall 1966):366-376. For the position of SPD leaders, see the speeches of Brandt and Schmidt at the 1966 Dortmund party convention, *Protokoll des SPD Parteitages in Dortmund, 1.-5. Juni 1966* (Bonn: Neuer Vorwärts Verlag, 1966), pp. 60-90.

33. Baron von Guttenberg in the Bundestag debate on the interpellation of the SPD, September 23, 1966, DBT/V/59, p. 2914.

34. SPD Chairman Willy Brandt, in his address to the SPD party convention in Dortmund, *SPD Parteitag in Dortmund*, p. 2890.

35. See note from the Soviet Union to the Federal Republic of Germany in reply to the German note of March 25, 1966, *American Foreign Policy: Current Documents, 1966*, ed. by the Department of State (Washington: Government Printing Office, 1967), pp. 395-402 (extracts in *Documents on Germany*, pp. 698-700).

36. See address by President Johnson to a conference of newspaper editorialists in New York, October 7, 1966 ("bridge-building speech").

37. Statement by Chancellor Kurt-Georg Kiesinger to the Bundestag, December 13, 1966, DBT/V/80, pp. 3656-65; also see *Aufgaben einer neuen Bundesregierung* (Bonn: Vorstand der SPD, 1966).

38. See Centre d'Etudes de Politique Etrangère, "Modèles de Sécurité Européenne", *Politique Etrangère*, 32 (1967):pp. 519-41.

39. Besides the above-cited statement of Kiesinger's to the Bundestag, December 13, 1966, see his *Entspannung in Deutschland, Friede in Europa: Reden und Interviews 1967* (Bonn: Presse- und Informationsamt der Bundesregierung, 1968); and *Reden and Interviews 1968* (Bonn: Presse- und Informationsamt der Bundesregierung, 1969).

40. Willy Brandt, "Realitäten des politischen Handelns," *Internationale Politik* (Belgrade), reprinted in *Bulletin*, June 5, 1968, pp. 593-95 (here p. 594). Also see his "German Policy Towards the East," *Foreign Affairs*, 46 (April 1968):476-86; *A Peace Policy for Europe* (New York: Holt, Rinehart & Winston, 1969).

41. On Brandt's concept of a European order of peace, see his radio interview with

Deutschlandfunk, July 2, 1967, reprinted in *Bulletin*, July 4, 1967, pp. 604-67; and his interview with *Sonntagsblatt*, February 14, 1968, reprinted in *Bulletin*, February 16, 1968, pp. 165-67. Also see his address to the Consultative Assembly of the Council of Europe in Strasbourg, January 24, 1967, *Bulletin*, January 26, 1967, pp. 59-61.

42. See Kiesinger's government policy statement to the Bundestag, December 13, 1966; also see Georg Ferdinand Duckwitz, "Gewaltverzicht und Interventionsrecht," *Aussenpolitik*, 19 (1968): 519-36.

43. See draft declaration on renunciation of force, February 7, 1967, *Dokumentation zum Gewaltverzicht* (Bonn: Auswärtiges Amt, 1968), p. 2. Most documents regarding the German-Soviet exchange on renunciation of force—except this one—are reprinted in *Die Politik des Gewaltverzichtes. Eine Dokumentation der deutschen und sowjetischen Erklärungen zum Gewaltverzicht, 1949 bis Juli 1968* (Engl.: *The Policy of Renunciation of Force: Documents on German and Soviet Declarations on the Renunciation of Force, 1949 to July 1968*). (Bonn: Press and Information Office, 1968); and, more selectively, in *Documents on Germany*.

44. "Statement of the Soviet Union to the Federal Republic of Germany Concerning Negotiations for a Treaty on the Renunciation of the Use of Force," October 12, 1967, *The Policy of Renunciation of Force*, pp. 7-8; "Memorandum From the Soviet Union to the Federal Republic of Germany Commenting on West German Draft Declarations on the Renunciation of the Use of Force," November 21, 1967, with two annexes, ibid., pp. 9-16 (here p. 9).

45. See Duckwitz, "Gewaltverzicht und Interventionsrecht," p. 523.

46. See remarks by Foreign Minister Brandt in the defense debate of the Bundestag, December 7, 1967, DBT/V/141, pp. 7229-33.

47. See "Statement from the Soviet Union to the Federal Republic of Germany," December 8, 1967, *The Policy of Renunciation of Force*, pp. 17-23; also see the parallel "Statement from the Soviet Union to the United States Alleging an Increase in Militarism and Neo-Nazism in West Germany," December 8, 1967, *Documents on Germany*, pp. 743-48.

48. See "Aide-mémoire from the Federal Republic of Germany to the Soviet Union," December 14, 1967, *The Policy of Renunciation of Force*, pp. 23-25. See aide-mémoire from the Federal Republic of Germany to the Soviet Union, December 14, 1967, and note from the Federal Republic of Germany to the Soviet Union, December 22, ibid., pp. 23-25.

49. See "Note from the Federal Republic of Germany to the Soviet Union in Reply to the Soviet Memoranda of October 12 and November 21, 1968," April 9, 1968, ibid., pp. 28-33.

50. See "Aide-mémoire from the Soviet Union to the Federal Republic of Germany," July 5, 1968, ibid., pp. 36-46.

51. See German note of April 9, 1968 and reply by the Bonn government upon an parliamentary inquiry concerning foreign policy and the debate on this inquiry on June 20, 1968, DBT/V/180, pp. 9702-25; also see speech by Foreign Minister Brandt at the NATO Ministerial Meeting in Reykjavik, June 24, 1968, *The Policy of Renunciation of Force*, pp. 35-36.

52. See Hans Ulrich Behn, "Chronik und Dokumente zum Vertrag mit Polen," in *Der Vertrag zwischen der Bundesrepublik Deutschland und der Volksrepublik Polen* (Engl.: *The Treaty Between the Federal Republic of Germany and the People's Republic of Poland*) (Bonn: Press and Information Office, 1971), pp. 103-249. Also see interview by Polish Foreign Minister Rapacki with *Trybuna Ludu*, January 7, 1968; and address by Foreign Minister Brandt to the Rhein-Ruhr Club in Düsseldorf, November 11, 1968, *Bulletin*, November 16, 1968, p. 38.

53. See Malcolm Mackintosh, "Die Sowjetunion und die europäische Sicherheit," *Europa-Archiv* 23 (1968):201-10; also see Richard Loewenthal, "The Sparrow in the Cage," *Problems of Communism*, 17 (November-December 1968):2-28. Duckwitz points out

that Moscow has used the dialogue with Bonn also to strengthen the cohesion of the Eastern bloc; see "Gewaltverzicht und Interventionsrecht," pp. 525-26.

54. On the initial position of the Grand Coalition, see Kiesinger's statement to the Bundestag, December 13, 1966; on the compromise reached, see address by Foreign Minister Brandt to the Foreign Correspondents' Club in Tokyo, May 11, 1967, *Bulletin*, May 17, 1967, p. 436.

55. Report by the government on "The State of the Nation in Divided Germany," March 11, 1968, DBT/V/158, pp. 8168-76.

56. See speech by Foreign Minister Brandt at the NATO Ministerial Meeting in Reykjavik, June 24, 1968.

57. In February 1967 the Warsaw Treaty member states agreed—under pressure from the GDR and the Soviet Union—on a common policy toward the Federal Republic. See Thomas S. Wolfe, *Soviet Power and Europe 1945-1970* (Baltimore: Johns Hopkins, 1970), p. 348 ff.

58. See Soviet statement to the Federal Republic, October 12, 1967, p. 7.

59. See speech by Chancellor Kiesinger in the Bundestag, April 25, 1969, DBT/V/229, pp. 12663-66.

60. See "Soviet Draft Declaration on the Use of Force in Relations with the Federal Republic of Germany," November 21, 1967, *Documents on Germany*, pp. 742-43. The Soviet Union has used the so-called "enemy states clauses" of the UN Charter for exerting political pressure on the Federal Republic, e.g., in connection with the talks on renunciation of force and Bonn's reluctance to sign the Non-proliferation Treaty. On Bonn's position, see Auswärtiges Amt, ed. *Die Auswärtige Politik der Bundesrepublik Deutschland* (Cologne: Wissenschaft und Politik, 1972) pp. 677-78; on the connection between the "enemy states clauses" and German *Ostpolitik*, see Knud Krakau, *Feindstaatenklauseln und Rechtslage Deutschlands nach den Ostverträgen* (Frankfurt: Alfred Metzner, 1975).

61. See Dietrich Frenzke, "Gewaltverzicht und Feindstaatenklauseln," *Europa-Archiv* 25 (1970):49-58. On the Soviet line of argumentation, see *The Policy of Renunciation of Force*. Moscow's claim to have a chartered right to intervene in German domestic affairs gained some appearance of plausibility with the reemergence of a neo-fascist movement in the Federal Republic. In the late 1960s, the National Democratic Party not only made headlines but also won enough votes to gain seats in a number of *länder* legislatures.

62. See statement by the Foreign Office, May 14, 1969, reprinted in *Die Auswärtige Politik der Bundesrepublic Deutschland*, pp. 677-678. In September 1968, upon Bonn's request, the three Western powers repeated their assurances originally given in connection with the Paris and Bonn Treaties of 1954 that their relationship with the Federal Republic would be guided solely by Article 2 of the UN Charter, and not by recourse to Articles 53 and 107. They repeated these assurances again when Bonn signed the Non-proliferation Treaty in 1969; see *Bulletin*, November 29, 1969, p. 1236. In the course of the negotiation on the German-Soviet Treaty of 1970, the Soviet Union issued similar assurances to Bonn.

63. See "Final Document of the Conference of Non-Nuclear-Weapon States: Measures to Assure the Security of Non-Nuclear-Weapon States (Resolution A)," *Documents on Disarmament 1968*, pp. 671-72; also see statement by Foreign Minister Brandt at this conference, September 3, 1968, *Europa-Archiv* 23 (1968):502-6.

64. See statement by Ambassador Bahr on the *German Television*, September 4, 1967, cited in Schwarzkopf, "Die Idee des Gewaltverzichts," p . 899.

65. See remarks by the chairman of the CDU/CSU parliamentary group, Rainer Barzel, at the Bundestag, February 1, 1967, DBT/V/90, pp. 4170-72.

66. Heinz Murmann, "Ein Jahr der aussenpolitischen Dürre," *Handelsblatt*, May 9, 1968.

67. Most visible was the change of direction within the FDP in its German policy. Prominent members of the FDP (Mischnik, Schollwer, Rubin) urged for a de facto recognition of the GDR and a normalization of relations with the other Eastern European states. See *Deutschlandpolitik der F.D.P.: Daten und Dokumente von 1945 bis heute* (Bonn: Bundesgeschäftsstelle der FDP, 1972). A parallel development was the resignation of Erich Mende and the election of Walter Scheel as party chairman in April 1967.

68. See address by Assistant Secretary of State Nicholas Katzenbach to the Assembly of the Western European Union, October 16, 1968, *U.S. Department of State Bulletin*, November 11, 1968, pp. 489-93.

69. See Sanne, "Zur Vorgeschichte des Vertrages," p. 79. Also see Günther Schmid, *Entscheidung in Bonn: Die Entstehung der Ost- und Deutschlandpolitik 1969/70* (Cologne: Wissenschaft und Politik, 1979), p. 174.

70. See interview by Foreign Minister Brandt with *German International*, July 31, 1969, reprinted in *Bulletin*, August 5, 1969, pp. 865-67. In turn, Bonn used the Soviet desire to have an all-European security conference convened to further its German policy; see Helga Haftendorn, *Sicherheit und Entspannung. Zur Aussenpolitik der Bundesrepublik Deutschland 1955-1982* (Baden-Baden: Nomos, 1983), p. 413 ff.

71. See Otto Wolff von Amerongen, "Aspects of German Trade With the East," *Aussenpolitik*, 21 (1970):83-89. Also see Stent, *From Embargo to Ostpolitik*, pp. 173-76.

72. See statement by Chancellor Brandt in the Bundestag, October 28, 1969, DBT/VI/5, pp. 20-34, extracts on Germany and European security are reprinted in *Documents on Germany*, pp. 815-16.

73. Foreign Minister Scheel, "Die deutsche Politik des Gewaltverzichts," *Frankfurter Allgemeine Zeitung*, July 15, 1970.

74. Statement by Chancellor Brandt in the Bundestag, October 28, 1969, p. 21. Also see report by Chancellor Brandt on "The State of the Nation," January 14, 1970, DBT/VI/22, pp. 839-47; extracts reprinted in *Documents on Germany*, pp. 824-29. Bonn knew that it didn't have much time, as a number of third world countries were intent on establishing diplomatic relation with the GDR.

75. On the various rounds of talks and negotiations see Schmid, *Entscheidung in Bonn*. On the genesis of Ostpolitik see Richard Löwenthal, "Vom Kalten Krieg zur Ostpolitik," in *Die zweite Republik: 25 Jahre Bundesrepublik Deutschland—Eine Bilanz*, ed. by Richard Löwenthal and Hans-Peter Schwarz (Stuttgart: Seewald, 1974), pp. 604-99; William E. Griffith, *The Ostpolitik of the Federal Republic of Germany* (Cambridge, Mass.: MIT Press, 1978).

76. Henry Kissinger, *White House Years* (Boston: Little, Brown, 1979), pp. 423-24.

77. See declaration and communiqué of the North Atlantic Council, December 5, 1969, *Texts of Final Communiqués 1949-1974* (Brussels: NATO Information Service, 1975), pp. 226-32; communiqué of the meeting of the North Atlantic Council in Rome, May 27, 1970, ibid., pp. 233-37.

78. The Group of Four was initiated by the U.S. administration in February 1957 to coordinate Western policy on Germany, and to give the Federal Republic a role in these deliberations. Its first task was to prepare a study on the problem of German reunification and its relationship to European security. During the Berlin crisis of 1958-61 it became known as "Berlin Contingency Group"; it was charged with coordinating the Western responses to Soviet actions, and to prepare the 1959 Geneva Foreign Ministers Conference as well as the abortive 1960 Paris Summit Conference. In 1961-62 it was plagued by a series of leaks which reduced the effectiveness of this group for a frank exchange of views and it ceased to meet on a regular basis. In its place a very similar mechanism evolved in Bonn, the so-called Bonn Group. Its members are the director of the political division in the German Foreign Office and the ambassadors or ministers of the

U.S., Great Britain, and France as the three powers with rights and responsibilities pertaining to Germany as a whole and to Berlin. During the negotiations on the Eastern treaties and on the Quadripartite Agreement on Berlin, this group often met daily to coordinate Western policy on Germany. It also dealt with issues on the agenda of the CSCE in Helsinki and Geneva, even with questions of East-West trade. In some respects this group had become a kind of steering committee within the Atlantic alliance on issues of East-West relations. It should not be overlooked, however, that the dividing line between consultation and information is very narrow. It has been up to the consulting country to decide to which degree it invited the consulted countries to participate in the process of decision-making. This has been no different in the Bonn Group, hence the controversy between Schmid and Kissinger to what degree Bonn had consulted its allies during the negotiations on the treaties with the Soviet Union and Poland in 1969 and 1970, see Schmid, *Entscheidung in Bonn*, p. 28 ff. and p. 251 ff.; and Kissinger, *White House Years*, p. 530 ff.

79. Interview of Secretary of State Egon Bahr by Günter Gaus on *Second German Television*, cited in Schmid, *Entscheidung in Bonn*, p. 48. Also see Gerhard Wettig, *Europäische Sicherheit: Das Europäische Staatensystem in der sowjetischen Aussenpolitik 1966-1972* (Düsseldorf: Bertelsmann, 1972), p. 101 ff.

80. This phrase was first used in the so-called Bahr Paper and later in the Moscow Treaty; see *Der Vertrag vom 12. August 1970*, p. 15 and pp. 7-8.

81. Given the intense domestic opposition, the Eastern policy of the Social-Liberal coalition was also plagued by a series of press leaks, especially by the Springer papers *Bild* and *Welt* as well as the magazine *Quick*. Both the Bahr paper and parts of the records of his talks with Falin and Gromyko were published to fuel the domestic debate. See details in Schmid, *Entscheidung in Bonn*, p. 366.

82. See "Bahr Paper," *Documents on Germany*, pp. 862-64, August 12, 1970. Also see Benno Zündorf (pseudonym), *Die Ostverträge. Die Verträge von Moskau, Warschau, Prag, das Berlin-Abkommen und die Verträge mit der DDR* (Munich: C.H. Beck, 1979), p. 27 ff.

83. Löwenthal, "Vom Kalten Krieg zur Ostpolitik," pp. 683-84.

84. These charges have been made, e.g., by Bonn's then-ambassador in Moscow, Helmut Allardt; see his *Moskauer Tagebuch: Beobachtungen, Notizen, Erlebnisse* (Düsseldorf: Econ, 1973), p. 280 ff. and 336 ff.

85. See Schmid, *Entscheidung in Bonn*, p. 34 ff.

86. See parliamentary inquiry by the CDU/CSU regarding policy on Germany, Eastern Europe, and European integration, April 27, 1970; the reply by the federal government, May 6, 1970; and the debate on both in the Bundestag, May 27 and June 17, 1970, DBT/VI/53, pp. 2665-2730, and DBT/VI/59, pp. 3219-52.

87. "Six-Point Declaration Setting Forth Guidelines for the Negotiation of the Treaty Between the Federal Republic of Germany and the Soviet Union," June 7, 1970, *Documents on Germany*, pp. 859-60.

88. See *Der Vertrag vom 12. August 1970*. The main documents: the treaty itself; an exchange of notes between the Federal Republic of Germany and the three Western powers, acknowledging quadripartite rights with regard to Germany and Berlin, August 7, 1970, and letter from the Federal Republic of Germany to the Soviet Union regarding German reunification, August 12, 1970, are reprinted in *Documents on Germany*, pp. 861-66.

89. Television address by Chancellor Brandt from Moscow, August 12, 1970, *Der Vertrag vom 12. August 1970*, p. 28. Also see statement by Chancellor Brandt at the Bundestag, September 18, 1970, DBT/VI/66, pp. 3632-33.

90. This phrase has been first used by Willy Brandt in his speech at the 1968 Nuremberg SPD party convention, cited in Behn, "Chronik und Dokumente zum Vertrag mit

der Volksrepublik Polen," p. 157. For the negotiations on the German-Polish treaty, also see Schmid, *Entscheidung in Bonn*, p. 97 ff.

91. Thilo Vogelsang, *Das geteilte Deutschland* (Munich: Deutscher Taschenbuch Verlag 1975⁶), p. 364. This phrase had been modeled after a similar sentence in the Görlitz Agreement between the GDR and Poland, July 6, 1950; see *Der Vertrag zwischen der Bundesrepublik Deutschland und der Volksrepublik Polen*, p. 109.

92. Chancellor Brandt in a statement before the Bundestag, April 29, 1970, DBT/VI/48, pp. 2417-18.

93. See *Der Vertrag zwischen der Bundesrepublik Deutschland und der Volksrepublik Polen*. The main documents: the treaty itself; a communiqué issued at the conclusion of talks between the two countries, December 8, 1970; an exchange of notes between the Federal Republic of Germany and the three Western powers, acknowledging quadripartite rights and responsibilities in the "Known Treaties and Agreements," November 19, 1970; and "Communication from the Government of Poland to the Government of the Federal Republic of Germany Regarding Certain Persons Wishing to Leave Poland for Either of the Two German States," November 20, 1970, are reprinted in *Documents on Germany*, pp. 884-86 and 872-73.

94. See Willy Brandt, *Begegnungen und Einsichten: Die Jahre 1960-1975* (Hamburg: Hoffmann & Campe, 1976), p. 383; for President de Gaulle's address to the Polish Sejm, see *Le Monde*, September 12, 1967.

95. See below, pp. 232–236. Also see Christian Hacke, *Die Ostpolitik der CDU/CSU: Wege und Irrwege der Opposition seit 1969* (Cologne: Wissenschaft und Politik, 1975).

96. The various agreements, arrangements, protocols, and letters are reprinted in *Documentation Relating to the Federal Government's Policy of Detente* (Bonn: Press and Information Office, 1978), pp. 40-66. Also see Helga Haftendorn, "Ostpolitik Revisited 1976," *The World Today*, 32 (June 1976):222-29. On the domestic debate on these agreements see Joachim Krause, "Aussenpolitische Opposition im und über den Bundesrat," *Zeitschrift für Parlamentsfragen*, 11 (1980):423-40.

97. Statement by Chancellor Kiesinger to the Bundestag, December 13, 1966, DBT/V/80, p. 3662.

98. See "Treaty on Mutual Relations Between the Federal Republic of Germany and the Czechoslovak Socialist Republic," December 11, 1973, *Documentation Relating to Detente*, pp. 67-69. On the history of this treaty see Zündorf, *Die Ostverträge*, pp. 96-97.

99. However, in the preamble it was stated that "the Munich Agreement of 29 September 1938 was imposed on the Czechoslovak Republic by the National Socialist regime under the threat of force," *Documentation Relating to Detente*, p. 67.

100. Ibid., p. 83.

101. *Der Vertrag vom 12. August 1970*, p. 167.

102. See remarks by President Nixon at the Siemens Factory in Berlin, February 27, 1969, *Documents on Germany*, pp. 799-801; address by Foreign Minister Gromyko to the Supreme Soviet of the USSR, extracts regarding Germany and Europe, July 10, 1969, ibid., pp. 812-13; statement by the Department of State announcing quadripartite talks on Berlin, February 27, 1970, ibid., p. 834. On the history of the negotiations on Berlin see "Der geschichtliche Hintergrund," *Die Berlin Regelung: Das Viermächte—Abkommen über Berlin und die ergänzenden Vereinbarungen* (Engl.: *The Quadripartite Agreement on Berlin of September 3, 1971*), (Bonn: Press and Information Office, 1971), pp. 211-60; also see Dennis L. Bark, *Agreement on Berlin: A Study of the 1970-72 Quadripartite Negotiations* (Washington: American Enterprise Institute, 1974).

103. See Kissinger, *White House Years*, p. 405 ff. and p. 529 ff.

104. On the negotiating procedures, see ibid., pp. 534, 807 ff. and 825 ff.; as well as interview by Ambassador Kenneth Rush on *German Television*, March 26, 1980 (mimeo.).

Also see John P. Leacocos, "Kissinger's Apparat," *Foreign Policy* (Winter 1971-72): 3-27.

105. Schütz is cited in Zündorf, *Die Ostverträge*, p. 117; Kennedy's radio and television address of July 25, 1961, in *Public Papers of the Presidents. John F. Kennedy, 1961* (Washington: Government Printing Office, 1962), pp. 533-40 (here p. 533). Also see Joseph W. Bishop, Jr., "The Origin and Nature of the Rights of the Western Allies in Berlin," in *West Berlin: The Legal Context*, ed. by Roland J. Stanger (Columbus: Ohio State University Press, 1966), pp. 23-51.

106. See Kissinger, *White House Years*, p. 823 ff. On the quadripartite negotiations, also see Honoré M. Catudal, Jr., *The Diplomacy of the Quadripartite Agreement on Berlin: A New Era in East-West Politics* (Berlin: Berlin Verlag, 1978); Erich Vogt, *Berlin and the Four-Power Negotiations in the Nixon Administration 1969-1971* (Berlin: Phil. diss., 1978).

107. Egon Bahr, "In Verantwortung für Deutschland," address commemorating the August 13, 1961, Berlin, August 13, 1981 (mimeo.).

108. For the German text of the Quadripartite Agreement on Berlin see *Die Berlin-Regelung*, pp. 157-60; for the English text, see ibid., pp. 329-32; for the GDR version, see Ministerium für Auswärtige Angelegenheiten der DDR/Ministerium für Auswärtige Angelegenheiten der UdSSR, ed. *Das Vierseitige Abkommen über Westberlin und seine Realisierung: Dokumente 1971-1977* (Berlin: Staatsverlag der DDR, 1978), pp. 44-47.

109. See "Agreement between the Government of the Federal Republic of Germany and the Government of the German Democratic Republic on Transit Traffic of Civilian Persons and Goods between the Federal Republic of Germany and Berlin (West)," December 17, 1971, *Documentation Relating to Detente*, pp. 111-14; "Arrangement between the Senat and the Government of the German Democratic Republic on the Regulation of the Enclaves Question by Exchange of Territory," December 20, 1971, ibid., pp. 137-45; "Arrangement between the Senat and the Government of the German Democratic Republic Concerning the Inclusion of the Territory of the Former Potsdam Railway Station in the Arrangement of 20 December on the Regulation of the Enclaves Question by Exchange of Territory," July 21, 1972, ibid., pp. 148-49.

110. See Jost Delbrück, "Die staatsrechtliche Stellung Berlins in der Rechtsprechung des Bundesverfassungsgerichts und der Bundesgerichte," in: *Ostverträge—Berlin-Status—Münchner Abkommen—Beziehungen zwischen der BRD und der DDR*, ed. by Institut für Internationales Recht an der Universität Kiel (Hamburg: Hansischer Gildenverlag, 1971), pp. 214-20.

111. This formula had been agreed upon by State Secretaries Frank and Falin in the summer of 1972. It reads: "This agreement shall, consistent with the Quadripartite Agreement of 3 September 1971, be extended to Berlin (West) in accordance with established procedures." See "Exchange of Letters on the Extension of Art. II and V of the German-Czech Treaty to Berlin (West)," *Documentation Relating to Detente*, pp. 70-71.

112. On the problems of the realization of the Berlin Agreement, see Günther van Well, "Die Teilnahme Berlins am internationalen Geschehen: Ein dringender Punkt auf der Ost-West-Tagesordnung," *Europa-Archiv*, 31:647-56; also see the GDR and Soviet position in *Das Vierseitige Abkommen über Westberlin und seine Realisierung*. The so-called Petersberg Formula on the "strict observance and full application of the agreement" had been agreed to during the visit of General Secretary Brezhnev to Bonn; see joint communiqué on this visit, May 22, 1973, *Current Digest of the Soviet Press*, June 13, 1973; S. 8-9 and 36.

113. See Manfred Görtemaker, *Die unheilige Allianz: Die Geschichte der Entspannungspolitik 1943-1979* (Munich: C.H. Beck, 1979), p. 111. For an evaluation of the Berlin Agreement, also see Honoré M. Catudal, *A Balance Sheet of the Quadripartite Agreement on Berlin: Evaluation and Documentation* (Berlin: Berlin Verlag, 1978); Günther Doeker et al., "Berlin

and the Quadripartite Agreement of 1971," *American Journal of International Law*, 67 (January 1973):44-62; Dieter M. Mahncke, "The Berlin Agreement: Balance and Prospects," *The World Today*, 27 (December 1971):511-21.

114. See statement by Chancellor Brandt to the Bundestag, October 28, 1969, DBT/VI/5, p. 21.

115. See Bahr's presentation at Tutzing, July 15, 1963, in *Die Deutsche Ostpolitik 1961-1970*, p. 48.

116. Foreign Minister Scheel in an interview with the wire service, *Associated Press*, October 31, 1969, reprinted in *Texte zur Deutschlandpolitik*, (Bonn: Innerdeutsches Ministerium, 1970), vol. 4, pp. 53-58 (here p. 57). The same line of argument is to be found in the Foreign Office circular. In an allusion to the Hallstein Doctrine, it has been called the "Scheel doctrine." Its contents had been leaked to the press, see *Die Welt*, November 6, 1969. Also see Günther Schmid, *Die Deutschlandpolitik der Regierung Brandt/Scheel* (Munich: tuduv, 1975), p. 73.

117. See letter from Chairman Ulbricht to President Heinemann transmitting a "Draft Treaty Concerning the Establishment of Equal Relations Between the German Democratic Republic and the Federal Republic of Germany," December 18, 1969, *Documents on Germany*, pp. 821-23.

118. See Brandt's "Report on the State of the Nation" to the Bundestag, January 14, 1970, DBT/VI/22, pp. 839-47, extracts reprinted in *Documents on Germany*, pp. 824-29.

119. See news conference remarks by Chairman Ulbricht in Berlin on negotiation of a treaty establishing equal relations with the Federal Republic, January 19, 1970, *Neues Deutschland*, January 20, 1970, extracts reprinted in *Documents on Germany*, pp. 829-32.

120. See letter from Chancellor Brandt to Minister-President Stoph proposing negotiations for an exchange of declarations renouncing the use of force, January 22, 1970; reply by Minister-President Stoph to Chancellor Brandt proposing immediate negotiations on normalization of relations, February 12, 1970; reply by Chancellor Brandt to Minister-President Stoph proposing a meeting to discuss the necessary technical preparations for negotiations, February 18, 1970, *Documents on Germany*, pp. 832-34.

121. For the statements by Minister-President Stoph and Chancellor Brandt at their meeting in Erfurt, March 19, 1970, see *Documents on Germany*, pp. 835-44. Brandt reported on this meeting to the Bundestag on March 20, 1970, see DBT/VI/41, pp. 2089-2091; Stoph one day later to the Volkskammer, see *Texte zur Deutschlandpolitik*, vol. 4, pp. 371-83. The meeting in Erfurt became a highly emotional affair with a huge crowd cheering the West German chancellor. The events demonstrated to a wide television public that personal relations between the representatives of the two German states were possible after all.

122. For the statements by Chancellor Brandt and Minister-President Stoph at their meeting in Kassel, May 21, 1970, see *Documents on Germany*, pp. 848-56. Brandt's "Twenty Points on Relations on the Basis of Equality Between the FRG and the GDR" are part of Brandt's opening statement at Kassel, ibid., pp. 849-51. They were derived from point six of the Bahr Paper.

123. See the exchange of letters between Minister-President Stoph and Berlin Governing Mayor Schütz, February 24 and 25, 1970, *Texte zur Deutschlandpolitik*, vol. 8, pp. 80-82. Concerned about an evolving intra-German dynamic, Kissinger sent a cautioning message to Bahr via the back channel, see Kissinger, *White House Years*, p. 825.

124. For the intra-German arrangements implementing the Quadripartite Agreement on Berlin see *Documentation Relating to Detente*, pp. 111-49. For an evaluation see Zündorf, *Die Ostverträge*, p. 184ff.

125. See news conference remarks by Chairman Ulbricht, January 19, 1970.

126. See address by First Secretary Erich Honecker to a National People's Army Audience on Rügen, January 6, 1972, *Neues Deutschland*, January 7, 1972.

127. See "Treaty between the Federal Republic of Germany and the German Democratic Republic on Traffic Questions," May 26, 1972, *Documents Relating to Detente*, pp. 159-74; and statements by both sides on signing this treaty, May 26, 1972, ibid., pp. 175-77. For an evaluation see Zündorf, *Die Ostverträge*, p. 202ff.

128. For First Secretary Honecker's speech in Sofia, April 18, 1972, see *Neues Deutschland*, April 19, 1972. This phrase has been coined the "Sofia formula." Also see interview of Honecker with the East German news agency ADN, *Neues Deutschland*, June 7, 1972.

129. See above, pp. 220-22. also see Zündorf, *Die Ostverträge*, p. 214ff.

130. Chancellor Brandt in an interview with *Der Spiegel*, April 20, 1970, p. 46.

131. See above, pp. 224-25.

132. For an overview of the positions taken by both sides, see *Texte zur Deutschlandpolitik*, vol. 11; also see Zündorf, *Die Ostverträge*, p. 211ff.

133. See "Treaty on the Basis of Relations between the Federal Republic of Germany and the German Democratic Republic, with Annexes," December 21, 1972, *Documentation Relating to Detente*, pp. 178-204.

134. See statement by the Foreign Office in Bonn, November 9, 1972, *Texte zur Deutschlandpolitik*, vol. 11, p. 325.

135. See "Letter on German Unity", December 21, 1972, *Documentation Relating to Detente*, p. 182.

136. See statement by Chancellor Brandt at a press conference in Bonn, November 9, 1972, *Texte zur Deutschlandpolitik*, vol. 11, pp. 320-24; also see "Erläuterungen zum Vertrag," ibid., pp. 302-5.

137. See resolution by CDU/CSU parliamentary group after deliberating the Basic Treaty, *Texte zur Deutschlandpolitik*, vol. 11, pp. 378-79. Also see *The Times*, December 20 and 21, 1972.

138. See interview of First Secretary Honecker with New York *Times*, November 25, 1972; and his closing address to the eighth meeting of the Central Committee of the SED, December 7, 1972, *Neues Deutschland*, December 8, 1972.

139. Statement by Foreign Minister Scheel on the day of the initialing of the Basic Treaty, November 7, 1972, *Texte zur Deutschlandpolitik*, vol. 11, p. 263-64.

140. See Zürdorf, Die Ostverträge, pp. 217-18; also see Karl E. Birnbaum, *East and West Germany: A Modus Vivendi* (Lexington, Mass.: Lexington Books, 1973; Wilhelm A. Kewenig, "Die Bedeutung des Grundvertrages für das Verhältnis der beiden deutschen Staaten," *Europa-Archiv*, 28 (1973):37-46; Wolfgang Wagner, "A Modus Vivendi in Germany," *German Tribune Quarterly Review*, March 22, 1973.

141. See "Grosse Anfrage der CDU/CSU-Fraktion zur Deutschland-, Ost- und Entspannungspolitik," April 27, 1970; the reply by the government, May 6, 1970; and the debate in the Bundestag on both, May 27, 1970, DBT/VI/53, pp. 2665-2730.

142. Resolution by parliamentary group and executive board of the CDU/CSU, August 27, 1970, cited in Hacke, *Die Ost- und Deutschlandpolitik der CDU/CSU*, pp. 36-37. Within the CDU Hacke differentiates between five foreign policy lines: a progressive line with Kiep and von Weizsäcker; an undecided line, for which Barzel stands; a center line with Gerhard Schröder, the former foreign minister; a conservative line with Dregger and the representatives of the expellees; and the CSU line. Ibid., pp. 75-76.

143. Letter from the chairman of the CDU/CSU parliamentary group, Rainer Barzel, to Chancellor Brandt on European policy, August 10, 1970, *Texte zur Deutschlandpolitik*, vol. 6, pp. 81-82.

144. See motion submitted by the CDU/CSU on "Beziehungen der Bundesrepublik

Deutschland und der Volksrepublik Polen," DBT/VI, calendar 6/1523, December 4, 1970. Also see resolution by CDU/CSU parliamentary group, October 15, 1970, *Texte zur Deutschlandpolitik*, vol. 6, pp. 164-65. For a vehement critique of the German Polish Treaty, see interview by the President of the Federation of Expellees, Czaja, with *Der Spiegel*, May 4, 1970, pp. 30-31.

145. On the increasing support for Ostpolitik, see Gebhard L. Schweigler, *National Consciousness in Divided Germany* (Beverly Hills, Calif.: Safe, 1975), p. 144ff.; for various pertinent public opinion polls see Elisabeth Noelle-Neumann, *The Germans: Public Opinion Polls 1967-1980* (Westport, Conn.: Greenwood Press, 1981), p. 119ff.

146. On the debate within the CDU/CSU parliamentary group and the positions taken, see Hacke, *Die Ost- und Deutschlandpolitik der CDU/CSU*, p. 46ff.

147. See address by Soviet Foreign Minister Gromyko before both houses of the Supreme Soviet on the occasion of the ratification of the Moscow Treaty, April 4, 1972, *Current Digest of the Soviet Press*, 44 (June 28, 1972): 11-12.

148. See *Die Welt*, April 18, 1972; *Quick*, April 26, 1972; also see (with a pro-bias), *Der Spiegel*, April 17, 1972, p. 21ff.; *Der Spiegel*, April 24, 1972, pp. 21-22.

149. See "Declaration of the Bundestag Setting Out the Mutual Position of the Parliamentary Groups on Foreign Policy and Inner German Relations," May 17, 1972, *Documentation Relating to Detente*, pp. 294-96.

150. On the legislative history of the Eastern treaties, see *Texte zur Deutschlandpolitik*, vol. 10.

151. See statement by the CDU/CSU foreign policy spokesman, Werner Marx, in the debate on ratification of the German-Czech Treaty, June 20, 1974, DBT/VII/110, p. 7453ff. Also see Hacke, *Die Ost- und Deutschlandpolitik der CDU/CSU*, p. 101ff.

152. See Krause, "Aussenpolitische Opposition im und über den Bundesrat."

153. Rolf Zundel, "Was sie früher sagten: CDU-Masstäbe für ein Berlin-Abkommen," *Die Zeit*, September 3, 1971.

154. Rolf Zundel, "Wohin will Barzel führen? Die Union vor der Wahl," *Die Zeit*, September 3, 1971. On the debate within the CDU/CSU parliamentary group on the Quadripartite Agreement and the positions taken, see Hacke, *Die Ost- und Deutschlandpolitik der CDU/CSU*, p. 41ff.

155. See press conference remarks by Chancellor Brandt in Bonn, November 9, 1972, *Texte zur Deutschlandpolitik*, vol. 11, pp. 320-21; also see address by Chancellor Brandt at the Dortmund SPD Convention, October 12, 1972, ibid., pp. 213-21; and address by Foreign Minister Scheel at the Freiburg FDP party convention, October 23, 1972, ibid., pp. 254-55.

156. See statement by the vice-chairman of the CDU, Schröder, at the Wiesbaden CDU party convention, October 10, 1972, and press conference remarks by the chairman of the CDU/CSU parliamentary group, Barzel, November 11, 1972, *Texte zur Deutschlandpolitik*, vol. 11, pp. 202-12 and 265-67.

157. See resolution of the CDU/CSU parliamentary group, December 19, 1972, *Pressemitteilung der CDU/CSU-Fraktion*, December 19, 1972; report by the Bundesrat on a bill concerning ratification of the Basic Treaty, February 2, 1973, Deutscher Bundesrat, calendar 640/72.

158. On the legislative history of the Basic Treaty, see *Texte zur Deutschlandpolitik*, vol. 12.

159. See Presse- und Informationsamt der Bundesregierung in Zusammenarbeit mit dem Bundesverfassungsgericht, ed. *Der Grundlagenvertrag vor dem Bundesverfassungsgericht* (Bonn: Presse- und Informationsamt der Bundesregierung, 1973), pp. 269 and 271.

160. See petition by the Bavarian State Government, May 28, 1973, *Der Grundlagenvertrag vor dem Bundesverfassungsgericht*, pp. 74-85.

161. See statement by the federal government, May 30, 1973, ibid., p. 25.

162. Decision by the Constitutional Court, July 31, 1973, ibid., pp. 383-403. Also see Rupert Dirnecker, "The Karlsruhe Decision and the Constitutionality of the Basic Treaty," in *German Unity: Documentation and Commentaries on the Basic Treaty*, ed. by Frederick W. Hess (Kansas City: Park College, Governmental Research Bureau, 1974), pp. 65-90; Wilhelm Kewenig, "Deutschlands Rechtslage heute," *Europa Archiv*, 29 (1974):71-82.

163. On the various theories of the continued existence (or demise) of the former "German Reich" and their political implications, see Rudolf Schuster, *Deutschlands staatliche Existenz im Widerstreit politischer und rechtlicher Gesichtspunkte 1945-1963* (Munich: Oldenbourg, 1963).

164. See decision by the Constitutional Court, p. 396.

165. Ibid., p. 398.

166. For a Soviet commentary on the decision of the Constitutional Court, see J. Rshewski, "Sowjetische Stellungnahme zum Grundlagenvertrag," *Meshdunarodnaja Shisn*, reprinted in *Neues Deutschland*, January 3, 1974.

167. See Egon Bahr as cited in Schmid, *Die Deutschlandpolitik der Regierung Brandt/Scheel*, p. 257.

168. These proposals by the GDR are reprinted in *Texte zur Deutschlandpolitik*, ser. 2, vol. 2, pp. 399-421. also see Dettmar Cramer, *Deutschland nach dem Grundvertrag* (Stuttgart: Bonn aktuell, 1973), for the earlier period.

169. See Deutsches Institut für Wirtschaftsforschung, ed., *DDR-Wirtschaft: Eine Bestandsaufnahme* (Frankfurt: Fischer Taschenbuch Verlag, 1974) pp. 116-118. Also see the regular reports on the GDR economy given by the same institute's *DIW-Wochenberichte*.

170. Address by Chancellor Brandt to the fifth German-French Conference of Chambers of Commerce in Hamburg, September 3, 1971, *Bundeskanzler Brandt: Reden und Interviews* (Bonn: Press- und Informationsamt der Bundesregierung, 1971), pp. 326-32 (here 327). To an even larger degree Chancellor Schmidt during his term of office has accentuated the importance of an active alliance and European policy for a successful Ostpolitik; see his "Report on the State of the Nation," January 30, 1975, DBT/VII/146, pp. 10034-41. With statements such as these the Bonn government reacted against the supposition that it was contemplating a *"renversement des alliances,"* a course directed toward a neutralization of the FRG, or even its achieving a status of subservience vis-à-vis Moscow as was alleged by Walter F. Hahn, "West Germany's Ostpolitik: The Grand Design of Egon Bahr," *Orbis*, 16 (Winter 1973):859-80; also see Hahn's *Between Westpolitik and Ostpolitik: Changing West German Security Views* (Beverly Hills, Calif.: Sage, 1957). The papers Hahn was referring to were not blueprints for a new foreign policy course of the Federal Republic, but rather analytical options drawn up in the planning staff of the Foreign Office in the late 1960s.

171. For an overview of the history of the CSCE, its proceedings, and its results, see Michael Palmer, *The Prospects for a European Security Conference* (London: Chatham House/PEP, 1971); Hans-Adolf Jacobsen, Wolfgang Mallmann, and Christian Meier, eds. *Sicherheit und Zusammenarbeit in Europa (KSZE): Analyse und Dokumentation*, 2 vols. (Cologne: Wissenschaft und Politik, 1973, 1978); Hermann Volle und Wolfgang Wagner, eds. *KSZE: Konferenz über Sicherheit und Zusammenarbeit in Europa in Beiträgen und Dokumenten aus dem Europa-Archiv* (Bonn: Verlag für Internationale Politik, 1976); Haftendorn, *Sicherheit und Entspannung*, pp. 413-516; Luigi Vittorio Ferraris, ed. *Report on a Negotiation: Helsinki—Geneva—Helsinki 1972-1975* (Leiden: Sijthoff, 1979).

172. On the concerns voiced in Paris and Washington, see Brandt, *Begegnungen und Einsichten*, pp. 347-48; Kissinger, *White House Years*, pp. 408ff. and 422ff. On Brandt's perception of an "European order of peace," see his radio interview with *Deutschlandfunk*, July 2, 1967.

173. On MBFR see above, pp. 134–135, and the references cited.

174. See Conference on Security and Cooperation in Europe: Final Act, Helsinki, 1975, *U.S. Department of State Bulletin,* Special Report, August 1975. For an evaluation, also see U.S. House of Representatives, ed. *First Semiannual Report by the President to the Commission on Security and Cooperation in Europe,* submitted to the Committee on Foreign Affairs (Washington: Government Printing Office, 1976); Stephen J. Flanagan, "The CSCE and the Development of Detente," in *European Security: Prospects for the 1980's,* ed. by Derek Leebaert (Lexington, Mass.: Lexington Books, 1979), pp. 189-232; Ferraris, *Report on a Negotiation,* p. 41ff.

175. See "The Belgrade Followup Meeting to the Conference on Security and Cooperation in Europe, October 4, 1977—March 9, 1978," *U.S. Department of State Bulletin,* Special Report, June 1978. Also see Hermann Volle and Wolfgang Wagner, *Das Belgrader KSZE Folgetreffen: Der Fortgang des Entspannungsprozesses in Europa in Beiträgen und Dokumenten aus dem Europa-Archiv* (Bonn: Verlag für Internationale Politik, 1978).

176. See Benoit d'Aboville, "Le projet de conférence Européenne sur le désarmement et l'échéance de Madrid," in *La sécurité de l'Europe dans les années 80: Les relations Est-Ouest et le théatre européen,* ed. by Pierre Lellouche (Paris: Ifri, 1980), pp. 393-403. Also see Jonathan Alford, *The Future of Arms Control: Part III. Confidence-Building Measures* (London: International Institute for Strategic Studies, 1979); F. Stephen Larrabee and Dietrich Stobbe, eds. *Confidence-Building Measures in Europe* (New York: Institute for East-West Security Studies, 1983).

177. See Concluding Document of the CSCE Review Meeting in Madrid, September 6, 1984, *U.S. Department of State Bulletin,* September 1984, pp. 28-29. Also see Nicole Gnesetto, "Conference on Disarmament in Europe opens in Stockholm," *NATO Review,* 31 (1983):1-5.

178. See, e.g., Peter Bender, *Das Ende des ideologischen Zeitalters: Die Europäisierung Europas* (Berlin: Severin & Siedler, 1981).

179. On the demise of detente, see Gebhard Schweigler, *Von Kissinger zu Carter: Entspannung im Widerstreit von Innen- und Aussenpolitik 1969-1981* (Munich and Vienna: Oldenbourg, 1982); also see Henry Kissinger's account in *Years of Upheaval* (Boston and Toronto: Little, Brown, 1982). On the resulting frictions in German-American relations when Bonn tried to keep its detente policy intact, see William E. Griffith, "Bonn and Washington: From Deterioration to Crisis?" *Orbis,* 26 (Spring 1982):117-33; Gebhard Schweigler, "Europe, America and detente," *The German Tribune,* August 29, 1982.

180. General Secretary Honecker in a speech on the occasion of the beginning of a new academic year at the SED party school in Gera, October 13, 1980, *Neues Deutschland,* October 14, 1980; also see Honecker's closing remarks at a delegates' conference in Berlin, February 15, 1981, *Neues Deutschland,* February 16, 1981. On the compulsory minimum currency exchange, see *Neues Deutschland,* October 10, 1980.

181. See joint communiqué on the visit by Chancellor Schmidt to the GDR, December 12, 1981, *Bulletin,* pp. 1033-35.

182. General Secretary Honecker in an interview with *Neues Deutschland,* December 16, 1981.

183. See Angela E. Stent, *Soviet Energy and Western Europe* (New York: Praeger, 1982); Harald Müller and Reinhard Rhode, *Osthandel oder Wirtschaftskrieg? Die USA und das Gas-Röhrengeschäft* (Frankfurt: Haag & Herchen, 1982).

184. Günter Gaus, "Die Elbe: Ein deutscher Strom, nicht Deutschlands Grenze," *Die Zeit,* January 30, 1981. With this interview, a lively debate on the state of the German nation was initiated. See the left-liberal weekly, *Die Zeit;* also see Egon Bahr, "Die nationale Frage: Das Problem der Wiedervereinigung und die Pflicht zum Frieden," *Die Zeit,* March 19, 1982; Günter Gaus, "Plädoyer für eine rationale deutsch-deutsche Politik," *Die Zeit,* June 4, 1982.

185. The necessity of a policy of detente, besides close cooperation with the alliance's partners in the West, has been acknowledged by Chancellor Kohl in his government policy statement, see DBT/IX/121, October 13, 1982, pp. 7213-29 (here p. 7225).

CHAPTER 5

1. See the announcement in July 1984 of a new credit by West German banks to the GDR, and of a visit by Party Secretary Honecker to the Federal Republic in September. Also see Jonathan Dean, "How to Lose Germany," *Foreign Policy* (Summer 1984):54-72.

2. On the Soviet-West European gas pipeline deal, see Angela E. Stent, *Soviet Energy and Western Europe* (New York: Praeger, 1982); Harald Müller and Reinhard Rode, *Osthandel oder Wirtschaftskrieg? Die USA und das Gas Röhren-Geschäft* (Frankfurt: Haag & Herchen, 1982).

3. On the demise of detente and the revitalization of containment, see Henry Kissinger, *Years of Upheaval* (Boston: Little, Brown, 1982); Gebhard Schweigler, *Von Kissinger zu Carter: Entspannung im Widerstreit von Innen- und Aussenpolitik 1969-71* (Munich and Vienna: Oldenbourg, 1982); William G. Hyland, *Soviet-American Relations: A New Cold War?* (Santa Monica, Calif.: Rand, 1981); Robert E. Osgood, "The Revitalization of Containment," *Foreign Affairs*, 60:465-502; John Lewis Gaddis, "The Rise, Fall and Future of Detente," *Foreign Affairs*, 62:354-77.

4. See Henry Kissinger, "NATO: The Next Thirty Years," *Survival*, 21 (November/December 1979):264-68; also see McGeorge Bundy, "The Future of Strategic Deterrence," ibid., pp. 268-72.

5. See address by President Reagan to the nation ("MX speech"), November 22, 1982, *The New York Times*, November 23, 1982; address to the National Press Club, November 18, 1981, *Public Papers of the Presidents of the United States*, 1981 (Washington: Government Printing Office, 1982), pp. 1062-67; to Eureka College, May 9, 1982, *U.S. Department of State Bulletin*, (June 1982):34-37.

6. See Peter Bender, *Das Ende des ideologischen Zeitalters: Die Europäisierung Europas* (Berlin: Severin & Siedler, 1981); Egon Bahr, "Europa in der Globalität," *Merkur*, 35 (August 1981):765-71.

7. See Friedrich Ruth, "Sicherheitspolitik der NATO: Abschreckung und Rüstungskontrolle," *Europa-Archiv*, 37 (1982): 135-144; John Newhouse, "Arms and Orthodoxy," *The New Yorker*, June 7, 1982.

8. See communiqué on the meeting of the NATO Council in Luxemburg, May 18, 1982, *NATO Final Communiqués* (Brussels: NATO Information Service, 1983), pp. 17-22.

9. See Helmut Schmidt, *The Balance of Power: Germany's Peace Policy and the Powers* (London: Kimber, 1971); Hans Dietrich Genscher, "Toward an Overall Western Strategy for Peace, Freedom and Progress," *Foreign Affairs*, 61 (Fall 1982):42-66.

10. Egon Bahr, "Gemeinsame Sicherheit: Gedanken zur Entschärfung der nuklearen Konfrontation in Europa," *Europa-Archiv*, 37 (1982):421-430; Günter Gaus, "Friedenspolitik für Deutschland," *Berliner Stimme*, November 12, 1981.

11. For three recent analyses of Germany's role in international affairs, see Ernst-Otto Czempiel, "Die Bundesrepublik—eine heimliche Grossmacht?" *Aus Politik und Zeitgeschichte*, June 30, 1979: pp 3-19; Fritz Stern, "Germany in a Semi-Gaullist Europe," *Foreign Affairs*, 58 (Summer 1977):867-86; Wolfram F. Hanrieder, "Germany as Number Two?" *International Studies Quarterly*, 26:57-86.

12. See Bender, *Das Ende des ideologischen Zeitalters*, p. 229.

Selected Bibliography

BIBLIOGRAPHIES

Bracher, Karl Dietrich; Jacobsen, Hans-Adolf; Tyrell, Albracht, eds. *Bibliographie zur Politik in Theorie und Praxis*. Düsseldorf: Droste, 1982.

Merritt, Anna J. and Richard L. Merritt, eds. *Politics, Economics, and Society in the Two Germanies, 1945-75: A Bibliography of English-Language Works*. Urbana: University of Illinois Press, 1978.

Bundesministerium für innerdeutsche Beziehungen, ed. *Bibliographie zur Deutschlandpolitik*, 2 vols. Frankfurt-am-Main: Alfred Metzner Verlag, 1975 and 1984.

PUBLIC DOCUMENTS

Die Auswärtige Politik der Bundesrepublik Deutschland. Ed. Auswärtiges Amt. Cologne: Wissenschaft und Politik, 1972.

Documentation Relating to the Federal Government's Policy of Detente. Bonn: Press and Information Office, 1978

Documents on Disarmament. Ed. Department of State (since 1961: Arms Control and Disarmament Agency). Washington: Government Printing Office, 1960.

Documents on Germany 1944-1970. Ed. U.S. Congress, Senate. Committee on Foreign Relations. 92nd Cong. 1st sess., 1971. Committee Print.

Dokumente zur Aussenpolitik der Regierung der Deutschen Demokratischen Republik. Berlin: Staatsverlag der DDR, 1960.

Dokumente zur Deutschlandpolitik. Ed. Bundesministerium für innerdeutsche Beziehungen. Frankfurt: Alfred Metzner, 1961ff.

NATO Final Communiqués 1979. Brussels: NATO Information Service 1980.

Texte zur Deutschlandpolitik. Bonn: Bundesministerium für gesamtdeutsche Fragen (since 1970: Bundesminister für innerdeutsche Beziehungen), 1967ff.

Texts of Final Communiqués 1949-1974. Brussels: NATO Information Service, 1975.

The North Atlantic Treaty Organization: Facts and Figures. Brussels: NATO Information Service, 1981.

The Policy of Renunciation of Force: Documents on German and Soviet Declarations on the Renunciation of Force, 1949 to July 1968. Bonn: Press and Information Office, 1968.

The Quadripartite Agreement on Berlin of September 3, 1971. Bonn: Press and Information Office, 1971.

The Treaty Between the Federal Republic of Germany and the People's Republic of Poland. Bonn: Press and Information Office, 1971.

The Treaty of August 12, 1970 Between the Federal Republic of Germany and the So-viet Socialist Republics. Bonn: Press and Information Office, 1970.

The White Paper 1970/71: The Security of the Federal Republic of Germany and the Development of the Federal Armed Forces. Ed. federal minister of defense. Bonn: Press and Information Office, 1971ff.

BOOKS AND ARTICLES

Adenauer, Konrad. *Erinnerungen,* 4 vols. Stuttgart: Deutsche Verlags-Anstalt, 1965-68. (English: Memoirs 1945-53. Chicago: Regnery, 1965. 1st vol. only).

——. *Reden 1917-1967. Eine Auswahl.* Hans-Peter Schwarz, ed. Stuttgart: Deutsche Verlags-Anstalt, 1975.

Alting von Geusau, Frans A.M., ed. *Allies in a Turbulent World: Challenges to U.S. and Western European Cooperation.* Lexington, Mass.: Lexington Books, 1982.

Andrén, Nils and Karl E. Birnbaum, eds. *Beyond Detente: Prospects for East-West Co-operation and Security in Europe.* Leyden: Sijthoff, 1976.

Ashkenasi, Abraham. *Reformpartei und Aussenpolitik: Die Aussenpolitik der SPD Berlin-Bonn.* Cologne and Opladen: Westdeutscher Verlag, 1968.

Backer, John H. *The Decision to Divide Germany: American Foreign Policy in Transition.* Durham, N.C.: Duke University Press, 1978.

Bahr, Egon. *Was wird aus den Deutschen?* Reinbek: Rowohlt, 1982.

Bandulet, Bruno. *Adenauer zwischen West und Ost. Alternativen der deutschen Aussenpolitik.* Munich: Weltforum Verlag, 1970.

Baring, Arnulf. *Aussenpolitik in Adenauers Kanzlerdemokratie: Bonns Beitrag zur Europäischen Verteidigungsgemeinschaft.* Munich and Vienna: Oldenbourg, 1969.

——. *Machtwechsel: Die Ära Brandt-Scheel.* Stuttgart: Deutsche Verlags-Anstalt, 1982.

——. *Sehr verehrter Herr Bundeskanzler! Heinrich von Brentano im Briefwechsel mit Konrad Adenauer 1949-1964.* Hamburg: Hoffmann and Campe, 1974.

Bark, Dennis L. *Agreement on Berlin: A Study of the 1970-72 Quadripartite Negotiations.* Washington: American Enterprise Institute, 1974.

Bender, Peter. *Das Ende des ideologischen Zeitalters: Die Europäisierung Europas.* Berlin: Severin & Siedler, 1981.

——. *Offensive Entspannung: Möglichkeiten für Deutschland.* Cologne: Wissenschaft und Politik, 1964.

Bertram, Christoph, ed. *The Future of Arms Control: 3 Parts.* London: The International Institute for Strategic Studies, 1978.

——. *Mutual Force Reductions in Europe: The Political Aspects.* London: The International Institute for Strategic Studies, 1972.

Besson, Waldemar. *Die Aussenpolitik der Bundesrepublik: Erfahrungen und Massstäbe.* Munich: Piper, 1970.

Birnbaum, Karl E., ed. *Arms Control in Europe: Problems and Prospects.* Laxenburg: Austrian Institute for International Affairs, 1980.

——. *East and West Germany: A Modus Vivendi.* Lexington, Mass.: Lexington Books, 1973.

——. *The Politics of East-West Communication in Europe.* Westmead, Farnborough, Hants.: Saxon House, 1979.

Bischoff, Detlef. *Franz Josef Strauss, die CSU und die Aussenpolitik.* Meisenheim-am-Glan: Hain, 1973.

Brandt, Peter and Herbert Ammon, eds. *Die Linke und die nationale Frage: Dokumente zur deutschen Einheit seit 1945.* Reinbek: Rowohlt, 1981.

Brandt, Willy. *Aussenpolitik-Deutschlandpolitik-Europapolitik: Grundsätzliche Erklärungen während des ersten Jahres im Auswärtigen Amt.* Berlin: Berlin Verlag, 1968.

——. *Begegnungen und Einsichten: Die Jahre 1960-1975.* Hamburg: Hoffmann and Campe, 1976.

——. *A Peace Policy for Europe.* New York: Holt, Rinehart and Winston, 1969.

Brzezinski, Zbigniew. *Alternative To Partition: For a Broader Conception of America's Role in Europe.* New York: McGraw-Hill, 1965.

Buczylowski, Ulrich. *Kurt Schumacher und die deutsche Frage: Sicherheitspolitik und strategische Offensivkonzeption vom August 1950 bis September 1951.* Stuttgart: Seewald Verlag, 1973.

Carstens, Karl und Dieter Mahncke, eds., *Westeuropäische Verteidigungskooperation.* Munich: Oldenbourg, 1972.

Catudal, Honoré M. *Kennedy and the Berlin Wall Crisis: A Case Study in U.S. Decision Making.* Berlin: Berlin-Verlag, 1980.

——. *A Balance Sheet of the Quadripartite Agreement on Berlin: Evaluation and Documentation.* Berlin: Berlin-Verlag, 1978.

——. *The Diplomacy of the Quadripartite Agreement on Berlin: A New Era in East-West Politics.* Berlin: Berlin-Verlag, 1978.

Coffey, Joseph I. *Arms Control and European Security: A Guide to East-West Negotiations.* London: Chatto and Windus, 1977.

Conradt, David P. *The German Polity.* New York and London: Longman, 1978.

Craig, Gordon A. *Europe Since 1815.* Alternative Edition. New York: Holt, Rinehart & Winston, 1974.

——. *Germany 1866-1945.* New York and Oxford: Oxford University Press, 1980.

DePorte, Anton W. *Europe between the Superpowers: The Enduring Balance.* New Haven & London: Yale University Press, 1979.

Deutsche Gesellschaft für Auswärtige Politik, ed. *Regionale Verflechtung der Bundesrepublik Deutschland: Empirische Analysen und theoretische Probleme.* Munich and Vienna: Oldenbourg, 1973.

Dönhoff, Marion. *Foe into Friend: The Makers of the New Germany from Adenauer to Helmut Schmidt.* London: Weidenfeld and Nicholson, 1982.

Edinger, Lewis J. *Kurt Schumacher: A Study in Personality and Political Behavior.* Stanford: Stanford University Press, 1965.

Epstein, Julius, "Die Quelle des Übels: Eine Dokumentation zur Genesis der deutsch-amerikanischen Verstimmung." *Rheinischer Merkur*, August 31, 1962.

Erler, Fritz. *Democracy in Germany.* Cambridge: Harvard University Press, 1965.

——. *Ein Volk sucht seine Sicherheit: Bemerkungen zur deutschen Sicherheitspolitik.* Frankfurt: Europäische Verlags-Anstalt, 1961.

Erler, Fritz und Richard Jäger. *Sicherheit und Rüstung: Beiträge von Fritz Erler und Richard Jäger.* Cologne: Wissenschaft und Politik, 1968.

Eschenburg, Theodor. *Jahre der Besatzung 1945-1949.* Stuttgart: Deutsche Verlags-Anstalt, 1983.

Etzold, Thomas H. and John Lewis Gaddis, eds. *Containment: Documents on American Policy and Strategy, 1945-1950.* New York: Columbia University Press, 1978.

Feld, Werner J. *The European Community in World Affairs. Economic Power and Political Influence.* Port Washington, N.Y.: Alfred Publishing, 1976.

——. ed. *Western Europe's Global Reach: Regional Cooperation and Worldwide Aspirations.* New York: Pergamon Press, 1979.

Ferraris, Vittorio, ed. *Report on a Negotiation: Helsinki-Geneva-Helsinki 1972-1975.* Leiden: Sijthoff, 1979.

Fontaine, André. *Un seul lit pour deux rêves. Histoire de la "detente" 1962-1981.* Paris: Fayard, 1981.

Forndran, Erhard. *Rüstungskontrolle: Friedenssicherung zwischen Abschreckung und Abrüstung.* Düsseldorf: Bertelsmann Universitätsverlag, 1970.

Forndran, Erhard and Paul J. Friedrich, eds. *Rüstungskonrolle und Sicherheit in Europa.* Bonn: 1979.

Fox, Willian T. R. and Warner R. Schilling, eds. *European Security and the Atlantic System.* New York and London: Columbia University Press, 1973.

Fritsch-Bournazel, Renata. *Die Sowjetunion und die deutsche Teilung: Die sowjetische Deutschlandpolitik 1945-1979.* Opladen: Westdeutscher Verlag 1979.

Gaddis, John Lewis. *Strategies of Containment: A Critical Appraisal of Postwar American Security Policy.* New York and Oxford: Oxford University Press, 1982.

Gaus, Günther. *Wo Deutschland liegt. Eine Ortsbestimmung.* Berlin: Severin and Siedler, 1983.

Goldmann, Kjell. *Detente: Domestic Politics as a Stabilizer of Foreign Policy.* Stockholm: Department of Political Science, University of Stockholm, 1984.

Görtemaker, Manfred. *Die unheilige Allianz: Die Geschichte der Entspannungspolitik 1943-1979.* Munich: C.H. Beck, 1979.

Gotto, Klaus, ed. *Konrad Adenauer: Seine Deutschland- und Aussenpolitik 1945-1963.* Munich: Deutscher Taschenbuch Verlag, 1975.

Grewe, Wilhelm. *Rückblenden. Aufzeichnungen eines Augenzeugen deutscher Aussenpolitik von Adenauer bis Schmidt.* Frankfurt-am-Main: Propyläen, 1980.

Griffith, William E. *The Ostpolitik of the Federal Republic of Germany.* Cambridge, Mass.: MIT Press, 1978.

Griffith, William E. *The Superpowers and Regional Tensions: The USSR, the United States, and Europe.* Lexington, Mass.: Lexington Books, 1982.

Grosser, Alfred. *The Western Alliance: European-American Relations Since 1945.* New York: Continuum, 1980.

Hacke, Christian. *Die Ostpolitik der CDU/CSU: Wege und Irrwege der Opposition seit 1969.* Cologne: Wissenschaft und Politik, 1975.

Haftendorn, Helga. *Sicherheit und Entspannung. Zur Aussenpolitik der Bundes-republik Deutschland 1955-1982.* Baden-Baden: Nomos, 1983.

Haftendorn, Helga et al., ed. *Verwaltete Aussenpolitik. Sicherheits- und entspan-nungspolitische Entscheidungsprozesse in Bonn.* Cologne: Wissenschaft Politik, 1978.

Hahn, Walter F. *Between Westpolitik and Ostpolitik: Changing West German Secu-rity Views.* Beverly Hills, Calif.: Sage, 1957.

Hanrieder, Wolfram F., ed. *Helmut Schmidt: Perspectives on Politics.* Boulder, Colo.: Westview, 1982.

——. *West German Foreign Policy: 1949-1979.* Boulder, Colo.: Westview, 1980.

——. *West German Foreign Policy 1949-1963: International Pressure and Domestic Response.* Stanford: Stanford University Press, 1967.

Hillenbrand, Martin J. *Germany in an Era of Transition.* Paris: The Atlantic Insti-tute for International Affairs, 1983.

Hinterhoff, Eugene. *Disengagement.* London: Stevens, 1959.

Holmes, Kim R. *The West German Peace Movement and the National Question.* Cambridge, Mass. and Washington, D.C.: Institute for Foreign Policy Analysis, 1984.

Huntington, Samuel P. *The Common Defense: Strategic Programs in National Poli-tics.* New York: Columbia University Press, 1969[3].

Jacobsen, Hans-Adolf; Wolfgang Mallmann and Christian Meier, eds. *Sicherheit und Zusammenarbeit in Europa (KSZE): Analyse und Dokumentation,* 2 vols. Cologne: Wissenschaft und Politik, 1973 and 1978.

Jansen, Thomas. *Abrüstung und Deutschland-Frage: Die Abrüstungsfrage als Prob-lem der deutschen Aussenpolitik.* Mainz: von Hase und Koehler, 1968.

Joffe, Josef. "The Foreign Policy of the German Federal Republic." Roy Macridis, ed. *Foreign Policy in World Politics.* Englewood Cliffs: Prentice-Hall, 1976, pp. 117-51.

Johnson, Nevil. *Government in the Federal Republic of Germany. The Executive at Work.* Oxford: Pergamon Press, 1973.

Kaiser, Karl. *German Foreign Policy in Transition: Bonn Between East and West.* London, Oxford, New York: Oxford University Press, 1968.

Kaiser, Karl and Markus Kreis, eds. *Sicherheitspolitik vor neuen Aufgaben.* Frank-furt: Metzner, 1977.

Kaiser, Karl and Hans-Peter Schwarz, eds. *America and Western Europe: Problems and Prospects.* Lexington, Mass.: Lexington Books, 1977.

Keliher, John G. *The Negotiations on Mutual and Balanced Force Reductions: The Search for Arms Control in Central Europe.* New York: Pergamon Press, 1980.

Kelleher, Catherine McArdle. *Germany and the Politics of Nuclear Weapons.* New York: Columbia University Press, 1975.

Kissinger, Henry. *White House Years.* Boston and Toronto: Little, Brown, 1979.

——. *Years of Upheaval.* Boston and Toronto: Little, Brown, 1982.

Kohl, Helmut, ed. *Konrad Adenauer 1876/1976.* Stuttgart und Zürich: Belser, 1976.

Kosthorst, Erich, Klaus Gotto, Hartmut Soell, eds. *Deutschlandpolitik der Nach-kriegsjahre.* Paderborn: Schöningh, 1976.

Krippendorff, Ekkehart and Rittberger, Volker, eds. *The Foreign Policy of West*

Germany: Formation and Contents. London and Beverly Hills: Sage Publications, 1980.

Leebaert, Derek, ed. *European Security: Prospects for the 1980's.* Lexington, Mass.: Lexington Books, 1979.

Legge, J. Michael. *Theater Nuclear Weapons and the NATO Strategy of Flexible Response.* Santa Monica, Calif.: Rand, 1983.

Lellouche, Pierre, ed. *La securité de l'Europe dans les années 80. Les relations Est-Ouest et le théatre européen.* Paris: Ifri, 1980.

———. *Pacifism et dissuasion: La contestation pacifiste et l'avenir de la sécurite de l'Europe.* Paris: Ifri, 1983.

Livingston, Robert Gerald, ed. *The Federal Republic of Germany in the 1980s.* New York: German Information Center, 1983.

Loewenberg, Gerhard. *Parliament in the German Political System.* Ithaca: Cornell University Press, 1966.

Löwenthal, Richard and Hans-Peter Schwarz, eds. *Die zweite Republik: 25 Jahre Bundesrepublik Deutschland—Eine Bilanz.* Stuttgart: Seewald, 1974.

Loth, Wilfried. *Die Teilung der Welt: Geschichte des Kalten Krieges 1941-1955.* Munich: Deutscher Taschenbuch Verlag, 1980.

Löwke, Udo F. *Für den Fall, dass. . .Die Haltung der SPD zur Wehrfrage 1949-1955.* Hannover: Verlag für Literatur und Zeitgeschehen, 1969.

Mahncke, Dieter. *Berlin im geteilten Deutschland.* Munich and Vienna: Oldenbourg, 1973.

———. *Nukleare Mitwirkung: Die Bundesrepublik Deutschland in der Atlantischen Allianz 1954-1970.* Berlin and New York: De Gruyter, 1972.

Mally, Gerhard, ed. *The New Europe and the United States.* Lexington, Mass.: D.C. Heath, 1974.

Markovits, Andrei S., ed. *The Political Economy of West Germany: Modell Deutschland.* New York: Praeger, 1982.

Mayntz, Renate and Scharpf, Fritz W. *Policy-Making in the German Federal Bureaucracy.* Amsterdam: Elsevier, 1975.

McGeehan, Robert. *The German Rearmament Question: American Diplomacy and European Defense After World War II.* Urbana, Ill.: University of Illinois Press, 1971.

Mechtersheimer, Alfred, ed. *Nachrüsten? Dokumente und Positionen zum NATO-Doppelbeschluss.* Reinbek: Rowohlt, 1981.

Meissner, Boris, ed. *Die deutsche Ostpolitik 1961-1970: Kontinuität und Wandel.* Cologne: Wissenschaft und Politik, 1970.

Merkl, Peter H. *The Origin of the West German Republic.* New York: Oxford University Press, 1963.

Militärgeschichtliches Forschungsamt, ed. *Verteidigung im Bündnis: Planung, Aufbau und Bewährung der Bundeswehr 1950-1972.* Munich: Bernhard and Graefe, 1975.

Moreton, Edwina N. *East Germany and the Warsaw Alliance: The Politics of Détente.* Boulder, Colo.: Westview, 1978.

Morgan, Roger. *The United States and West Germany 1945-1973: A Study in Alliance Politics.* London: Oxford University Press, 1974.

———. *West Germany's Foreign Policy Agenda.* Beverly Hills, Calif.: Sage, 1978.

Mutz, Reinhard. *Konventionelle Abrüstung in Europa: Die Bundesrepublik Deutschland und MBFR.* Baden-Baden: Nomos, 1984.

Myers, Kenneth A., ed. *NATO: The Next Thirty Years.* Boulder, Colo.: Westview, 1980.

Nerlich, Uwe, ed. *Soviet Power and Western Negotiating Policies.* 2 vols. Cambridge, Mass.: Ballinger, 1983.

Noelle-Neumann, Elisabeth. *The Germans. Public Opinion Polls 1967-1980.* Westport, Conn.: Greenwood Press, 1981.

Nolte, Ernst. *Deutschland und der Kalte Krieg.* Munich: Piper, 1974.

Olive, Marsha McGraw and Jeffrey D. Porro, eds. *Nuclear Weapons in Europe: Modernization and Limitation.* Lexington, Mass.: Lexington Books, 1983.

Osgood, Robert E. *The Case for the MLF: A Critical Evaluation.* Washington: The Washington Center of Foreign Policy Research, 1964.

———. *NATO: The Entangling Alliance.* Chicago: Chicago University Press, 1962.

Pirker, Theo. *Die SPD nach Hitler: Die Geschichte der Sozial-demokratischen Partei Deutschlands 1945-1964.* Munich: Rütten and Leoning, 1965.

Planck, Charles R. *Sicherheit in Europa: Die Vorschläge für Rüstungsbeschränkung und Abrüstung 1955-1965.* Munich: Oldenbourg, 1968.

Pöttering, Hans-Gert. *Adenauers Sicherheitspolitik 1956-63. Ein Beitrag zum deutsch-amerikanischen Verhältnis.* Düsseldorf: Droste, 1975.

Poppinga, Anneliese. *Meine Erinnerungen an Konrad Adenauer.* Munich: Deutscher Taschenbuch-Verlag. 1972.

Record, Jeffrey. *Force Reductions in Europe. Starting Over.* Cambridge, Mass. and Washington: Institute of Foreign Policy Analysis, 1980.

Richardson, James L. *Germany and the Atlantic Alliance: The Interaction of Strategy and Politics.* Cambridge: Harvard University Press, 1966.

Ruehl, Lothar. *MBFR: Lessons and Problems.* London: The International Institute for Strategic Studies, 1982.

Rupp, Hans Karl. *Ausserparlamentarische Opposition in der Ära Adenauer: Der Kampf gegen die Atombewaffnung in den fünfziger Jahren.* Cologne: Pahl Rugenstein, 1980.

Scheuner, Ulrich and Lindemann, Beate, eds. *Die Vereinten Nationen und die Mitarbeit der Bundesrepublik Deutschland.* Munich and Vienna: Oldenbourg, 1973.

Schierbaum, Hansjürgen. *Intra-German Relations: Development-Problems-Facts.* Munich: tuduv, 1979.

Schlesinger, Arthur. *A Thousand Days: John F. Kennedy in the White House.* Boston: Houghton Mifflin, 1965.

Schmid, Carlo. *Erinnerungen.* Bern, Munich, Vienna: Scherz, 1979.

Schmid, Günther. *Die Deutschlandpolitik der Regierung Brandt/Scheel.* Munich: tuduv, 1975.

———. *Entscheidung in Bonn: Die Entstehung der Ost- und Deutschlandpolitik 1969/70.* Cologne: Wissenschaft and Politik, 1979.

Schmidt, Helmut. *The Balance of Power: Germany's Peace Policy and the Powers.* London: Kimber, 1971.

———. *Beiträge.* Stuttgart: Seewald, 1967.

———. *Defense or Retaliation: A German View.* New York: Praeger, 1962.

Scholz, Arno and Walter G. Oschilenski. *Turmwächter der Demokratie: Ein Lebensbild von Kurt Schumacher; Reden und Schriften.* Berlin-Grunewald: Arani, 1953.

von Schubert, Klaus. *Sicherheitspolitik der Bundesrepublik Deutschland: Dokumentation 1945-1977.* 2 vols. Cologne: Wissenschaft Politik, 1979.

Schwarz, Hans-Peter. *Die Ära Adenauer. Gründerjahre der Republik 1949-1957.* Stuttgart: Deutsche Verlags-Anstalt, 1981.

——. "Das aussenpolitische Konzept Adenauers," in Klaus Gotto, ed. *Konrad Adenauer: Seine Deutschland- und Aussenpolitik 1945-1963.* Munich: Deutscher Taschenbuch Verlag, 1975.

——. *Vom Reich zur Bundesrepublik Deutschland im Widerstreit der aussenpolitischen Konzeptionen in den Jahren der Besatzungsherrschaft 1945-1949.* Neuwied and Berlin: Luchterhand, 1966.

Schwarz, Klaus-Dieter, ed. *Sicherheitspolitik: Analysen zur politischen und militärischen Sicherheit.* Bad Honnef-Erpel: Osang, 1976.

Schwartz, David N. *NATO's Nuclear Dilemmas.* Washington, D.C.: Brookings Institution, 1983.

Schweigler, Gebhard. *Von Kissinger zu Carter: Entspannung im Widerstreit von Innen- und Aussenpolitik 1969-1981.* Munich and Vienna: Oldenbourg, 1982.

——. *West German Foreign Policy: The Domestic Setting.* New York: Praeger, 1984.

Siegler, Heinrich von, ed. *Wiedervereinigung und Sicherheit Deutschlands: Eine dokumentarische Diskussionsgrundlage.* 2 vols. (1964-1967). Bonn, Vienna, Zürich: Siegler and Co., 1968.

Smyser, William R. *German-American Relations.* Beverly Hills, Calif.: Sage, 1981.

Soell, Hartmut. *Fritz Erler. Eine politische Biographie,* 2 vols. Bonn-Bad Godesberg: Dietz, 1976.

Stanger, Roland J., ed. *West Berlin: The Legal Context.* Columbus: Ohio State University Press, 1966.

Stent, Angela. *From Embargo to Ostpolitik: The Political Economy of West German-Soviet Relations, 1955-1980.* Cambridge: Cambridge University Press, 1981.

——. *Soviet Energy and Western Europe.* New York: Praeger, 1982.

Strauss, Franz Josef. *Challenge and Response: A Program for Europe.* New York: Athenäm, 1970.

——. *The Grand Design: A European Solution to German Reunification.* New York: Praeger, 1966.

Stützle, Walther. *Kennedy und Adenauer in der Berlin-Krise 1961-1962.* Bonn-Bad Godesberg: Verlag Neue Gesellschaft, 1973.

Thiel, Elke. *Dollar-Dominanz, Lastenteilung und amerikanische Truppenpräsenz in Europa: Zur Frage kritischer Verknüpfungen währungs- und stationierungspolitischer Zielsetzungen in den deutsch-amerikanischen Beziehungen.* Baden-Baden: Nomos Verlag, 1979.

Treverton, Gregory F. *The Dollar Drain and American Forces in Germany: Managing the Political Economics of Alliance.* Athens, Ohio: Ohio University Press, 1978.

Tucker, Robert W. and Linda Wrigley, eds. *The Atlantic Alliance and its Critics.* New York: Praeger, 1983.

Van B. Cleveland, Harald. *The Atlantic Idea and its European Rivals*. New York: McGraw Hill, 1966.

Vogelsang, Thilo. *Das geteilte Deutschland*. Munich: Deutscher Taschenbuch Verlag, 1975[6].

Volle, Hermann and Wolfgang Wagner. *Das Belgrader KSZE Folgetreffen: Der Fortgang des Entspannungsprozesses in Europa in Beiträgen und Dokumenten aus dem Europa-Archiv*. Bonn: Verlag für Internationale Politik, 1978.

——. *Konferenz über Sicherheit und Zusammenarbeit in Europa in Beiträgen und Dokumenten aus dem Europa-Archiv*. Bonn: Verlag für Internationale Politik, 1976.

Wallace, Helen; William Wallace and Carde Webb, eds. *Policy-Making in the European Communities*. Chichester and New York: John Wiley & Sons, 1977.

Wassermann, Sherri L. *The Neutron Bomb Controversy: A Study in Alliance Politics*. New York: Praeger, 1983.

Herbert Wehner. Wandel und Bewährung: Ausgewählte Schriften 1930-1967, ed. by Hans-Werner Graf Finckenstein and Gerhard Jahn. Frankfurt-am-Main: Ullstein, 1968.

Wettig, Gerhard. *Entmilitarisierung und Wiederbewaffnung in Deutschland 1943-1955: Internationale Auseinandersetzungen über die Rolle der Deutschen in Europa*. Munich: Oldenbourg, 1967.

——. *Europäische Sicherheit: Das europäische Staatensystem in der sowjetischen Aussenpolitik 1966-1972*. Düsseldorf: Bertelsmann, 1972.

Whetten, Lawrence. *Germany's Ostpolitik. Relations Between the Federal Republic and the Warsaw Pact Countries*. London and New York: Oxford University Press, 1971.

Wilker, Lothar. *Die Sicherheit der SPD 1955-1966: Zwischen Wiedervereinigungs- und Bündnisorientierung*. Bonn-Bad Godesberg: Neue Gesellschaft, 1977.

Willis, F. Roy. *France, Germany and the New Europe, 1945-1963*. Stanford: Stanford University Press, 1965.

Windsor, Philip. *Germany and the Atlantic Alliance: Lessons from the 1980 Crisis*. London: The International Institute for Strategic Studies, 1981.

——. *Germany and the Management of Détente*. London: Chatto and Windus, 1971.

Wolfe, Thomas W. *Soviet Power and Europe 1945-1970*. Baltimore and London: The Johns Hopkins Press, 1970.

Yost, David S., ed. *NATO's Strategic Options. Arms Control and Defense*. New York: Pergamon Press, 1981.

Ziebura, Gilbert. *Die deutsch-französischen Beziehungen seit 1945. Mythen und Realitäten*. Pfullingen: Neske, 1970.

Zündorf, Benno. *Die Ostverträge. Die Verträge von Moskau, Warschau, Prag, das Berlin-Abkommen und die Verträge mit der DDR*. Munich: C.H. Beck, 1979.

INDEX

About the Author

Helga Haftendorn is professor of international relations at the Free University of Berlin. Until 1978 she was associate professor and professor at the University of Hamburg and at the Armed Forces University, also at Hamburg, Germany. From 1960-69 she was with the Deutsche Gesellschaft für Auswärtige Politik in Bonn. She has taught frequently in the United States, most recently in 1982-83 as a visiting professor in comparative West European studies at Stanford University.

Dr. Haftendorn has published widely in the areas of foreign policy and international relations. A German version of this book has been published as *Sicherheit und Entspannung* by Nomos Verlag, Baden-Baden, in 1983. Her articles have appeared in *Adelphi Papers, Europa-Archiv,* and *Politische Vierteljahresschrift,* among others.

Dr. Haftendorn holds a German equivalent to a M.A. and a Dr. phil. (Ph.D.) from the University of Frankfurt (1959 and 1960). She received her *venia legendi* from the University of Hamburg in 1972.